Employment in the Service Economy

Canadian Cataloguing in Publication Data

Main entry under title:

Employment in the service economy

Issued also in French under title: Tertiarisation et polarisation de l'emploi.
ISBN 0-660-13825-5
DSS cat. no. EC22-172/1991E

1. Labor Supply – Canada. 2. Service industries – Canada. 3. Canada – Industries. 4. Employment forecasting – Canada. I. Economic Council of Canada.

HD5728.E46 1991   331.12'0971   C91-098555-3

Employment in the Service Economy

A research report prepared for the
Economic Council of Canada by:

Gordon Betcherman, project leader

Marcel Bédard
Christina Caron
Surendra Gera
Norm Leckie
Kathryn McMullen
Harry Postner
Syed Sajjadur Rahman
Tom Siedule

Juliette Beauger-Legault, secretary
Lucie Marier, secretary

1991

© Minister of Supply and Services Canada 1991

Available in Canada through

Associated Bookstores
and other booksellers

or by mail from

Canada Communication Group – Publishing
Ottawa, Canada K1A 0S9

Catalogue No. EC22-172/1991E
ISBN 0-660-13825-5

Contents

Foreword	ix
1 Introduction	1

Part A: The Service Economy

2 The Service Sector	**7**
The Concept of "Services"	7
Convergence between Goods and Services	8
A Typology of the Service Industries	8
Dynamic Services	8
Traditional Services	9
Nonmarket Services	10
Four Dimensions of the Service Sector	10
Technology	10
Trade in Services	15
Location of Services	20
Firm Size	27
Conclusion	29
3 Sectoral Interdependencies and the Growth in Service Employment	**31**
The Shift to Services: Some Common Explanations	31
Consumer Demand	31
Productivity Growth	32
Contracting-Out	34
Intermediate Demand	35
Summary	38
The Interdependence of Goods and Services	38
The "Manufacturing Matters" Debate	38
Policy Simulations of a Sectoral Econometric Model	39
Interindustry Transactions	44
Medium-Term Prospects	52
Conclusion	53

Part B: The Emerging Labour Market

4 The Shift to Services and Labour Adjustment	**57**
The Shift to Services	57
An International Comparison	59
Aggregate Implications of the Shift to Services	61
Sectoral Shifts and the Aggregate Unemployment Rate	61
The Growth of Services and Business-Cycle Fluctuations	61

	The Labour Adjustment of Individuals and the Shift to Services	63
	Patterns of Job Separation	63
	Postseparation Experience	64
	Conclusion	68
5	**Nonstandard Employment**	**71**
	Nonstandard Employment in the United States and Europe	71
	Nonstandard Employment in Canada	72
	Part-Time Employment	72
	Short-Term and Temporary Employment	77
	Temporary-Help Agency Work	79
	Own-Account Self-Employment	79
	Aggregate Nonstandard Employment	81
	Employment and Worker Characteristics	81
	Why Is Nonstandard Employment Growing?	82
	Labour Force Composition	83
	Industrial Structure	84
	Labour Market Conditions	85
	Policy Issues	86
	Conclusion	87
6	**Jobs and Skills in a Service Economy**	**89**
	Literature Review	89
	Occupational Shifts and Their Skill Implications	90
	Occupational Trends by Sector	92
	Educational and Skill Implications	93
	Information Content of Jobs	95
	Occupational-Trait Measures of Skill	96
	Skill Shifts	96
	Relative Skill Levels of Industries	98
	Skill Shifts within Industries	99
	Skill Measures Based on Reports by Workers	101
	Job Complexity	103
	Training Requirements	105
	Autonomy and Control	106
	Occupational-Trait and Self-Report Skill-Measure Comparisons	107
	Conclusion	109
7	**Issues in Human-Resource Development**	**111**
	Education and Employment Outcomes	111
	The Education-Employment Relationship over Time	112
	The School-to-Work Transition	118
	Education and Labour Market Adjustment	121
	Canada's Training Infrastructure	122
	Employer-Sponsored Training	123
	Government-Sponsored Training	129
	Conclusion	136

8   The Distribution of Earnings **137**
  Trends in Compensation Levels   137
    Wages and Salaries   137
    Supplementary Labour Income   139
  Trends in the Distribution of Earnings   140
    Results   142
  Explanations of Increased Earnings Disparity   149
    Supply-Side Explanations: A Changing Labour Force   149
    Demand-Side Explanations: The Shift to Services   153
  The Durability of the Declining Middle   156
    Changing Labour Force Demographics   156
  Conclusion   157

Part C: Conclusions

9   Conclusions and Policy Implications **161**
  Strengthen the Commitment to the Development of Human Resources 162
    Education   162
    Training and Labour Adjustment   163
    Policies Aimed at "Unattached" Workers   163
    Employer-Based Human-Resource Development   166
  Promote Economic Security for Workers   168
    Employment Standards   169
    Public Benefit Programs   169
    Pensions   169
  Recognize the Role of Services in Economic Growth   170
    Industrial Policy   170
    Linking Goods and Services   170
    Service Infrastructure   171
    Regional Development   172
    Measuring the Service Economy   172

Appendices

A   The Calculation of Stimulative Power by Industry   177
B   Income Distribution Analysis: Methodology   183

Notes   185

List of Tables, Charts, and Figures   201

Project Contributors   207

Foreword

In 1990 the Economic Council of Canada released *Good Jobs, Bad Jobs*, a Statement on employment in the service economy. The motivation for that publication was the rapid growth of services and the need to know more about its implications for the well-being of Canadians.

Good Jobs, Bad Jobs has attracted a great deal of attention since its release. Its analysis of the economic role of services and the nature of employment in a service economy has pointed to a number of fundamental changes in the operation of the labour market, and in the content of work and how it is organized. It also underlined the point that many of our traditional approaches no longer "fit"; policies need to be reshaped in order to support job creation and maximize the contribution of Canada's human resources in the changing environment.

This volume presents the details of the Council's research on employment and the service economy. It considers the topics highlighted in *Good Jobs, Bad Jobs* in much more depth and with the benefit of an additional year of analysis. The first part of this report is concerned with the nature of service industries, how they are changing, and their growing linkages to the goods sector. The second part addresses a set of trends that are redefining the labour market as employment becomes increasingly concentrated in service industries: the problems certain groups are experiencing in adjusting to the changing industrial structure, the proliferation of nonstandard jobs, the growth of work with high skill content, the increasing importance of training and education, and the polarization of earnings. In the third part, the recommendations put forward by the Council in *Good Jobs, Bad Jobs* are reproduced.

The research assembled in *Employment in the Service Economy* is the product of a number of studies undertaken both by the Economic Council staff and outside researchers (the authors of individual chapters are identified at the back of the report). The results are a comprehensive and up-to-date picture of the Canadian labour market and suggest the dominant trends that are likely to shape employment and earnings as we approach the next century.

The research team, led by Gordon Betcherman, was supported by an Advisory Committee consisting of three Council members and five outside experts. I would like to thank the committee, and particularly Diane Bellemare who chaired it, for its contribution to our research.

Judith Maxwell
Chairman

READER'S NOTE

The reader should note that various conventional symbols similar to those used by Statistics Canada have been used in the tables:

- .. figures not available
- ... figures not appropriate or not applicable
- – – amount too small to be expressed
- – nil or zero

Details may not add up to totals because of rounding.

1 Introduction

The industrial makeup of the Canadian economy has undergone a dramatic transformation within the space of just two generations. As recently as the 1950s, the goods-producing industries – natural resources, manufacturing, and construction – accounted for the major share of production and employment. Canada's economic profile in the 1990s, however, can no longer be accurately sketched out by farms, forests, and factories. While the goods sector is still crucial, service activities have become fundamental to the Canadian economy.

Given the magnitude of the changes in the economic structure, surprisingly little attention has been paid to the rapid growth of services and its implications for the nature of economic activity and public policy. Even into the 1980s, the diverse group of industries which comprise the service sector remained underresearched by economists and often overlooked by policymakers. Now this is finally changing: the federal government has sponsored a major research initiative on Canada's service industries and a number of studies have been undertaken by provincial governments.[1] As well, service-sector analysis is gathering momentum in other advanced industrial countries and in international organizations. As we begin to learn more about the service economy, it is apparent that both conventional economic concepts and measures, and traditional policy approaches require some refashioning.

The Economic Council of Canada's research on the growth of services has focused, in particular, on the changes in employment that have occurred along with the transformation of the industrial structure. And nowhere has the shift from goods to services been more striking than in the labour market. While the share of employment in the service sector increased gradually in the first half of this century, the pace of the transition has been rapid over the past three decades. In the 1950s, most Canadian workers were employed in the goods sector; today, over 70 per cent work in service industries (Chart 1-1). Over the past 40 years nearly 90 per cent of net employment creation in Canada has taken place in the service sector.

This concentration of job growth in services and the attendant shift in the sectoral composition of employment

Chart 1-1

Employment Share of the Goods and Service Sectors, Canada, Selected Years, 1946-89[1]

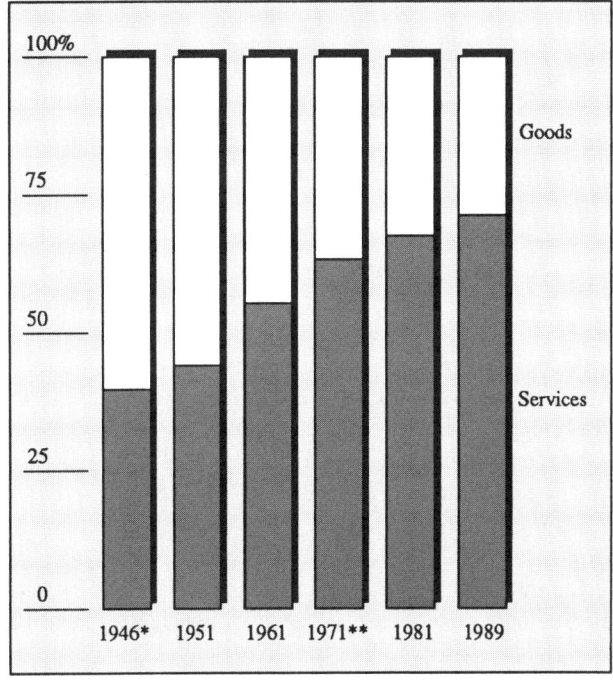

*Population 14 years and over for 1946, 1951, and 1961.
**Population 15 years and over for 1971, 1981, and 1989.
1 Includes Newfoundland from 1951 onward.
SOURCE Estimates by the Economic Council of Canada, based on data from Statistics Canada, the Labour Force Survey.

has engendered a number of important debates. Why has employment in the services expanded so rapidly? Are there limits to the growth of services? Is it possible that, in a country like Canada, virtually every worker will eventually be employed in the service industries? Does the growth of services lead to more and more "good" jobs or, alternatively, more "bad" ones? What are the effects of the shift to services on the skill content of jobs? What are the implications for human-resource development? Is the growth of services likely to make the location of jobs more "footloose," thereby reducing urban-rural and interregional disparities? What are the implications of the growth of services for compensation levels and the distribution of earnings?

Given the importance of questions such as these, the Economic Council has undertaken a wide range of studies on employment in a service economy. These studies and their policy implications were summarized in a Council Statement, *Good Jobs, Bad Jobs*.[2] In the present report we present the details of the research highlighted in that Statement.

The report is organized into three parts. Part A is concerned with the nature of the service economy. We begin in Chapter 2 by looking at conceptual issues associated with services, the factors which have traditionally distinguished service activity from the production of goods, and how innovations in technology and industrial organization are altering these orthodox distinctions. Our focus then turns to the service sector itself. That sector – as it has been defined – includes a very heterogeneous group of industries, thus tending to preclude useful analysis on a sector-wide basis. Consequently, we have developed a typology for services which organizes the sector into three subsectors – dynamic, traditional, and nonmarket services. After presenting this model, selected characteristics of these three subsectors are discussed, including technology, trade, the geographic location of employment, and industrial organization.

Chapter 3 focuses on explanations for the rapid expansion of the service sector. We begin by considering the four most common hypotheses, which are based on consumer demand, productivity growth, contracting-out, and intermediate demand. We then offer a different perspective by looking at the growth of services through that sector's relationship with the goods sector. Two related exercises were undertaken. The first was a series of policy simulations, using a model designed to offer an overall view of the intersectoral relationship. The second employed input-output data to quantify the transactions between individual goods and service industries.

After examining the service sector, we turn in Part B to the specific focus of our research, employment in a service economy. Chapter 4 documents the shift from goods to services and details the employment growth in the three service subsectors. Canadian trends are then compared with those of other OECD countries. The remainder of the chapter investigates the implications of the rapid growth of services for labour adjustment.

One dimension of the emerging employment structure that has attracted a great deal of attention in recent years has been the increase in "nonstandard" employment – jobs that depart from the traditional full-time, essentially permanent arrangement. The implications of this trend have been subject to differing interpretations. In Chapter 5, we examine the issue of nonstandard employment in Canada. After reviewing existing research in Europe and the United States, we consider the four major types of nonstandard employment in Canada: part-time, short-term, temporary help, and "own-account" self-employment. We then assess various explanations for the rapid growth of these work forms. Finally, policy issues associated with the increase in nonstandard employment are discussed.

The focus of Chapter 6 is on the skill content of jobs. There has been considerable debate surrounding the skill implications of the shift to a service-dominated, high-technology economy. Some observers have argued that the overall effect is to upgrade the aggregate skill level of the job structure, while others argue that downgrading is the result. Empirical research has done little to resolve this disagreement, in no small part because of methodological difficulties associated with the conceptualization and measurement of the skill content of work. We have carried out three different types of quantitative analysis. The first considers longitudinal trends in the composition of the occupational structure, looking in particular at the impact of the growth of services. The second is based on measures from the national occupational classification system, which estimates the training and education requirements and the nature of the skills and responsibilities associated with each occupation. In the third study, we have put together a new perspective on skills using data from two surveys of workers.

The emergence of a high-technology, service economy has heightened awareness of the importance of education and training. In Canada, as in all industrialized countries, the objective of building a competent, flexible, and technically skilled work force is gathering momentum among policymakers. Chapter 7 addresses two sets of issues associated with human-resource development. The first is concerned with the relationship between human capital and employment outcomes. We begin with an analysis of how the relationship has changed over time. We then examine how the transition from school to work, and adjustments to changes in employment differ according to educational attainment. The second considers Canada's capacity for developing human resources, with a particular focus on the training infrastructure in this country. The objective is to assess the opportunities for skill-formation outside the formal education sector. We review the evidence regarding training within Canadian industry, and then consider the recent activities of the federal government and selected provincial governments in providing opportunities for human-resource development.

The distribution of earnings represents one of the most controversial issues associated with the emergence of a service economy. Studies carried out in the United States indicate that incomes in that country have become more polarized over the past few decades. In Canada, this topic has not been researched to the same extent, and the findings have been less conclusive than those in the United States. Chapter 8 reports the results of a major Economic Council study of income distribution trends. After documenting the existence of a "declining middle," or a polarization of earnings since the 1960s, we consider the role of various factors that may have altered the earnings distribution. We conclude the chapter by examining whether earnings polarization is likely to be a durable trend or a transitory phenomenon of the period.

The third part of this report, Chapter 9, presents conclusions and policy implications. This chapter is reproduced from *Good Jobs, Bad Jobs* and puts forth the argument that public policy has not kept up with the changing labour market. As a consequence, many of our traditional institutions and policy approaches require some refitting. To offer a direction for the future, we identify and discuss three general and mutually reinforcing principles that the Council believes must be at the centre of any strategy to achieve high employment and to maximize the contribution of human resources in a service economy: 1) to strengthen the commitment to the development of human resources; 2) to promote economic security for workers; and 3) to recognize the role of services in economic growth.

Part A: The Service Economy

2 The Service Sector

The purpose of Chapters 2 and 3 is to set the scene for the analysis of labour market issues that are the main subject of this report. This chapter provides an overview of the changing nature of service activity; in doing so, it dispels many myths about service industries. Canadians often perceive the service sector as consisting of the cashier in the local supermarket, the sales clerk in the department store, the barber, and the dry-cleaner. What is not clearly understood is that a relatively large and rapidly growing part of the service sector does not deal with final consumers at all, but instead with business; that service sector firms employ a large majority of Canadian workers; that the service sector accounts for over half the output and value-added in the economy; and that many of the industries that make up the service sector are undergoing rapid technological change and productivity growth.

In this chapter, we contrast the traditional view of the service sector with a currently evolving one that recognizes the many organizational changes and the new technologies that are transforming it. In a number of important respects, the traditional distinctions between goods and services no longer hold as services increasingly acquire many characteristics traditionally associated with goods, and goods production acquires some service-like qualities. This "convergence" of goods and services, together with some of the conceptual and measurement issues that it raises, is treated in the first section of this chapter. Given the large size and considerable diversity of the service sector, we have developed a descriptive and analytical typology of service industries, which is presented in the second section. It organizes the sector into three subsectors: dynamic services, traditional services, and nonmarket services. This typology is largely based on a consideration of four dimensions of the service sector – technology, trade, location, and firm size. The third section is a detailed examination of the service sector in relation to these four dimensions. The final section is a summary that outlines how general perceptions regarding the service sector need to be modified to reflect the very fundamental changes in the service sector.

The Concept of "Services"[1]

"Services" have been subject to rather strange treatment by economists in the past. In fact, it was not until the turn of the century that most services were included in official measures of economic output. Even then, however, the particular characteristics of service production were not defined. Indeed, services were regarded as merely a residual activity, after "primary" output (agriculture, fishing, forestry, and mining) and "secondary" output (manufacturing and construction) were accounted for. Sometimes services were referred to as "tertiary" output,[2] but this nomenclature had no special significance. It is only in the past decade or two that economists and statisticians have begun to analyse the special features of service production vis-à-vis goods production (i.e., output from the primary and secondary sectors).

Economists have tried to identify characteristics which distinguish "services" from "goods." In the conventional view, a "good" is defined as a physical object which, once produced, is transferable between the producer and the consumer. An essential feature of goods production is a clear separation between the process of production and the ultimate consumption. On the other hand, a "service" is traditionally defined as a *change* in the condition of an economic unit resulting from the activity of another unit; consumption cannot be separated from production. Services are consumed as they are produced and so service consumption and production are aspects of the same process.[3]

These definitions have led to the following conventional distinctions between goods and services: 1) tangibility vs. intangibility; 2) no direct contact vs. direct contact between the producer and consumer; 3) transferability vs. nontransferability; and 4) storability vs. nonstorability. Given these characteristics, it is not surprising that services have been viewed as difficult to measure, at least in contrast to goods.[4] Among the many measurement problems are difficulties associated with decomposing the current valuations of services into their "price" and "quantity" components. Moreover, price indices for services are difficult to construct and ambiguous, which makes economic comparisons over time – including those related to the measurement of productivity – complex and confused. (These issues are examined in greater detail in Chapter 3.) A less well-known measurement issue is the fact that the nonstorability of services makes the conventional concept of "excess supply" (or demand) inoperable.[5] This has implications for the traditional economic price-adjustment process and for the measurement apparatus (new and unfilled orders, productive capacity, and inventories) which underlies business-cycle analysis.[6] In the final analysis, the key conceptual and measurement issue is not so much how services differ from goods, but that the perception of services, and the development of measures, economic theory, and policy relating to services, are still at an early stage.

Convergence between Goods and Services

While we believe that goods and services can still be usefully distinguished, a rigid distinction is likely to be less and less tenable in the future. In addition, innovations in technology and industrial organization are changing the nature of both goods and services to the point where the borderline between the two is becoming increasingly blurred. Indeed, when we turn to labour market developments in Part B, it will be evident that a number of important trends are affecting both the goods and the service sectors.

First, it should be recognized that what is officially classified as a "good" or as a "service" is mainly a reflection of the particular final form in which an economic transaction occurs. The production of any commodity increasingly incorporates both services and goods; a great deal of service-type activity is embodied in the value-added of goods production while some goods activity is typically inherent in the value-added of service production. There is also an increasing tendency to "bundle" goods and services into an integrated package that is contributing to the convergence process; for example, tying training and maintenance contracts into equipment sales. Second, goods production is not always characterized by the conventional features noted above. For example, in manufacturing and construction, it is not unusual for production to be customized, which often involves direct contact between the producer and consumer. This trend towards more user-oriented goods production is being reinforced by organizational and technological innovations associated with the "just-in-time" method of operation. Third, just as goods production is taking on service-like characteristics, services are becoming more like goods in some respects. Like goods producers, service producers purchase other services as intermediate inputs into their own production; these service inputs may then be processed further or could even be transferred, just like tangible goods. It is also possible to find examples of services being subject to "delivery lags," a phenomenon conventionally associated with goods production.

Many of the changes in the nature of service activity are being driven by innovations in computer and telecommunications technology. The outputs of many business and information services – for example, computer software, consultants' reports, audio-visual presentations – can be put in physical form and stored for future use. Advances in telecommunications mean that a growing number of services no longer require direct contact between the producer and the consumer. And many personal services, such as fast food and banking, can be provided in standardized form, with characteristics normally associated with goods production.

The changing nature of services is becoming recognized in business accounting theory and practice. It is no longer true that service inputs must be immediately expensed and that service outputs must be immediately treated as revenue. The latest business accounting standards permit cost deferment for some service inputs, and do not automatically treat service output as revenue until certain specified conditions are satisfied. This, in effect, means that the accounting rules associated with the concepts of inventory accumulation and decumulation are coming to be applied to services as well as to goods. In addition, it is becoming more common to recognize the "capital investment" nature of business activities related to "intangible" services like research and development, training, employer health expenditures, and even advertising and marketing.

A Typology of the Service Industries

As we have noted, the service sector includes a wide range of diverse industries. In order to create a meaningful structure for the conceptual, descriptive, and analytical work underlying this report, we have organized the service sector into three subsectors, each of which has its own distinctive characteristics and employment patterns (see box). These are the dynamic services and traditional services – which together make up commercial services – and nonmarket services. Wherever possible, statistics (including tables and charts) have been organized according to this typology. However, in some cases the data do not permit this.

Dynamic Services

The dynamic-service subsector includes four major industry divisions; two are distribution industries (transportation, communications, and utilities; and wholesale trade) and two are producer-service industries (finance, insurance, and real estate; and business services). There are a number of characteristics that make these industries "dynamic." They are high-value-added industries that, for the most part,

> **The Structure of the Service Sector***
>
> **Dynamic Services**
>
> Transportation, communications, and utilities
>   Air, rail, and water transport
>   Ground transportation
>   Pipelines
>   Storage and warehousing
>   Broadcasting – radio, television, cable
>   Telephone systems
>   Postal and courier services
>   Utilities – electricity, gas, water, and sewage systems
> Wholesale trade
>
> Finance, insurance, and real estate
>   Banks and trust companies
>   Credit unions and mortgage companies
>   Insurance companies
>   Investment dealers
>   Real estate operators
> Business services
>   Employment agencies
>   Advertising services
>   Architectural, scientific, engineering, and computing services
>   Legal services
>   Management consulting
>
> **Traditional Services**
>
> Retail trade
>   Food stores
>   Drug stores and liquor stores
>   Shoe and clothing stores
>   Furniture, appliances, furnishings, and stereo stores
>   Car dealers, gas stations, and auto repair shops
>   Department stores
>   Jewellery stores and photographic stores
> Accommodation, food, and beverages
>   Hotels, motels, and tourist courts
>   Camping grounds and travel trailer parks
>
> Restaurants
> Amusement and recreation
>   Motion picture, audio and video production and distribution
>   Motion picture exhibition
>   Sports and recreation clubs and services
>   Bowling alleys and billiard parlours
> Personal services
>   Barber and beauty shops
>   Laundries and cleaners
>   Funeral services
>
> **Nonmarket Services**
>
> Education services
>   Schools, colleges, and universities
>   Libraries, museums, and archives
> Health services
>   Hospitals
>   Doctors and dentists
>   Medical laboratories
>
> Social services
>   Daycare, meal services, and crisis centres
>   Psychologists and social workers
>   Religious organizations
> Public administration
>
> *This classification scheme is organized according to Statistics Canada's Standard Industrial Classification (1980).

have become more and more involved in globally competitive markets. They are also being more traded internationally and they are becoming increasingly critical ingredients in the production and distribution of goods, a point we return to in Chapter 3.

Traditional Services

The traditional-service subsector consists of retail trade; accommodation, food, and beverages; amusement and recreation; and personal services.[7] These industries are "traditional" in the sense that they represent the old "Main Street" variety of services. It would be a mistake, however, not to recognize the changes that are taking place within this subsector. Most notable, perhaps, is the emergence of megacorporations – in the fast-food industry, for example – and their progressive application of mass-production technologies, inventory systems, and marketing techniques. In retailing, commercial innovations such as self-service and automated at-home buying have been developed and are increasingly being adopted. Nevertheless, the traditional services remain, on balance, relatively insulated from the trends towards globalization and international competitiveness that are driving the goods sector and the dynamic-service subsector. Much of the traditional-service subsector still tends to operate in local, or at most national, markets; its value-added tends to be lower than for dynamic services; there is less emphasis on productivity growth; and the importance of technological change is less pronounced.

Nonmarket Services

The third subsector – nonmarket services – includes education, health, social services, and public administration. While competition has traditionally not been a significant factor in this subsector, nonmarket services are extremely relevant to economic competitiveness, for two reasons. First, the efficiency with which these services are produced will affect the level of public financing that is needed. And second, nonmarket services provide inputs into the activity of all private-sector firms. Those inputs include, for example, infrastructure (such as transportation systems), education and health services (which have an important bearing on the quality of the work force), and regulatory services. The nature of the nonmarket-service sector has been changing in recent years. The role of competition has been growing as the pressures for deregulation and privatization increase, and renewed attention is being focused on changing management practices. Productivity growth and technological change are also becoming increasingly important to the nonmarket sector. Education and health services are encountering the need to change as a result of factors relating to costs and demographics. These changes reflect the growing awareness of the public sector's role in overall competitiveness and the fiscal pressures associated with the drive to reduce the public debt.

Four Dimensions of the Service Sector

The typology described above provides a brief summary of the major characteristics that distinguish the many industries that form the service sector. This section elaborates upon that theme, providing detailed information on the service sector with respect to four dimensions – technology, trade, location, and firm size. These four dimensions are now shaping the labour market, affecting skills and employment – including the location of that employment and the nature of workers' attachment to the labour market.

Technology

In the past few decades, the Canadian economy has been transformed by technological change. While computer-based technologies first appeared in the 1960s, they did not begin to penetrate industries widely until the development of the microchip in the 1970s. Since then, technological change within the computer industry has resulted in exponential growth in its capabilities that has led to these technologies being adopted with remarkable rapidity throughout the economy. In this section, we identify the extent to which the service sector has participated in the process of technological change and also differences among the industries that make up the service sector, and make observations about the extent to which the spread of computer-based technological change and the growth of services are linked.

Three types of indicators are used to assess technological change in the various service industries. The first set of indicators is spending on machinery and equipment. This is the broadest measure, since it includes expenditures not only on office machines, telecommunications equipment, and professional and scientific equipment, but also on items such as furniture and transportation equipment. Given the wide range of capital goods included in the definition of machinery and equipment, indicators based on this measure can be considered only as a proxy for investment in high technology. The next set of indicator – narrower in its focus – is the extent to which industries have been involved in the introduction of computer-based technologies. The third indicator, narrower still, is spending on R&D by industries. It focuses more on the producers of new technology than on the wider universe of its users, though technology adoption often involves some R&D spending.

As seen in Table 2-1, the average annual growth of investment in machinery and equipment in the service sector over the period 1966-88, at 6.4 per cent, was higher than that in the goods sector, which was 3.7 per cent. As a result, the share of total machinery and equipment capital stock accounted for by the service sector increased substantially over the period, from 40.8 to 55.3 per cent. Unfortunately, the data cannot be disaggregated to correspond to the standard service-sector typology used throughout this report; particularly troublesome is the fact that business services are included in "other services" along with a range of traditional services. However, the industry detail that is available shows significant differences across the service industries. In particular, the "other services" and finance, insurance, and real estate industries showed very strong average annual growth in investment in machinery and equipment capital stock between 1966 and 1988. And while the average annual rates of growth shown by the remaining service industries were lower in comparison, they still exceeded the average rate shown by the goods sector. By 1988, the share of total machinery and equipment capital

Table 2-1

Average Annual Growth in Machinery and Equipment Capital Stock, 1966-88, and Share of Total Machinery and Equipment Capital Stock, Selected Years, 1961-88, by Industry, Canada

	Average annual growth, 1966-88	Share of total 1961	1971	1981	1988
	(Per cent)	(Per cent)			
Service sector	6.4	40.8	43.5	48.8	55.3
Transportation, communications, and utilities	5.4	28.6	28.5	29.3	29.4
Finance, insurance, and real estate	11.4	0.6	1.0	1.3	2.9
Wholesale and retail trade	4.6	5.3	4.9	4.6	4.7
Education, health, and social services	5.1	1.6	3.0	2.3	2.5
Public administration	6.8	3.1	3.2	3.7	4.6
Other services[1]	13.2	1.6	3.0	7.6	11.2
Goods sector	3.7	59.2	56.5	51.2	44.7
Total	5.0	100.0	100.0	100.0	100.0

1 Includes business services; accommodation, food, and beverages; amusement and recreation; and personal services.
SOURCE Estimates by the Economic Council of Canada, based on data from Statistics Canada.

stock accounted for by "other services" reached 11.2 per cent after starting from a level of 1.6 per cent in 1961. By far the largest part of the increase in the service sector's share of machinery and equipment capital stock was accounted for by the "other services" industry; of the remainder, almost half was due to increases in finance, insurance, and real estate.

Table 2-2 shows the machinery and equipment share of total investment in the goods and service sectors and in the service industries from the 1960s to the 1980s. The goods sector experienced relatively little change; the service sector, on the other hand, showed a large increase. Large relative increases were shown by education, health, and social services; finance, insurance, and real estate; and public

Table 2-2

Machinery and Equipment Investment as a Share of Total Investment, by Industry, Canada, 1960s, 1970s, and 1980s; and 1988

	Annual average			
	1960s	1970s	1980s	1988
	(Per cent)			
Service sector	23.1	33.3	41.8	45.2
Transportation, communications, and utilities	33.2	42.4	47.2	51.7
Finance, insurance, and real estate	11.4	12.3	18.9	22.9
Wholesale and retail trade	48.5	58.4	63.4	65.1
Education, health, and social services	12.4	20.9	27.8	28.5
Public administration	7.0	11.0	18.0	21.5
Other services[1]	58.1	72.9	82.5	84.3
Goods sector	56.0	58.5	52.9	59.7

1 Includes business services; accommodation, food, and beverages; amusement and recreation; and personal services.
SOURCE Estimates by the Economic Council of Canada, based on data from Statistics Canada.

administration; all three of which started from low bases in the 1960s. The "other services" industry stands out as allocating a very large proportion (84 per cent) of total investment to machinery and equipment in 1988, with high levels also being recorded by transportation, communications, and utilities, and wholesale and retail trade.

The value of machinery and equipment capital stock per employee in constant (1981) dollars in 1966 and 1988 for the goods and service sectors is shown in Table 2-3. The capital-intensiveness of the transportation, communications, and utilities industry is particularly striking, exceeding even the value of machinery and equipment per employee in the goods sector by a factor of two-and-a-half to one in 1988. Wholesale and retail trade and education, health, and social services, on the other hand, have very low levels of machinery and equipment per employee. In terms of change over time, again the "other services" and the finance, insurance, and real estate industries show the strongest performances, with the former showing an average annual growth rate of 8.1 per cent and the latter 7.3 per cent for the period 1966-88.

Table 2-3

Expenditure on Machinery and Equipment per Employee, 1966 and 1988, and Average Annual Growth Rate, 1966-88, by Industry, Canada

	1966	1988	Average annual growth rate, 1966-88
	(1981 dollars)		(Per cent)
Service sector	8,390	16,307	3.1
Transportation, communications, and utilities	36,422	83,246	3.8
Finance, insurance, and real estate	2,168	10,131	7.3
Wholesale and retail trade	3,779	5,604	1.8
Education, health, and social services	2,330	3,177	1.4
Public administration	6,335	14,518	3.8
Other services[1]	2,491	13,706	8.1
Goods sector	17,213	32,149	2.9

1 Includes business services; accommodation, food, and beverages; amusement and recreation; and personal services.
SOURCE Estimates by the Economic Council of Canada, based on data from Statistics Canada.

Together these indicators draw a picture of a service sector that has been actively involved in the introduction of new machinery and equipment since the 1960s. Two sets of service industries in particular had very high rates of growth in investment in machinery and equipment – finance, insurance, and real estate and "other services." While the available data on business investment do not allow more detailed disaggregation of the latter industry category, the evidence on the introduction of computer-based technologies and on R&D suggests that much of the growth in investment in machinery and equipment by "other services" consists, in fact, of investment by the business-service industry.

The second set of indicators focuses on more explicit indicators of technological change in services. Information on the introduction of computer-based technologies by the service industries in the 1980s is drawn from two special surveys, the first conducted by the Economic Council of Canada in 1985, and the second conducted by Statistics Canada in 1989.[8]

Table 2-4 shows the performance of a number of service industries on two measures of technological intensity based on the Council's survey. Since public administration was excluded from the sample, the table focuses on the adoption of computer-based technological change in the dynamic- and traditional-service subsectors in the period 1980-85. The first measure of technological intensity is the percentage of establishments in each industry reporting the introduction of computer-based technologies between 1980 and 1985. The dynamic-service subsector, at 79.8 per cent, exceeded the all-industry average of 75.5 per cent. The traditional-service subsector, at 67.6 per cent, was below the average for all industries, while the performance of the goods sector was about average. Very high levels of innovation were shown by establishments in four dynamic-service industries – wholesale trade; communications and utilities; business services; and finance, insurance, and real estate. The second measure of technological intensity is the percentage of employees in each establishment working with computers in 1985. Again, the dynamic-service subsector, at an establishment mean of 22.7 per cent of all employees, was well above the all-industry average, and the same four dynamic-service industries ranked high. The traditional-service subsector was also above average; this is because of the relatively strong performance of the retail trade industry which saw the spread of new technologies such as point-of-sale (POS) equipment in the early 1980s. The goods sector, on the other hand, ranked below the all-industry average in terms of this measure.

Statistics Canada's 1989 survey of the diffusion of computer-based technologies in the service sector also finds

Table 2-4

Adoption of Computer-Based Technology, by Service Industry, Canada, 1980-85

	Proportion of establishments introducing computer-based technologies, 1980-85	Proportion of employees working with computers (establishment mean), 1985
	(Per cent)	
Dynamic services	79.8	22.7
Transportation and storage	60.0	16.8
Communications and utilities	87.5	23.4
Wholesale trade	91.1	22.6
Finance, insurance, and real estate	79.2	25.2
Business services	81.7	23.3
Traditional services	67.6	18.2
Retail trade	74.4	25.3
Accommodation, food, and beverages	60.7	12.6
Other traditional services[1]	63.0	11.0
Goods sector	76.1	13.4
All industries[2]	75.5	16.1

1 Includes amusement and recreation, and personal services.
2 Includes nonmarket services except public administration.
SOURCE Based on the Working with Technology Survey, Economic Council of Canada, 1985.

that establishments in communications, wholesale trade, finance and insurance, and business services were most likely to have introduced computer-based technologies. Accommodation, food, and beverage industries and retail trade usually had the lowest incidence of computer-technology use. In terms of technologies with general applications in all industries, the more established office automation technologies such as personal computers, on-line terminals, and mini-computers have been widely adopted in the service industries. The next phase of computer-based technological change is expected to emphasize technologies that are oriented to networking, such as local area networks, facsimile, private electronic mail, and electronic data interchange.

The Statistics Canada survey also found that some industries have high levels of adoption of industry-specific technologies. For example, use of electronic funds transfer (EFT) is 18 per cent overall and is expected to increase to 27 per cent by 1992. Finance and insurance industries are the dominant users, reporting employment by 41 per cent of establishments. Within this industry, the deposit-accepting institutions indicate use by 50 per cent of establishments, and this is expected to grow to almost 70 per cent by 1992. As the deposit-accepting institutions must have the capability to perform EFT in order for other industries to adopt it, adoption by these institutions will play an important role in setting the pace at which other industries may employ it.[9] Another example is POS terminals, employed predominantly in the retail industry, where 47 per cent of establishments included in the survey reported their use in 1989, and in the accommodation, food, and beverages industry, where the figure is 43 per cent.[10]

Table 2-5 shows expenditures on R&D as a proportion of sales for 1979, 1983, and 1987. In its analysis of R&D activity, Statistics Canada focuses on current R&D spending

Table 2-5

Current Intramural R&D Expenditures as a Proportion of Performing Company Sales (Revenues), by Industry, Canada, 1979, 1983, and 1987

	1979	1983	1987
	(Per cent)		
Dynamic services			
Transportation, communications, and utilities	0.5	0.5	0.6
Wholesale trade	0.4	0.8	1.1
Finance, insurance, and real estate	1.5	0.6	0.9
Business services	6.8	9.1	11.3
Traditional services			
Retail trade	..	0.3	0.1
Nonmarket services			
Education, health, and social services	..	..	34.0
All other services	0.9	0.8	4.0
Goods sector			
Agriculture; fishing and trapping; logging and forestry	11.0	8.0	5.5
Manufacturing and mining	0.8	1.3	1.5
All industries	0.8	1.2	1.4

SOURCE Estimates by the Economic Council of Canada, based on data from Statistics Canada.

and excludes capital expenditures, since the latter consists of investments in land, buildings, and major items of R&D equipment and so can fluctuate widely from year to year. To the extent permitted by the data, R&D/sales ratios are shown for industries grouped according to the dynamic-, traditional-, and nonmarket-service categories.

With the exceptions of business services and health and social services, no striking, consistent trends emerge from Table 2-5. Within the dynamic-service subsector, the transportation, communications, and utilities industry shows no real change in the R&D/sales ratio from 1979 to 1987; wholesale trade shows a small increase, after starting from a very small base; and the finance, insurance, and real estate industry shows a decrease, with some recovery by 1987. Very little detail is available for traditional and nonmarket services, though the ratio of 4.0 per cent for "other services" suggests that the all-industry average of 1.4 per cent may be exceeded in at least parts of the service sector not included in dynamic services.

What is striking, however, is the very high R&D/sales ratios shown by business-service and health- and social-service industries. Within business services, very strong performances are shown by the engineering- and scientific-service industry and by the computer-service industry. Much of that R&D activity is for the use of the R&D performing companies in those industries. However, part of that activity also represents R&D conducted on behalf of other companies that have contracted for those services. Unfortunately, the data do not show the magnitude of such interindustry flows of R&D funding. Nevertheless, they do strongly suggest that the business-service industry makes an important contribution to innovation in other parts of the economy; indeed, it has been argued that producer services (business services and finance, insurance, and real estate), by playing a major role in investment, innovation, and technological change, play a strategic role in the economy.[11] The high ratio of R&D to revenues for the health- and social-service industry, on the other hand, reflects the special role of that part of the nonmarket sector in medical research. Governments provide a major part of the funding for that research which is associated with high social rates of return.[12]

Together, these indicators draw a picture of the substantial technological change that is under way in the service sector. The dynamic services – in particular, business services and finance, insurance, and real estate – have shown a growing orientation to investment in machinery and equipment, and the amount of capital per worker within these industries has increased. Furthermore, the results of the surveys of the diffusion of computer-based technological change in the service sector suggest quite strongly that an important part of that growth in investment in machinery and equipment consists of computer technology, both of a generic nature and with industry-specific applications.

The picture drawn by these indicators, however, is a sketchy one at best, for it fails to reflect the full extent of the transformation of the service sector. To do that we must step back and take a broader view of services within the economic system as a whole and of technological change and its impacts.

Technologies such as "telematics" – interrelated computer and telecommunications technologies – are transforming both the nature of service activities and the contribution they make to economic growth. Indeed, as noted previously, technological change is rendering some of the conventionally held views on the distinctive features of service activity less relevant. For example, information-based services are increasingly transferable through digital telecommunications systems, and some services – software systems and expert systems, for example – are now storable. Consequently, as we have noted, direct contact between the service producer and consumer is no longer necessary for a growing number of service transactions.

Technological change, particularly telematics, has also generated new types of information-based service activities. Computers have created the potential for the collection and analysis of huge amounts of complex information quickly and cheaply. At the same time, revolutionary progress in telecommunications has made it possible to link physically separate units through information-transmission systems. This ability to process and communicate vast amounts of information quickly has become recognized as a valuable business management tool which has generated a demand for even greater quantities of information.

The process of innovation in the service sector has received very little discussion in the literature. Statistics on R&D, such as those presented in Table 2-5, are used as a standard indicator of the technological orientation of industries. However, they capture only a small part of that orientation since much innovation takes place outside a formal R&D setting. And, given the invisible nature of much service output and the central role played by the organization of service production, it might be expected that the nature of service-sector R&D and technological change would differ intrinsically from that of goods industries.

Some pioneering work by Barras argues that the process of innovation in services is the reverse of the standard innovation model identified as prevailing in the sectors which produce the capital goods embodying the new technology.[13] In the standard model, innovation progresses from product innovation through radical process innovation to more incremental process innovation, as the new producer goods industries move from takeoff through growth to maturity. Barras contends that in the adopting industries such as services, the progression is in the opposite direction, with early applications of the new technology producing incremental process innovations designed to reduce costs and improve efficiency, followed by more radical process innovation which improves product quality, and finally by product innovations which create completely new types of services.

To offer one example, in the mid-1960s and early 1970s, securities trading houses faced the physically overwhelming task of handling the 10 to 12 million shares which were being transferred daily. Once this was mastered through automated trading, they found that they also had the capacity to introduce a variety of new products such as cash management accounts tailored to customers' needs. As automation spread internationally and as world financial markets became increasingly integrated, countries began changing their trading rules to maintain national competitiveness and large industrial companies increasingly became directly involved in placing their own securities on world markets. This linkage of financial markets internationally has changed the very nature of international competition.[14]

Two related sets of factors play key roles in the process of computer-based technological change in services. The first is the evolution of computer technology itself, which, according to many observers, is still in its early stages.[15] The second is the telematics infrastructure that links suppliers of information products with business and personal users.[16] As these technologies continue to evolve both technically and in their penetration into business and home markets, their range of potential applications will widen, leading to growth in the size of the market for information products. Given this view of innovation in services, the real explosion of new types of services and of new types of service employment is still to come.

The nature and scale of service activity in the late 20th century are entangled, then, in the growth of information demand, of information-processing technologies, of suppliers of information products, and of the physical infrastructure that allows the transmission of information. Canada, along with other developed countries, is witnessing a major transformation of its economic structure – a transformation mediated through computer and telecommunications technologies. Underlying this transformation are fundamental changes in production methods, organizational and network structures, and product characteristics. One important aspect of this has been growing linkages between the customers for new information products and the suppliers of those products. As will be shown in Chapter 3 of this report, that demand originates largely in the goods sector, which fuels the growth of information suppliers in the service sector, particularly in the dynamic-service subsector. Indeed, that the successful exploitation of this synergy between goods and dynamic services is a key to growth in the emerging economy is one of the principal conclusions of our research.

Trade in Services

This discussion of trade in services has two purposes. First, it will describe the nature of service trade. Analysis of the available data leads to the conclusion that the content of service trade has been undergoing substantial change in recent years; the trend of those changes could have important implications for the size and nature of service trade in the future. The second purpose, which reflects the principal focus of this report, is to identify the employment implications of trade in services.

At the outset, some mention should be made of the problems associated with measuring service trade. The view that services are non-tradeable, with the corollary that demand for services is generated purely by domestic service demand, has been both reinforced by, and reflected in, the official data on trade in services. For a number of reasons, those data fail to capture the full extent of service trade.

The measurement of trade in services is more complex than the measurement of trade in goods. Services, as intangibles, are not subject to the border measures of tariffs and quotas applied to goods trade. Also, trade in services often takes place within multinational corporations and the monetary value placed on that trade reflects the internal pricing practices of those companies. The bundling of services together with goods in a single package, identified earlier in this chapter, represents another measurement problem; in the context of an analysis of trade, the value of services such as installation and training can be difficult to distinguish from the value of goods which are exported. And finally, since much of the new trade in services is transferred electronically, it tends to be invisible, and so has not been fully captured in the official statistics on trade in services.[17]

In the balance of international payments accounts there are five broad categories of service trade: travel; freight and shipping; business services; government transactions; and "other services." All of these services enter into international commerce via direct cross-border trade. No attempt is made in these data to measure the volume of services that are exported or imported indirectly in a form embodied in some physical output. Furthermore, since for many services a foreign direct investment is necessary for the conduct of business abroad, revenues, generated when branches in foreign countries do business with the nationals of that country, are considered part of investment income and do not enter into international trade statistics. Only when service producers located in one country provide services for consumption in another country does international trade in services take place. Therefore, for some industries, notably banking, the data do not adequately distinguish between service trade and investment activity, and trade in banking services is not included in the data on trade in services.[18]

The value of Canadian service trade has increased substantially in recent decades – in the period 1961-88 service exports grew from $1.3 to $20 million, and service imports grew from $1.7 to $26 million. Nevertheless, that growth has still been less than the increases shown by merchandise imports and exports. As a result, service exports and imports as a percentage of total exports and imports have been falling (Table 2-6). The signing of the Canada-U.S. Auto Pact in 1965, however, led to significant growth in the volume of cross-border trade in auto parts and vehicles, in a sense inflating the volume of merchandise trade. When service trade is compared to that part of Canada's international trade which excludes transactions relating to the Auto Pact, a slightly different picture emerges. Service trade is

Table 2-6

Service Exports and Imports as a Proportion of Total and Non-Auto-Pact Exports and Imports, Canada, Selected Years, 1961-88

	1961	1971	1981	1988
	(Per cent)			
Service exports				
Total exports	17.9	16.0	12.8	12.7
Non-auto-pact exports	17.9	19.9	14.9	16.5
Service imports				
Total imports	23.3	21.6	17.1	16.9
Non-auto-pact imports	23.3	27.3	20.7	21.4

SOURCE Based on J. J. McRae, "An exploratory analysis of Canada's international transactions in service commodities," paper prepared for the Economic Council of Canada, November 1989; and data from Statistics Canada, Cat. 67-001.

Table 2-7

Service Exports and Imports of Major OECD Countries, 1984

	Exports	Imports	Balance	Service exports as a proportion of total exports
	(Millions of US $)			(Per cent)
United States	53,687	53,890	−203	24.6
Japan	23,386	35,364	−11,978	13.8
West Germany	32,521	37,842	−5,321	19.0
France	51,277	42,685	8,592	55.1
United Kingdom	28,436	23,456	4,980	30.2
Italy	19,554	15,161	4,393	26.6
Canada	10,856	14,253	−3,397	12.5
Austria	7,243	4,408	2,835	46.1
Belgium-Luxembourg	13,007	10,926	2,081	25.1
Denmark	7,304	7,127	177	45.9
Netherlands	14,501	13,998	503	22.1
Norway	6,961	7,026	−65	36.9
Portugal	1,731	1,239	492	33.5
Spain	12,631	5,105	7,526	53.7
Sweden	6,920	6,095	825	23.6
Australia	3,796	6,363	−2,567	15.5
Total	293,811	284,938	8,873	25.4

SOURCE Based on McRae, "An exploratory analysis of Canada's international transactions in service commodities."

still only a fraction of total trade in 1988, but it rises from a ratio of 17 per cent of all imports to a ratio of more than one fifth of non-auto-pact imports. The increase is slightly smaller for service exports, increasing in 1988 from 13 per cent of all exports to 17 per cent of non-auto-pact exports.

Compared to other major OECD countries, Canada's service trade performance is not outstanding (Table 2-7). Canada ranked 10th out of 16 countries in terms of service export volume in 1984, well behind the four leading countries, which were the United States, France, West Germany, and the United Kingdom. Further, Canada ranked last when the value of service exports was taken as a percentage of total exports. When the balance of service trade is considered, Canada again turned in a relatively weak performance. The Canadian deficit on service trade was the third largest in 1984, after Japan and West Germany. Ten countries, on the other hand, reported surpluses on their international service-sector account, with the largest shown by France, Spain, the United Kingdom, and Italy.

Table 2-8 shows the content of Canadian service trade between 1961 and 1989. In 1961, international travel, and freight and shipping, which together represent the "traditional" categories of service trade, accounted for 76 per cent of service exports and for 70 per cent of service imports. In 1989, their share, while still dominant, had fallen considerably. Government transactions, which refer to military and diplomatic activities of the provincial and federal governments not included elsewhere in the balance of payments, decreased as a percentage of service trade between 1961 and 1989. Trade in "other services" remained only a very small proportion of service trade. (The "other services" category includes items such as wages and dues payable to international unions, expenditures by Canadian students abroad and by foreign students in Canada, recreational and cultural transactions, and the earnings of commuters and migrant workers.)

Very striking, however, is the surge in the relative importance of trade in business services on both the import and export side. The share of business services in service exports more than doubled over the period, increasing from 14 to 33 per cent. Business services accounted for a larger share of service imports over the period.

The composition of the Canadian trade in business services in 1969 and 1988 is shown in Table 2-9. In 1969, close to half of all business-service exports consisted of commissions earned by wholesale merchants and brokers on merchandise trade, transportation-related services, and tooling and other automotive charges. Some important changes took place, however, in the structure of business-

Table 2-8

Distribution of Service Exports and Imports by Service-Trade Category, Canada, Selected Years, 1961-89

	1961	1971	1981	1989
	(Per cent)			
Service exports				
Travel	37.7	36.8	30.2	34.6
Freight and shipping	38.1	34.9	34.5	26.2
Business services	14.3	19.1	29.2	33.5
Government transactions	7.0	5.2	3.6	3.3
Other services	2.7	4.0	2.6	2.4
Total	100.0	100.0	100.0	100.0
Service imports				
Travel	37.0	34.3	30.7	38.5
Freight and shipping	32.8	28.3	24.3	17.1
Business services	22.3	30.5	37.2	38.3
Government transactions	7.3	5.0	6.0	4.7
Other services	0.6	1.9	1.7	1.4
Total	100.0	100.0	100.0	100.0

SOURCE Based on McRae, "An exploratory analysis of Canada's international transactions in service commodities"; and data from Statistics Canada, Cat. 67-001.

service exports over the period: while the shares of service exports accounted for by commissions and by transportation-related services were still relatively large in 1988 compared to the other business-service export categories, they were nevertheless substantially smaller than their 1969 shares. R&D exports grew considerably over the period.

Changes in the composition of business service imports are also evident. In 1969, the largest shares of business service imports consisted of royalties, patents, and trademarks; the residual "other" category; and tooling and other automotive charges. In 1988, insurance and royalties, patents, and trademarks represented the largest categories of business-service imports, but management and administrative services, and R&D have also become important.

A comparison of the export/import balance in 1969 and 1988 leads to the following observations. The share of R&D services in both exports and imports grew substantially over the period, particularly on the export side, as did communications services. Canada's export performance in consulting and other professional services was also strong, while the share of imports represented by these services

Table 2-9

Exports and Imports of Selected Business Services,[1] by Type of Service, Canada, 1969 and 1988

	Proportion of Exports, 1969	Proportion of Imports, 1969	Proportion of Exports, 1988	Proportion of Imports, 1988
	(Per cent)			
Consulting and other professional services	7.3	9.0	10.3	5.2
Transportation-related services	14.9	7.1	10.9	8.3
Management and administrative services	6.6	10.1	6.8	11.2
R&D	3.1	5.3	11.5	8.5
Commissions	22.4	7.5	11.1	5.6
Royalties, patents, and trademarks	0.7	12.5	1.6	12.6
Films and broadcasting	1.7	3.9	0.3	1.9
Advertising and promotional services	2.3	2.8	0.9	1.4
Insurance	9.3	7.6	10.6	14.3
Other financial services	0.0	0.0	5.8	6.9
Computer services	0.0	0.0	3.5	1.6
Equipment rentals	10.7	6.3	3.5	3.0
Franchises and similar rights	0.0	0.8	--	0.3
Communications	1.0	1.3	6.4	4.5
Refining and processing services	0.0	...	1.5	...
Tooling and other automotive charges	11.0	12.4	11.4	7.4
Other	8.9	13.3	3.8	7.4
Total	100.0	100.0	100.0	100.0

1 Services here correspond to National Account entries and are therefore not strictly comparable to industry categories shown in the box on p. 9.
SOURCE Based on McRae, "An exploratory analysis of Canada's international transactions in service commodities"; and data from Statistics Canada, Cat. 67-203.

decreased. On the other hand, the trade deficit on royalties, patents, and trademarks was large in both 1969 and 1988; the deficit on management and administrative services increased; and insurance services showed a strong increase in imports.

Among Canada's trading partners, the United States predominates. Nearly 70 per cent of the value of business-service imports in 1986 originated in the United States, which was the almost exclusive source of imports of tooling and other automotive charges, computer services, R&D, advertising and promotional services, and management and administrative services. On the other hand, for communications services, other financial services, and consulting and other professional services, the European Economic Community and other foreign countries were the major sources in 1986.

Business-service exports show a less concentrated pattern of trade. In 1986, 56 per cent of the value of Canadian business-service exports had the United States as their destination; in contrast, 77 per cent of Canadian merchandise exports went to the United States. In particular, a very high proportion of consulting and other professional services and of communications services were exported to non-U.S. destinations.

Differences between business-service imports and exports are also apparent when the main vehicles of trade are examined. Intracorporate transactions are much larger in relative terms for imports, while for exports, arm's-length transactions predominate. To a large extent, the pattern and content of Canadian business-service imports reflects the relative importance of U.S. foreign direct investment in Canada; intracorporate charges for imports into Canada of tooling and other automotive services, R&D, management and administrative services, and royalties, patents, and trademarks are especially notable. The predominance of arm's-length transactions on the export side, especially when those exports are directed to countries other than the United States, suggests that Canadian business-service exporters, especially in the fields of communications, refining and processing services, equipment rentals, and consulting and other professional services, are achieving a certain degree of success in international competition, independently of intracorporate ties. Further, Canadian-controlled companies accounted for two thirds of the exports of business services in 1986, while business-service imports were accounted for primarily by foreign-controlled – especially U.S.-controlled – establishments. However, just over one third of business-service imports – a considerable amount – were accounted for by Canadian-controlled firms.[19]

Employment Implications of Service Exports

Because information on the amount of service-sector employment that is directly involved in international trade is simply not available, we have adopted a new approach. Our estimates are based on an indirect analysis of export-dependent service trade; hence, they should be considered only as an approximation of the actual magnitudes involved. First, we focus on the direct export of services, that is, services that are exported via a communications network or by the temporary movement of suppliers or customers. The second part of our discussion takes a broader view of service trade to include indirect-service exports; that is, services embodied in goods that are exported.

The information for the estimation of service-sector jobs which are dependent on direct-service exports was taken from Harris and Cox.[20] They developed an input-output model using data for 1981 to determine the share of industry output accounted for by each of final demand, intermediate demand, and exports. Since they used input-output data from Statistics Canada, the analysis refers to all business activities in the economy, and excludes all government-financed activities.

The direct-export share for each of the 15 service industries in 1988 included in the Harris-Cox model is shown in Table 2-10. To calculate the amount of export-dependent employment in each industry, that export share of output was also taken to represent the proportion of employment in each of those industries that is dependent on exports. When applied to employment data for 1988, this methodology yields an estimate of 250,000 service-sector jobs that were dependent on exports, which represented only 3.6 per cent of all service-sector jobs. However, as was shown above, some important differences exist within the service sector, notably between industries in the dynamic-service subsector and in the traditional-service groups. On the whole, the dynamic-service subsector is much more export-oriented than is the traditional-service subsector; indeed, the typology of the service sector discussed at the beginning of this chapter is based in part on the extent to which industries in the two groups are oriented to exports. When applied to the employment data for 1988, it is found that close to 230,000 jobs in dynamic services – almost 9 per cent of all jobs in that subsector – were dependent upon direct-service exports.

However, Harris and Cox estimate that the magnitude of indirect-service exports – that is, of services embodied in exported goods as a result of intermediate-demand transactions – is about 50 per cent greater than that of direct-service exports.[21] If the effects of both direct- and indirect-service exports on employment are considered, then the total employment effect of service trade is more significant.

Table 2-10

Exports as a Proportion of Output and Export-Dependent Employment in the Service Sector, Canada, 1988

	Export proportion of output	Export-dependent employment
	(Per cent)	
Dynamic services	8.7	227,935
Transportation		
Air	5.0	2,985
Rail	31.9	24,483
Truck	21.2	24,405
Other transportation and storage	20.3	42,444
Communications	2.2	4,892
Electric power	11.8	10,308
Other utilities	0.9	1,155
Wholesale trade	11.8	64,850
Finance, insurance, and real estate[1]	1.1	7,031
Business services	8.7	45,382
Traditional and nonmarket services[2]	0.5	21,766
Retail trade	0.3	3,753
Accommodation, food, and beverages	--	102
Amusement and recreation	0.2	318
Personal services	0.7	2,264
Health and education	0.8	15,329
Total services	3.6	249,701

1 Excludes banking.
2 Nonmarket services excludes social services and public administration.
SOURCE Based on McRae, "An exploratory analysis of Canada's international transactions in service commodities."

Furthermore, as is shown later in this report, it is the dynamic-service industries that are most closely linked to the goods sector. Therefore, most of those indirect-service exports will involve the dynamic services, and more than 20 per cent of the jobs in the dynamic services may be dependent on exports.

It is clear that in terms of direct trade, services form only a small component of overall trade. However, for some parts of the service sector, trade in services is significant, and technological change and the lowering of barriers to market access internationally may work to further increase the relative importance of trade in selected services in the future. Indeed, interest in service trade has been growing internationally, which is perhaps best reflected in the high priority given to service trade discussions in the current Uruguay Round of GATT negotiations. The interest is growing in Canada also; detailed research on Canadian service trade was conducted recently as part of the federal government's larger study of services.

To a large extent, the structure of Canadian service imports reflects patterns of foreign direct investment in Canada and the resulting content and magnitude of intracorporate service transfers. Thus Canada shows a tendency to import R&D and management and administrative services. However, while Canada's weak performance respecting trade in services compared to a number of OECD countries partly reflects the relative magnitude of foreign direct investment in Canada, it also reflects a relatively weak performance on the service-export side. The trends in service trade in Canada (especially given the context of the Canada-U.S. Free-Trade Agreement) and other countries suggest that, increasingly, domestic-service companies can expect to encounter foreign competition at home. As service markets become increasingly global, domestic-service producers – whether they engage directly in service trade or not – will need to be internationally competitive.

There are some positive signs on the export side. Particularly strong performances have been shown in recent years by consulting and professional services and communications. Arm's-length transactions by Canadian-controlled firms predominate and markets in a range of countries outside the United States are increasingly being tapped, demonstrating that many Canadian service firms can compete globally.

At the same time, much of the service trade takes place indirectly through the export of goods. The interdependence of goods and service producers is a major theme of this report. One of the implications of that interdependence is that, whether through direct participation in service exports, through the meeting of foreign competition at home, or through the contribution made to goods which are exported or which compete with imported goods, services clearly play a role in the competitiveness of the Canadian economy.

Location of Services

Service activities have always had an affinity for urban locations. Historically, service producers tended to locate close to their customers since service transactions relied heavily on direct contact between customers and suppliers. Minimum market-size requirements varied across the service sector, however, so that some services were found only in larger urban centres. Most villages, for example, contained a general store, while larger towns and cities would contain many retail outlets, perhaps a hospital to serve the regional population, and lawyers' offices. Services, therefore, were distributed throughout the urban hierarchy according to their market-size requirements.

While computer-based technological change has had a number of major impacts on the service sector, two are of particular relevance here. First, the computer allows the processing of vast amounts of information quickly and relatively cheaply, and its importance as a business management tool is rapidly growing. The demand for, and supply of, that information has grown exponentially. One outcome has been rapid growth in the size of the business-service industry. Second, computer-based technological change has relaxed some of the constraints that previously tied many service producers to their customers. No longer must information be exchanged on a face-to-face basis – information is now storable and transferable and its value is often enhanced in the process.

The conjunction of these two outcomes – the growth in business services and the relaxation of some of the market/location constraints – has led some observers to argue that an important part of the new growth in jobs could become "footloose" in terms of location and so could decentralize away from metropolitan areas to peripheral locations. Business services, in particular, have attracted attention as a potential tool for stimulating growth in regions where economic development is lagging, for four reasons.[22] First, the business-service industry has shown strong output and employment growth in recent years. Second, many of the jobs generated in business services are considered to be "good" jobs in that their average skill levels and earnings tend to be high. Third, the growth of these services in interregional and international trade makes them a potential engine of growth. And, fourth, business services play a very strategic role in investment, innovation, and technological change; by being a locus of competitive advantage, they may contribute to spatial variations in economic development.

However, rather than being footloose, the dynamic-service industries in general, and the business services and finance, insurance, and real estate industries in particular, show a strong tendency to locate in large metropolitan areas. In 1981, this tendency was most pronounced for computer services, personnel and executive-search services, advertising agencies, management consultants, architects and urban designers, and engineering and scientific services.[23] Business represents by far the main class of customer for each of these industries. Legal and accounting services also showed a tendency to concentrate in large metropolitan areas, but that tendency was less pronounced, in part because final consumers form a significant portion of their customer base.

The trend towards metropolitan concentration of key service-sector industries continued to 1986. Table 2-11 shows the extent to which Canadian cities and towns have more of a given industry's labour force than would be expected given their share of the national labour force. An index of greater than 100 indicates that the industry's workers are disproportionately located in the city; an index of less than 100 shows the extent to which that industry is underrepresented. Indexes are shown in the table for cities and towns of various sizes in all regions of the country.

Clearly, the dynamic-service industries are not spatially indifferent. Note, for example, the very high index for finance, insurance, and real estate in Toronto, and for business services in Calgary, Toronto, Ottawa-Hull, Vancouver, and Montreal. This pronounced concentration, which has been observed in other countries as well, suggests that the dynamic services respond strongly to very particular locational requirements.

Similar patterns are found when the analysis is based on occupations rather than industries (Table 2-12). In fact, the tendency for highly skilled occupations to be found in large metropolitan areas is even more pronounced. This reflects the fact that, in addition to the concentration of dynamic services in those locations, employment in the goods sector also shows a strong tendency towards occupational differentiation across locations; management and administrative, technical, and office occupations tend to be concentrated in large metropolitan areas, while goods occupations associated with resource extraction and traditional processing tend to be found in smaller urban centres.[24]

The following picture therefore emerges. Dynamic services and the head (or divisional) offices of goods-producing firms tend to locate in the largest urban areas.[25]

Also, while activities in the primary sector and traditional manufacturing industries are more commonly found in peripheral regions and in smaller urban centres, medium and high-value-added manufacturing tend to be located in large urban centres and in central regions.[26] This tendency to locate disproportionately in the larger urban centres is paralleled by the highly skilled occupations – the managerial and administrative, and professional groups.

There are several reasons for this urban concentration. All of these activities need to have access to information, and they also need to have face-to-face contact. The contention that new telecommunications technologies will relax the constraint on location imposed by the need for information suppliers and users to exchange information directly is valid for a significant portion of information exchanges, but usually only where routine information is involved. The type of information which is exchanged in the process of complex decision making at high levels in the management hierarchy, on the other hand, has thus far proved less amenable to indirect personal contact. The end result, therefore, has been somewhat perverse – the computer-based technologies, rather than stimulating the decentralization of management functions, have increased the ability of head offices to exert control over routine functions from a distance.[27]

That is not to say that the tendency towards concentration of information-intensive functions will not change in coming decades. In many respects, computer-based technological change is still in its early phases. New advances in telecommunications technologies that will allow visual contact in distance communications, such as improvements in video-conferencing, may well act to reduce or eliminate the need for direct personal contact. Socio-cultural innovations that encourage new working arrangements on a wide scale may reduce or eliminate the need for most people to commute to jobs in large central office complexes. And growing diseconomies associated with very large metropolitan areas – congestion, soaring housing costs, crime, lack of office space, and the very high costs of office space that is available – may act as a stimulus to many businesses and workers to seek more attractive locations in smaller urban areas and in peripheral locations.

The high degree of locational correspondence between firms in the dynamic-service sector and the central offices of goods-producing firms reflects not only their common need for information, but also the fact that they show very close industrial linkages. Most goods industries are heavily dependent on the inputs of dynamic-service firms for the production of goods, as will be seen in Chapter 3. At the same time, dynamic services need the demand which

Table 2-11

Index of Employment Concentration, Dynamic Services, Selected Cities and Towns, Canada, 1986[1]

	Toronto, Ont.	Montreal, Que.	Vancouver, B.C.	Edmonton, Alta.	Ottawa-Hull	Calgary, Alta.	Winnipeg, Man.	Quebec, Que.	Halifax, N.S.	Saskatoon, Sask.	St. John's, Nfld.
	(Thousands)										
Population	3,427	2,921	1,381	785	819	671	625	603	296	201	162
						(Canada = 100)					
Dynamic services	134	121	133	113	98	129	121	99	111	105	107
Transportation, communications, and utilities	97	117	130	120	87	111	141	77	116	99	113
Wholesale trade	136	122	123	114	61	112	122	87	100	132	120
Finance, insurance, and real estate	157	119	135	105	93	121	116	137	121	94	95
Business services	166	130	147	111	157	185	93	101	101	100	102

Table 2-11 (cont'd.)

	Saint John, N.B.	Sydney, B.C.	Kelowna, B.C.	Sault Ste. Marie, Ont.	Fredericton, N.B.	Lethbridge, Alta.	Charlottetown, P.E.I.	Prince Albert, Sask.	New Glascow, N.S.	Brandon, Man.
	(Thousands)									
Population	121	119	90	85	66	59	54	41	39	39
					(Canada = 100)					
Dynamic services	116	74	92	74	95	90	79	84	75	99
Transportation, communications, and utilities	152	109	80	87	105	91	94	95	113	114
Wholesale trade	116	70	93	70	106	96	82	92	79	130
Finance, insurance, and real estate	96	58	113	71	72	83	73	83	57	93
Business services	81	40	84	63	95	89	58	60	31	51

The Service Sector 23

Table 2-11 (concl'd.)

	Corner Brook, Nfld.	Grande Prairie, Alta.	Campbellton, N.B.	Cranbrook, B.C.	Summerside, P.E.I.	Swift Current, Sask.	Matane, Que.	White-horse, Yukon	Thompson, Man.	Carbonear, Nfld.
					(Thousands)					
Population	34	26	17	16	16	16	15	15	15	13
					(Canada = 100)					
Dynamic services	88	104	63	117	75	93	73	107	73	76
Transportation, communications, and utilities	88	125	92	148	90	112	96	169	140	84
Wholesale trade	149	109	66	129	103	119	59	83	42	144
Finance, insurance, and real estate	69	94	48	103	46	81	73	65	41	46
Business services	48	75	30	70	55	48	48	74	30	30

1 The index is measured as each industry's share of total employment in each city or town, as a proportion of that industry's share of total employment in Canada, multiplied by 100.
SOURCE   Based on data from Statistics Canada, Census of Canada.

24 Employment in the Service Economy

Table 2-12

Index of Employment Concentration, by Occupation, Selected Cities and Towns, Canada, 1986[1]

	Toronto, Ont.	Montreal, Que.	Vancouver, B.C.	Edmonton, Alta.	Ottawa-Hull	Calgary, Alta.	Winnipeg, Man.	Quebec, Que.	Halifax, N.S.	Saskatoon, Sask.	St. John's, Nfld.
						(Thousands)					
Population	3,427	2,921	1,381	785	819	671	625	603	296	201	162
						(Canada = 100)					
Managerial, administrative, and related	128	117	110	104	147	119	100	126	103	94	111
Professional											
Natural sciences, engineering, and mathematics	126	114	101	123	186	210	97	149	115	105	106
Social sciences and related	107	101	124	112	157	114	120	129	101	111	117
Religion	61	83	73	91	90	75	123	139	90	147	135
Teaching and related	86	102	86	102	102	87	103	132	109	113	137
Medicine and health	81	109	107	110	96	90	120	137	130	125	147
Artistic, literary, recreation, and related	140	145	123	97	149	106	105	125	106	93	86
Clerical and related	123	115	109	110	124	118	115	110	114	96	118
Sales	108	103	122	113	88	116	109	105	108	115	101
Service	81	88	113	105	105	104	105	113	141	114	105
Farming, horticultural, and animal husbandry	25	18	42	59	33	42	37	24	16	90	21
Fishing, trapping, and related	1	2	83	2	2	3	3	3	69	9	160
Forestry and logging	5	6	45	14	14	8	9	18	15	7	12
Mining and quarrying (including oil and gas fields)	5	13	20	176	8	101	12	12	35	124	67
Processing	65	89	76	53	32	40	59	56	34	64	77
Machining and related	111	92	72	98	33	66	100	57	47	56	34
Product-fabricating, assembling, and repairing	115	124	74	70	46	61	103	65	60	67	51
Construction trades	78	72	94	114	89	95	91	74	99	113	103
Transport-equipment operating	80	95	101	106	74	94	103	86	99	97	103
Material-handling and related	126	101	113	72	39	66	86	54	94	76	103
Other crafts and equipment-operating	126	125	81	100	100	92	120	94	95	102	95
All occupations	100	99	100	100	98	100	100	99	100	98	100

Table 2-12 (cont'd.)

	Saint John, N.B.	Sydney, B.C.	Kelowna, B.C.	Sault Ste. Marie, Ont.	Fredericton, N.B.	Lethbridge, Alta.	Charlotte-town, P.E.I.	Prince Albert, Sask.	New Glascow, N.S.	Brandon, Man.
					(Thousands)					
Population	121	119	90	85	66	59	54	41	39	39
					(Canada = 100)					
Managerial, administrative, and related	95	66	86	69	114	86	111	81	78	76
Professional										
Natural sciences, engineering, and mathematics	94	50	55	101	162	92	78	37	84	55
Social sciences and related	102	90	97	100	135	119	125	140	69	147
Religion	156	134	120	60	159	122	181	246	116	121
Teaching and related	95	123	82	107	133	112	95	119	97	114
Medicine and health	134	131	111	109	96	111	141	106	117	176
Artistic, literary, recreation, and related	67	59	102	72	114	85	87	74	50	83
Clerical and related	109	83	90	90	111	97	107	90	89	90
Sales	103	103	135	99	97	114	90	115	98	132
Service	110	109	117	115	111	123	117	139	85	129
Farming, horticultural, and animal husbandry	29	24	138	30	39	76	113	142	42	54
Fishing, trapping, and related	70	323	13	24	12	0	248	0	207	0
Forestry and logging	46	68	142	85	145	2	53	158	335	18
Mining and quarrying (including oil and gas fields)	24	781	90	40	8	87	28	43	88	43
Processing	89	137	87	208	39	73	64	49	84	66
Machining and related	83	61	68	142	35	62	62	49	203	47
Product-fabricating, assembling, and repairing	72	66	95	90	57	74	54	57	132	65
Construction trades	129	148	119	140	103	122	120	118	132	118
Transport-equipment operating	104	116	83	86	75	95	95	100	92	105
Material-handling and related	137	102	98	161	72	80	61	72	112	44
Other crafts and equipment-operating	135	83	52	75	99	78	91	103	129	119
All occupations	100	98	100	100	98	98	101	98	98	98

Table 2-12 (concl'd.)

	Corner Brook, Nfld.	Grande Prairie, Alta.	Campbellton, N.B.	Cranbrook, B.C.	Summerside, P.E.I.	Swift Current, Sask.	Matane, Que.	White-horse, Yukon	Thompson, Man.	Carbonear, Nfld.
					(Thousands)					
Population	34	26	17	16	16	16	15	15	15	13
					(Canada = 100)					
Managerial, administrative, and related	79	83	90	98	66	72	92	118	62	63
Professional										
Natural sciences, engineering, and mathematics	56	105	54	55	27	74	46	125	122	33
Social sciences and related	106	112	169	116	107	109	114	191	134	55
Religion	115	101	408	72	94	208	53	120	169	145
Teaching and related	118	110	119	99	71	96	118	118	120	132
Medicine and health	130	91	249	70	106	122	113	55	86	84
Artistic, literary, recreation, and related	56	60	31	90	77	102	139	89	52	77
Clerical and related	94	87	80	96	85	89	97	108	82	71
Sales	116	118	90	110	79	121	101	81	69	88
Service	102	102	120	116	210	129	108	109	112	82
Farming, horticultural, and animal husbandry	15	46	27	26	85	122	30	34	16	12
Fishing, trapping, and related	322	9	60	0	349	0	118	15	0	645
Forestry and logging	136	134	516	554	45	9	504	84	64	41
Mining and quarrying (including oil and gas fields)	19	526	14	231	24	293	67	356	2,078	55
Processing	167	86	91	104	145	42	125	29	109	323
Machining and related	37		36	64	23	62	45	27	76	53
Product-fabricating, assembling, and repairing	56	61	61	74	65	85	76	72	73	101
Construction trades	130	77	127	103	102	114	104	137	115	207
Transport-equipment operating	113	134	113	156	94	86	133	122	132	95
Material-handling and related	129	152	67	79	105	80	126	64	108	141
Other crafts and equipment-operating	71	71	63	89	93	129	86	98	28	50
All occupations	98	123	101	98	98	98	99	98	98	98

1 The index is measured as each occupation's share of total employment in each city or town, as a proportion of that occupation's share of total employment in Canada, multiplied by 100.

SOURCE Based on data from Statistics Canada, Census of Canada.

originates in the goods sector. Typically, head offices act as the central control unit for their branch plants. As a consequence, those branch plants – which are usually dispersed geographically – have less need for the direct local acquisition of many dynamic services since they are often provided through head offices.[28] Branch plants, therefore, create less demand for services produced locally, while head offices create firm-wide demand in central locations for dynamic services.

A third factor encouraging the concentration of dynamic services and other information-based activities in large urban areas is access to skilled labour. The shift to services has been accompanied by substantial growth in the workforce share of highly skilled occupations with high educational requirements in financial, business, and nonmarket services, and low-skilled occupations in traditional services (see Chapter 6). And while large metropolitan areas are not the exclusive source of highly skilled labour, they are a large source. The importance of skilled labour to some industries, however, also provides skilled workers with some leverage regarding the location of employment. For example, medical and educational occupations tend to be found in middle-sized urban areas in both central and peripheral locations.[29] In fact, regional centres based on specialized research skills often develop in association with universities, industrial research centres, or other specialized facilities.

It would appear, therefore, that the effect of the growth of dynamic services and other information-based activities on the location of employment is spatial segmentation in the labour market, on several scales – between large metropolitan regions and smaller urban areas, between urban locations and rural areas, and between central and peripheral regions. Some observers have argued that for most countries, the largest metropolitan area will act as the national information centre, and that the urban hierarchy of information centres will extend to the international scale where a few "world-cities" will dominate the global information economy.[30] Differentiation throughout the national economy in terms of the "information-intensiveness" of different locations will translate into spatial variations in occupational mix, skill levels, and earnings. In Canada, there are distinct regional variations in the distribution of very large metropolitan areas. Based on the size of the largest urban centres and the shape of the urban hierarchy, the overall position of the Atlantic provinces could be viewed as being not as strong in relative terms as that of central Canada and the western provinces, though Halifax continues to be a regional centre of some importance.

It is likely, therefore, that the locational characteristics of service-sector industries and of information-based occupations will have implications for regional development in Canada. To an important extent, these issues reflect the interaction of computer and telecommunications technologies, on the one hand, and industry supplier-customer relationships, on the other. In fact, many observers have stressed the critical part played in regional performance by these technologies, stressing their role as "enablers" in the economic development process.[31] The research reported here leads to similar conclusions.

Firm Size

The last dimension that we examine in this chapter is the structure of the service sector in terms of firm size. Although it may be expected that firm size will have an important bearing on such things as employment and output growth, and technological change, our primary interest is in looking at firm size as it relates to the main theme of this report, namely, the changing nature of employment in the service economy. In this section we compare the firm sizes of the goods and service sectors to determine whether small firms are particularly characteristic of the service sector.

Table 2-13 shows the distribution of employment growth between 1978 and 1986 in the goods and service sectors across the three firm-size categories. Since medium-sized (20-99 employees) and large firms (100 or more employees) in the goods sector actually contracted over the period, all net growth in that sector occurred in the small-firm category (less than 20 employees). In the service sector, on the other hand, 32 per cent of the job growth took place in firms with 100 or more employees, and 58 per cent of the growth took place in small firms with less than 20 employees. Thus small firms have played an important role in employment growth overall, more so in the goods sector than in the service sector. The contribution of the goods sector to total employment growth, however, was relatively small, since service-sector firms accounted for 93 per cent of the net job growth in Canada between 1978 and 1986.

Another way to compare the firm-size structure of the goods and service sectors is to examine the two sectors over time (Table 2-14). In 1978, 18 per cent of total employment was found in small firms with less than 20 employees; by 1986, the small-firm share of employment had risen to 27 per cent. And, in each of 1978, 1984, and 1986, the differences between the goods sector and the service sector in terms of the share of employment found in small firms were actually very small, contrary to the popular notion that small firms dominate the service sector more than the goods sector. Furthermore, in both sectors, the share of employment found in large firms of more than 100 employees fell,

Table 2-13

Distribution of Employment[1] Growth in the Goods and Service Sectors by Firm Size, Canada, 1978-86

	Less than 20	20-99	100 or more	Total
	(Per cent)			
Service sector	57.8	9.9	32.3	100.0
Goods sector[2]	400.4	–3.2	–296.7	100.0
Total	74.6	9.5	15.9	100.0

Firm size (number of employees)

1 Defined as the number of "average labour units" calculated for a business as its total annual payroll divided by the average wages in its industry and province.
2 Firms with 20 or more employees experienced employment contractions.
SOURCE Estimates by the Economic Council of Canada, based on Statistics Canada, unpublished LEAP data.

while the share found in medium-sized firms of 20-99 employees remained relatively stable.

These data on employment by firm size are based on the concept of the "average labour unit" per firm developed by Statistics Canada.[32] They are calculated by taking firm payroll and dividing it by the average wage in the industry and province where the payroll is earned. They are thus an artificial construction rather than an enumeration of the actual number of employees in each firm. The average labour unit is used here because actual employee counts are not available for historical periods. Table 2-15, however, provides the most recent information available on employment by firm size and industry. It is based on a count of the actual number of paid employees in each firm. Because the data-set underlying Table 2-15 is based on a different definition of employment, comparisons with the previous tables should not be made.

The purpose of Table 2-15 is to show differences across the various industries *within* the service sector. The share of employment accounted for by small firms varied considerably from industry to industry within that sector in 1989. The largest percentage of employment found in small firms was shown by the traditional services. There is a great deal of variation, however, within dynamic services. Small firms were least characteristic of transportation, communications, and utilities, and also represented a smaller share of employment in finance, insurance, and real estate compared to other dynamic services and to traditional services. In contrast, roughly one third of employment in business services and wholesale trade in 1989 was in firms with fewer than 20 employees. The firm-size structure of nonmarket services clearly stands out as being very different from the rest of the service sector; small firms account for only 2 per cent of employment in education, for 17 per cent of employment in health and social services, and for less than 1 per cent of employment in public administration.

This short overview of firm size points to the conclusion that small firms are not much more characteristic of the service sector than they are of the goods sector. However, the small-firm phenomenon is important because it has accounted for by far the largest proportion of new jobs in recent years. Since most employment growth has taken place in the service sector, it follows that job creation by small service-sector firms has been the predominant source of new jobs in Canada. Data presented by Birch[33] for the United States, Sweden, the United Kingdom, and Canada also show that, with the exception of Sweden, where most job growth has taken place in very large firms, small firms

Table 2-14

Distribution of Employment[1] in the Goods and Service Sectors by Firm Size, Canada, 1978, 1984, and 1986

	Less than 20	20-99	100 or more	Total
	(Per cent)			
Goods sector				
1978	14.8	17.0	68.2	100.0
1984	20.2	..	..	100.0
1986	25.4	16.4	58.2	100.0
Service sector				
1978	19.2	15.0	65.8	100.0
1984	24.8	..	..	100.0
1986	26.6	14.0	59.3	100.0
Total				
1978	17.8	15.6	66.5	100.0
1984	24.0	14.6	61.4	100.0
1986	26.5	14.7	58.9	100.0

Firm size (number of employees)

1 Defined as the number of "average labour units" calculated for a business as its total annual payroll divided by the average wages in its industry and province.
SOURCE Estimates by the Economic Council of Canada, based on Statistics Canada, unpublished LEAP data.

Table 2-15

Distribution of Employment¹ by Firm Size, Canada, First Half of 1989

	Firm size (number of employees)				
	Less than 20	20-49	50-99	100 or more	Total
	(Per cent)				
Service sector	23.6	9.9	6.6	60.1	100.0
Dynamic services	23.4	11.1	7.8	57.7	100.0
Transportation, communications, and utilities	12.1	5.7	4.5	77.6	100.0
Wholesale trade	31.5	17.3	9.9	41.3	100.0
Finance, insurance, and real estate	21.9	10.0	6.7	61.3	100.0
Business services	33.9	14.3	11.7	40.1	100.0
Traditional services	36.7	15.6	8.3	39.4	100.0
Retail trade	40.4	12.2	6.2	41.3	100.0
Accommodation, food, and beverages	34.8	21.9	12.8	30.5	100.0
Amusement and recreation	32.0	14.8	9.2	44.0	100.0
Personal services	57.7	15.9	6.9	19.7	100.0
Nonmarket services	7.4	3.3	3.8	85.5	100.0
Health and social services	17.0	6.4	7.1	69.6	100.0
Education	2.2	1.9	2.1	93.8	100.0
Public administration	0.2	0.5	1.2	98.1	100.0
Goods sector	18.5	11.4	9.7	60.4	100.0
Total	22.3	10.3	7.4	60.0	100.0

1 An employee is defined as any person drawing pay for services rendered or for paid absences and for whom the employer is required to complete a Revenue Canada T-4 Supplementary form.
SOURCE Estimates by the Economic Council of Canada, based on data from Statistics Canada, Survey of Employment, Payroll, and Hours (SEPH).

have been the predominant source of new jobs in recent years. Therefore, the Canadian trends resemble those found in similar countries.

According to Birch, one of the important characteristics of small firms is their orientation towards innovation. Another characteristic of the small-firm phenomenon is its volatility – a large number of new firms appear each year, some grow rapidly while others decline, and a large number go out of business. In Birch's view, a strong small-firm sector and a vibrant economy are characterized by both a strong orientation to innovation and high levels of volatility, features that are characteristic of the Canadian service sector.

Conclusion

In many respects the term "service sector" is an anachronism. The service sector is clearly composed of a large number of diverse industries that behave in quite different ways. And many of the traditionally held views on the service sector – that services are neither tradeable nor storable, and that service transactions require direct contact between the customer and the supplier – are no longer valid.

Our analysis identifies a few of the differences among the industries that make up the service sector and highlights some of the characteristics that distinguish the dynamic-service industries from the traditional-service industries and how those in turn differ from the nonmarket-service industries. The dynamic-service subsector, in particular, showed a strong orientation to investment in the 1980s, with an important part of that investment consisting of the introduction of computer-based technologies. And while the direct involvement of dynamic services in Canada's international trade is still small, the content of service trade has been undergoing important changes, which are reflected in an expanding role for business-service and communications transactions across borders. It may be expected that dynamic-service industries – and service trade in general – will grow in the future, in part as a result of new opportunities made possible through technological change.

The dynamic-service subsector differs from the two other service subsectors in another important respect. The dynamic services, particularly business services, and finance, insurance, and real estate, show a marked tendency to locate in the larger metropolitan areas. That tendency parallels a similar locational pattern for office functions in the goods sector, and so, at least for the present, reinforces current rural-urban and regional differences in job opportunities.

Small firms appear to be no more characteristic of the service sector than of the goods sector; in both cases, employment growth in the 1980s has taken place primarily in small firms. And while small firms may be a source of economic vibrancy, they also offer a wide range of jobs, both good jobs – well-paid and highly skilled – and bad jobs, poorly paid, low-skilled, and with weak attachment to the labour market.

3 Sectoral Interdependencies and the Growth in Service Employment

In this chapter we will consider various explanations of why the shift to services is taking place. The first section considers a number of explanations found in the literature. These fall into four major groups, which are: 1) changes in the composition of final demand; 2) sectoral differences in productivity growth; 3) contracting-out; and 4) changes in the nature of intermediate demand for services. Ultimately, although each appears to have played some role in the shift to services, none provides a comprehensive explanation.

In the second section of this chapter, therefore, we present a series of analyses whose aim is to examine and shed further light on the causes of service-sector employment growth. We begin by reviewing the "manufacturing matters" debate, a discourse that has occupied an important place in the recent literature, especially in the United States. At its most fundamental level, this debate is over which of the two sectors – goods or services – plays the pivotal role in generating growth in the U.S. economy. The remainder of this section consists of an analysis of the relationship in the Canadian economy between the goods and service sectors. What is the nature of that relationship? Has it changed over time? What can be learned about the dynamic processes behind the growth of services by looking at these sectoral interactions?

Our research consisted of two related projects. The first was a series of policy simulations using a sectoral econometric model that was specially designed to give an overall view of the relationship between the goods and the service sectors and of the impacts of aggregate spending patterns on employment and output growth in the sectors. However, because the model deals with the sectors at the aggregate level, and because it works with gross domestic product (that is, value-added outputs), it cannot treat linkages that occur at the level of individual goods and service industries. Therefore we undertook a complementary research project that used input-output data to analyse the nature of demand and supply relationships between industries in Canada. The results of our research highlight the significant differences among the various service subsectors. We find, for example, that production in the goods sector and the dynamic-service subsector is highly interdependent. Because of the relationships between demand, output, and employment, goods-production growth stimulates service-production growth. But equally important, goods producers depend on the service industries for many of their intermediate inputs. However, the growth in the traditional-service subsectors is attributable to the more common explanations such as productivity growth and final demand effects.

The third section discusses the prospects for service-sector growth in Canada, and the final section summarizes the major conclusions of the research reported in this chapter.

The Shift to Services: Some Common Explanations

The shift to services has attracted a fair amount of attention in the literature from analysts attempting to identify its causes. As early as 1940, Colin Clark argued that a high propensity to consume services was an important explanation for the relatively fast growth of employment in the service sector.[1] In the late 1960s, William Baumol's "Macroeconomics of unbalanced growth" and Victor Fuchs' *The Service Economy* addressed the topic.[2] Recently, analysts have expressed concern about the relative decrease in the size of the goods sector,[3] a topic that has become the subject of the "manufacturing matters" debate.

Among the explanations for the shift in employment to the service sector, four predominate: first, that consumer demand for services has increased faster than for goods; second, that labour-productivity growth has been slower in services than in goods; third, that goods producers now are simply contracting out for services that were formerly performed in-house; and fourth, that there has been strong growth in the intermediate demand for services as inputs to the production process.

Consumer Demand

Proponents of this explanation argue that as incomes rise, consumers tend to spend proportionately more on services than on goods. To test this argument, we used Statistics Canada's National Income and Expenditure Accounts data to calculate personal expenditures on goods and on services for the period 1971-86. We found that, contrary to expectations, approximately $0.44 of every additional dollar in disposable income was spent on goods and about $0.32 was spent on services.[4] Based on the estimated equations, the income elasticities of demand for goods and for services at the midpoint of the consumption expenditure curves were calculated. For goods, the elasticity was 0.93; for services, it was 0.88. After allowing for statistical noise, the two estimates may be taken as approximately equal. Admittedly, consumption function analysis is a rich and controversial field of economic research and there is no agreement on the definitive estimates of the income elasticity of demand for goods and services. However, other attempts to verify the income elasticity argument also have met with little success.[5] For example, Grubel and Walker analyse consumer expenditures on nine types of services in 1974 and 1984, and conclude that "the income elasticity of demand for services is not high; on average it is about one. If this generalization is correct and holds in the future, consumer spending on services may be expected not to provide much stimulus for demand and output even if Canadian incomes on average continue to rise."[6] All this evidence suggests that there are sufficient grounds to be doubtful about the income elasticity argument.

Another method of testing the service-demand hypothesis is to examine the distribution of total final expenditures. A complete analysis of trends in final expenditures patterns must take account not only of personal expenditures on goods and services, but also of government current expenditures on goods and services, government investment, business investment, exports of goods and services, and imports of goods and services.

The results of such an analysis is presented in Table 3-1. Between 1971 and 1988, the share of total domestic expenditures accounted for by personal consumption of services increased from about 22.3 per cent in 1971 to 25.5 per cent in 1988. However, government current expenditures (roughly 93 per cent of which consists of services) decreased over the period from 20.8 per cent of total domestic expenditures to 17.8 per cent, while business investment in goods increased from 16.3 per cent of total domestic expenditures to 22.1 per cent. Service exports and imports showed some small changes but remained relatively minor components of total domestic expenditures. Thus the small increase in personal expenditures on services as a share of total domestic expenditures between 1971 and 1988 was more than offset by changes in the government and business components of total expenditures. Consequently, the shares of total domestic expenditures accounted for by goods and by services remained essentially stable over the period. These results, then, also point to the conclusion that shifts in the composition of final demand cannot provide a satisfactory explanation for the shift to services.

Productivity Growth

A second popular explanation of the shift to services, and one that has attracted a great deal of attention in the literature, argues that the rapid postwar growth in service employment is attributable to relatively slow growth in the labour productivity of the service industries compared to

Table 3-1

Distribution of Total Final Expenditures on Goods and Services, Canada, 1971, 1981, and 1988

		1971	1981	1988
		(Per cent)		
Total domestic expenditures on goods[1]		59.2	58.7	59.6
Total domestic expenditures on services[2]		40.8	41.3	40.5
Personal expenditures on goods	A	31.0	30.7	30.6
Personal expenditures on services	B	22.3	24.3	25.5
Government current expenditures on goods and services	C	20.8	19.3	17.8
Government investment	D	3.9	2.6	2.5
Total business investment	E	16.3	21.9	22.1
Goods exports	F	20.8	23.7	31.2
Service exports	G	3.7	3.5	3.0
Goods imports	H	14.2	21.7	28.3
Service imports	I	4.5	4.5	4.3

1 Total final expenditures on goods = $A + (1-a)C + D + E + F - H$, where a is the ratio of government expenditures on services to total government current expenditures on goods and services, calculated from the input-output tables.
2 Total final expenditures on services = $B + aC + G - I$.
SOURCE Estimates by the Economic Council of Canada, based on data from Statistics Canada.

goods industries.[7] We tested this hypothesis using data on gross domestic product (1981 dollars) per worker for the goods sector and for the three service subsectors for the period 1967-89.[8]

It should be pointed out that the measurement of output is extremely poor for many service industries. Nevertheless, economists still use these data to compare the relative productivity performance of the goods and service sectors. We caution, therefore, that the discussion which follows should be regarded as indicative rather than conclusive evidence (we return to a consideration of some of the problems associated with estimating output and productivity in services later in this section).

The labour-productivity growth performances of goods and service industries, as currently measured, varied considerably from year to year. However, when averaged over the whole of the period 1967-89, the goods sector's rate of productivity growth, at 1.8 per cent, is superior to that of the service sector at 1.4 per cent (Table 3-2). This was due to the poor performance of the traditional and nonmarket services, where annual labour-productivity growth rates averaged 0.7 per cent and –0.2 per cent, respectively. In fact, the average annual performance of the dynamic services, at 2 per cent, was superior to that of the goods sector.

When productivity performance is compared with employment growth (see Chapter 4), the productivity argument loses ground as a comprehensive explanation of the shift to services. While it is true that employment growth has been relatively high in the traditional-service subsector, where productivity growth has been low, that pattern is not characteristic of nonmarket services and dynamic services. Since the early 1970s, nonmarket services' share of total employment has stabilized in the range of between 21 and 23 per cent, despite its poor measured productivity growth performance. And despite strong productivity growth in dynamic services, that subsector's share of total employment has increased significantly. In other words, there has been no consistent trend across the three service subsectors concerning employment and productivity growth.

Perhaps the best-known problem of measurement concerns the method used to estimate output in many service industries. Sharpe, for example, uses information from Statistics Canada to estimate the magnitude of the output measurement problem for the goods and service sectors, and for individual industries.[9] He finds that Statistics Canada's "poor quality" rating of the official data affects 1.6 per cent of the output measured in the goods sector, 15.1 per cent of output in the commercial component of the service sector, and 9.3 per cent of output in the noncommercial-service sector which, being based on input-output data, excludes public administration. Further, while labour input is used to estimate output in some commercial-service industries and even in some goods industries, the use of this measure predominates in the noncommercial-service sector, where 51.6 per cent of the output is measured by labour input and depreciation. Overall, Sharpe estimates that 37.2 per cent of the output of business services and personal services is measured either by labour input or is classified by Statistics Canada as being of poor quality. He concludes that the "very poor productivity performance in recent years in this sector may thus be linked to productivity measurement problems."[10]

A less-known problem is the price deflators used to determine an industry's real output. It is increasingly felt by some experts that the deflators used introduce biases into the measurement of real output growth, with the result that the estimate of labour productivity in the service industries is biased downward and the estimate of labour productivity in the goods industries is biased upward. In other words, rather than invalidating the usefulness of the productivity growth comparisons discussed above, analysis of the nature of the measurement biases related to price deflation methods reinforces our general conclusions that productivity growth in the dynamic-service subsector is stronger than in the goods sector.

How are these biases introduced and what is their impact on productivity as it is measured in the goods and the service industries? In order to accurately estimate an industry's productivity growth, the theoretically "correct" double-deflation procedures are used to measure the industry's real outputs. The double-deflation procedure to measure real value-added (or real net output) involves deflating the value

Table 3-2

Average Annual Rate of Growth in Output[1] per Employee, Canada, 1967-89

	(Per cent)
Service sector	1.4
Dynamic services	2.0
Traditional services	0.7
Nonmarket services	–0.2
Goods sector	1.8
Total	1.4

1 Gross domestic product (1981 dollars).
SOURCE Estimates by the Economic Council of Canada, based on data from Statistics Canada.

of industry's total gross output and total intermediate inputs, in current prices, by the appropriate price indices. Therefore, real value-added (or real net output), which is the usual numerator in productivity calculations, is equal to real (deflated) gross output minus real (deflated) intermediate inputs.

However, recognition is growing that price deflators (or their implicit equivalents) for gross output for many service industries are probably biased upward,[11] so estimates of real gross output for these industries are too low. This is because for many services, appropriate price deflators are not available, so growth in those industries' inputs is used to simulate growth in their real value-added (or real net output). If that output growth is more or less equal to the input growth, then the productivity growth measures are biased towards zero. Also price deflators do not typically reflect improvements in quality. Therefore, when the quality of inputs is improved, the industry consuming the input appears to experience a decrease in real costs and a corresponding increase in measured real net output relative to labour inputs. In other words, productivity growth in user industries, according to conventional measurement techniques, would be biased upward. Unfortunately, the precise magnitude of these measurement biases is not known and so the measures of real output cannot be corrected.

A significant portion of the output of many service industries – notably dynamic services – is consumed by other industries, particularly in the goods sector, as intermediate inputs. Therefore, given the suspected bias in the deflator for gross output in many service industries and the false attribution of output growth to industries purchasing higher quality inputs from suppliers, it follows that biases are introduced into the productivity growth measures for goods as well. For services, the likely result is to bias productivity growth measures downward; for goods, the result is probably an upward bias, since part of the gain in productivity achieved by suppliers of intermediate services is falsely attributed to the goods industry purchasing those services as inputs.[12] Furthermore, because the magnitude of purchases of services by the goods sector as a whole has been increasing, it is likely that the extent of the bias for both services and goods has been growing in recent years.

Contracting-Out

Some economists have argued that the growth of service-sector employment relative to goods-sector employment is merely a statistical artifact, reflecting the fact that services that were formerly performed within goods-producing firms are now increasingly purchased – that is, contracted out – from specialists in the service sector. According to this hypothesis, the rapid expansion of the service sector – particularly the dynamic services, which tend to be closely linked to goods production – represents a replacement of part of the value-added and associated employment by goods-producing industries. In the final analysis, therefore, what is observed is simply a change in how the production process is organized rather than any real growth in the share of value-added (and growth in output and employment) accounted for by services. The extent to which the "contracting-out" argument can explain the shift to services has been studied in background research done for the Council by Postner.[13] That research is summarized here.

The economic theory underlying the question of contracting-out is largely derived from the field of industrial organization. A good summary of the basic principles can be found in Grubel and Walker[14] who identify four factors encouraging the contracting-out of services by goods-producing firms: 1) the increasing complexity of business operations which makes it more difficult to monitor performance of nonproduction employees (and easier to obtain service inputs from outside suppliers); 2) increasing specialization and technological change, which makes it more profitable to hire service expertise in the market than to produce it in-house; 3) the decreasing cost of information and communications which makes it less costly to obtain services in the market than to produce them within the firm; and 4) increasing total employment costs (including nonwage costs), particularly for manufacturing firms, relative to those of small service-firms that are less affected by constraints such as the regulatory environment and unionization. On the other hand, Grubel and Walker also identify economic forces that favour the in-house production of services, such as the need to prevent disclosure of firm-specific information, and the ability to provide services that may previously have been acquired locally to distant parts of the firm, as a result of innovations in communications.

McFetridge and Smith[15] recently completed a major Canadian study of contracting-out. They find a small but significant occurrence of contracting-out of certain services that presumably were previously produced in-house; the extent, however, is not uniform across the various goods-producing industries and service inputs. Since contracting-out is difficult to measure directly, McFetridge and Smith use various indirect techniques based on a number of assumptions which may not hold true. As a result, they draw their conclusions cautiously and call for further research and better data to clarify the issue.

Some insights into the contracting-out question also can be gained from research conducted for the Council by

Postner and Wesa.[16] They find evidence of above-average increases in the outside purchase by goods-producing industries of some services, notably communications, financial services, and business-management services. At the same time, however, a number of other producer-service inputs grew at a lower-than-average rate, for example, wholesale trade and transportation services. But the question remains: To what extent do these observed trends reflect replacement rather than augmentation of in-house service production by goods-producing industries? Postner and Wesa use occupational data to help answer that question, and again, the evidence is rather mixed. They found that contracting-out for the services of accountants, lawyers, and communication specialists, for example, did replace in-house production of those services to some extent. But they found the opposite trend was true for service specialists such as managerial personnel, and professional and technical workers, where the trend was towards more in-house employment in goods-producing industries. Other studies have produced similar results.[17]

There are a number of shortcomings in the empirical work on contracting-out which arise out of a lack of data at the appropriate statistical level, and which have been overlooked in the literature reviewed above. For example, the theoretical arguments relating to contracting-out place it within the context of firm-level transactions; the empirical work, however, is largely based on establishment-level information. Much of the contracting-out which is at the establishment level may in fact represent intrafirm transactions and therefore should not be counted. At the same time, those transactions occurring between diverse production units within conglomerates operating in widely different industries probably should be counted as true contracting-out.[18]

There are two other statistical problems which should be mentioned briefly.[19] First, neither research at the level of the establishment nor at the level of the firm documents in-house service activities of goods producers. It is very difficult, then, to identify when contracting-out *replaces* in-house activities, which is an essential aspect of the contracting-out question. Second, there is reason to be concerned about the reliability of the measurement of purchased service inputs.[20] Ideally, these data should be provided by company head offices and related ancillary units; none of the standard statistical surveys, however, are directed to these units.

In response to the deficiencies in the data on contracting-out, Statistics Canada recently conducted an experimental survey for the period 1984-87, with projections to 1990.[21] The results indicate increases in the consumption by goods producers of both services produced in-house and contracted-out services. They also suggest the value of contracting-out as a proportion of all services consumed grew moderately over the study period. Even this survey has its deficiencies, however. The goods sector and producer services were only partially covered in the survey, and the period studied is really too limited to establish significant trends. It would also be useful if the data collection were extended to include information on the extent of contracting-out compared to in-house production of goods and services by service producers. Hopefully the survey will be modified and extended, and improved data on the question of contracting-out in Canada and its role in service-sector growth will become available.

Overall, the evidence which is available suggests that there is a trend towards increased contracting-out for services by goods producers, but that activity is too small to account for more than a part of the overall shift to services. We can conclude from this that: 1) given the growth in service-related employment in both service-sector and goods-sector firms, the official statistics on employment by industry probably underestimate the *level* of total service employment in the economy; 2) since there has been some trend towards increased contracting-out of services and since that, implicitly at least, partly replaces some service activities formerly performed in-house, the official statistics would overestimate the *rate of growth* of service employment overall; and 3) the fact of contracting-out will affect observed *distribution* of employment by industry. For example, if a wholesale-trade firm or a manufacturing firm contracts out to a business-service firm, the economic activity it generates would be allocated to the business-service industry, although, in fact, the activity would be undertaken in support of the purchaser. However, the extent to which contracting-out would affect the observed industrial distribution of economic activity has not been empirically investigated.

Intermediate Demand

Earlier in this chapter we considered the role of shifts in the composition of final demand in the growth of the service sector. Final demand expenditures, however, account for only a part of service-sector output; the other part is accounted for by intermediate demand: that is, the consumption of services by businesses as inputs for the production of goods and other services. Economists have tended to focus on the role of consumer demand in service-sector growth. But consumer demand can explain a significant part of that growth only if it accounts for a large part of the consumption of outputs of service industries – and for many service producers, that simply is not the case. For many service industries, in fact, intermediate demand is far more important than final demand (Table 3-3). For example, in 1985, the transportation and the business-service industries each sold more than three quarters of their output to other industries as intermediate inputs; final consumers accounted for only 17 and 6 per cent, respectively, of their output. In fact, with the exception of wholesale trade, each of the dynamic-service industries sold at least half of its output as intermediate inputs. Only in the cases of communications, finance and real estate, and insurance did consumers purchase a significant portion of the output.[22] On the other hand, final demand, and consumer demand in particular, was of much greater relative importance in traditional services.[23] Therefore, while consumer demand for services undoubtedly played a role in the growth of traditional services, its impact on dynamic services was small in comparison to the impact of intermediate demand.

Some attention has been paid in the literature to the question of the impact of intermediate demand on service-sector growth. Clearly, since the economy as a whole has grown over time, the total demand for services as intermediate inputs also must have increased, in absolute terms. Therefore, the focus of the intermediate demand argument must be changes in the relative demand by individual producers for services as intermediate inputs; specifically, that more service inputs are required today to produce one unit of output than in the past.

To test this hypothesis, we used input-output data to trace industry inputs and outputs over the period 1971-85. Two indicators were developed: first, the proportion of all intermediate inputs that consisted of services; and second, the ratio of total service inputs (including services produced in-house and purchased services) to gross output. Of a total of 28 goods-producing industries, only two – mining, and crude petroleum and natural gas – showed any significant increase in the ratio of service inputs to total intermediate inputs over time (Chart 3-1). While some goods-producing industries showed minor increases over the period 1971-85 in the ratio of service input to gross output, most showed a decrease over 1981-85 (Chart 3-2). Nor does there

Table 3-3

Distribution of Service Industry Output[1] According to Intermediate and Final Demand, Canada, 1985

	Intermediate input	Consumer expenditures	Other	Total demand
	(Per cent)			
Dynamic services				
Transportation	77.3	17.3	5.4	100.0
Pipeline transport	58.8	0.9	40.3	100.0
Storage	76.8	17.6	5.6	100.0
Communications	57.4	34.4	8.2	100.0
Utilities	50.8	7.2	42.0	100.0
Wholesale trade	47.2	2.9	50.0	100.0
Finance and real estate	51.2	40.7	8.1	100.0
Insurance	51.2	41.3	7.5	100.0
Business services	81.1	5.6	13.3	100.0
Traditional services				
Retail trade	12.9	5.5	81.6	100.0
Accommodation, food, and beverages	16.4	83.7	–	100.0
Amusement and recreation	24.6	75.4	–	100.0
Personal services	49.4	30.0	20.7	100.0
Other services[2]	52.8	26.6	20.6	100.0

(Output sold as: Final demand = Consumer expenditures + Other)

1 Gross domestic product (1981 dollars).
2 Includes equipment and vehicle rental, and photographic, repair, and building services.
SOURCE Estimates by the Economic Council of Canada, based on input-output data from Statistics Canada.

Sectoral Interdependencies 37

Chart 3-1

Total Service Input as a Proportion of Total Intermediate Input, by Goods Industry, Canada, 1971, 1981, and 1985

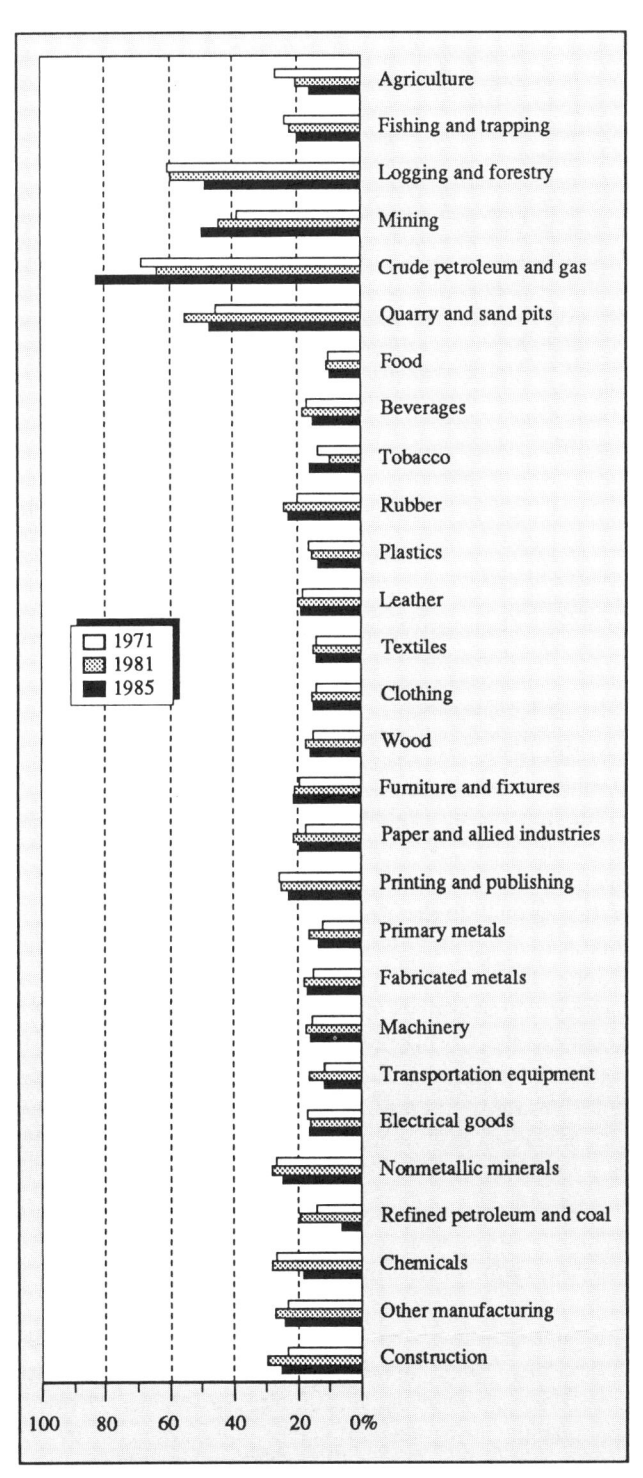

[Bar chart showing values from 0% to 100% for the following industries, with bars for 1971, 1981, and 1985:
Agriculture, Fishing and trapping, Logging and forestry, Mining, Crude petroleum and gas, Quarry and sand pits, Food, Beverages, Tobacco, Rubber, Plastics, Leather, Textiles, Clothing, Wood, Furniture and fixtures, Paper and allied industries, Printing and publishing, Primary metals, Fabricated metals, Machinery, Transportation equipment, Electrical goods, Nonmetallic minerals, Refined petroleum and coal, Chemicals, Other manufacturing, Construction]

SOURCE Estimates by the Economic Council of Canada, based on data from Statistics Canada.

Chart 3-2

Total Service Input as a Proportion of Gross Output, by Goods Industry, Canada, 1971, 1981, and 1985

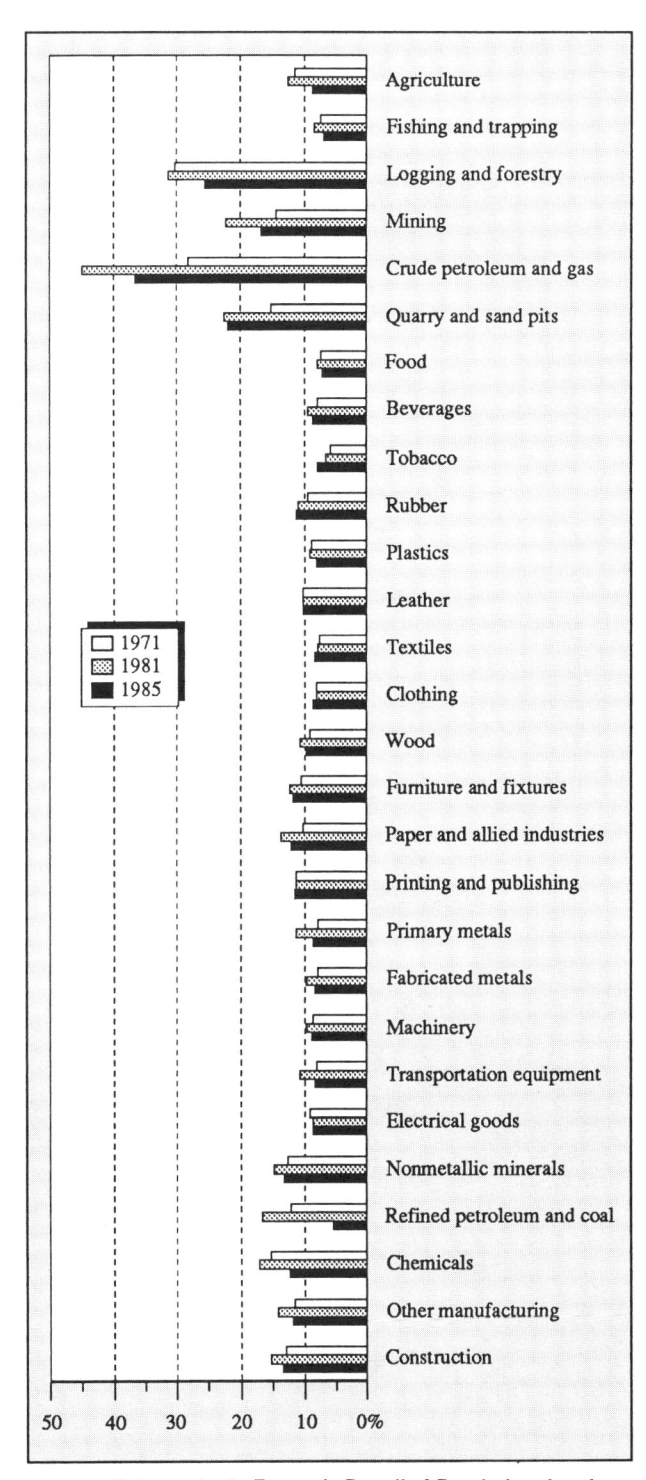

[Bar chart showing values from 0% to 50% for the following industries, with bars for 1971, 1981, and 1985:
Agriculture, Fishing and trapping, Logging and forestry, Mining, Crude petroleum and gas, Quarry and sand pits, Food, Beverages, Tobacco, Rubber, Plastics, Leather, Textiles, Clothing, Wood, Furniture and fixtures, Paper and allied industries, Printing and publishing, Primary metals, Fabricated metals, Machinery, Transportation equipment, Electrical goods, Nonmetallic minerals, Refined petroleum and coal, Chemicals, Other manufacturing, Construction]

SOURCE Estimates by the Economic Council of Canada, based on data from Statistics Canada.

appear to have been any significant trend towards growing service consumption on the part of the service industries themselves. Of a total of 18 service-producing industries, none showed any increase in the ratio of service input to total intermediate input. And few showed any significant increases in the ratio of service input to gross output between 1981 and 1985 except for storage and communications (Chart 3-3).

These results suggest that there was not any substantial increase in the extent to which services are used as intermediate inputs by individual producers in either the goods or the service sectors between 1971 and 1985. The results of the analysis of contracting-out, though, suggest that some shift may have occurred in the source of those services; that is, slightly more services are being acquired from outside the firm today than previously.

Summary

A review of some of the explanations of the shift to services leads to rather ambiguous conclusions. All four explanations – a shift in the composition of final demand, differences in goods- and service-sector productivity growth, contracting-out, and changes in the level of intermediate demand for services – appear to account for a part of the overall growth of the service sector, but the individual contribution of each appears to be small relative to the magnitude of the shift. Furthermore, rigorous testing of the hypotheses is seriously constrained by the lack of appropriate data, an indication of the inadequacy with which services have been treated by economists and policymakers alike. This point is taken up again in the final chapter of this report.

The Interdependence of Goods and Services

Another weakness in the research on the shift to services is that it often focuses on only the direct impact of each factor. However, the real world is rarely quite so simple. In fact, growth in the size of the economy, along with the increasing complexity of the production process, have worked to increase both the number of actors and the number of transactions in the economy. As a result, the indirect effects of economic interactions have now assumed significant importance. To adequately address the question of the causes of the shift to services, therefore, it is necessary to take account of how the economic system functions as a whole. It is to this that we now turn.

The "Manufacturing Matters" Debate

For the past few years, policy analysts and economists in the United States have debated whether an economy can thrive without a large manufacturing base. Popularly termed the "manufacturing matters" debate, some argue that in the future only services will be necessary for a vibrant economy, others argue that the most important source of growth and wealth will be the manufacturing sector, and still others

Chart 3-3

Total Service Input as a Proportion of Gross Output, by Service Industry, Canada, 1971, 1981, and 1985

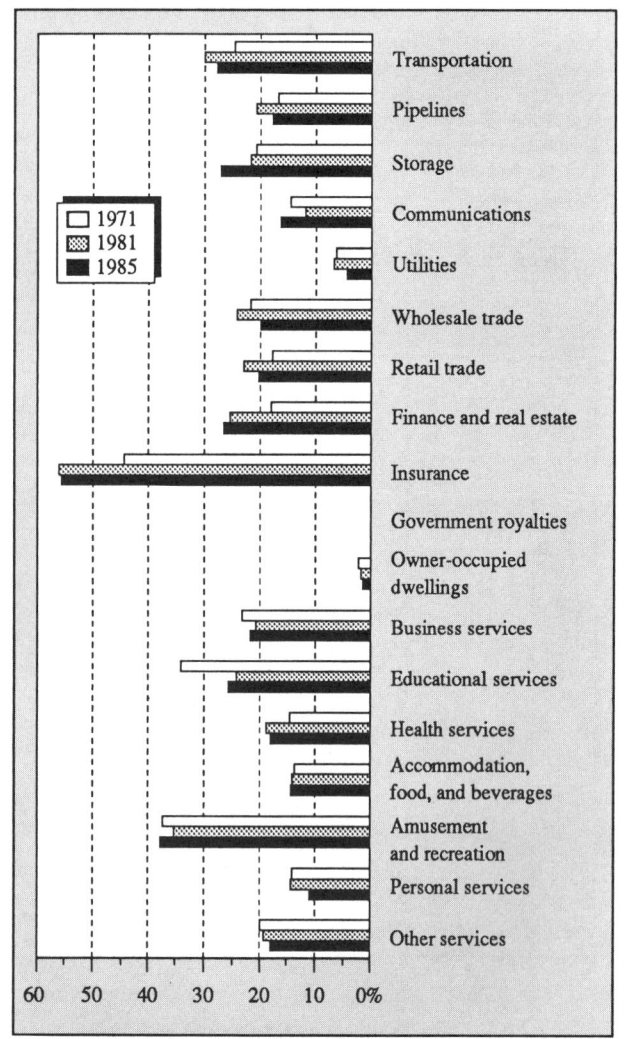

SOURCE Estimates by the Economic Council of Canada, based on data from Statistics Canada.

argue that both manufacturing and service activities will be necessary.

Those who subscribe to the view that only services will matter in future argue that the most highly developed economies naturally evolve towards what has been termed the "post-industrial society."[24] Taken to the extreme, this view implies that, just as the balance of employment shifted from agriculture to manufacturing in the decades following the industrial revolution, so will modern economies see a shift out of manufacturing and into services. The logical conclusion is that, eventually, the service sector will be the primary generator of wealth in the economy. Whether the evolution to a post-industrial society involves a shift in the industrial structure of employment, or output, or both, is rarely specified.

Those that argue that, on the contrary, manufacturing will remain the most vital component of a national economy, claim that because it is the locus of R&D activity, it generates by far the greater part of exports and provides high-wage jobs.[25] They also argue that because the manufacturing sector is the source of an important part of the demand for inputs from other sectors, manufacturing is the primary generator of economic activity.

The third argument is that increasing complexity in the production process, accompanied by changes in the organizational structure of production, has resulted in the lengthening of the chain of linkages between economic activities.[26] Services form a vital part of those linkages and therefore both manufacturing and services, particularly producer services, are vital components of the economy. At the same time, because manufacturing does matter, the shift to services cannot continue indefinitely to the point where goods production disappears altogether; the presence of both a strong manufacturing sector and a strong service sector is necessary for an economy to thrive.

Our results indicate that manufacturing, and goods producers more generally, play a key role in generating production in both the goods and the service sectors. They also highlight the fact that goods producers are highly dependent on services as large and important sources of intermediate inputs. Consequently, the quality (and cost) of those service inputs will have a critical impact on the competitiveness of the goods sector, and that competitiveness will ultimately determine whether the goods sector grows. The main conclusion of our analysis, therefore, is that the two sectors are mutually interdependent, and the vitality of one will affect the vitality of the other. To our knowledge, the current study is the first attempt to measure the strength of the linkages between the two sectors in a Canadian context.

Policy Simulations of a Sectoral Econometric Model

In order to gain an overall view of the relationship between the goods and the service sectors, we undertook a series of policy simulations using an econometric model specially designed by Curtis and Murthy for this purpose.[27] The model is unique in that it is decomposed into three interrelated sectors, which reflect the typology outlined in Chapter 2. The three sectors are: goods (primary industries, manufacturing, and construction); commercial services (dynamic and traditional services); and nonmarket services (health, education, and public administration). The model focuses on the relationship between economic growth and the demand for goods and services, and in turn their relationship to sectoral output and employment levels. Aggregate supply is derived from the goods sector, commercial services, and nonmarket services; and aggregate demand is disaggregated according to final expenditures on goods and services.

The model builds upon explanations of the shift to services found in the literature, incorporating contemporary macroeconomic theory. The structure of output (supply) is explained primarily by the pattern of aggregate expenditures (demand). Aggregate expenditures are driven and structured by the effects of income, wealth, relative prices, interest rates, and government expenditures. Employment is defined by sectoral employment equations and is explained by sectoral output, capital stock, and wage rates. Most importantly, all these aspects of the structure of the aggregate economy are reconciled in a consistent dynamic-model framework. The model is based on quarterly data, seasonally adjusted when appropriate, from National Income and Expenditure Accounts and other data supplied by Statistics Canada, for the period 1967-86.

The Simulations and Their Results

Before discussing the simulation analysis, a few introductory remarks are appropriate. First, a variety of simulations based on changes of varying magnitude to different parameters could be useful for understanding the historical development of the goods and service sectors; in this section, we present three possible simulations, referring interested readers to the detailed background study for a discussion of alternate specifications. Second, it should be emphasized from the outset that the analysis reported here was specifically designed to focus on the interactions between the three sectors, it is not intended to provide lessons for macroeconomic policymaking.[28]

The purpose of the simulation analysis was to increase our understanding of the dynamics underlying the shift of output and employment to the service sector observed in Canada in 1967-86. The results offer interesting insights into the dynamics of the interactions between the goods sector, commercial services, and nonmarket services. They show the differences in the responses of the sectors to various policy measures, and how those differences affect the process of structural change and the performance of the aggregate economy.

We begin with the observation that, over the study period, the service sector as a whole grew faster than the goods sector. We then ask the question: How different would that pattern be if changes were made to selected parameters in the model such that the level of economic activity of the goods sector was boosted relative to that of services? To help answer that question, a number of simulations were performed, three of which are reported here.

The first simulation consisted of a set of changes that either stimulated goods production directly or that were more favourable to the goods sector than to services, in relative terms. As in model simulation generally, each of the changes that was introduced was arbitrarily imposed in the sense that the values of selected model parameters that were determined on the basis of historical experience were replaced with new, hypothetical values, determined by the researcher. In each case, those imposed values were different enough from the actual experience to cause a discernible change in outcome, but were not so different as to cause an unrealistic departure from the historical experience. Specifically, the policy package in this simulation involved making three changes:

1 Personal income taxes were lowered slightly on an annual basis over the study period. That involved changing two tax parameters in the model. The result was that the ratio of "direct tax on persons and other transfers from persons to gross national product" was lowered; for example, from 14.6 per cent (actual) to 14.1 per cent (hypothetical) in 1972, and from 18 per cent (actual) to 15 per cent (hypothetical) in 1986. As a consequence, personal disposable income increased. From the estimated equations of consumption of goods and services, we know that people spent slightly more of their additional income on goods than on services – in the model, the marginal propensity to consume goods was 0.44, while the marginal propensity to consume services was 0.32. Therefore, an increase in disposable income would stimulate the final demand for goods more than for services.

2 A portion of government current expenditures over the period 1971-86 was reallocated to government expenditures on capital. Government current expenditures consist of outlays for goods and services by the federal, provincial, and local governments. In contrast to the capital expenditures component which consists of spending on buildings, machinery, and equipment, a relatively large portion of the money for government current expenditures (about 93 per cent) was spent on services. In the hypothetical scenario, government current expenditures was set at 92 per cent of its historical value; the other 8 per cent was reallocated to the government capital expenditures account.

3 The last policy change in this first simulation involved lowering the interest rate. Interest rates in Canada have been high by historical standards since 1979. In keeping with the desire to simulate plausible scenarios, high interest rates were lowered for each year by between 1 and 2 percentage points for the period 1979-84 when interest rates peaked. Because actual interest rates fell below 10 per cent in 1985 and 1986, the decreases for these years were less than 1 percentage point. In the model, these interest-rate reductions would stimulate the demand for goods while having little direct impact on the demand for services, for two reasons. First, since the cost of capital would decrease, capital investment would increase; second, lower interest rates would, by reducing the cost of debt financing, stimulate the demand for consumer durables – many of which are "big-ticket" items – relatively more than the demand for services which, though increasingly purchased on credit, are often relatively less expensive.

An additional feature of the policy package should be highlighted. Since governments are concerned with the size of the deficit, in order to make the simulation as realistic as possible, the policy changes were designed so as to cause little difference between the size of the federal deficit in the simulated economy compared to the actual economy. The decrease in government revenues resulting from the reduction in the personal tax rate was balanced by the reduced interest rate, which led to a decrease in the amount of interest paid by governments on the public debt and to a widening of the tax base through stimulation of the economy as a whole.

The results of this simulation are summarized in Table 3-4. Total output, employment, and personal disposable income were higher in the hypothetical scenario than in the actual economy throughout the period 1971-86 and the unemployment rate was lower. Furthermore, output and employment levels in each of the goods and commercial-service sectors also were higher in the simulated case. The levels of output and employment in nonmarket services, however, did not change. That is because they are determined in the model by the level of total government expenditures, which remained the same in the simulated case as in the actual case.

The higher levels of economic activity in the goods and commercial-service sectors are to be expected, given the expansionary impact of the reduction in personal income taxes and interest rates. However, as explained earlier, the reduced personal income tax and interest rates, along with the reallocation of a portion of government expenditures away from services to goods, also should have had a disproportionately larger expansionary impact on the goods sector relative to commercial services and nonmarket services. In 1986 the goods sector's share of employment did increase, but only from 29 per cent in 1986 in the actual case to 30 per cent in the simulated case; the share of commercial services decreased by 0.6 percentage points; and the balance of the reduction in share was accounted for by nonmarket services. In terms of output, the share of the goods sector increased by 0.9 percentage points while the decreases accounted for by commercial services and nonmarket services were 0.3 and 0.7 percentage points, respectively. Clearly, despite the stimulation given to the goods sector, the actual gains shown by that sector in the hypothetical case were very small in relative terms.

Because this simulation involved changes to three different model parameters, identifying the impact of any one of those changes on its own is difficult. In particular, the impact of the direct stimulation of the goods sector compared to services is not easily differentiated from the effects of the expansionary economic climate generally. The second simulation, therefore, is a subset of the first. It focuses on the impact of one of the changes described above, namely, the transfer of 8 per cent of the historical value of government current expenditures to government capital expenditures. That change affected the level of spending on goods directly, representing an increase of $6 billion in spending on goods in 1986 and, equally important, a decrease of $6 billion in spending on services.

The results of the second simulation are summarized in Table 3-4. What is immediately striking is how similar these results are to those of the first simulation. Notably, total output and personal disposable income were higher in the hypothetical scenario than in the actual economy throughout the period, the unemployment rate was lower, and employment levels were slightly elevated. The goods sector's share of employment increased, but by only 0.7 percentage points; the share of employment accounted for by commercial services decreased by 0.5 percentage points; and the remainder of the decrease was accounted for by nonmarket services. Similarly, small differences are apparent when the output shares are compared. Again, despite the stimulation given to the goods sector at the expense of the service sector, the relative sizes of the two sectors changed very little.

The results of the first two simulations can be explained as follows. The level of goods output was increased directly by a shift in government spending from services to goods; it was also increased indirectly by the increase in personal disposable income resulting from the tax reduction and by the increase in the attractiveness of spending on consumer durables due to the reduction in the interest rate. Together, these led to a larger relative increase in the direct demand for goods compared to services. But, in the model, a complementarity exists between goods and commercial services in consumption and production. Goods expenditures commonly involve the purchase of a package that includes the good itself along with services such as delivery, financing, and repairs. Therefore, in addition to the initial effect of stimulating aggregate demand, higher levels of goods production and consumption also had the indirect effect of stimulating the production of services. Expenditures on many services, by contrast, usually involve consumption of the service only – for example, the purchase of legal services, dry-cleaning services, and entertainment – and tend to have relatively small indirect effects on goods consumption. Furthermore, when goods output increased, total employment also increased. As a result, national income and personal disposable income increased as well, which also caused the demand for both goods and services to increase. In other words, because of linkages among output, employment, income, and expenditures, it was not possible for the goods sector to grow significantly at the expense of the service sector.

The first two simulations were designed to stimulate goods-producing activity. The results suggest that that stimulation does indeed lead to growth in the level of economic activity – not only in the goods sector, but also in commercial services – with relatively small impacts on the nonmarket sector. The third simulation (see Table 3-4) approaches the question of the impact on the structure of the economy of shifts in the sectoral allocation of expenditures from the opposite direction, and poses the question: Would stimulation of the service sector at the expense of the goods sector lead to similar growth in the overall level of economic activity and in employment and output levels in both the service and the goods sectors? In the model, personal consumption of goods and services is behaviourally determined by two separate equations which take into account real disposable income, real net financial wealth, relative sector prices, and nominal interest rates. In this simulation, 10 per cent of the actual historical values of personal expenditures on goods in each year from 1971 to 1986 was taken away from goods and added to personal expenditures on services.

Employment in commercial services showed some small gains, but the size of those increases was insignificant and

42 Employment in the Service Economy

Table 3-4
Sectoral Interdependency: Selected Indicators of the Impacts of Three Sets of Policy Simulations on Goods- and Service-Sector[1] Growth, Canada, Selected Years, 1971-86

	Actual economy					Simulation 1[2]			
	1971	1976	1981	1986	Average 1972-86	1971	1976	1981	1986	Average 1972-86
	(Billions of 1981 dollars)					(Billions of 1981 dollars)			
Personal disposable income	144.9	204.0	237.7	259.3		146.1	213.6	248.8	284.8	
Consumer expenditures[3]										
Goods sector	73.0	99.5	109.5	124.0		73.6	104.4	116.0	136.7	
Service sector	52.4	71.5	86.7	101.1		52.8	75.3	89.9	107.4	
Gross domestic product										
Goods sector	92.8	109.3	117.8	133.2		94.4	112.9	122.7	141.5	
Commercial services	78.3	110.4	144.0	168.0		78.5	112.0	146.2	173.0	
Nonmarket services	43.8	53.3	57.8	63.3		43.8	53.3	57.8	63.3	
	(Millions of persons)					(Millions of persons)			
Employment										
Goods sector	3.0	3.3	3.6	3.4		3.0	3.3	3.7	3.6	
Commercial services	3.4	4.2	5.1	5.7		3.4	4.2	5.2	5.7	
Nonmarket services	1.8	2.0	2.3	2.5		1.8	2.0	2.3	2.5	
	(Per cent)								
Annual rate of real output growth										
Goods sector					2.5					2.8
Commercial services					5.3					5.4
Nonmarket services					2.5					2.5
Annual rate of employment growth										
Goods sector					1.0					1.2
Commercial services					3.6					3.6
Nonmarket services					2.5					2.5
Output share										
Goods sector	43.2	40.0	36.9	36.6		43.6	40.6	37.6	37.5	
Commercial services	36.4	40.4	45.1	46.1		36.2	40.3	44.8	45.8	
Nonmarket services	20.4	19.5	18.1	17.4		20.2	19.2	17.7	16.7	
Employment share										
Goods sector	36.9	34.4	32.5	29.4		37.0	34.6	32.9	30.3	
Commercial services	41.4	44.2	46.5	48.9		41.4	44.2	46.3	48.3	
Nonmarket services	21.7	21.4	20.9	21.7		21.6	21.3	20.8	21.5	
Unemployment rate	6.2	7.1	7.5	9.6		5.9	6.7	6.8	8.5	

Table 3-4 (concl'd.)

	Simulation 2[4]					Simulation 3[5]			
	1971	1976	1981	1986	Average 1972-86	1971	1976	1981	1986	Average 1972-86
Personal disposable income	145.2	(Billions of 1981 dollars) 207.5	244.9	270.5		144.0	(Billions of 1981 dollars) 197.1	225.7	241.1	
Gross domestic product										
Goods sector	94.1	111.9	121.4	138.5		90.4	103.9	110.9	123.3	
Commercial services	78.4	111.0	145.2	170.3		78.1	109.0	141.4	163.4	
Nonmarket services	43.8	532.3	57.8	63.3		43.8	53.3	57.8	63.3	
Employment	(Millions of persons)						(Millions of persons)			
Goods sector	3.0	3.3	3.6	3.5		2.9	3.2	3.4	3.1	
Commercial services	3.4	4.2	5.1	5.7		3.4	4.2	5.2	5.8	
Nonmarket services	1.8	2.0	2.3	2.5		1.8	2.0	2.3	2.5	
				(Per cent)						
Annual rate of real output growth										
Goods sector					2.7					2.2
Commercial services					5.3					5.1
Nonmarket services					2.5					2.5
Annual rate of employment growth										
Goods sector					1.1					0.4
Commercial services					3.6					3.7
Nonmarket services					2.5					2.3
Output share										
Goods sector	43.5	40.5	37.4	37.2		42.6	39.0	35.8	35.2	
Commercial services	36.2	40.2	44.8	45.8		36.8	41.0	45.6	46.7	
Nonmarket services	20.2	19.3	17.8	17.0		20.6	20.0	18.6	18.1	
Employment share										
Goods sector	37.0	34.6	32.8	30.1		36.6	33.8	31.5	27.4	
Commercial services	41.4	44.1	46.3	48.4		41.6	44.7	47.5	50.8	
Nonmarket services	21.6	21.3	20.8	21.6		21.8	21.5	21.0	21.7	
Unemployment rate	5.9	6.8	7.1	8.9		6.7	7.6	8.2	10.8	

1 In the simulations, commercial services include dynamic and traditional services.
2 Simulation 1 entailed: 1) decreasing personal income taxes annually from 1972 to 1986; 2) transferring 8 per cent of government current expenditures to government capital expenditures; and 3) decreasing the interest rate annually from 1972 to 1986.
3 For the sake of simplicity, consumer expenditures are not shown for simulations 2 and 3.
4 Simulation 2 entailed transferring 8 per cent of government current expenditures to government capital expenditures.
5 Simulation 3 entailed reallocating 10 per cent of the actual historical value of personal expenditures on goods in each year from 1971 to 1976 to expenditures on services.

SOURCE Estimates by the Economic Council of Canada, based on data from Statistics Canada, and an econometric model from D.C.A. Curtis and K.S.R. Murthy, "Goods sector-service sector structural change and Canadian economic growth," paper prepared for the Economic Council of Canada, 1989.

not nearly enough to offset the employment decrease in the goods sector. By 1986, commercial services' share of total employment in the simulated economy was 1.9 percentage points higher than in the actual economy, and the goods sector's share was 2 percentage points lower. However, that gain in commercial services' share of employment was won at the cost of a weaker economy overall, as reflected in lower total employment, lower total output, and lower personal disposable income compared to the actual economy in 1971-86.

The simulation analyses reported here point to the following conclusions. First, direct stimulation of the goods sector at the expense of the service sector leads to growth in the level of economic activity in both the goods and the service sectors. And while the share of output and employment accounted for by the goods sector did increase, the increase was very small because of the resulting growth in the service sector. Second, direct stimulation of the service sector at the expense of the goods sector did not have indirect growth effects; on the contrary, the resulting decrease in the level of total employment was larger than the gains experienced by the service sectors. Consequently, the service sector's share of employment did increase, but the overall level of economic activity decreased. These results suggest that there are fundamental differences in the roles played by the goods and the service sectors in the economy.

The sectoral model that forms the basis for the simulation analysis provides a useful picture of how aggregate spending patterns affect the distribution of employment and output across the sectors. However, a complete accounting of how the goods and service sectors relate is more complex because final demand represents only one component of total demand for services. The other important component is intermediate demand; that is, demand by other industries for goods and services as inputs to the production process. The fact that the econometric model that formed the basis for the simulation exercises contains only three broad sectors means that it cannot provide insights into how demand and supply linkages at the level of individual industries contribute to output growth in different industrial sectors. Accordingly, we used input-output data in the next stage of our analysis to define the role played by intermediate demand.

Interindustry Transactions

Before we describe the input-output analysis, some comments on the data should be noted. While the simulation results reported above are based on National Income and Expenditure Accounts data and include goods, commercial services, and nonmarket services, an analysis of interindustry transactions requires information at the industry level on sources of inputs and the allocation of outputs. Statistics Canada's input-output tables provide this information. They trace interindustry transactions, but only in the private sector. The input-output analysis which follows, then, includes all business activities in the goods and commercial-service sectors, but excludes all government-financed activities in the economy. The analysis, which focuses on the period 1971-85, is based on the "medium" (M) aggregation in the input-output tables which provides raw data for 50 industries and 100 commodities.

A Sectoral Input-Output Analysis

Industrial interdependence is a fact of life in a developed economy. To illustrate this using the example of the agriculture industry, the total output of agriculture in 1985 was $23,301 million (1981 dollars). From this gross output, $4,615 million worth was used by agriculture itself as intermediate inputs, $9,977 million was used by the food-processing industry, $56.1 million by the beverage industry, $201 million by the tobacco products industry, and $34.3 million by wholesale trade, with the remaining $8,418 million going to other industries as intermediate inputs and to final demand. Thus a large proportion of the output of one industry becomes inputs for other industries.

Although input-output data point to the importance of interindustry transactions, they do not automatically provide a systematic evaluation of the details of that interdependence. For example, when the food-processing industry produces a given amount of output, it purchases services from service industries, and commodities from the agriculture, fishing and trapping, forestry, and refined petroleum and coal products industries. Those industries, in turn, also require other goods and services as inputs to fill the orders of the food-processing industry. The process involves many transactions which together are considered as taking place within a single "production pass," that is, all of the intermediate demand flows arising out of an increase in production in a given industry are treated as taking place within a single unit of time (Figure 3-1). This is different from the concept of the "long-run multiplier," which requires successive rounds of consumer spending before the total multiplier effect is realized. Raw input-output data show only the direct supply and demand linkages between industries. In order to measure the total output effect of production in a given industry, both the direct and the indirect effects – that is, the requirements of supplying industries for inputs to produce their output – must be taken into account, which requires more sophisticated treatment of the raw data.

Figure 3-1

Partial Illustration of the Types of Intermediate Transactions Involved in Production, Food-Processing Industry, Canada, 1985[1]

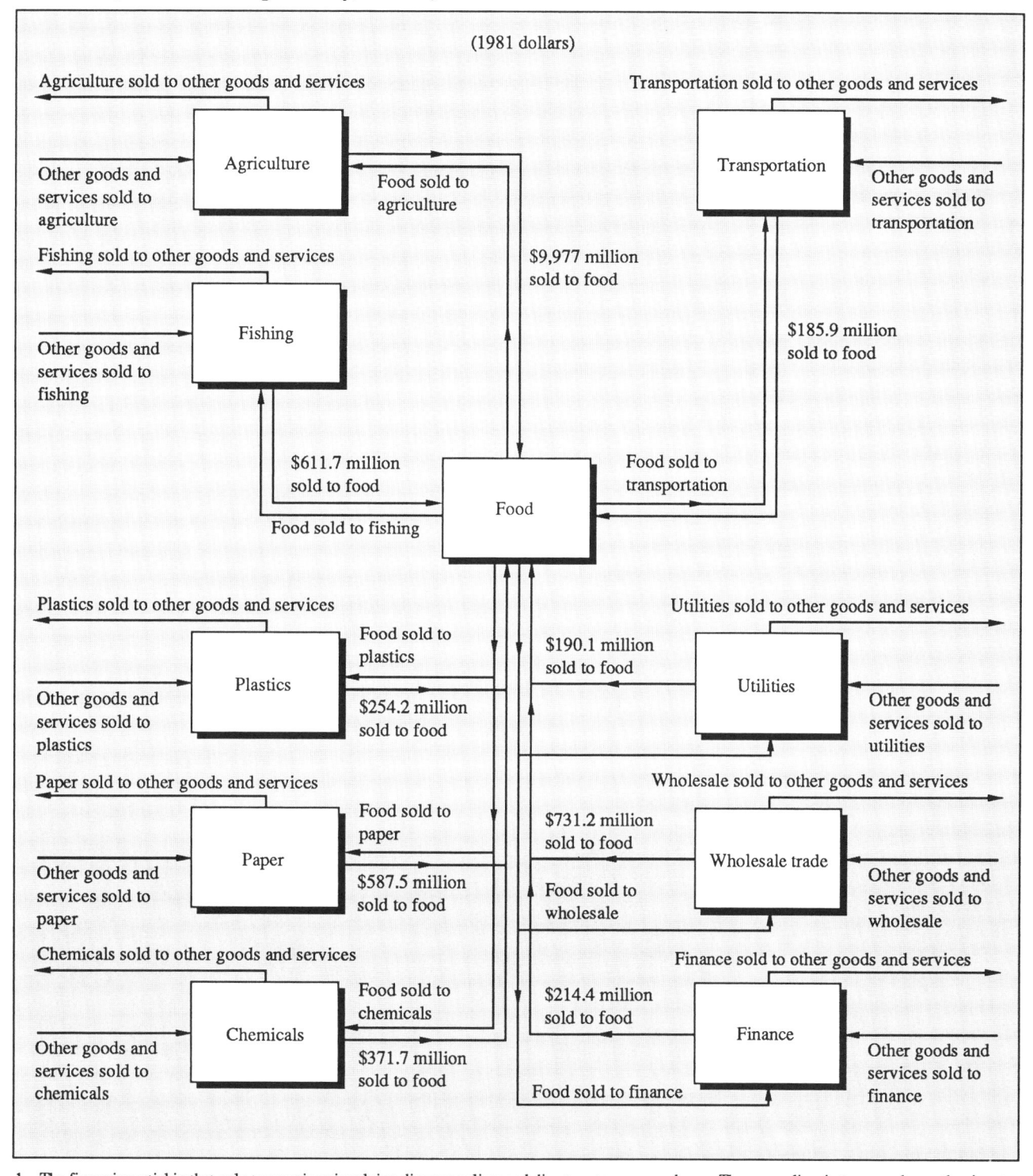

(1981 dollars)

- Agriculture sold to other goods and services
- Other goods and services sold to agriculture
- Food sold to agriculture
- $9,977 million sold to food
- Transportation sold to other goods and services
- Other goods and services sold to transportation
- $185.9 million sold to food
- Food sold to transportation
- Fishing sold to other goods and services
- Other goods and services sold to fishing
- $611.7 million sold to food
- Food sold to fishing
- Plastics sold to other goods and services
- Other goods and services sold to plastics
- Food sold to plastics
- $254.2 million sold to food
- $190.1 million sold to food
- Utilities sold to other goods and services
- Other goods and services sold to utilities
- Paper sold to other goods and services
- Other goods and services sold to paper
- Food sold to paper
- $587.5 million sold to food
- $731.2 million sold to food
- Wholesale sold to other goods and services
- Food sold to wholesale
- Other goods and services sold to wholesale
- Chemicals sold to other goods and services
- Other goods and services sold to chemicals
- Food sold to chemicals
- $371.7 million sold to food
- $214.4 million sold to food
- Finance sold to other goods and services
- Food sold to finance
- Other goods and services sold to finance

1 The figure is partial in that only transactions involving direct suppliers and direct customers are shown. Those suppliers in turn purchase other inputs and sell to other customers.

SOURCE Estimates by the Economic Council of Canada, based on data from Statistics Canada.

Input-output analysis has been used extensively to evaluate the impacts of changes in final demand on the economy since the pioneering work of Leontief.[29] For example, economists have calculated the direct and indirect effects on domestic industry outputs of a given increase in consumer spending on durable goods and of a given increase in domestic exports.[30] While these analyses do take into account the interdependence of economic activities, they focus on the ultimate impact of final demand shifts on the economy rather than on the details of sectoral interdependencies (and of the linkages between individual industries) that play a role in shaping that impact. Defining such intermediate input-output transactions is central to the analysis of this chapter. The only work that addresses this issue extensively is that of Miyazawa.[31] The research in this section uses Miyazawa's technique, adapted for Canadian input-output data, for an analysis of industrial interdependence as the basis of a definition of intermediate input-output transactions. A detailed description of the methodology is found in Appendix A.

The analysis treats the goods and the service sectors separately and calculates the "propagation effects" of each, based on the internal interactions of each of the goods and service industries.[32] For the goods sector, the internal interactions come from each goods industry's need to purchase other goods as intermediate inputs. For example, for each goods industry to produce one dollar's worth of output, it has to buy goods from other industries as inputs to meet its production requirements. Those other industries, in turn, also require goods as intermediate inputs to meet their production requirements. The cumulative effect of a one-dollar increase in output in each goods industry, therefore, is much greater in magnitude than the initial increase in output since each industry must meet not only the requirement to increase its own output by one dollar, but also the input needs of other industries as well. When combined with information on each goods industry's requirement for service inputs to produce one unit of output, the sectoral input-output analysis estimates the total demand of the goods sector for services, or the "stimulative power" of the goods sector on service production. The same technique is used to calculate the stimulative power of the service sector on goods production. (The analysis of stimulative power was conducted for the period 1971-85; for descriptive convenience, however, the discussion of the analytical results refers only to 1985.)

Analytical Results — Stimulative power is first calculated for each industry and then summed to give aggregate information at the sectoral level. The matrix showing the stimulative power of each goods industry on each service industry in 1985 is shown in Table A-1. Table A-2 shows the stimulative power of each service industry on each goods industry (see Appendix A).[33]

Chart 3-4 shows the stimulative power of each goods industry on the service sector as a whole. For example, in 1985, one dollar of agricultural output generated $0.13 worth of demand for services, one dollar of output in the fishing industry generated $0.09 worth of demand for services, and so on. Overall, the crude petroleum and natural gas industry had very strong stimulative power on the

Chart 3-4

Stimulative Power of Goods Industries on Service-Sector Output,[1] Canada, 1985

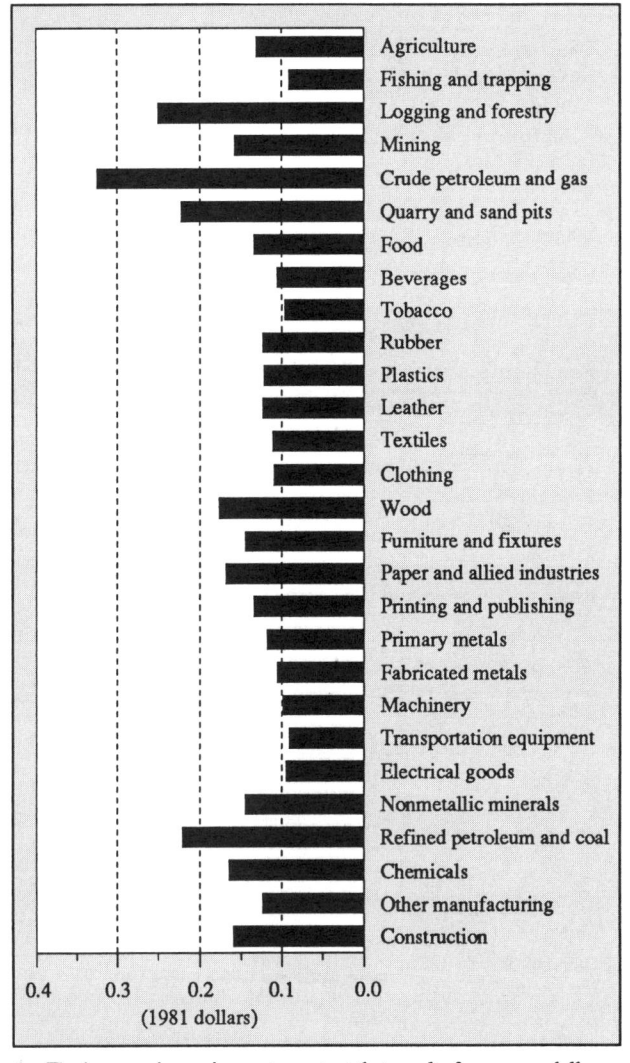

[Bar chart showing stimulative power values in 1981 dollars (x-axis from 0.4 to 0.0) for the following industries:
Agriculture, Fishing and trapping, Logging and forestry, Mining, Crude petroleum and gas, Quarry and sand pits, Food, Beverages, Tobacco, Rubber, Plastics, Leather, Textiles, Clothing, Wood, Furniture and fixtures, Paper and allied industries, Printing and publishing, Primary metals, Fabricated metals, Machinery, Transportation equipment, Electrical goods, Nonmetallic minerals, Refined petroleum and coal, Chemicals, Other manufacturing, Construction]

1 The increase in service-sector output that results from a one-dollar increase in the output of each goods industry.
SOURCE Estimates by the Economic Council of Canada, based on data from Statistics Canada.

service sector, as did all of the primary industries, with the exception of fishing and trapping. The manufacturing industries also stimulated production in the service industries, although on the whole their stimulative power was less than that of the primary industries. Among the manufacturing industries with the strongest stimulative power on the service sector were refined petroleum and coal products, wood products, paper and allied industries, and the chemical industry.

The stimulative power of the individual service industries on the goods sector as a whole is shown in Chart 3-5. When compared to Chart 3-4, it is immediately clear that the stimulative power of the service industries on the goods sector is less than that of the goods industries on the service sector, which is consistent with the simulation results reported earlier. Only in the cases of the accommodation, food, and beverages industry and the transportation industry does stimulative power match the levels seen for the goods industries.

The concept of stimulative power also can be examined from the perspective of the stimulated industries, giving a picture of the "sensitivity" of individual industries to output in either the goods or the service sector. The sensitivity of the service industries to output increases in the goods sector is shown in Chart 3-6. For example, one dollar of output in each of the goods-producing industries summed over the whole of the goods sector generated a total demand of $0.96 for finance and real estate services and of $0.85 for wholesale trade services. Six service industries, which together make up the bulk of dynamic services, were particularly dependent on demand from the goods industries for their output: finance and real estate, wholesale trade, utilities, business services, transportation, and communications. Together, these industries accounted for 56 per cent of gross

Chart 3-5

Stimulative Power of Service Industries on Goods-Sector Output,[1] Canada, 1985

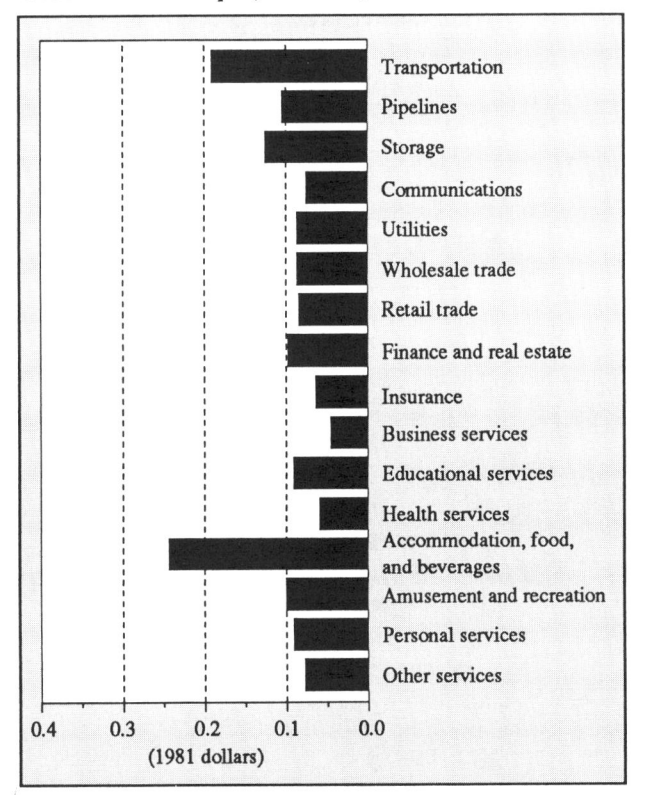

[1] The increase in goods-sector output that results from a one-dollar increase in the output of each service industry.
SOURCE Estimates by the Economic Council of Canada, based on data from Statistics Canada.

Chart 3-6

Sensitivity of Service Industries to Goods-Sector Output,[1] Canada, 1985

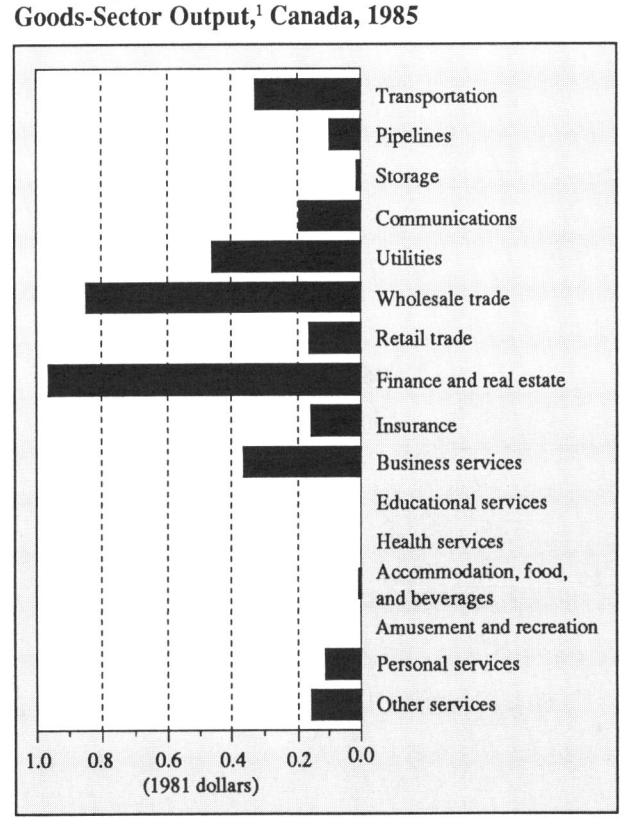

[1] The increase in the output of each service industry that results from a one-dollar increase in the output of the goods sector.
SOURCE Estimates by the Economic Council of Canada, based on data from Statistics Canada.

domestic product in the service sector in 1988 and 36 per cent of gross domestic product in the economy as a whole. When considered along with the proportion of output in the other service industries that was dependent on intermediate demand originating in the goods sector, the role played by goods production in generating service-sector activity is substantial.

Chart 3-7 shows the sensitivity of each goods-producing industry to service-sector output in 1985.[34] The goods industries, on the whole, are less sensitive to demand for their output generated by the service sector. Those which are most sensitive to service-sector demand are construction, refined petroleum and coal, food, and printing and publishing.

The discussion so far has focused on the nature of interindustry transactions across sectoral boundaries. However, industries are also involved in intrasectoral input-output relationships. What is the stimulative power of a

Chart 3-7

Sensitivity of Goods Industries to Service-Sector Output,[1] Canada, 1985

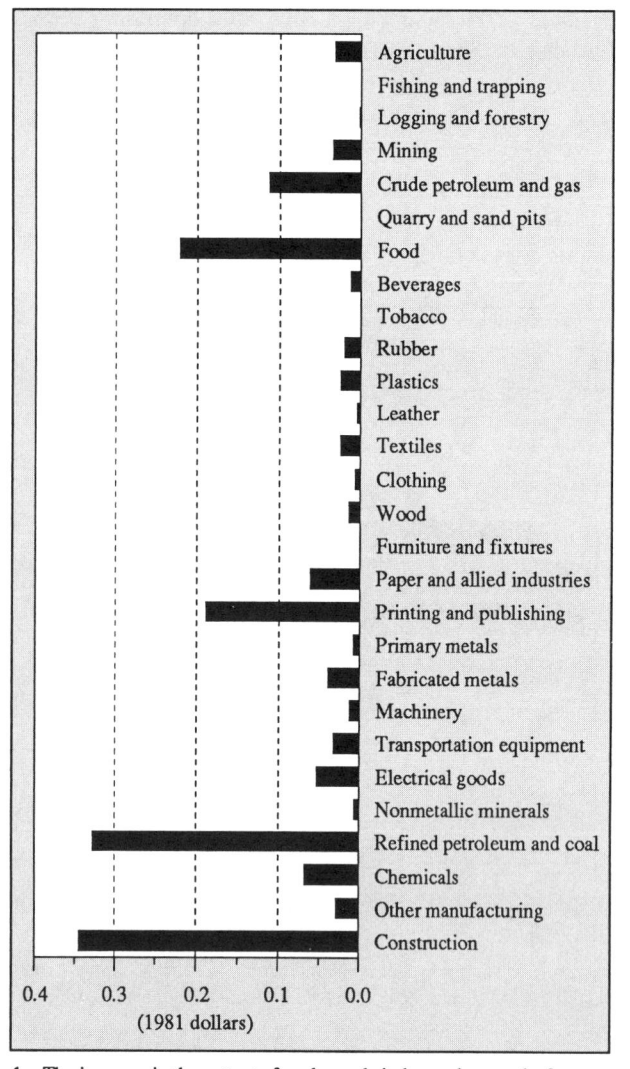

[Horizontal bar chart with x-axis from 0.4 to 0.0 (1981 dollars), showing bars for: Agriculture, Fishing and trapping, Logging and forestry, Mining, Crude petroleum and gas, Quarry and sand pits, Food, Beverages, Tobacco, Rubber, Plastics, Leather, Textiles, Clothing, Wood, Furniture and fixtures, Paper and allied industries, Printing and publishing, Primary metals, Fabricated metals, Machinery, Transportation equipment, Electrical goods, Nonmetallic minerals, Refined petroleum and coal, Chemicals, Other manufacturing, Construction]

1 The increase in the output of each goods industry that results from a one-dollar increase in the output of the service sector.
SOURCE Estimates by the Economic Council of Canada, based on data from Statistics Canada.

Chart 3-8

Stimulative Power of Each Goods Industry[1] on All Other Goods Industries, Canada, 1985

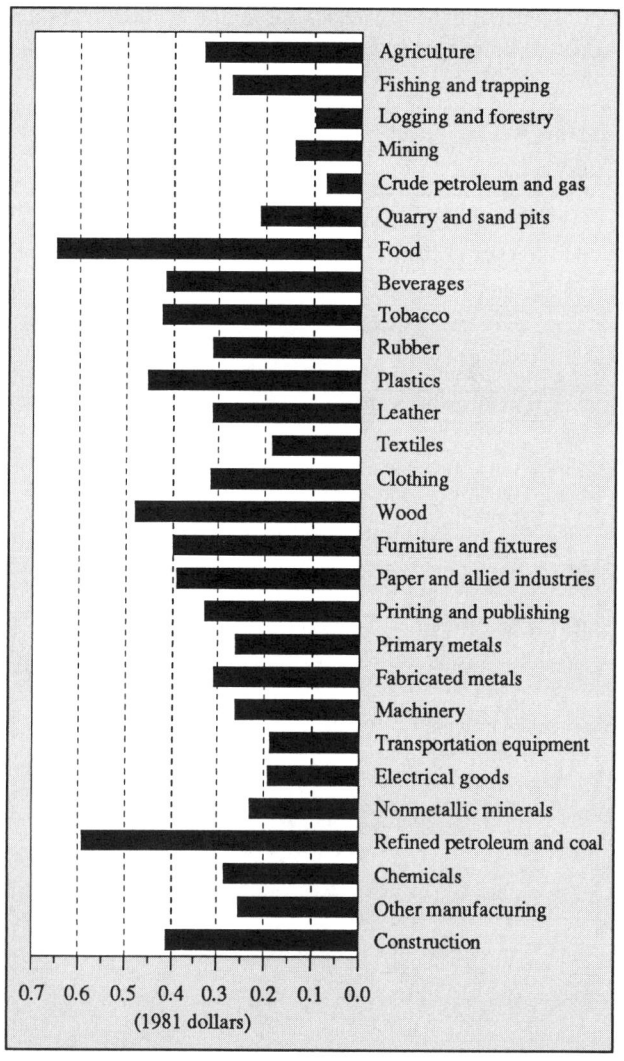

[Horizontal bar chart with x-axis from 0.7 to 0.0 (1981 dollars), showing bars for: Agriculture, Fishing and trapping, Logging and forestry, Mining, Crude petroleum and gas, Quarry and sand pits, Food, Beverages, Tobacco, Rubber, Plastics, Leather, Textiles, Clothing, Wood, Furniture and fixtures, Paper and allied industries, Printing and publishing, Primary metals, Fabricated metals, Machinery, Transportation equipment, Electrical goods, Nonmetallic minerals, Refined petroleum and coal, Chemicals, Other manufacturing, Construction]

1 The impact of a one-dollar increase in the output of each goods industry on the output of the remaining goods industries as a whole.
SOURCE Estimates by the Economic Council of Canada, based on data from Statistics Canada.

Chart 3-9

Stimulative Power of Each Service Industry[1] on All Other Service Industries, Canada, 1985

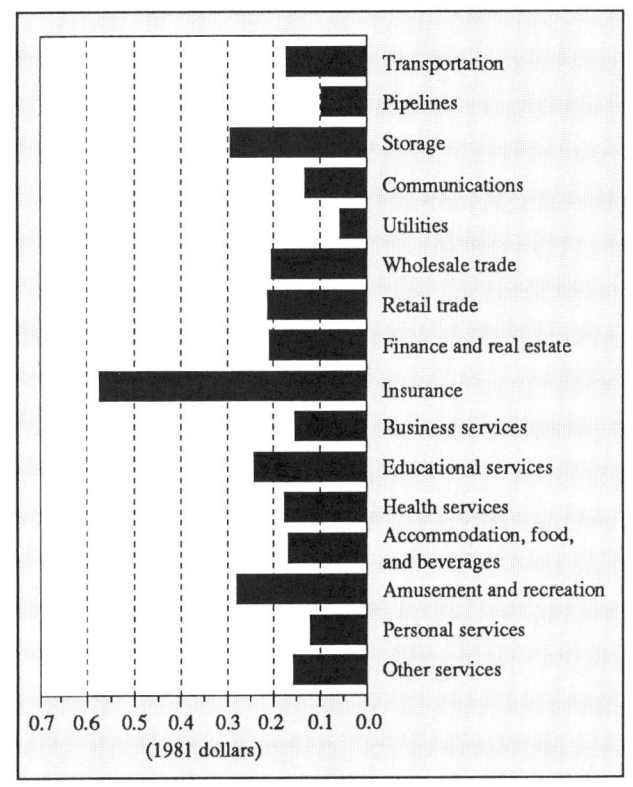

Transportation	
Pipelines	
Storage	
Communications	
Utilities	
Wholesale trade	
Retail trade	
Finance and real estate	
Insurance	
Business services	
Educational services	
Health services	
Accommodation, food, and beverages	
Amusement and recreation	
Personal services	
Other services	

0.7 0.6 0.5 0.4 0.3 0.2 0.1 0.0
(1981 dollars)

1 The impact of a one-dollar increase in the output of each service industry on the output of the remaining service industries as a whole.
SOURCE Estimates by the Economic Council of Canada, based on data from Statistics Canada.

sector's industries on that sector's output? Overall, goods industries generate substantially more demand for goods output than service industries do for service output. In 1985, for example, in 20 of the goods industries studied, one dollar's worth of output generated at least $0.25 worth of demand in the rest of the goods sector (Chart 3-8). In contrast, only four of the service industries generated an intrasectoral demand of similar magnitude (Chart 3-9).

These results further highlight the complexity of production in the modern Canadian economy. Today, goods producers require a broad variety of inputs to support the production process. This, it could be argued, reflects two complementary trends. First, goods producers have become increasingly specialized, at least at the plant level, reducing the in-house production of inputs so as to increase efficiency and quality. Second, technological change has increased the complexity of products themselves; new materials, the introduction of microchips, and innovations in product capabilities in order to meet a widely differentiated consumer base are examples of technological changes that have radically altered the nature of the output for many goods producers. The microwave oven is as different from the gas stove of 30 years ago as a compact-disc system is from a gramophone. Goods producers require both goods and service inputs; the producers of each of those inputs in turn need goods and service inputs, and so on down the chain of production. At the sectoral level, the implications of high levels of industrial interdependence are that the goods industries need the outputs of service producers as inputs while the service industries need the demand for their inputs that arises from the goods sector (Figure 3-2).

Comparison over Time — The results of the sectoral input-output analysis for 1985 lead to the conclusion that the stimulative power of goods industries on the service sector is greater than that of service industries on the goods sector. That raises the question: Has the stimulative power of goods on services changed over time? To answer that question we will review the time series of the empirical results.

Chart 3-10 shows the stimulative power of goods industries on the service sector for 1971 and 1981.[35] Of a total

Figure 3-2

Links between Goods and Services

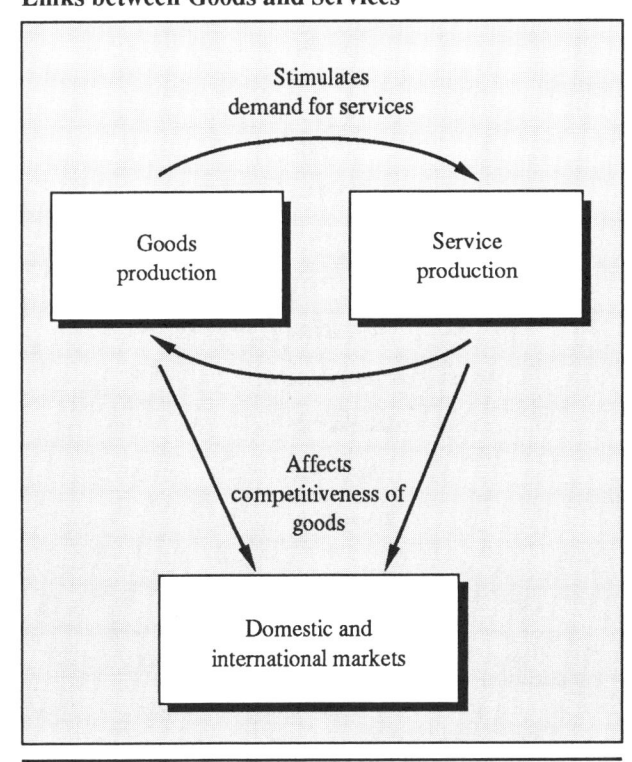

Goods production → (Stimulates demand for services) → Service production

Goods production and Service production → (Affects competitiveness of goods) → Domestic and international markets

Chart 3-10

Stimulative Power of Goods Industries on Service-Sector Output,[1] Canada, 1971 and 1981

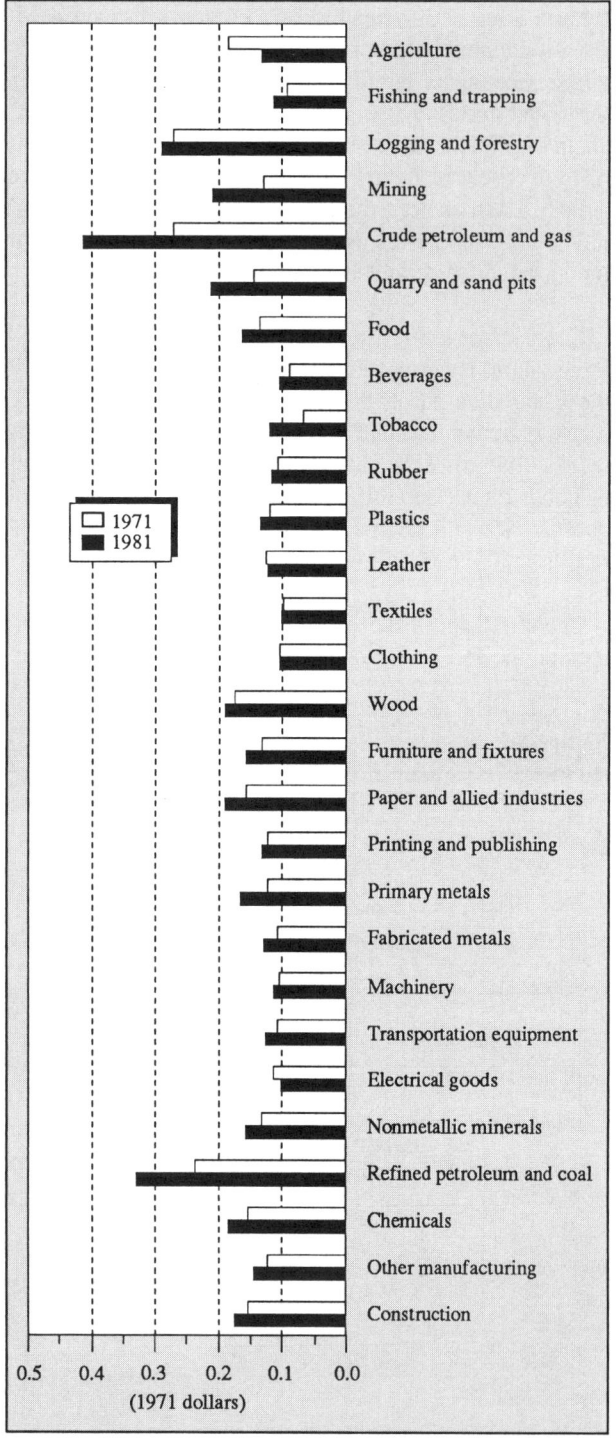

[Bar chart showing values for: Agriculture, Fishing and trapping, Logging and forestry, Mining, Crude petroleum and gas, Quarry and sand pits, Food, Beverages, Tobacco, Rubber, Plastics, Leather, Textiles, Clothing, Wood, Furniture and fixtures, Paper and allied industries, Printing and publishing, Primary metals, Fabricated metals, Machinery, Transportation equipment, Electrical goods, Nonmetallic minerals, Refined petroleum and coal, Chemicals, Other manufacturing, Construction. Legend: □ 1971, ■ 1981. X-axis: 0.5, 0.4, 0.3, 0.2, 0.1, 0.0 (1971 dollars)]

1 The increase in service-sector output that results from a one-dollar increase in the output of each goods industry.
SOURCE Estimates by the Economic Council of Canada, based on data from Statistics Canada.

of 28 goods industries, 24 had higher stimulative power in 1981 than in 1971. This suggests that the stimulative power of goods production on service production did grow over time, though the magnitude of stimulus given to individual service industries may have changed.

What causes the change in stimulative power over time? The stimulative power of the goods sector is determined by 1) the matrix of demand for intermediate goods inputs required to produce one unit of output in each goods industry, and 2) the corresponding matrix of demand for intermediate service inputs to produce that output. The shape of these matrices is determined by the structure of production in the goods industries. Comparing matrices over time is difficult since there is no systematic way to aggregate changes in individual components. Nevertheless, the matrix of service inputs for the goods industries reveals no large or systematic changes in the magnitude of service input required by individual goods producers.

However, the total demand for service inputs by goods producers has increased as a result of the interaction of three factors: 1) goods producers require many intermediate goods inputs to meet their production requirements; 2) each goods industry, in turn, also requires intermediate service inputs; and 3) total output levels in the goods sector as a whole have increased. Those higher production volumes in the goods sector naturally feed back to stimulate corresponding increases in the volume of production by service suppliers. In other words, while it may be that no one goods industry has increased its "service inputs per unit of output" ratio, the fact that goods industries purchase many inputs from other goods industries means that total demand for service inputs has grown as output levels in the goods sector have increased. If, on the other hand, goods industries needed only services as intermediate inputs, the overall level of demand for intermediate services would not be very large, since there would be no secondary stimulatory effect. Further, it should be noted that the increase in the stimulative power of the goods industries on services between 1971 and 1981 was not strictly a necessary condition for the goods sector to drive service activity; the key point is that the stimulative power of goods on services was always higher than services on goods. As long as output levels in the goods industries grew over time, the service industries grew automatically, because of the stimulative power effect.

The sensitivity of service producers to output in the goods sector through time is shown in Chart 3-11. The bulk of the traditional services – retail trade; accommodation, food, and beverages; amusement and recreation; and personal services – showed either no change in the extent to which changes in the level of output in the goods sector feed

Sectoral Interdependencies 51

Chart 3-11

Sensitivity of Service Industries to Goods-Sector Output,[1] Canada, 1971 and 1981

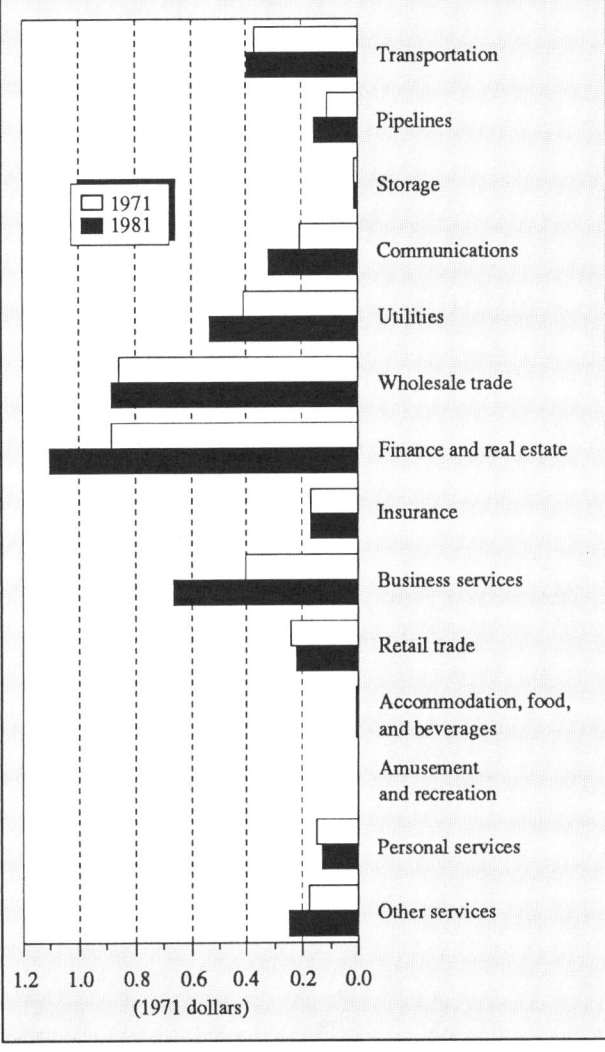

[Bar chart showing sensitivity values for 1971 (white bars) and 1981 (black bars) across service industries: Transportation, Pipelines, Storage, Communications, Utilities, Wholesale trade, Finance and real estate, Insurance, Business services, Retail trade, Accommodation, food, and beverages, Amusement and recreation, Personal services, Other services. X-axis ranges from 1.2 to 0.0 in 1971 dollars.]

1 The increase in the output of each service industry that results from a one-dollar increase in the output of the goods sector.
SOURCE Estimates by the Economic Council of Canada, based on data from Statistics Canada.

through the system to stimulate (or reduce) their output levels, or a decrease in their sensitivity to changes in the level of goods output. The dynamic services, on the other hand – most notably business services, communications, utilities, and finance and real estate – showed increases in the extent to which their output levels depended on output in the goods sector.

As we will detail in Chapter 4, the dynamic services have experienced strong output and employment growth in recent years. This analysis of stimulative power and sensitivity also shows that there has been a simultaneous strengthening of linkages between dynamic services and the goods sector. These results, then, further reinforce the conclusion that growth in national output and the existence of intermediate demand linkages have together contributed significantly to the shift to services.

Differences in labour productivity levels have also played a role in determining the distribution of economic activity across the goods and service sectors. Throughout the period 1966-89, the level of gross domestic product per worker was always lower in the service sector as a whole than in the goods sector (Table 3-5). Therefore, even if output in both sectors were to expand by equal amounts, more jobs would be created in services than in goods. However, note that the aggregate service-sector productivity level masks differences among the three service subsectors. In fact, real domestic product per worker was higher in the dynamic-service subsector than in the goods sector throughout the study period; the nonmarket services occupied the middle ground; and the traditional-service subsector showed the lowest levels. However, the trend was for output per worker to increase in traditional services and decrease slightly in nonmarket services over the period.

These differences in both productivity levels and the stimulative power effect have combined to shape the sectoral distribution of employment and output in the following ways. First, dynamic-service output has grown rapidly because it is most sensitive to output growth in the goods sector, and goods-sector output growth has induced

Table 3-5

Output[1] per Employee, by Sector, Canada, 1966, 1981, and 1989

	Output per employee		
	1966	1981	1989
	(Thousands of 1981 dollars)		
Service sector	21.8	27.2	29.8
Dynamic services	32.2	42.8	50.9
Traditional services	14.0	14.8	16.1
Nonmarket services	24.5	24.3	23.3
Goods sector	27.2	32.9	40.9
Total	24.0	29.1	33.0

1 Gross domestic product.
SOURCE Estimates by the Economic Council of Canada, based on data from Statistics Canada.

employment growth in the dynamic-service subsector, despite that subsector's strong productivity performance, because of intermediate linkage effects. Second, the stimulative power of the goods sector on traditional services, though lower than on dynamic services, nevertheless induces some output growth. The lower productivity level of the traditional services, however, meant that the increase in output necessary for one job to be created in that sector was smaller than was the case for the goods sector. Therefore, when output in those services grew, employment increased relatively faster than employment in goods.

Medium-Term Prospects

What of the medium-term future? Will the shift to services continue? In order to gain some insight into the growth of the sectors in the medium term, we carried out projections using the sectoral econometric model described earlier in this chapter. The projection is based on all of the exogenous assumptions of the base-case projection of *Legacies*, the Economic Council of Canada's 26th Annual Review.[36] Specifically, the projected economy sees an average annual rate of growth of 2.7 per cent in real gross domestic product and of 1.5 per cent in total employment between 1989 and 1993.

Table 3-6 summarizes the results of the projection that bear on the sectoral shift. Because goods-sector output is expected to grow only moderately – at an average of 1.5 per cent annually – between 1989 and 1993, and because the growth rate in real gross domestic product per worker in that sector will be 1.6 per cent per annum, employment growth in the goods sector is expected to be nil. However, output growth in the goods sector stimulates output growth in commercial services, and since the rate of growth in real domestic product per worker in commercial services will be lower than the rate of growth in output, employment in commercial services is expected to grow. Last, since labour productivity growth in nonmarket services is expected to be negligible, its rate of employment growth will almost match the projected rate of real output growth.

The historical trends, then, are likely to continue in the medium term. The employment share of the goods sector is projected to decline from 29 per cent in 1988 to 27 per cent in 1993; the commercial services' share will increase from 49 to 51 per cent in 1993; and the employment share of nonmarket services, which had already started to decline in the early 1980s, will continue to decrease slightly.

The econometric model used to produce both the simulations and the projection was designed to focus on

Table 3-6

Growth in Gross Domestic Product[1] and Employment, by Sector, Canada, 1972-88 and Projected 1989-93

	Average annual rate of growth	
	1972-88	1989-93
	(Per cent)	
Real gross domestic product		
Goods sector	2.7	1.5
Commercial services[2]	5.4	3.8
Nonmarket services	2.3	2.2
Employment		
Goods sector	1.1	0.0
Commercial services[2]	3.3	2.2
Nonmarket services	2.9	2.0
Real gross domestic product per employee		
Goods sector	1.6	1.6
Commercial services[2]	2.1	1.5
Nonmarket services	–0.5	0.2

1 In 1981 dollars.
2 Includes traditional and dynamic services.
SOURCE Estimates by the Economic Council of Canada, based on data from Statistics Canada.

the relationships between the major sectors of Canadian industry, so it uses data at the aggregate sectoral level. However, one of our major objectives in this chapter is to look at the differences between the dynamic and traditional services. Accordingly, the model projections were supplemented with additional analysis at the sub-sector level using information on employment trends to provide slightly more disaggregated projections of employment shares. That analysis finds that the dynamic-service subsector's share of employment in the commercial-service sector is expected to decrease slightly from 47.3 per cent in 1988 to 46.6 per cent in 1993; the share of commercial services accounted for by the traditional-service subsector will increase accordingly from 52.7 to 53.4 per cent. While these changes may appear to be very small, the projection period is, it should be remembered, very short. Furthermore, these changes accord well with what would be expected given the relationship between interdependency and differences in sectoral productivity growth discussed in the subsection "Comparison over Time"; because productivity levels are higher in the dynamic services than in traditional services, the employment growth in commercial services that is induced by the moderate increase in goods output shifts slightly to traditional services.

Conclusion

The shift to services is an empirical phenomenon that has involved rapid and large-scale growth in the share of output and employment accounted for by the service industries. The reasons for the shift have been little understood. The causes that are usually cited, such as the composition of final demand and productivity differentials, have indeed played a role in the shift. But these only partially explain the phenomenon. The main thesis of this chapter is that industrial linkages are playing a very important role in that shift, a factor to which very little attention has been paid in the literature.

The importance of industrial interdependence for understanding the shift to services is borne out by the analyses of the relationships between goods and services at the sectoral level and at the level of individual industries. We found that the goods industries are the source of a substantial part of the demand for the output of the service industries, and likewise, the service industries are the source of a substantial part of the inputs required by goods producers. It is this mutual dependency, in conjunction with differences in productivity levels across the two sectors, that explains why the shift to services has occurred.

Our research revealed that output growth in the goods sector leads to output growth in the service sector, for two reasons. First, economic growth causes both incomes and the demand for goods and services to grow. To meet that demand, producers in the goods and the service sectors increase their output. To produce that output, goods producers require a large number of intermediate inputs from other goods producers and from service producers, and those producers, in turn, also require other goods and service inputs. Because the stimulative power of goods production on services is higher than that of service production on goods, more service production is generated by the increase in goods output than if service output increased.

Differences in productivity levels across the two sectors also play a role. Within the service sector, it is the dynamic services that are most sensitive to output levels in the goods sector. Therefore, because of the stimulative power of goods on dynamic services, these have experienced high relative rates of employment growth despite high productivity levels and high rates of productivity growth. The traditional services, on the other hand, are less sensitive to output levels in the goods sector. But they too have experienced high rates of employment growth, in part because of their low productivity levels and low rates of productivity growth, and in part because they are more sensitive to changes in final demand than dynamic services.

The results of the analysis of industrial interdependency also bear on the "manufacturing matters" debate. Our analysis suggests that manufacturing does indeed matter. However, in Canada the resource industries matter a great deal as well; in fact, the stimulative power of the resource industries on the service sector is greater than that of manufacturing.

What conclusions can be drawn from our analysis of sectoral interdependencies? On the one hand, a significant part of service-sector growth derives from growth in the level of economic activity in the resource and manufacturing industries; on the other hand, services, and especially dynamic services, by providing many important inputs for the production of goods, are key factors in the performance of the goods industries. Therefore, the quality of those services and the quality of the linkages between goods and service producers play a critical role in determining the competitiveness of goods producers. That competitiveness, in turn, determines the output performance of the goods sector, and so the circle continues. Viewed in this light, it is clear that neither the goods sector nor the service sector is of less intrinsic value in relative terms. Rather, the two sectors work in unison as partners in the process of production.

In summary, in order to understand why the shift to services has occurred, it is necessary to take a broad view of the Canadian economy as a complex system composed of many closely linked economic actors. No single factor can explain the change in industrial structure that has taken place in the last three or four decades; rather, the explanation lies in the conjunction of many factors that affect the economic system simultaneously.

These conclusions have important implications for industrial policy. If it fails to recognize and build upon the complementary contributions of goods and services to economic growth, then it cannot be fully effective in pursuing the goal of economic development. Since the shift to services has not been completely understood, it is likely that the treatment of the service sector within the context of industrial policy in general has been less than adequate. The research reported in this chapter, therefore, should contribute to identifying some of the first steps that are necessary to integrate services into industrial policy and build upon the contribution they make to economic growth.

Part B: The Emerging Labour Market

4 The Shift to Services and Labour Adjustment

Having looked at the service sector in the preceding two chapters – its composition, the characteristics of its industries, and the dynamics of its growth – we now turn in Part B of our report to employment in a service economy. This chapter raises the curtain on our employment analysis by considering the implications of the sectoral shift for the Canadian labour market. We begin by documenting the shift itself: the rapid growth of service employment, both in absolute and relative terms, and how the Canadian experience compares with that of other OECD countries.

We then examine various ways that the labour market is adjusting to the sectoral shift. It is well known that a great deal of adjustment occurs continuously in the labour market as jobs are created and eliminated, and individuals enter and leave the work force. In the past three decades, one context for this "churning" has been an employment structure tilting rapidly towards services. We ask how this has affected labour market adjustment at both the aggregate and individual levels. At the aggregate level, we look at the impact of the shift to services on the overall level of unemployment; within this broader question, we go on to consider the hypothesis that cyclical fluctuations are reduced in a service economy. For individuals, employment is increasingly concentrated in the service sector; the chapter concludes, then, with an analysis of how well Canadian workers are adjusting to this changing industrial structure.

The Shift to Services

The growth of the service sector in Canada has been a remarkable phenomenon. By 1989, services accounted for almost 65 per cent of the measured domestic output in this country, and the service sector employed well over twice as many Canadians as did the goods sector. And our projections suggest that the relative importance of services will continue to increase in the medium term (see Chapter 3).

Looking at it from a historical perspective, the dominance of service industries is the result of a structural transformation that has been under way for much of this century. In terms of employment, 40 per cent of Canadian workers held jobs in the service sector in 1946; by 1989 that share had increased to 71 per cent. On the other hand, the goods sector's share of total employment decreased over this period from 60 to 29 per cent.

Tables 4-1 and 4-2 detail the sectoral trends over the period 1967-89 in output and employment, organized according to the typology of service industries presented in Chapter 2. We will look first at output, always keeping in mind the problems regarding the measurement of output in some service industries, which probably lead to an overall underestimation (see Chapter 3). The service sector showed strong growth over the period – the average annual rate of increase over these years in the real domestic product of services was 4.7 per cent, compared to 2.7 per cent for goods (see Table 4-1).

Output growth was particularly strong in the dynamic-service subsector which had an average annual growth rate of 5.3 per cent. Business services experienced the fastest expansion by a considerable margin; in fact, all of the dynamic services recorded output growth rates that were well above average. And even the performance of the traditional and nonmarket services has been higher than that of the goods sector in terms of real domestic product growth since 1967.

As a result, the proportion of overall economic output accounted for by the service sector increased from 54.8 per cent in 1967 to 64.2 per cent in 1989, and the goods sector's share declined from 45.2 to 35.8 per cent. The dynamic services' share grew nearly 10 percentage points over the period, reaching 36 per cent by 1989; indeed, output in dynamic services now exceeds output in goods.

The increase in the importance of services over the past two decades has been even more dramatic in terms of employment. Overall, the average annual rate of employment growth in the service sector in 1967-89 was over three times the rate experienced by the goods sector (see Table 4-2). While dynamic services stood out with respect to output expansion, the three service subsectors had relatively similar job-creation performances, with annual growth rates around 3 per cent. Here too, however, business services had by far the fastest rate of increase of any industry, with average annual employment gains of 7.3 per cent. Rapid gains were also recorded in "other traditional services," which includes accommodation, food and beverages; amusement

58 Employment in the Service Economy

Table 4-1

Output Growth, 1967-89, and Output Share, 1967 and 1989, by Industry, Canada

	Average annual rate of growth, 1967-89	Share of total 1967	Share of total 1989
	(Per cent)		
Service sector[1]	4.7	54.8	64.2
Dynamic services	5.3	26.6	36.0
Transportation, communications, and utilities	5.2	8.7	11.4
Wholesale trade	5.4	4.5	6.2
Finance, insurance, and real estate	4.8	11.9	14.8
Business services	7.9	1.6	3.7
Traditional services[2]	3.4	8.4	11.1
Retail trade	..	..	6.4
Accommodation food, and beverages	..	..	2.2
Amusement and recreation	..	..	0.9
Personal services	..	..	1.5
Nonmarket services	3.1	19.8	16.0
Health and social services	4.1	5.1	5.2
Education	2.4	7.1	4.8
Public administration	2.9	7.6	6.0
Goods sector	2.7	45.2	35.8
Total	3.8	100.0	100.0

1 Other services (equipment and vehicle rental; photographic, repair, and building services) is excluded from the traditional-service subtotal but included in the service-sector total.
2 The data do not allow comparisons between industries within the traditional-service subsector in 1967.
SOURCE Estimates by the Economic Council of Canada, based on data from Statistics Canada.

relative size of the service sector was distributed fairly evenly among dynamic, traditional, and nonmarket services, with each currently including slightly less than one quarter of overall employment.

Table 4-2

Employment Growth, 1967-89, and Employment Share, 1967 and 1989, by Industry, Canada

	Average annual rate of employment growth, 1967-89	Share of total employment 1967	Share of total employment 1989
	(Per cent)		
Service sector[1]	3.2	60.1	71.0
Dynamic services	3.2	19.8	23.4
Transportation, communications, and utilities	1.7	9.3	7.7
Wholesale trade	2.7	4.3	4.5
Finance, insurance, and real estate	3.7	4.2	5.9
Business services	7.3	1.9	5.3
Traditional services	2.8	21.3	22.6
Retail trade	2.7	12.3	13.0
Other traditional services[2]	4.2	7.1	9.6
Accommodation, food, and beverages	..	..	5.9
Amusement and recreation	..	..	1.2
Personal services	..	..	2.5
Nonmarket services	3.3	19.0	22.7
Health and social services	3.8	7.1	9.4
Education	3.2	5.7	6.5
Public administration	2.9	6.2	6.8
Goods sector	0.9	39.9	29.0
Total	2.4	100.0	100.0

1 Excludes other services.
2 Accommodation, food, and beverages; amusement and recreation; and personal services are grouped together because data are not available to measure employment for these industries individually before 1974. The annual average growth rate shown is for 1974-89.
SOURCE Estimates by the Economic Council of Canada, based on data from Statistics Canada.

and recreation; personal services; education, health, and social services; and finance, insurance, and real estate.

With these growth rates, the share of total employment accounted for by the service sector increased from 60 per cent in 1967 to 71 per cent in 1989. The increase in the

An International Comparison

All the major industrialized nations have experienced a shift to services since World War II. But there are marked variations in the pace and nature of that shift as a result of differences in national public policies and areas of comparative advantage. Chart 4-1 shows the distribution of jobs between the goods and service sectors in a number of OECD countries in the early 1960s, 1973, and 1984. In all the countries, the service sector's share increased substantially over the period. In 1984, that share was highest in the United States, which already had a dominant share of service sector compared to goods sector employment in 1960. In terms of the timing and the magnitude of the sectoral transition, the Canadian experience most closely resembles that of the United States.

The share of employment found in services in the United Kingdom and Sweden also was high in 1984, after starting from a much lower base (just under 50 per cent of all jobs) in the early 1960s. Compared to the other countries, the proportion of employment in services is lower in West Germany and Japan, reflecting the strength of the goods sectors in these countries; nevertheless, in both, the majority of workers were employed in services by the mid-1980s. A moderate position was held by France in all three years.

Table 4-3 considers international trends in the structure of employment within the service sector in selected years from 1960 to 1984. There are some similarities in all the countries. For example, nonmarket services was the largest service subsector in most countries by 1984 (Japan was a prominent exception). In every case, including Canada but excepting West Germany, dynamic services accounted for about 20 per cent (or slightly more) of total employment by that time. On the other hand, there were also some important differences in the structure of service employment among these countries. In the United States, as in Canada, service-sector employment is distributed fairly evenly across the dynamic, traditional, and nonmarket services. In Sweden, nonmarket services clearly dominate, accounting for over one third of total employment. They are also

Chart 4-1

Goods and Service Sectors' Share of Total Employment, Selected OECD Countries,[1] Early 1960s, 1973, and 1984

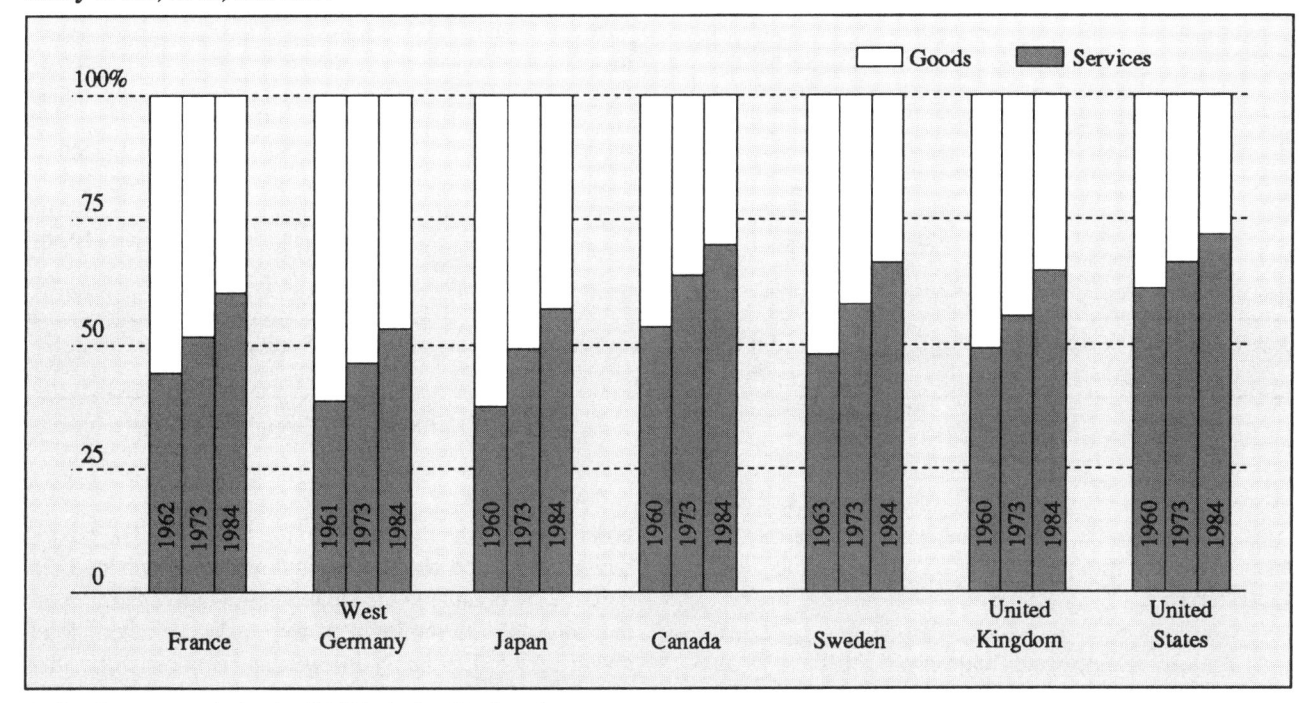

1 The data were manipulated to fit Elfring's classification scheme.
SOURCE Estimates by the Economic Council of Canada, based on Tom Elfring, *Service Sector Employment in Advanced Economies* (Aldershot: Avebury, 1988); and data from Statistics Canada, the Labour Force Survey.

Table 4-3

Distribution of Employment by Sector, Selected OECD Countries, Early 1960s, 1973, 1982, and 1984; and Canada, 1984

	Year	Goods sector	Dynamic services	Traditional services	Nonmarket services	Service sector	Total
			(Per cent)				
France	1962	55.9	12.6	15.6	16.0	44.1	100.0
	1973	48.7	16.1	16.0	19.2	51.3	100.0
	1982	41.3	18.5	16.4	23.8	58.7	100.0
	1984	39.6	18.9	16.5	25.0	60.4	100.0
West Germany	1961	61.4	13.4	14.9	10.3	38.6	100.0
	1973	53.9	14.8	15.0	16.3	46.1	100.0
	1982	47.9	15.7	15.7	20.7	52.1	100.0
	1984	46.8	15.6	16.1	21.4	53.2	100.0
Japan	1960	62.5	12.9	16.4	8.2	37.5	100.0
	1973	50.9	19.1	19.5	10.5	49.1	100.0
	1982	43.9	21.9	21.9	12.4	56.1	100.0
	1984	42.9	22.0	22.2	12.9	57.1	100.0
Sweden	1963	52.3	14.6	16.8	16.3	47.7	100.0
	1973	42.3	16.4	15.1	26.2	57.7	100.0
	1982	34.7	17.6	13.2	34.5	65.3	100.0
	1984	33.7	18.0	13.3	35.0	66.3	100.0
United Kingdom	1960	51.2	14.2	18.7	15.8	48.8	100.0
	1973	44.6	16.5	18.0	20.8	55.4	100.0
	1982	37.0	18.8	19.8	24.4	63.0	100.0
	1984	35.2	19.3	20.8	24.8	64.8	100.0
United States	1960	38.9	17.0	22.9	21.2	61.1	100.0
	1973	33.6	18.8	22.2	25.3	66.4	100.0
	1982	28.9	21.4	23.2	26.4	71.1	100.0
	1984	28.2	22.2	23.7	25.9	71.8	100.0
Canada	1984	30.0	22.2	24.7	23.1	70.0	100.0

SOURCE Estimates by the Economic Council of Canada, based on Elfring, *Service Sector Employment*; and data from Statistics Canada, the Labour Force Survey.

relatively dominant in West Germany. In Japan, on the other hand, there are stronger traditional- and dynamic-service subsectors.

At a more disaggregated industry level, there is also consistency among the high-growth industries. The strongest growth is shown by finance, insurance, real estate, and business services. These industries, which are commonly referred to as "producer services," are an important part of the dynamic-service subsector. The contribution of producer services to employment growth has been particularly notable in the United States and Japan. Important increases in employment were also characteristic of social services, notably in Sweden. However, the job-creation role of these industries – which include health, education, and social services, and public administration – has been levelling off in most countries in recent years, largely because of cutbacks in public expenditures.[1]

Aggregate Implications of the Shift to Services

The shift to services has important implications for the process of matching people and jobs in the labour market. As the economic structure is transformed, individuals must adjust to changes in the location of business activity, the form of employment, and the skill profile required, for example. Before considering the individual adjustment process, we will look briefly at the implications of this adjustment as it is manifested at the aggregate level. Has the shift to services helped or hindered adjustment in the labour market? Has it created additional unemployment pressures? Has it affected the impact of business-cycle fluctuations on employment?

Sectoral Shifts and the Aggregate Unemployment Rate

The implications of the sectoral shift for the aggregate unemployment rate has been an important question in the economics literature. There are two conflicting positions on this issue. One argues that the rapid growth of services has reduced unemployment levels by absorbing workers released from declining goods industries. The other argues that the sectoral shift has been a source of structural unemployment because of adjustment problems resulting from mismatches between the requirements of firms in the expanding service industries and the skills of workers displaced from the goods sector.

As we will see, it is very difficult to resolve this debate empirically; ultimately the impact of the sectoral transition on the level of unemployment remains unclear. Certainly, as we will document later in this chapter, the service sector has played a role in absorbing workers displaced from goods industries. At the same time, however, some major trends are consistent with the hypothesis that structural changes in the economy have created adjustment problems and, as such, have been a source of some unemployment. For example, the aggregate unemployment rate has ratcheted upwards over the past four decades – the period corresponding with the shift from goods to services. Looking more closely at the 1970s and 1980s, it appears that structural unemployment has been an important component of the overall picture. Indeed, this was the conclusion drawn by the Economic Council in its analysis of unemployment trends undertaken for *Back to Basics*, the 25th Annual Review, in 1988.[2] Citing rises in the "natural rate of unemployment," the incidence of vacancies at a given level of unemployment, and the long-term unemployment rate, the Council argued that the persistence of relatively high jobless rates over this period has stemmed from structural factors which have resulted in growing mismatches between labour demand and supply.

While mismatching may have been an important element of the Canadian unemployment experience of the past two decades, there have been a number of other structural developments over this period about whose role there is no consensus. These include commodity shocks, and changes in the demographic composition of the work force, technology, and the product-demand mix. Disentangling the effects of these closely interrelated factors has been a major problem for researchers.

There have been attempts to systematically estimate the impact of the shift to services on the aggregate unemployment rate. For example, Lilien in the United States and Samson in Canada have concluded that the uneven growth among sectors has indeed created adjustment problems which have led to additional unemployment.[3] These studies used an index of employment dispersion across industries to estimate the degree of growth imbalance, and hence the magnitude of the sectoral shift.[4] Using econometric techniques, they then estimated the empirical relationship between this index and the unemployment rate. Recently, however, employment-dispersion measures – and the conclusions that have resulted from them – have been criticized on the grounds that they are influenced significantly by a range of factors with the result that changes in the index cannot be attributed to industry-structure shifts alone. For example, some Canadian studies now suggest that the employment-dispersion measure has, in fact, captured cyclical developments and energy-price trends which have had a greater impact on the unemployment rate than the sectoral shift itself.[5]

The Growth of Services and Business-Cycle Fluctuations[6]

The question of whether the rapid growth of services has affected aggregate employment and unemployment patterns by altering business cycles and their impact on the labour market has also been addressed by some economists. One proposition often put forward in this context is that cyclical fluctuations are moderated as services become more dominant in the economy. According to this argument, some characteristics of service activity – such as the nonstorability of services, which precludes the possibility of inventory buildup; the essential nature of some services which are largely unaffected by income fluctuations; the relative insulation of the public and quasi-public sectors from cyclical pressures; and the labour-intensive production processes in many of these service industries – in fact promote a relatively stable, noncyclical pattern of overall employment. Indeed, research in the United States suggests that the growing importance of services has reduced the length and depth of recessions and their impact on employment levels in that country.[7]

In order to examine the Canadian experience, we analysed the pattern of employment behaviour during the three most recent periods of recession and recovery in this country – 1974-75, 1979-80, and 1981-82 (Table 4-4).[8] That analysis reveals considerable differences between the goods and service sectors. All of the industries in the goods sector, except construction in 1974-75, suffered job declines during each of the recessionary periods. The service sector, on the other hand, experienced employment losses only in the severe recession of 1981-82. In the other two periods, service employment not only increased, but in fact the gains in that sector also more than offset the declines in the goods sector; as a result, aggregate employment rose during those earlier downturns.

During the two earlier recessions, among the service industries only wholesale and retail trade in 1979-80 experienced employment losses of any significance. In the 1981-82 recession, however, each of the commercial-service industries registered job declines, although in relative terms the employment losses were still much smaller than those suffered by goods industries. During that downturn, the only employment buffer was provided by the nonmarket services; nevertheless, the gains in this subsector were not enough to offset the massive job losses in the rest of the economy.

In addition to having a generally moderating influence on employment levels during recessions, service industries have accounted for a disproportionate share of the employment growth which took place in the ensuing recovery and expansion periods. After the recessions of 1974-75, 1979-80, and 1981-82, the service sector's share of the net job creation was 77 per cent, 78.9 per cent, and 76.1 per cent, respectively. In the recoveries after the first and third periods, commercial services played a particularly major role, with over 55 per cent of the subsequent employment growth occurring in these industries. On the other hand, in the short recovery following the 1979-80 downturn, commercial services were less important (47.7 per cent of the new jobs) and nonmarket services provided a relatively significant impetus to growth (accounting for 31.2 per cent of new jobs).

The data suggest that aggregate cyclical trends over the past 15 years have affected the sectors differently, with services moderating the employment impacts of recessions. According to our research, this reflects differences in the output and expenditure patterns of the goods and service sectors. Most notably, during recessions output levels (from which employment levels are derived) have tended to decline in nonagricultural goods industries, but much less so in service industries. In each of the three downturns since the mid-1970s, the production of goods (excluding agriculture) decreased in real terms; in contrast, service-sector output increased during the two earlier periods and declined slightly during the severe 1981-82 recession (Table 4-5). An important factor underlying the more stable output in the service sector appears to have been the income inelasticity of consumer demand for services relative to goods. During the three recessions we examined, consumer

Table 4-4

Changes in Employment between Business Cycle Peaks and Troughs, by Industry, Canada, 1970s and 1980s

	Changes in employment during		
	1974Q1–1975Q1	1979Q4–1980Q2	1981Q2–1982Q4
	(Thousands)		
Nonagricultural goods sector	–112	–28	–464
Other primary	–12	6	–65
Manufacturing	–117	–11	–316
Construction	17	–23	–83
Service sector	249	93	–92
Commercial services	168	49	–143
Transportation, communications, and utilities	43	–3	–30
Wholesale and retail trade	26	–19	–62
Finance, insurance, and real estate	17	57	–11
Business and personal[1]	82	14	–40
Education, health, and social services	43	19	43
Public administration	37	25	8
All industries	137	65	–556

1 Includes business services, accommodation, food, and beverages, amusement and recreation, and personal services.
SOURCE Estimates by the Economic Council of Canada, based on data from Statistics Canada.

expenditures on services increased and those on goods were less favourable, particularly in the case of durable goods where there were decreases in each of the last two periods (Table 4-6).

It should be noted that the impact of the service sector on cyclical fluctuations may be changing as a result of current developments; for example, while the nonmarket-service subsector has represented a major countercyclical force in the labour market in the past, public finance pressures and changing views about the role of government may render the employment buffer provided by these services less effective. As well, transformations taking place within commercial services appear to be making these industries less immune to the effects of the business cycle; most notable in this regard are the growing linkages between the service and goods sectors, which we documented in Chapter 3.

Table 4-5

Changes in Real GDP during Recessions, by Industry, Canada, 1970s and 1980s

	Average quarterly change		
	1974Q2-1975Q2	1980Q1-1980Q2	1981Q3-1982Q4
	(Per cent)		
Agriculture	2.410	2.446	0.858
Nonagricultural goods sector	−2.320	−2.151	−2.177
Other primary	−5.005	−1.555	−0.462
Manufacturing	−2.182	−2.906	−3.429
Construction	1.120	−0.660	−0.555
Service sector	0.822	0.732	−0.621
Commercial services	0.772	0.744	−0.867
Transportation, communications, and utilities	0.754	−0.230	−0.967
Wholesale and retail trade	−0.264	0.326	−1.200
Finance, insurance, and real estate	0.495	1.075	−0.526
Business services	1.363	2.776	−0.390
Personal services[1]	0.809	1.216	0.439
Education, health, and social services	0.990	0.694	0.338
Public administration	1.522	0.705	0.724
All industries	−0.624	−0.622	−0.989

1 Includes accommodation, food, and beverages, amusement and recreation, and personal services.
SOURCE Estimates by the Economic Council of Canada, based on data from Statistics Canada.

Table 4-6

Changes in Real Consumer and Government Expenditures during Recessions, Canada, 1970s and 1980s

	Average quarterly change		
	1974Q2-1975Q2	1980Q1-1980Q2	1981Q3-1982Q4
	(Per cent)		
Consumer expenditures	0.784	0.267	−0.574
Durable goods	0.522	−2.563	−2.560
Nondurable goods	0.346	0.701	−0.453
Services	1.234	1.420	0.087
Government expenditures			
Goods and services	1.766	1.473	0.933
All sectors	1.046	0.576	−0.178

SOURCE Estimates by the Economic Council of Canada, based on data from Statistics Canada.

The Labour Adjustment of Individuals and the Shift to Services

Underlying the aggregate labour market statistics, of course, are the experiences of individual workers. In this section, we consider the question of how well Canadians are adjusting to this new employment structure, where job opportunities are now so heavily concentrated in the service sector. Our analysis begins with patterns of job separation and then goes on to examine re-employment. With respect to the latter, we will look at what happens to workers who lose or leave their employment. Who finds a second job? How long are the periods between jobs? What kinds of new positions do the job finders obtain?

Patterns of Job Separation

Although the magnitude and patterns of job separations determine the extent of labour adjustment required, there have been relatively few detailed studies of separations in

Canada, largely because of shortcomings in the data. However, a new administrative data base, recently developed by Statistics Canada with assistance from the Economic Council, provides a source for estimating separations in the Canadian labour market. This longitudinal file was built on the basis of the Record of Employment (ROE) form that employers are required to file for employees who have an interruption of earnings. The following brief discussion of separations is based on an analysis by Picot and Baldwin that uses the ROE administrative file over the period 1978-87.[9]

The ROE file reinforces the contention that there is a great deal of movement in the Canadian labour market. Of the 12.2 million people who held jobs at some time during 1986, for example, over 4.5 million experienced a separation of some kind. This churning is also evident from the perspective of jobs, rather than workers – in 1986, there were 6.1 million separations from 16.1 million "person-jobs" (i.e., people employed in a firm at any time during the year).[10]

Table 4-7 presents job separation rates in 1986 by industry and according to the nature of the separation. Regarding the latter, two distinctions are drawn: first, between permanent and temporary separations, and second, by the reason for separation. In the case of permanent separations, the ROEs have been organized into three categories: "quits," "layoffs," and "other" (including discharge, contract termination, return to school, maternity leave, and early retirement). For temporary separations, where "quits" generally do not represent a relevant category, a simple distinction is made between "layoffs" and "nonlayoffs" (which also includes work-sharing, apprenticeship training, and labour disputes).

Our particular interest is in the sectoral differences in separation patterns. The high incidence of layoffs in goods, which accounted for almost two thirds of the layoffs registered in 1986, was the major difference here. Both permanent and temporary layoffs were particularly frequent in the primary industries and construction, reflecting the volatile and seasonal nature of these industries. In the service sector, the highest separation rates were in traditional services. In fact, the incidence of quits in these industries was the highest of all the industries; as we will see in Chapter 8, the traditional services are a low-wage subsector which, according to Picot and Baldwin, underlies the high quit rate. Nonmarket services had the lowest incidence of separations, while distributive and information services – the dynamic subsector – were in the middle position.

Postseparation Experience

What happens to the roughly one third of individuals in the work force that separate from jobs in a given year? Our analysis of the individual adjustment process is based on

Table 4-7

Job Separation Rates,[1] by Industry Group, Canada, 1986

	Permanent				Temporary			Total separations
	Quits	Layoffs	Other	Total	Layoffs	Nonlayoffs	Total	
	(Per cent)							
Primary industries	6.1	17.3	6.0	29.4	20.1	6.3	25.2	54.6
Manufacturing	8.0	6.2	6.4	20.8	13.2	8.4	19.9	40.7
Construction	6.1	26.8	5.4	38.4	22.9	5.7	27.4	65.8
Distributive services[2]	6.6	5.3	5.9	17.9	6.7	5.2	11.5	29.4
Information services[3]	8.2	4.9	6.3	19.4	3.5	5.5	8.8	28.2
Traditional services	12.3	6.0	9.0	27.3	4.9	6.8	11.4	38.7
Nonmarket services	2.8	2.1	5.5	10.4	6.3	9.4	15.2	25.6
All industries	7.7	6.9	6.8	21.3	9.6	8.3	17.0	38.3

1 Number of separations as a percentage of total "person-jobs" (number of persons employed by a firm at any time during 1986).
2 Includes transportation, communications, and utilities; and wholesale trade.
3 Includes finance, insurance, and real estate; and business services.
SOURCE Estimates by the Economic Council of Canada, based on Garnett Picot and John Baldwin, "Patterns of quits and layoffs in the Canadian economy," *Canadian Economic Observer* (October 1990).

data from the Labour Market Activity Survey (LMAS) for 1986-87, which permits us to track the employment history of individuals. We will focus on those workers who separated from jobs sometime in 1986 and observe their postseparation experiences through the end of 1987.[11]

Re-employment and Sectoral Mobility

When workers separate from their jobs, they typically try first to find another one within the same industry or in a related one, where they have experience and where they are likely to have appropriate skills and good information about job vacancies. However, with new employment opportunities concentrated in the service sector, people losing or leaving jobs in goods industries often have to change sectors to find another position. Indeed, of the LMAS respondents who separated from goods-sector jobs and who did become re-employed, nearly 40 per cent found their next job in services (Table 4-8). On the other hand, only 17.2 per cent of respondents leaving or losing jobs in services changed sectors in order to get another position.

Table 4-8 offers a comparison of the characteristics of workers who changed sectors and those who did not. Overall, there were only minor differences in the profiles. Those who had quit their jobs were slightly more likely to stay in the same sectors than those who had been laid off. On the other hand, older workers and females had higher-than-average incidences of remaining in the same sector; in the case of women, this is due to a strong employment concentration in services, while for older workers it reflects their immobility.

Table 4-8

Profile of Job Finders: Distribution by Sectoral Movement, Canada, 1986-87[1]

	Same sector	New sector	Total
	(Per cent)		
All job finders	76.7	23.3	100.0
From goods sector	61.8	38.2	100.0
From service sector	82.8	17.2	100.0
Reason for separation			
Quit personal	75.8	24.2	100.0
Quit nonpersonal	78.3	21.7	100.0
Involuntary	74.0	26.0	100.0
Age			
16-19	77.8	22.2	100.0
20-24	76.1	23.9	100.0
25-34	75.5	24.5	100.0
35-44	75.5	24.5	100.0
45-54	81.6	18.4	100.0
55-64	79.9	20.1	100.0
Sex			
Males	72.0	28.0	100.0
Females	82.5	17.5	100.0
Region			
Atlantic	74.6	25.4	100.0
Quebec	78.7	21.3	100.0
Ontario	77.4	22.6	100.0
Prairies	76.5	23.5	100.0
British Columbia	78.2	21.8	100.0

1 Based on a sample of workers who separated from a job in 1986 and found another one before the end of 1987.
SOURCE Estimates by the Economic Council of Canada, based on Statistics Canada, the Labour Market Activity Survey.

Labour Force Status of Job Separators

Obviously, general labour market conditions have a major impact on the adjustment process. They affect the incidence and nature of separations; they also significantly influence the likelihood of finding another job.[12] At any given point in time, however, the adjustment experience can vary considerably among different types of workers. As our analysis of the period 1986-87 indicates, some people appear to be very mobile, while others find the adjustment very difficult.

Of those individuals who had separated from their employment in 1986, 78.6 per cent had found another job before the end of 1987 (Table 4-9).[13] Of the remaining 21.4 per cent, roughly three quarters (15.7 per cent) reported that, for various reasons, they did not wish to be re-employed; over 5 per cent of the 1986 job separators, then, wanted to find new work but had been unable to by the end of 1987.[14]

According to the LMAS data, the likelihood of finding re-employment varies considerably among different groups. Significant differences existed according to the type of separation. Note that we have categorized the reasons for separation into four classes: quit for personal reasons (e.g., illness, residence change, retirement); quit for nonpersonal reasons (e.g., job dissatisfaction, return to school, found a new job); involuntary layoff (permanent or temporary); and a miscellaneous category.

Table 4-9

Profile of Job Separators: Distribution by Postseparation Status, Canada, 1986-87[1]

	Found another job	Did not find another job[2] Job wanted	Did not find another job[2] Job not wanted	Total
	(Per cent)			
All job separators	78.6	5.6	15.7	100.0
From goods sector	75.7	7.5	16.8	100.0
From service sector	79.9	4.9	15.3	100.0
Reason for separation				
Quit personal	68.7	4.3	27.0	100.0
Quit nonpersonal	88.4	2.1	9.5	100.0
Involuntary	76.0	9.6	14.5	100.0
Other	84.6	4.4	11.1	100.0
Age				
16-19	82.1	2.5	15.4	100.0
20-24	86.8	3.4	9.8	100.0
25-34	82.1	6.6	11.4	100.0
35-44	79.2	7.8	13.0	100.0
45-54	68.5	10.0	21.5	100.0
55-64	36.3	9.4	54.3	100.0
Sex				
Males	82.9	5.4	11.7	100.0
Females	73.9	5.9	20.2	100.0
Region				
Atlantic	77.2	5.8	17.0	100.0
Quebec	81.0	4.7	14.3	100.0
Ontario	79.7	4.6	15.7	100.0
Prairies	78.7	6.3	15.0	100.0
British Columbia	76.7	6.7	16.7	100.0

1 Based on a sample of workers who separated from a job in 1986.
2 Labour force status in the last week of 1987.
SOURCE Estimates by the Economic Council of Canada, based on Statistics Canada, the Labour Market Activity Survey.

As Table 4-9 indicates, individuals who quit for nonpersonal reasons had the highest re-employment rate (88.4 per cent), while those who quit for personal reasons had the lowest (68.7 per cent). A closer examination, however, reveals that the laid-off group had the most serious re-employment problems after separation. While a very high proportion of those who quit for personal reasons and had not found re-employment did not want another job, the same was not true for laid-off individuals. Of the workers who had lost their jobs because of a layoff in 1986, 9.5 per cent wanted to find new work but still had not succeeded by the end of 1987. Considering that the majority of these layoffs originated in the goods sector, the adjustment difficulties faced by these workers are likely to be considerable.

Clearly, re-employment prospects diminished with age (see Table 4-9). This was particularly true for those between 55 and 64 years of age, only slightly more than one third of whom had found re-employment by the end of 1987. Note that the majority of respondents in this group reported that they did not want to find other work; however, on the basis of existing research on older workers, it seems probable that a significant proportion of these individuals left the work force because they were discouraged about their chances.[15] While the 45-54 age group did report a much higher incidence of re-employment, 10 per cent were still involuntarily unemployed at the end of 1987, at least one year after separating from their jobs.

Concerning gender and the original sector of employment, males were more likely than females to have found re-employment (82.9 per cent versus 73.9 per cent); however, this difference was accounted for by a much higher proportion of women than men withdrawing from the labour force (i.e., not wanting another job).

Of particular interest for this study is a comparison of the experiences of workers according to the sector from which they separated (see Table 4-9). The re-employment rate was slightly higher for those losing or leaving jobs in the service sector (79.9 per cent) relative to those separating from employment in the goods sector (75.7 per cent); at the same time, the incidence of involuntary unemployment was greater in the latter group (7.5 per cent versus 4.9 per cent).

Duration of Joblessness

Another important dimension of the adjustment process is the amount of time workers spend between jobs (Table 4-10). According to the duration data for those in the LMAS sample who found re-employment, experiences varied widely: while 43.2 per cent were without work for just four weeks or less, 21.9 per cent were jobless for between 27 and 52 weeks and 6.5 per cent did not get a another job for at least 53 weeks.

The reason for the original separation was one important determinant of duration of joblessness. Workers who left their jobs (quit, nonpersonal) tended to get new positions much more quickly than those who lost their jobs (through layoff); 76.1 per cent of the former were without work for

Table 4-10

Profile of Job Finders: Distribution by Duration of Joblessness, Canada, 1986-87[1]

	Weeks of joblessness				
	4 or less	5-26	27-52	53 or more	Total
	(Per cent)				
All job finders	43.2	28.4	21.9	6.5	100.0
Reason for separation					
Quit personal	16.4	28.8	44.5	10.4	100.0
Quit nonpersonal	76.1	15.5	5.9	2.5	100.0
Involuntary	29.6	39.9	23.0	7.5	100.0
Age					
16-19	33.1	25.7	34.6	6.6	100.0
20-24	42.0	28.5	24.2	5.4	100.0
25-34	50.3	28.5	15.7	5.5	100.0
35-44	48.8	30.2	12.5	8.4	100.0
45-54	39.0	30.3	21.2	9.5	100.0
55-64	36.7	32.3	21.3	9.7	100.0
Sex					
Males	44.8	28.2	21.8	5.1	100.0
Females	41.2	28.7	21.9	8.2	100.0
Region					
Atlantic	38.1	29.3	25.2	7.4	100.0
Quebec	39.2	30.2	24.0	6.7	100.0
Ontario	46.4	25.6	22.3	5.8	100.0
Prairies	46.5	28.7	18.6	6.2	100.0
British Columbia	47.4	28.0	18.3	6.2	100.0
Sectoral movement					
Goods to goods	43.7	27.4	22.8	6.1	100.0
Goods to services	36.7	30.1	26.0	7.3	100.0
Services to services	44.9	28.1	20.4	6.6	100.0
Services to goods	40.3	30.0	23.7	6.1	100.0

1 Based on a sample of workers who separated from a job in 1986 and found another one before the end of 1987.
SOURCE Estimates by the Economic Council of Canada, based on Statistics Canada, the Labour Market Activity Survey.

four weeks or less, while the corresponding figure for the latter was just 29.6 per cent. About 30 per cent of the job losers had at least 27 weeks of joblessness, compared to less than 10 per cent of job leavers. Overall, the mean duration without work was twice as long for involuntary than for voluntary job changers (22 weeks versus 11 weeks).

Prime-aged workers (25-34 and 35-44 years of age) tended to experience shorter periods between jobs than either younger or older individuals (see Table 4-10). The differences in duration of joblessness between the sexes were not significant. In terms of region, the jobless period was generally shorter for workers separating from jobs in Ontario and the West than in the Atlantic provinces and Quebec (where unemployment rates were higher). Finally, in comparison to workers who changed sectors to find new positions, those who found jobs within the sector where they had previously been employed were more likely to have short spells of unemployment (4 weeks or less) and slightly less likely to have long ones (at least 27 weeks).

Wages and Job Change

Obviously, an important consideration in the labour-adjustment process involves the impact of re-employment on job quality. We examined this issue by comparing the pre- and postseparation (hourly) wages of job changers. According to this analysis, the majority were better off in their new jobs, with 58.1 per cent reporting higher wages. Note, however, that a significant minority (33.5 per cent) experienced wage decreases (Table 4-11).

Wage outcomes tended to vary significantly in different situations. Certainly the reason for the initial separation is an important factor. Those who quit their initial positions were much more likely to find higher-paying subsequent jobs than those who had been laid off. Two thirds of the former registered wage increases compared to one half of the latter; at the same time, laid-off workers had a higher incidence of wage loss (40.6 per cent versus 26.7 per cent).

Age also appears to be a significant variable. The probability of a job change leading to a higher wage decreased with each age category, beginning with 63.4 per cent among workers aged 16-19 years and falling to 48.3 per cent for those aged 55-64 (see Table 4-11). At the same time, the probability of a cut in pay increased with age; while 27.2 per cent of the youngest group reported lower wages in their subsequent job, the corresponding figure in the oldest group was 40.4 per cent.

While gender differences were relatively modest, female job changers, on average, had slightly more favourable wage outcomes than their male counterparts. There were no major differences across regions, although, unexpectedly, job changers in Atlantic Canada had the highest incidences of wage gains and the lowest incidences of wage losses.

Finally, wage outcomes were affected by sectoral adjustment patterns (see Table 4-11). Wage levels tended to be affected most where workers changed sectors, with the goods sector being a far more favourable destination than the service sector. Job changers moving from goods to services were actually more likely to experience wage losses than wage gains (48.1 per cent compared to 45.9 per cent); from our analysis of separation patterns, we know that layoffs were important here. In contrast, a shift in the other direction was more apt to benefit the job changer than any other adjustment pattern: 64.8 per cent of those moving from jobs in services to jobs in goods registered wage increases, while just 28.4 per cent reported wage cuts. Workers who remained in their original sector occupied a middle position.

Table 4-11

Profile of Job Finders: Distribution by Wage Outcome, Canada, 1986-87[1]

	Wage increase	No change	Wage decrease	Total
	(Per cent)			
All job separators	58.1	8.4	33.5	100.0
Reason for separation				
Quit personal	59.0	7.8	33.2	100.0
Quit nonpersonal	66.4	7.0	26.7	100.0
Involuntary	49.7	9.7	40.6	100.0
Age				
16-19	63.4	9.4	27.2	100.0
20-24	59.7	8.2	32.1	100.0
25-34	57.3	7.8	34.9	100.0
35-44	55.1	8.0	36.9	100.0
45-54	50.1	9.0	40.9	100.0
55-64	48.3	11.3	40.4	100.0
Sex				
Males	56.2	8.8	35.0	100.0
Females	60.5	8.0	31.6	100.0
Region				
Atlantic	59.7	8.4	31.8	100.0
Quebec	58.3	9.2	32.6	100.0
Ontario	56.8	10.2	33.0	100.0
Prairies	58.3	7.1	34.6	100.0
British Columbia	55.4	7.9	36.7	100.0
Sectoral movement				
Goods to goods	57.0	11.8	31.2	100.0
Goods to services	45.9	6.0	48.1	100.0
Services to services	59.4	8.2	32.5	100.0
Services to goods	64.8	6.9	28.4	100.0

1 Based on a sample of workers who separated from a job in 1986 and found another one before the end of 1987.
SOURCE Estimates by the Economic Council of Canada, based on Statistics Canada, the Labour Market Activity Survey.

Conclusion

The considerable structural change that has characterized the shift to services has had important implications for how efficiently people and jobs are matched in the labour market. In some ways, the rapid growth of services has contributed positively to that process. For example, in recent decades, the sector has been able to absorb large numbers of new work force entrants at a time when the job-creation capacity of goods industries has been very limited. As well, the growth of services has moderated cyclical fluctuations in employment, although there are reasons to suspect that this influence may be attenuated somewhat in the future.

In other ways, however, the unevenness of the sectoral pattern of growth and the emerging job structure are problematic. Certainly, many Canadians appear to be very mobile, moving into new and often better jobs with evidently very little dislocation. Our analysis suggests, however, that some groups are experiencing special difficulties. Two stand out – older workers, and people who have been laid off (largely from goods industries). Individuals in these categories have a higher-than-average probability of not finding re-employment after separating from jobs; they tend to have longer periods of joblessness even when they do find new work, and often experience cuts in wages when they are re-employed.

This chapter has introduced our analysis of the labour market in a service-dominated economy. It is to the nature of that labour market that we turn in the remaining chapters of this report.

5 Nonstandard Employment

The growth of work arrangements that differ from the traditional model of full-year, full-time employment has aroused a good deal of interest in recent years. These work forms have been variously referred to as "nonstandard" or "atypical" employment, "precarious" or "contingent" work, and a "flexible" component of the labour force, depending on the perspective of the observer. Generally, however, they are understood to encompass part-time, short-term and contract jobs, certain types of self-employment, and work within the temporary-help industry.

These employment forms are attracting attention in industrialized economies because in recent years they have grown more rapidly than more standard types of employment. In Canada, nonstandard employment has been a major source of job creation during the past decade, while in some European countries it has accounted for virtually all new employment growth. This development poses a challenge to policymakers who have continued to design labour market policies around a traditional concept of what constitutes the employment norm.

Nonstandard employment has also aroused a certain amount of controversy because of differing interpretations regarding the implications of its growth. From one perspective, the increasing prevalence of these arrangements is seen as a response to legitimate needs of both business and labour for more flexible forms of work.[1] Nonstandard employment forms offer employers a means to realize cost savings and an enhanced capacity to adjust their work forces rapidly to changing market conditions. This augments the efficiency and competitiveness of individual businesses and, by extension, of Canadian industry as a whole. At the same time, the availability of part-time and short-term jobs is perceived as meeting a need in certain segments of the labour force – most notably, students, and parents of small children – for work that falls outside the rigid boundaries of traditional full-time, full-year employment.

There is also a sceptical view that focuses on the inferior compensation, security, and career advancement opportunities that typically characterize nonstandard employment. Some equate the new labour market flexibility with labour market insecurity and view many varieties of nonstandard work as arrangements that transfer business-related risk from the firm to the worker.[2] There are concerns that these employment forms may, in fact, be giving rise to a new type of dual labour market consisting of one sector with workers in relatively secure jobs, with adequate compensation, and access to benefits and training and promotion opportunities; and another composed of marginalized "contingent" workers in nonstandard jobs with none of these attributes.[3] Sceptics also point to the evidence that significant numbers of nonstandard employees are involuntary in the sense that they would prefer more permanent, full-time jobs.

This chapter considers the phenomenon of nonstandard employment in Canada. We begin with a review of research that has been undertaken in other countries. We then focus on the Canadian experience, analysing part-time employment, short-term work, temporary-help agency work, and "own-account" self-employment. For each of these nonstandard work forms, we examine statistical trends and details on the nature of the employment and the work force. We conclude the chapter with a discussion of the growth of nonstandard employment in the aggregate, the factors underlying its expanding labour market share, and the policy issues that are being raised by its proliferation.

Nonstandard Employment in the United States and Europe

Although nonstandard employment has not been extensively analysed in Canada,[4] a number of empirical studies have been undertaken in other industrialized countries. In considering the results of this research, it is important to recognize that there is no broadly accepted convention as to what precise work forms should be included under the rubric "nonstandard employment." Despite this absence of consensus as to exact definitions (due in large part to differences in data availability across countries), recent studies generally estimate that the incidence of nonstandard work has been rising and that these employment forms now account for between one quarter and slightly over one third of total employment in the major industrialized countries.

In the United States, discussion of nonstandard work has focused on the notion of "contingency," emphasizing the conditional and transitory nature of the employment relationship, which is usually dependent on the employer's need for labour. In terms of theory, researchers in that country have tended to argue that contingent workers should be identified primarily on the basis of the absence of any long-term (implicit or explicit) affiliation with an employer.[5]

In practice, analysis in the United States has been affected by the lack of data that distinguishes between temporary and permanent (or indefinite) employment. The operational definition of "contingent employment" has thus become any arrangement which differs from full-time, permanent, wage and salary employment, and includes part-time work, temporary work, employee-leasing, self-employment, contracting-out, and home-based work.[6]

In an international study, Hakim defined the "flexible work force" in the United States as those people with some employment experience in a given year who worked less than full time and year round; in 1985, that was 41 per cent of the total American work force.[7] A recent study by Belous yielded similar results using a different methodology.[8] In this analysis, the "contingent work force" was defined to include four categories of workers: part-timers, the self-employed, temporary-help agency workers, and those employed in the business-service industry.[9] Belous estimates that between 25 and 30 per cent of the U.S. labour force could be described as "contingent" in 1988, accounting for between 33 and 55 per cent of new jobs created between 1980 and 1988.

In comparison to that of the United States, European research on nonstandard employment has benefited from the greater availability of data on temporary (and fixed-term) work. Hakim was able to include in the section of her work dealing with the "flexible work force" in the European Community those who described their jobs as temporary, in addition to part-time workers and the self-employed. She found that 33 per cent of the total EC work force in 1985 was in one of these employment forms.[10]

In a study of nonstandard employment in West Germany, Büchtemann and Quack include in their definition part-time work, self-employment, fixed-term employment contracts, and temporary-agency work.[11] They estimate that nonstandard employment was 35 per cent of total employment in 1987. Büchtemann and Quack note that this proportion has expanded continuously since the beginning of the 1980s. They also observe that in Germany, nonstandard employment growth has occurred almost entirely at the expense of standard employment forms: between the early 1970s and the mid-1980s, the number of full-time jobs dropped by about one million while the number of part-time jobs rose by approximately the same number.

Nonstandard Employment in Canada

We focus here on four categories of nonstandard employment: part-time, short-term and temporary, work within the temporary-help industry, and "own-account" self-employment. Part-time employment is defined as positions for which the usual hours of work are less than 30 per week. We define short-term work as a job lasting six months or less, while a temporary job is one where a permanent attachment was never intended. Employment within the temporary-help industry is work with agencies that, for a fee, supply workers to employers on a temporary basis. The own-account self-employed are self-employed persons who do not themselves have employees.

It is important to recognize that in Canada, as in the United States and a number of other countries, labour force data still do not permit accurate estimates of all nonstandard work forms. While excellent data are available on part-time workers and, to a lesser extent, the own-account self-employed, less are available on short-term, particularly temporary employment.

Part-Time Employment

Magnitude and Growth

Part-time employment is the largest of the nonstandard employment forms. In 1989, there were 1.9 million part-time workers in Canada, accounting for 15.1 per cent of total employment. As in most industrialized economies, the incidence of part-time work in Canada has grown since World War II (Chart 5-1). During the 1950s and 1960s, the rate of increase was rapid, with the part-time share of total employment rising from 3.8 per cent in 1953 to 12.3 per cent by 1970. After slowing down in the 1970s, the incidence of part-time work started to accelerate in the first half of the 1980s (from 13 per cent of total employment in 1980 to a peak of 15.5 per cent in 1985).[12]

Between 1980 and 1989, the number of part-time workers increased by almost 500,000; this represents over one quarter of the net employment creation in Canada during the decade (Table 5-1). About one third of this growth in part-time jobs was "involuntary"; that is, the workers would have preferred to work full time.

Employment and Worker Characteristics

Part-time employment is overwhelmingly a service-sector phenomenon; in 1989, virtually 90 per cent of all part-time

Chart 5-1

Part-Time Employment as a Proportion of Total Employment, Canada, 1953-89[1]

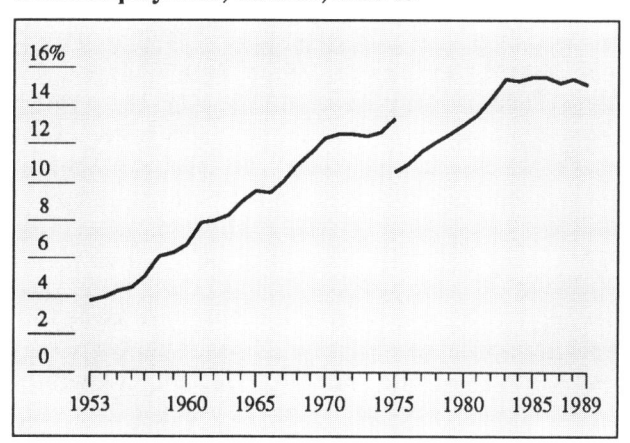

1 A series break occurred in 1975. Before 1975, part time was defined as less than 35 hours work per week. From 1975 on, it is defined as less than 30 hours per week.
SOURCE Estimates by the Economic Council of Canada, based on data from Statistics Canada.

Table 5-2

Distribution and Incidence of Part-Time Employment by Industry Group, Canada, 1989

	Part-time employment	
	Distribution	Share of total industry employment
	(Per cent)	
Goods sector	11.2	5.9
Primary industries	4.2	11.2
Manufacturing	4.4	4.0
Construction	2.5	6.2
Service sector	88.9	18.9
Dynamic services	14.0	9.1
Traditional services	49.4	29.8
Nonmarket services	25.5	17.0
All industries	100.0	15.1

SOURCE Estimates by the Economic Council of Canada, based on Statistics Canada, the Labour Force Survey, unpublished data.

Table 5-1

Net Employment Growth, by Employment Status, Canada, 1980-89

	Increase	Distribution of total increase
	(Thousands)	(Per cent)
Part-time employment	497	27.9
Voluntary	322	18.1
Involuntary	175	9.8
Full-time employment	1,282	72.1
Total employment	1,779	100.0

SOURCE Estimates by the Economic Council of Canada, based on Statistics Canada, the Labour Force Survey.

workers were employed in this sector (Table 5-2). Within the service sector, by far the largest concentration of part-time jobs is in traditional services, which accounts for slightly less than one half of total part-time employment in Canada.

Incidence rates by industry offer another view of the association between part-time employment and the service sector, particularly the traditional-service subsector (Table 5-2). In 1989, 18.9 per cent of service-sector workers were employed part-time; in the goods sector, on the other hand, the corresponding figure was 5.9 per cent. The incidence rate was especially high in traditional services where the part-time share of total employment in the subsector was 29.8 per cent. Part-time work was prevalent throughout the traditional subsector, with incidence rates of 32.8 per cent in personal services, 32.4 per cent in accommodation, food, and beverages, 30.9 per cent in amusement and recreation, and 29.1 per cent in retail trade.

Given the industrial distribution, it is not surprising that part-time employment is concentrated in the clerical, sales, and service occupations; together these three groups accounted for 65.3 per cent of all part-time workers in 1989. The highest incidence rates were in service and sales occupations where the part-time share of total employment was 30.5 and 25.1 per cent, respectively. It is interesting to note that there was a relatively high incidence of part-time work among managers and other professionals as well (11 per cent).

As Table 5-3 indicates, there is also a strong relationship between part-time work and firm size. Data from the Labour Market Activity Survey job file indicates that part-time jobs

74 Employment in the Service Economy

Table 5-3

Distribution of Part-Time and Full-Time Paid Jobs by Firm Size, Canada, 1987

	Distribution of	
	Part-time paid jobs	Full-time paid jobs
	(Per cent)	
Number of employees		
19 or less	37.2	25.7
20 to 99	16.1	18.4
100 to 499	12.5	15.3
500 or more	34.2	40.6
Total	100.0	100.0

SOURCE Estimates by the Economic Council of Canada, based on Statistics Canada, the Labour Market Activity Survey, unpublished data.

are considerably more likely to exist in very small organizations than are full-time jobs, and significantly less likely to be in large ones. In 1987, 37.2 per cent of all part-time jobs were in firms with less than 20 employees, compared with just 25.7 per cent of full-time jobs. On the other hand, while firms with at least 500 workers accounted for 40.6 per cent of full-time jobs, these large organizations accounted for only 34.2 per cent of total part-time jobs.

In 1989, women and people under 25 accounted for nearly 90 per cent of the total part-time labour force. Over 70 per cent of part-time workers in Canada are women. Currently, working women are roughly three times more likely to be employed part-time than are men; the part-time incidence rate in 1989 was 24.5 per cent for females, compared to 7.7 per cent for males. Note, however, that the part-time share of total employment has increased more for men than for women over the past decade; in 1979, for example, the incidence rates were 23.3 per cent and 5.7 per cent for women and men, respectively.

The conventional explanation for the high incidence of part-time employment among women is that it enables them to combine work and childrearing. And there is a strong correlation between part-time work and the presence of children. For instance, in married-couple families, part-time work is the dominant mode of employment for women with children below the age of 18: in 1986, 61 per cent of employed women in this category worked part time or part year.[13] Among employed married women with children under the age of five, the proportion rises to 73 per cent.

However, the pattern of female part-time work indicates that there are also other factors at play. For instance, single as well as married women are significantly more likely than men with the same marital status to work part time. Furthermore, women between the ages of 25 and 44 – the group with the heaviest overall childrearing responsibilities – are less likely than either younger or older women to work part time. Additional research is needed, then, to clarify the reasons for the high incidence of part-time employment among women, which are more complex than has been supposed.

In terms of age, in 1989, 42.2 per cent of part-time workers were between the ages of 15 and 24. Among young workers, part-time employment is strongly associated with student status; as well, within the 15-24 age group, women are significantly more likely than men to work part time. The part-time incidence rate is much higher for young workers than for the other age categories; in 1989, 33.6 per cent of the employed work force aged between 15 and 24 held part-time jobs, while the corresponding shares for the 25-44 and 45 and over age groups were 9.8 and 12.8 per cent, respectively (Chart 5-2). Comparing the 1989 incidence rates by age group with the 1979 rates, we can see that the part-time share of total employment grew by far the most in the young-worker category; however, relative increases were also recorded in the other two age classes.

Labour Force Attachment

The majority of part-time workers cannot be considered "casual" labour market participants. According to data from

Chart 5-2

Part-Time Employment as a Proportion of Total Employment, by Age Group, Canada, 1979 and 1989

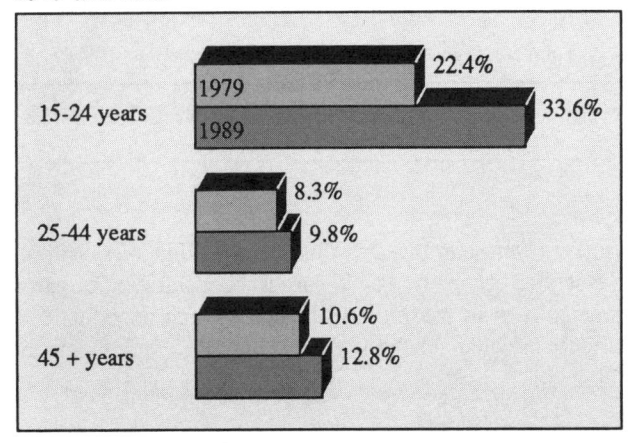

Age group	1979	1989
15-24 years	22.4%	33.6%
25-44 years	8.3%	9.8%
45 + years	10.6%	12.8%

SOURCE Statistics Canada, the Labour Force Survey.

the Labour Market Activity Survey, for example, 70 per cent worked year round (50 to 52 weeks) in 1986; by comparison, 81 per cent of full-time paid workers worked at least 50 weeks that year.

Further evidence of a significant labour market attachment on the part of most part-time workers comes from the data on "involuntary" part-time employment. This involuntary component, which consists of part-time workers who would have preferred full-time jobs, represents an increasingly important aspect of the part-time phenomenon. In 1989, 420,000 part-time employees were classified as "involuntary."

Traditionally, involuntary part-time employment has followed a distinct cyclical pattern; as Chart 5-3 indicates, its share has tended to rise fairly quickly during and immediately after recessions and then to subside once the expansion is well established. However, the general upward slope evident in Chart 5-3 also reveals a secular increase during the past 15 years in the incidence of involuntary part-time work. It is noteworthy that, at a given level of labour market tightness, the voluntary part-timers' share has risen over this period. For example, comparing 1975, 1980, and 1989 – when the annual unemployment rate was between 6.9 and 7.5 per cent – the proportion of part-time work that was involuntary rose from 11 to 17.6 per cent in 1980 and 22.2 per cent in 1989. In fact, over one third of the part-time employment growth during the 1980s was involuntary; overall, almost 10 per cent of all jobs created between 1980 and 1989 were classified as "involuntary part-time" (see Table 5-1).

Job Stability and Compensation

One issue that has been the subject of some debate is the stability of part-time work. By a considerable degree, part-time workers are more likely to be employed in short-term jobs than are full-time workers. Furthermore, the proportion of part-time workers with short tenure has increased appreciably during the past decade and that of full-time workers has changed only marginally; according to Labour Force Survey data, the share of the part-time work force with less than three-months' job tenure rose from 17.2 to 22.1 per cent between 1978 and 1989, while the corresponding rise for full-time workers was from 8.6 per cent in 1978 to 9.2 per cent in 1989. Although part-time employment does tend to be more short-term than full-time work, it should be noted that a substantial segment of the part-time work force is employed in relatively long-term jobs. In 1988, 55 per cent of part-time workers aged 25 years and over reported that they had been in their job for at least two years.

The pattern of hours worked also represents an important dimension of job stability. In 1986, three quarters of part-time workers usually worked the same number of hours each month; however, this is significantly lower than the corresponding figure for full-time workers (94 per cent).[14] Among part-time workers with variable hours, 51 per cent said that they had an "on-call" arrangement with their employer. The typical part-time employment pattern is to work a few days each week: in 1986, 92 per cent of the part-time work force reported that they worked four weeks per month, with the most typical workweek consisting of two or three days. In that year, part-time employees worked an average of 18 hours per week, with the most frequently reported work schedule having between 12 and 24 hours a week.

Generally, compensation for part-time workers is significantly inferior to that for full-time workers. According to the Labour Market Activity Survey, average hourly earnings in 1987 for part-time jobs were slightly less than three quarters of those reported by full-time workers.[15] As well, access to fringe benefits is much lower; for example, only about 11 per cent of part-time jobs in 1987 had work-related pension plans (compared to 46 per cent of full-time jobs).[16]

There are several reasons for this. First, part-time employment patterns are concentrated in firms, industries, and occupations that tend to have low levels of compensation.

Chart 5-3

Involuntary Part-Time Employment as a Proportion of Total Part-Time Employment, and Unemployment Rate, Canada, 1975-89

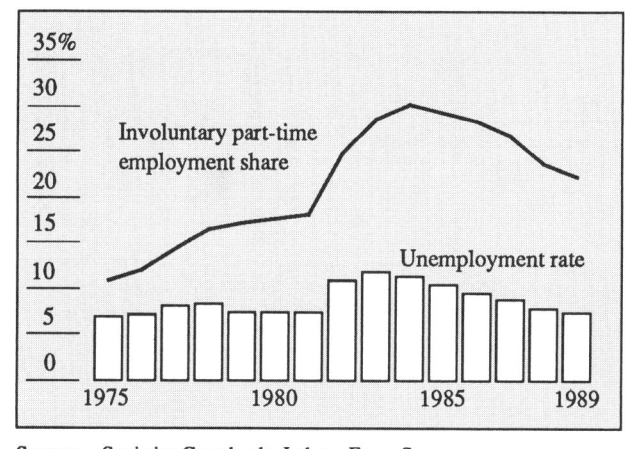

SOURCE Statistics Canada, the Labour Force Survey.

As we have seen, part-time jobs are disproportionately located in small firms, which generally pay less than larger companies: in 1987, for example, according to data from the Labour Market Activity Survey, average hourly earnings in organizations with fewer than 20 employees were $8.45, compared with $12.97 in firms employing 500 or more. Similarly, about one half of the part-time work force is employed in the traditional-service subsector, which is by far the lowest-paid of all the major industry groups: average hourly wages in traditional services in 1987 were less than two thirds of the all-industry standard. Finally, nearly two thirds of all part-time workers are in service, sales, or clerical positions; jobs in these groups are among the lowest-paid of all occupational groups, with average hourly earnings in 1987 of only 67 per cent, 79 per cent, and 85 per cent of the national average, respectively.

Although part-time employment is concentrated in relatively poorly paid segments of the labour market, this does not completely explain the low compensation levels. Within industries, occupations, and firm-size categories, part-time hourly earnings are generally lower than those of comparable full-time workers. Significant hourly-wage differentials exist between part-time and full-time jobs in all major industry sectors (Table 5-4). Mean part-time earnings in 1987 ranged from 63 per cent (sales occupations) to 92 per cent (professional occupations) of full-time levels. And part-time jobs in firms of all sizes are paid less than their full-time counterparts; as Chart 5-4 shows, this differential is greatest in large organizations.

The composition of the part-time labour force itself undoubtedly has some bearing on these lower earnings. As we have noted, over 40 per cent of part-time workers are between the ages of 15 and 24, lack work experience, and often have lower levels of educational attainment than prime-aged workers. This is reflected in their wages; on average, young part-time workers earn 60 per cent of the hourly wages of part-time workers aged over 25. (It is worth noting, however, that young part-timers also earn considerably less than young full-time workers.) Furthermore, over 70 per cent of part-time workers are women, and many studies of women's earnings have identified a male-female earnings gap even after controlling for such factors as occupational and industrial distribution, education, and work experience.

In addition to age and gender composition, another factor to consider in explaining the inferior part-time compensation is the low incidence of unionization in this segment of the work force. In 1986, union membership rates were 20.8 per cent for part-time employees and 37.6 per cent for full-time workers.[17] It is well known that unionized workers

Table 5-4

Part-Time Paid Jobs: Average Hourly Earnings and Earnings Relative to Full-Time Earnings, by Industry Group, Canada, 1987

	Average hourly earnings[1]	
	Part-time paid jobs	Part-time as a proportion of full-time paid jobs
	(Dollars)	(Per cent)
Goods sector	9.56	80.0
Primary industries	9.02	79.6
Manufacturing	9.26	77.2
Construction	10.57	86.2
Service sector	8.41	73.6
Dynamic services	9.74	77.8
Traditional services	6.02	75.7
Nonmarket services	11.47	85.6
All industries	8.54	73.7

1 Wages and salaries only.
SOURCE Estimates by the Economic Council of Canada, based on Statistics Canada, the Labour Market Activity Survey, unpublished data.

Chart 5-4

Hourly Earnings of Part-Time Paid Jobs Relative to Full-Time Paid Jobs, by Firm Size, Canada, 1987

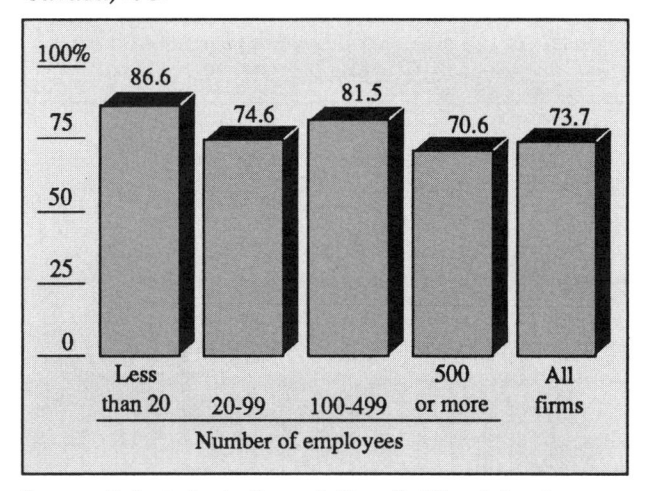

Number of employees	Per cent
Less than 20	86.6
20-99	74.6
100-499	81.5
500 or more	70.6
All firms	73.7

SOURCE Estimates by the Economic Council of Canada, based on Statistics Canada, the Labour Market Activity Survey, unpublished data.

generally earn more than their nonunionized counterparts. Indeed, the union wage premium appears to be very significant within the part-time population, where, according to the Labour Market Activity Survey, nonunionized part-time jobs were paid just 63 per cent of the wages paid to unionized part-time jobs. As well, consistent with the fact that wage differentials of all types tend to be reduced in unionized industries, the gap between part-time and full-time earnings was significantly smaller in the unionized sector. Among unionized jobs, part-time wages were 89 per cent of full-time wages, while the corresponding proportion for nonunionized jobs was only 74 per cent.

Short-Term and Temporary Employment

Magnitude and Growth

As we have already noted, research on short-term employment in Canada is constrained by inadequate data. Most notably, information on fixed-term or temporary employment (outside of temporary-help agency work) is lacking. However, one source of such data is the Labour Market Activity Survey, in which respondents separating from jobs were asked why their employment had ended. According to this survey, of the 4.8 million paid jobs that were terminated in 1987, 11.3 per cent were identified as having been terminated because they were temporary positions.[18]

Without a great deal of information on temporary jobs, most of our analysis on short-term employment has been based on job duration and job tenure statistics. While these data can be used to sketch out the incidence of short-term employment, they cannot distinguish between those jobs that are explicitly temporary in nature and those that terminate in a short period of time for other reasons.

In our analysis, a "short-term" job has been defined as one which lasts for no more than six months. To identify short-term employment, then, information on completed job duration is required. The most recent comprehensive source of such data is the Labour Market Activity Survey which we used to analyse job duration patterns in 1987. In order to calculate the share of employment that was short-term, we focused on those paid jobs that existed in the first 26 weeks of that year.[19] Of the 12.9 million jobs reported during that period, 1.7 million (or 13.1 per cent) were identified as short-term (i.e., with a completed duration of no more than 26 weeks).

While the LMAS affords a "snapshot" view, there is no time series of completed job spells. In order to track the incidence of short-term employment over time, we used ongoing job tenure data from the Labour Force Survey (which are available from 1975 on). In the past, researchers have used information on job tenure as a proxy measure for completed job duration; in fact, making some assumptions, the percentage of those employed at a given point in time with less than three months' tenure corresponds to the proportion of workers in jobs with an eventual duration of no more than six months.[20]

According to our analysis of the LFS job tenure data, there was a modest increase in the incidence of short-term employment during the second half of the 1980s. In the period 1975-84, the proportion of workers reporting ongoing job tenure of less than three months remained relatively stable, fluctuating between 8.6 per cent in 1982 and 10.2 per cent in 1979 and 1981. This figure increased somewhat after 1985, reaching a peak of 11.6 per cent in 1987 before retreating slightly to 11.2 per cent in 1989.

Employment and Worker Characteristics

Turning now to the nature of temporary and short-term employment,[21] we have already noted that 11.3 per cent of all paid jobs that ended in 1987 were temporary jobs. Overall, there was very little difference between the sectors, with temporary jobs accounting for 11.8 per cent of all goods-sector employment terminating in 1987, compared to 11.1 per cent for the service sector. Within these sectors, temporary employment was most significant in nonmarket services and construction, where it accounted for 21.6 and 19.6 per cent of all job terminations, respectively.[22]

The incidence of short-term employment (lasting 26 weeks or less) was slightly higher in the goods sector than in the service sector (Table 5-5). At the industry-group level, the highest rates were reported in construction, primary industries, and traditional services. Short-term employment also appears to be related to firm size; the incidence rate was greatest in firms with less than 20 employees (20.6 per cent of paid jobs) and it declined in each successive size-category, accounting for only 7.5 per cent in firms with 500 employees or more. Finally, part-time jobs were particularly likely to be of short duration: 17.6 per cent of part-time employment terminated within six months compared to 12 per cent of full-time jobs.

The job tenure data from the Labour Force Survey paint a similar picture of short-term employment. In 1989, when 11.2 per cent of the employed work force reported ongoing tenure of less than three months, the highest rates were in construction (17.5 per cent), traditional services (16.4 per

Table 5-5

Incidence and Distribution of Short-Term Paid Jobs[1] by Industry Group, Canada, 1987

	Short-term paid jobs	
	Proportion of all paid jobs in each industry	Distribution
	(Per cent)	
Goods sector	15.7	33.1
Primary industries	22.4	6.9
Manufacturing	10.5	14.6
Construction	28.0	11.6
Service sector	12.1	66.9
Dynamic services	9.5	15.9
Traditional services	17.7	33.8
Nonmarket services	8.8	17.3
All industries	13.1	100.0

1 Duration of less than 26 weeks, based on all paid jobs reported in the first six months of 1987.
SOURCE Calculations by the Economic Council of Canada, based on Statistics Canada, the Labour Market Activity Survey, unpublished data.

Chart 5-5

Short-Term Paid Jobs,[1] as a Proportion of All Paid Jobs, by Age, Canada, 1987

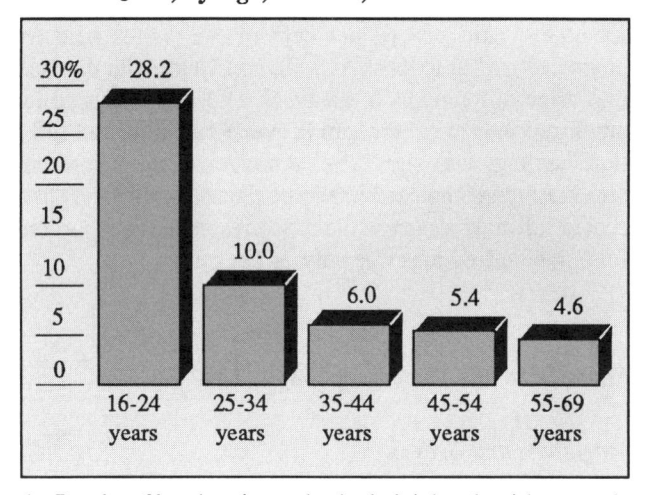

Age group	Per cent
16-24 years	28.2
25-34 years	10.0
35-44 years	6.0
45-54 years	5.4
55-69 years	4.6

1 Duration of less than six months. Analysis is based on jobs reported in the first six months.
SOURCE Statistics Canada, the Labour Market Activity Survey.

cent), and primary industries excluding agriculture (14.6 per cent). The LFS data also show a strong association between short-term and part-time work; in 1989, 22.1 per cent of part-time employees reported job tenure of less than three months while the corresponding figure for full-time employees was just 9.2 per cent.

The incidence of temporary employment is relatively neutral between sexes and across age groups. The proportion of jobs terminating in 1987 that were temporary was 11.1 per cent among males and 11.6 per cent among females. By age, the highest rates were in the 35-44 and 45-54 age groups with older workers (55 years and over) and younger workers (16-24 years) reporting below-average incidence levels.

On the other hand, the predominant characteristic of short-term employees is their youth. Well over one half (59 per cent) of the jobs lasting six months or less in the LMAS sample were held by workers between the ages of 16 and 24. As Chart 5-5 shows, the incidence of short-term employment among this group was almost three times as high as that for any other age category. According to the LFS data, 27.4 per cent of the 15-24 age group were in short-tenure jobs in 1989, compared to just 7.4 per cent for those 25 years and over. According to both the LFS and the LMAS, women are slightly more likely than males to be in short-term jobs: in the LMAS, the 1987 short-term incidence rate was 13.2 per cent for women and 12.9 per cent for men, while the corresponding figures for the LFS in 1989 were 12.3 per cent and 10.3 per cent.

Compensation

Compensation levels for temporary and short-term employees are usually lower than those of other workers. The mean hourly wages earned in temporary jobs terminating in 1987 were 90.6 per cent of those earned in nontemporary jobs. The differential was considerably larger for short-term jobs: average hourly earnings for short-term jobs were 65.4 per cent of those in positions lasting more than six months.

The wage gap, specifically for short-term workers, is due partly to the fact that these employees, like those who work part-time, are often employed in sectors of the labour market – notably traditional services and small firms – that are associated with low pay. But, again similar to part-time jobs, wages and salaries for short-term employees are generally lower than for other workers in the same broad industry and occupational groups. In many respects this is not surprising: short-term workers, by definition, lack significant firm-specific experience or skills; they have no seniority; they are less likely to be unionized; and they are disproportionately young and thus have lower levels of education and labour force experience.

In addition, short-term workers often do not have access to a broad range of employment benefits. For instance, many employers routinely exclude such employees from most nonstatutory benefits, or require a minimum period of service (typically, several months) before extending coverage. With respect to pensions, virtually no short-term workers get benefit entitlements, as even those who are covered fall short of the usual two-year minimum service requirement for vesting of pension credits. Some worker benefits guaranteed by employment standards legislation also have minimum-service periods for eligibility. In some cases these are quite short – for instance, between 15 and 90 days for statutory holiday pay, depending on the jurisdiction – while at the other extreme, most jurisdictions require twelve months' continuous service as a condition of eligibility for maternity leave. Many short-term workers are also effectively excluded from some public benefit plans due to minimum requirements regarding employment duration (for example, Unemployment Insurance) or annual earnings (for example, the Canada/Quebec Pension Plans).

Temporary-Help Agency Work

Employment and Worker Characteristics

Employment in the temporary-help industry has increased almost two-and-a-half times in the 1980s to reach about 82,000 in 1989.[23] Over one half of temporary-help workers are in clerical occupations, compared with just 18 per cent of all workers.[24] However, the proportion in professional, transport, and general labour positions has increased in recent years. Those industries with the highest incidence of temporary-help workers relative to total employment are government and finance, insurance, and real estate, while manufacturing is the single largest industry client of temporary-help services. These three industry groups account for over half of all temporary-help placements.[25]

Employers generally make use of temporary agencies either because of changes in worker availability or because of fluctuations in workload that are unplanned, short, or of uncertain duration. A 1987 survey found that the main reasons companies brought in temporary office workers were to replace employees who were ill or on holidays (28 per cent), to handle an unexpected overload of work (23 per cent), or to assist with a special project (13 per cent).[26]

About three quarters of the temporary-help agency work force are female. As well, they are more likely than the labour force at large to be young and single: 35 per cent are between the ages of 16 and 24 (compared with 25 per cent of other workers) and 45 per cent are single (compared with 30 per cent of other workers). Temporary-help agency employees are also relatively well educated: 54 per cent have some postsecondary education (compared with roughly 40 per cent of all Canadian workers).[27]

Two separate surveys of temporary-help employees have found that a substantial minority – 36 per cent in 1984 and 41 per cent in 1987 – were engaged in this type of work because they could not find full-time employment.[28] This finding is reinforced by comments of industry executives that attracting and retaining qualified employees becomes very difficult in fields with low unemployment rates. Of those workers who are voluntarily employed by temporary-help agencies, the most important reasons for choosing this kind of work are to obtain variety and challenge and to permit attendance at an educational institution.[29]

Compensation

While temporary-help wages vary substantially according to local labour market conditions, they are generally below those for full-time salaried workers in the same occupational groups.[30] In 1986, for instance, the mean hourly wage for temporary-help clerical employees was 83 per cent of the average wage for all clerical workers.[31] For specific clerical occupations, temporary-help wages ranged from 70 per cent of equivalent hourly wages for permanent receptionists, to 88 per cent in the case of office-machine operators.[32] In only two occupational groups – systems analysts and domestics and nannies – did temporary-help wages exceed those of permanent workers.[33]

Own-Account Self-Employment

Magnitude and Growth

The final nonstandard group we analysed is the "own-account" self-employed (OASE) – that is, self-employed individuals who do not themselves have employees.[34] In 1989 this group represented 54 per cent of all self-employed persons. Unlike the self-employed with paid help who are usually incorporated, about 90 per cent of the OASE population do not have incorporated businesses.[35]

In the period since the mid-1970s, self-employment has increased relatively rapidly in Canada. The own-account group has followed this larger trend: between 1975 and 1989, OASE rose faster than employment as a whole, increasing its share of total employment from 6.2 to 7.2 per cent; it accounted for 10 per cent of the job growth during these years.[36]

Employment and Worker Characteristics

Table 5-6 presents data on the incidence of own-account self-employment by industry group for 1975 and 1989. The OASE share of total employment in 1989 was slightly higher in the goods (9 per cent) than in the service sector (6.5 per cent); over the period 1975-89, however, these rates converged somewhat as the growth of OASE was more rapid in services than in goods. By 1989, almost two thirds of the own-account self-employed were in services.

As one might expect, own-account self-employment is particularly important in agriculture, where over two fifths of the employed work force fell into this category in 1989. While OASE is not nearly as prevalent in any of the other major industry groups represented in Table 5-6, this work form did account for over 10 per cent of the total employment in construction and traditional services.[37] Traditional services accounted for 37 per cent of all own-account self-employment and agriculture 20 per cent.

In comparison with all classes of paid workers (which excludes OASE), the own-account self-employed are sig-

Table 5-6

Own-Account Self-Employment as a Share of Total Employment, by Industry, Canada, 1975 and 1989

	1975	1989
	(Per cent)	
Goods sector	9.2	9.0
Agriculture	44.7	42.1
Other primary industries	4.6	7.3
Manufacturing	0.8	1.1
Construction	8.6	13.0
Service sector	4.7	6.5
Traditional services	10.0	10.8
Dynamic services	3.5	6.7
Nonmarket services	0.8	1.6
All industries	6.2	7.2

SOURCE Estimates by the Economic Council of Canada, based on Statistics Canada, the Labour Force Survey, unpublished data.

Table 5-7

Distribution of Paid Employees and Own-Account Self-Employed by Sex and Age, Canada, 1989

	Paid employees	Own-account self-employed
	(Per cent)	
Sex		
Males	53.8	63.4
Females	46.2	36.5
Age		
15-24	20.9	10.9
25-44	55.2	49.4
45-64	23.0	34.0
65 and over	0.9	5.7
Total	100.0	100.0

SOURCE Estimates by the Economic Council of Canada, based on Statistics Canada, the Labour Force Survey, unpublished data.

nificantly more likely to work in primary, artistic and literary, sales, and service occupations and much less likely to be employed in clerical, managerial, processing and fabricating, and professional jobs.[38] However, the industrial composition of own-account self-employment is changing and with it the occupational composition; particularly notable is the relative decline of OASE in primary occupations.

The demographic composition of the own-account self-employed is distinctly different from that of other nonstandard workers. While young workers and women are overrepresented in the part-time, short-term, and temporary-help agency populations, the own-account self-employed are disproportionately male and tend to be older than the work force at large (Table 5-7).

The employment patterns of OASE women and men differ considerably. Among the women, 40 per cent worked part time, and almost two thirds were in traditional services in 1989. Among men, on the other hand, own-account self-employment is much more likely to be found in goods-sector industries, particularly agriculture (26 per cent of OASE males in 1989) and construction (17 per cent). Only 11 per cent of own-account self-employed men worked part time.

Just as the kind of work performed by the own-account self-employed is changing, however, so too are the characteristics of those who perform it. In fact, in the group with the highest OASE incidence – men aged 45 and over – there was little growth in own-account self-employment in the 1980s. The greatest proportion of job growth in this employment category occurred among women (58 per cent). Among the age groups, the 25-44 group provided over four fifths of new recruits to own-account self-employment.

Employment and Compensation Patterns

Data collected by Statistics Canada on the self-employed suggests that there is a high degree of variability in the hours of the own-account self-employed. Within the OASE population, more than one quarter usually work less than 30 hours per week (in comparison to 16.5 per cent of paid workers), while at the other end of the scale, nearly one third work over 50 hours per week (compared to only 7 per cent of paid workers). The hours worked by the full-time, own-account self-employed are generally longer than those worked by paid employees (44 hours per week in comparison with 37), while those worked by part-timers are usually shorter (11 hours per week rather than 15).

In contrast with other kinds of nonstandard jobs, the duration of own-account self-employment tends to be relatively long. In 1986, the average tenure of full-time OASE individuals was 10.9 years, compared with 7.5 years for paid workers. Similarly, among part-timers, average tenure was 5.4 years for the own-account self-employed and 3.4 years for paid workers. The incidence of short-term work was almost identical for both groups: 12.3 per cent of the own-account self-employed and 12 per cent of paid workers reported tenure of three months or less in 1986.

Earnings of the own-account self-employed are lower, in most industries and occupations, than those of paid workers: in 1985, when mean annual earnings for full-year paid workers were $24,300, the corresponding figure for the OASE group was just $16,200. The relative disparities are even greater for median earnings, reflecting the fact that while a minority of the self-employed with high earnings raise the overall average, the majority of the own-account self-employed have very low incomes. In 1985, the respective median earnings for full-year workers were $23,200 for paid workers and $11,800 for the own-account self-employed. Just over half of the OASE group earned less than $10,000, compared with 27 per cent of paid workers. The OASE situation stands in sharp contrast to that of the self-employed with paid help, who generally earn more than paid workers in the same occupations and industries: the 1985 mean and median earnings for the full-year self-employed with paid help were $29,700 and $22,900, respectively.[39]

Aggregate Nonstandard Employment

According to our estimates, there were approximately 3.5 million nonstandard workers in Canada in 1989.[40] This represented 28 per cent of all employment in that year. Taking definitional differences into consideration, the incidence of nonstandard employment in this country appears to be similar to that of the United States and the European Economic Community.[41]

Chart 5-6 shows a steady increase in the nonstandard share of total employment over the past 15 years; the incidence rate was 23.7 per cent in 1975, 25.4 per cent in 1980, and 27.9 per cent in 1985. Overall, nonstandard work forms accounted for about 44 per cent of all employment growth in the 1980s and 41 per cent of the growth since 1975.

Chart 5-6

Nonstandard Employment as a Proportion of Total Employment, Canada, 1975-89

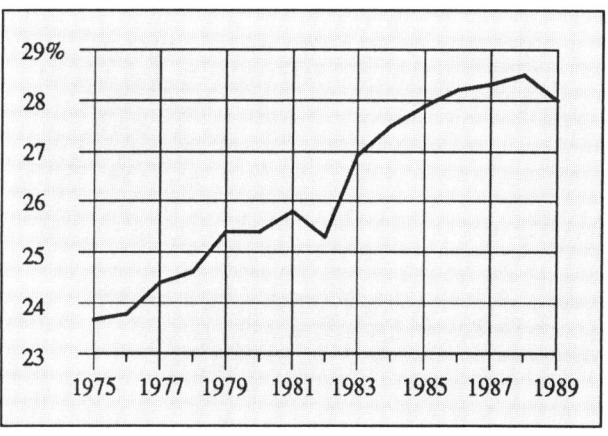

SOURCE   Calculations by the Economic Council of Canada, based on Statistics Canada, the Labour Force Survey, unpublished data.

Employment and Worker Characteristics

Since it is the only data base for estimating nonstandard employment over time, the Labour Force Survey has been used as the source for the incidence rates shown in Chart 5-6. In order to examine the characteristics of nonstandard jobs and the workers who occupy them, however, we have based our analysis on the Labour Market Activity Survey for 1987. There are two major advantages to this data base: first, it provides information on completed job spells (for estimating short-term employment), and, second, it identifies temporary jobs. According to the LMAS,

33.8 per cent of all jobs that existed in the first six months of 1987 were nonstandard – part-time, short-term, temporary, and own-account self-employment.[42]

The incidence and distribution of aggregate nonstandard employment by industry group are presented in Table 5-8. It is somewhat more prevalent in services, where 36.3 per cent of all jobs were nonstandard, compared to 27.7 per cent in goods. The relatively high incidence in the service sector was due, in large part, to traditional services where virtually one half (49.5 per cent) of total jobs were nonstandard; this subsector accounted for 38.7 per cent of all nonstandard jobs in the economy. Above-average incidence rates were also reported in the primary industries and construction, while the lowest rate by a considerable margin was in manufacturing.

Women are disproportionately represented in the nonstandard work force. As Table 5-9 indicates, the majority (53.8 per cent) of nonstandard jobs in the first half of 1987 were occupied by women, despite the fact that females still accounted for a minority of total employment. This is due to a significant difference in the incidence rates for men and women (27.9 per cent versus 41.4 per cent). The overrepresentation of women is a result of their dominance in the part-time labour market: recall that over 70 per cent of part-time workers – the largest component of nonstandard workers – are female; among full-timers, men outnumber women in the temporary, short-term, and self-employment categories.

Young people below the age of 25 constitute the largest single age group of nonstandard workers, filling 40.4 per cent of all nonstandard jobs (Table 5-9). Over half (54.6 per cent) of the jobs filled by young workers were nonstandard; the incidence rate declines for the prime-aged categories and then rises again for workers between 55 and 69 years of age.

Why Is Nonstandard Employment Growing?

As we have seen, the proliferation of nonstandard employment appears to be a fairly widespread phenomenon throughout the industrialized economies. Any explanation for its growth, therefore, must encompass generalized, rather than country-specific, factors. The hypotheses that have been advanced can be grouped into three types of candidate explanations: supply-side, demand-side, and cyclical.

Table 5-9

Distribution and Incidence of All Nonstandard Jobs by Sex and Age, Canada, 1987[1]

	Distribution	Share of all jobs in each group
	(Per cent)	
Sex		
Males	46.2	27.9
Females	53.8	41.4
Age		
16-24	40.4	54.6
25-34	23.7	27.7
35-44	16.9	24.9
45-54	10.7	25.2
55-69	8.3	31.5
Total	100.0	33.8

1 Based on all jobs reported in the first six months of 1987.
SOURCE Estimates by the Economic Council of Canada, based on Statistics Canada, the Labour Market Activity Survey, unpublished data.

Table 5-8

Distribution and Incidence of All Nonstandard Jobs by Industry, Canada, 1987[1]

	Distribution	Share of all jobs in each industry
	(Per cent)	
Goods sector	23.5	27.7
Primary industries	8.6	45.8
Manufacturing	7.7	16.1
Construction	7.2	39.8
Service sector	76.4	36.3
Dynamic services	16.3	25.3
Traditional services	38.7	49.5
Nonmarket services	21.4	31.5
All industries	100.0	33.8

1 Based on all jobs reported in the first six months of 1987.
SOURCE Estimates by the Economic Council of Canada, based on Statistics Canada, the Labour Market Activity Survey, unpublished data.

Supply-side hypotheses start with the proposition that the impetus for the growth in nonstandard employment has come from the labour force. They contend that, because of changes in the composition of the work force, there is now a stronger preference for work forms that differ from the traditional full-time, full-year paid arrangement, pointing to the increasing labour force participation of females and young people, who often have responsibilities outside the labour market. It is argued, then, that as the work force involvement of women and youth has increased, so too has the potential supply of nonstandard employees.

Demand-side hypotheses focus on the role of employers in generating nonstandard jobs. They argue that in the wake of the recession of the early 1980s and the subsequent heightening of competitive pressures, many firms have adopted an employment strategy aimed at maximizing flexibility and minimizing costs through the use of part-time, short-term, and temporary labour. This strategy often follows a "core-periphery" duality whereby firms maintain a basic or "core" labour force of workers with long-term employer attachment that is then supplemented by "peripheral" nonstandard workers who can be hired or let go as needed.

There are a number of distinct advantages for employers in pursuing a strategy involving nonstandard employment: surplus labour can be shed rapidly and with minimal termination costs during economic downturns or when labour-saving technology is introduced; the work force can be quickly augmented in response to short-term demands; low wages and benefit coverage for nonstandard workers allows firms to reduce unit labour costs; nonstandard employees are often more difficult to organize into unions; and labour standards do not always apply to them. While these would undoubtedly be seen as advantages for many employers, they may be especially attractive to small companies with strong cost constraints, and to service-sector firms who are unable to store their product and require the flexibility to directly respond to market demands.

Explanations focusing on cyclicality emphasize the role of slack labour markets in the expansion of nonstandard employment. According to this argument, nonstandard jobs – with relatively poor compensation, protection, and career prospects – will typically be taken up by many workers only when full-time, more permanent positions are not available; as a consequence, employers are able to successfully pursue a nonstandard employment strategy when there is a surplus of labour. Exponents of this view point to the relatively rapid growth of some components of nonstandard work – especially involuntary part-time work – during periods of recession, and suggest that a dearth of standard employment opportunities may force workers to accept "second-best" job opportunities.

We examined nonstandard employment trends in light of these hypotheses. With respect to the supply-side argument, we used shift-share analysis to estimate the impact of the shifting age and sex composition of the work force on nonstandard incidence rates.[43] Aspects of the demand-side argument – especially changes in employer strategies – are more difficult to capture quantitatively. We can, however, use shift-share analysis to estimate the impact of the employment shift towards service industries with a high propensity for nonstandard work forms. Finally, in order to consider the cyclicality explanation, we tracked the incidence patterns of nonstandard employment relative to labour market conditions since 1975.

Labour Force Composition

In order to assess the impact of changes in the makeup of the labour force on the level of nonstandard employment, we calculated hypothetical nonstandard incidence rates for 1988, holding the age and sex distributions of the employed work force constant at their 1975 levels. By comparing the hypothetical rates with the observed ones, we can gain some insight into the effects of the shifting age and sex structure of the labour force. In Table 5-10, we show the results of this shift-share analysis for the part-time, short-term, and own-account self-employed, as well as for nonstandard work in the aggregate. In all cases, our calculations suggest that the impact of the changing makeup of the work force has been very moderate, with the effects of the shifts in the age and sex structure operating in opposite directions.

We have seen in this chapter that nonstandard employment is most concentrated among women and young people. Looking first at women, their share of total employment increased from 36.4 per cent in 1975 to 43.8 per cent in 1988. If that share had remained at the 1975 level, *ceteris paribus*, the amount of nonstandard work and its largest categories would have been only slightly lower in 1988 than it actually was: the 1975-88 increase in the incidence of part-time, short-term, and aggregate nonstandard employment would have been 3.5, 1.4, and 3.8 percentage points (based on Table 5-10*a*) instead of the observed 4.8, 1.5, and 4.8 percentage points. Most of the nonstandard growth, then, is not explained by the increasing participation of women in the work force over this period. Of greater importance was the rising incidence of nonstandard employment among both women and men; according to our calculations, the incidence rate for all forms of nonstandard work among females increased from 31 to 36.1 per cent between 1975

84 Employment in the Service Economy

Table 5-10

Shift-Share Analysis of Nonstandard Employment Trends, Canada, 1975 and 1988 (Actual) and 1988 (Hypothetical)

	Incidence rate[1]			
	Part-time employment	Short-term employment	Own-account self-employment	Total nonstandard employment[2]
	(Per cent)			
1975	10.6	10.0	6.2	23.7
1988	15.4	11.5	7.4	28.5
1988 (hypothetical)[3]				
a Gender-constant	14.1	11.4	7.6	27.5
b Age-constant	16.9	12.6	7.5	30.5
c Sector-constant	14.6	11.4	7.7	28.2

1 Employment in nonstandard work forms as a proportion of total employment.
2 Not a sum because the overall rate removes the overlap among nonstandard work forms.
3 Assumes no change between 1975 and 1988 in the composition of employment by gender, age, and industry group.
SOURCE Estimates by the Economic Council of Canada, based on Statistics Canada, the Labour Force Survey.

and 1988, while that for males rose from 19.5 to 22.6 per cent over the same period.

To what extent can the growth of nonstandard employment be attributed to the shifting age composition of the labour force over the past 15 years? In fact, the shift-share analysis suggests that changes in the age structure have acted to limit the growth of these work forms. Although participation rates for young workers – by far the most likely to be nonstandard workers – have risen during the period in question, the declining numbers in the 15-24 population have led to a reduction in that group's share of the employed work force, from 25.6 per cent in 1975 to 19.5 per cent in 1988. In our hypothetical scenario where the age structure remained frozen according to its 1975 makeup, the 1988 incidence of nonstandard employment and each of its constituent elements was actually higher than the observed rates (see Table 5-10*b*). With an older work force in 1988, then, the employed labour force has actually been moving towards an age profile with a lower propensity to work in nonstandard jobs. The important factor, however, has been rising incidence rates in all age groups, and especially the youngest and oldest categories: between 1975 and 1988, the nonstandard share of total employment increased 13.8 and 13.6 percentage points for those 15-24 and 65 years and over, and 3.9 and 4.7 percentage points for the 25-44 and 45-64 age groups.

Industrial Structure

It has been argued that a significant factor in the growth of these work forms has been the shift to service industries where production typically cannot be stored, and where labour flexibility is therefore required to accommodate fluctuations in demand. As we saw in Table 5-8, the incidence of nonstandard employment is greater in services than in goods, with a particularly high degree of concentration in traditional services. Moreover, during the period 1975-88, the service-sector share of total employment increased from 65.8 to 70.9 per cent, with the largest gains in traditional services.

How important have these trends been in the growth of nonstandard employment? To consider this question, we calculated hypothetical 1988 incidence rates for nonstandard employment in the aggregate and for each of its particular forms based on the 1975 industrial structure (see Table 5-10*c*). Our results suggest that the changing composition of industry has contributed, but only slightly, to the growth of nonstandard work. If the structure had remained as it was in 1975, the aggregate nonstandard share would have been smaller, but only by 0.3 percentage points; part-time employment would have been smaller (by 0.8 percentage points), but the short-term rate would have remained the same and the figure for the own-account self-employed would have been slightly higher. Again, rising incidence rates within each group were more important than shifts in relative sizes of the groups: the share of total employment in nonstandard jobs increased in the goods sector (excluding agriculture), traditional services, dynamic services, and nonmarket services by 3.4, 6.0, 5.9, and 5.2 percentage points, respectively, between 1975 and 1988.

Labour Market Conditions

As we have noted, slack labour markets represent a favourable environment for most forms of nonstandard work and during the past 15 years, when nonstandard employment has expanded so much, unemployment rates have typically been high by historical standards. To what extent, then, has the growth of nonstandard jobs been the result of prevailing labour market conditions?

A review of the period 1975-89 indicates that there is certainly a cyclical element to nonstandard employment trends. The biggest single annual increase in the nonstandard incidence rate (1.6 percentage points) occurred between 1982 and 1983 when the economy was in the depths of a recession; in fact, over the 15-year period we have analysed, about one half of the overall increase in the incidence of nonstandard employment (2.2 of 4.3 percentage points) took place between 1982 and 1984.

On the other hand, however, it is clear that slack labour markets cannot explain all of the growth in nonstandard employment since the mid-1970s. The incidence of these work forms has continued on an upward trend throughout the past 15 ears regardless of labour market conditions (see Chart 5-6). In fact, in only two years since 1975 has nonstandard employment expanded at a slower rate than total employment. Moreover, during the postrecession period, the incidence of nonstandard work continued to increase, despite the fact that the labour market became progressively tighter for five consecutive years; as the unemployment rate fell from 11.9 per cent in 1983 to 7.8 per cent in 1988, the nonstandard share of total employment rose from 26.9 to 28.5 per cent.

Chart 5-7 provides a closer look at the role of labour market conditions by tracking the relationship over the period 1975-89 between the national unemployment rate and each of the three major nonstandard work forms in turn. To interpret these figures, note that the curve moves along a path between the lower-left corner (low incidence, low unemployment) and the upper-right corner (high incidence, high unemployment) where nonstandard employment trends are cyclical; between the upper-left (high incidence, low unemployment) and the lower-right (low incidence, high unemployment) where trends are countercyclical; and in no clear pattern where the cyclical relationship is indeterminate.

Chart 5-7

Incidence of Nonstandard Employment Forms[1] and Unemployment Rate, Canada, 1975-89

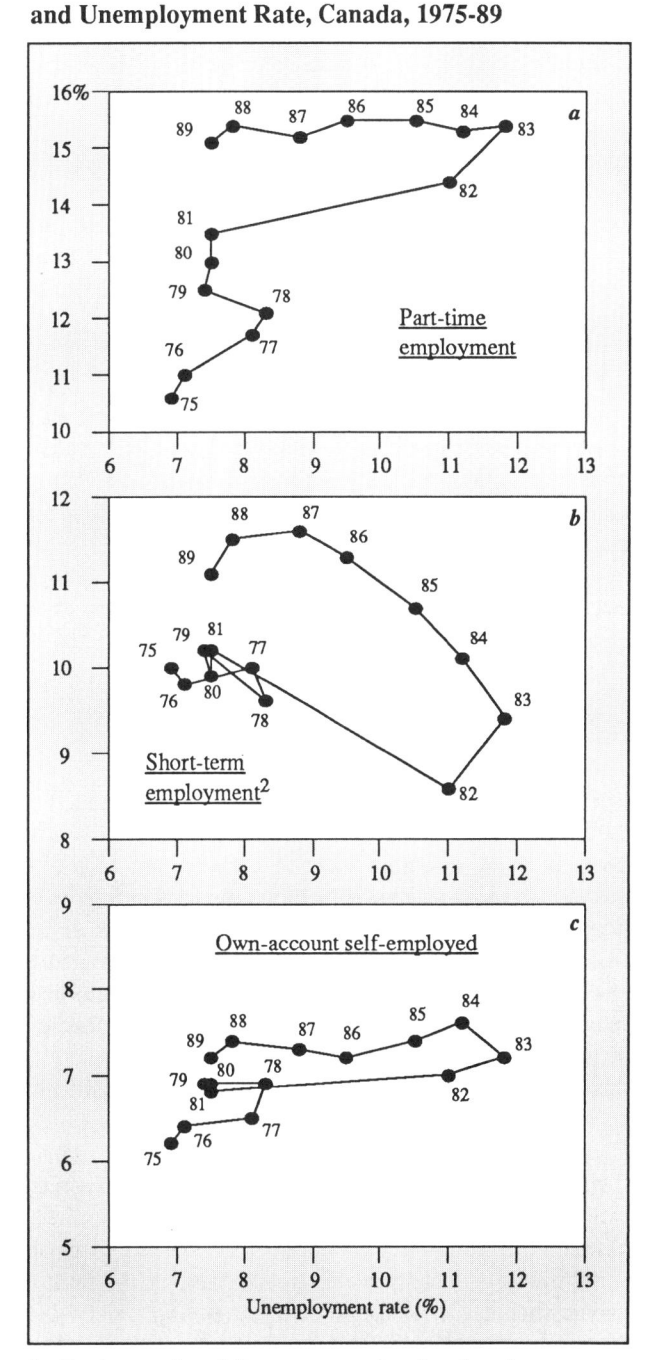

1 Employment in each form as a proportion of total employment.
2 Job tenure of less than three months.
SOURCE Statistics Canada, the Labour Force Survey.

Looking first at part-time employment (Chart 5-7a), it is evident that incidence rates grew significantly in periods of major increases in unemployment (1976-78 and, particularly, 1981-83). Part-time employment trends did not behave in a cyclical fashion, however, when labour market conditions remained unchanged or when they improved; during 1979-81 when the unemployment rate was essentially constant, there was a major increase in part-time employment, while between 1983 and 1989, as unemployment fell, the level of part-time work fluctuated very little. Turning now to short-term and own-account self-employed workers, Chart 5-7b and c indicate that, compared to part-time workers, there has been less change in the share of the employment in these two work forms. (Note that the vertical axes in b and c are on a larger scale than a.) Moreover, the patterns would imply that there is little relationship between the rate of unemployment and both short-term work and own-account self-employment.

The experience of the past 15 years, then, does not offer strong support for the hypothesis that nonstandard employment patterns primarily reflect labour market conditions. While nonstandard employment in the aggregate – particularly part-time employment – has displayed some cyclical fluctuations, the dominant trend has been a secular upward movement which has been relatively independent of cyclical conditions.

Policy Issues

Two findings stand out in our research into nonstandard employment. First, these work forms constitute a large and growing share of employment in Canada, and have accounted for a large part of job creation during the past decade. Second, nonstandard employment tends to be characterized by inferior compensation and job and income insecurity: to put it bluntly, many nonstandard jobs are "bad jobs." Together these findings point to a troubling conclusion: a large number of the jobs being created in today's labour market are, on a number of different levels, *substandard* as well as nonstandard.

At the same time, however, it is important to recognize that these modes of employment clearly respond to the changing needs of many employers and the preferences of certain groups of workers. This suggests that the policy debate should not lie in the direction of specifically attempting to curtail growth in these work forms, but rather in considering what steps need to be taken to reduce the possibility that workers who fill these jobs do not become a new employment underclass. In Chapter 9 of this report, we reproduce the policy recommendations designed to improve the economic security of nonstandard workers that were put forward by the Economic Council of Canada in *Good Jobs, Bad Jobs.*

An important step must be recognition by policymakers that this segment of the labour market should not be neglected. Nonstandard jobs and the workers who occupy them can no longer automatically be considered "marginal"; the reality now is that jobs are no longer exclusively from nine to five, five days a week, for a single, long-term employer. In making this observation, it is important to note not only the numbers of nonstandard jobs, but also the strong labour force attachment of many workers who occupy them.

Historically, the lack of concern regarding the terms and conditions of nonstandard employment has been due largely to the perception that most of the individuals in nonstandard jobs were "casual" members of the work force. Accordingly, employment-standards legislation and benefit plans have excluded those deemed to have insufficient labour force attachment. Changes in the labour market in recent decades, however, call into question the validity of this distinction. Now, most individuals in nonstandard jobs are, in fact, committed to the labour force over the longer term. Furthermore, it is important to recognize that many people are involuntarily in part-time, short-term, or temporary positions and would prefer full-time, full-year employment. Significant numbers of workers, then, have a strong labour force attachment, but for various reasons do not have a consistent attachment to a particular employer.

The aspect of nonstandard employment that has been explored most thoroughly by policymakers in Canada is part-time work.[44] The discussions have typically focused on the differences in compensation and economic security between part-time and full-time workers. This has raised questions about whether governments should act to reduce these disparities. Most often, the policy instrument considered for pursuing this objective is to require that part-time workers have prorated access to the same employment benefits – both employer-sponsored and public – as their full-time counterparts.

In regard to employer-sponsored benefits, this would mean that contribution and benefit levels would be established in relation to the number of hours worked. At present, Canadian jurisdictions do not have such requirements in their employment-standards legislation, except with respect to pension plans. After an active decade of pension reform, the majority of the jurisdictions now place part-time workers meeting certain standards of attachment (in terms of years employed, hours worked, or earnings) on an equal footing with full-time employees regarding pension-plan membership.

With respect to benefits legally mandated under employment-standards legislation and to public-benefit plans, the prorating of benefits would imply certain changes. Pay for statutory holidays provides one example. Several provinces require that an employee work 15 or more days during the 30 calendar days immediately preceding a statutory holiday in order to receive holiday pay; consequently, part-time employees who work less than four days per week (about two thirds of all part-time employees) are excluded, while people who work the same number of hours spread over a four- or five-day week are covered. In terms of public-benefit plans, the major employment-related programs – Unemployment Insurance, the Canada/Quebec Pension Plans, and Workers' Compensation – provide for the inclusion of both full-time and part-time workers; however, all three plans have some criteria that effectively exclude some part-timers. For example, in order to qualify for unemployment insurance (UI) benefits, workers must earn at least 20 per cent of the UI earnings ceiling or work 15 or more hours per week for the same employer. According to our estimates, these conditions exclude over one quarter of part-time workers from benefit entitlement: two fifths work fewer than 15 hours per week, and only a third of these have sufficiently high wages to meet the earnings requirement.

The policy implications of the growth of the other forms of nonstandard work generally have not been addressed in Canada. The major concerns, at least for short-term, temporary, and temporary-help agency employment, are also employment and income security.[45] In some respects, however, the issues here are more complex. First, the relative lack of data makes it very difficult to consider many policy questions with any degree of certainty. Second, there are important differences between part-time work and short-term and temporary employment. Notably, while a substantial minority of part-time jobs are also short-term, most part-time workers do become part of their employer's ongoing, permanent work force; on the other hand, short-term and temporary employees are more often "casual."

In the final analysis, policy responses to issues raised by the proliferation of nonstandard employment must take into account a number of competing factors. For example, the conventionally held notion of "labour force attachment" is changing and there is therefore a need to reconsider who should have access to employer-sponsored and public benefits. There are also other arguments in favour of policy intervention in support of nonstandard workers. One is a straightforward equity consideration – that is, equal compensation for work of equal worth; in this regard, the overrepresentation of women in the nonstandard work force is of particular concern. Another is that better employment-related benefits will reduce the numbers of transfer-payment recipients, thus promoting economic security.

The idea of enhancing the compensation of nonstandard workers – by prorating benefits for example – has given rise to some areas of concern. The principal one is that the costs to employers and to taxpayers would be excessive. Furthermore, in the case of employer-sponsored benefits, it is argued that higher costs would create a disincentive for firms to hire nonstandard workers, which ultimately would be to the detriment of certain groups, such as women and young people, who are overrepresented in nonstandard employment. The extent of disemployment would depend on the actual magnitude of the incremental costs and on whether nonstandard workers confer any particular advantages on their employers, such as additional flexibility.[46]

Conclusion

In this chapter, we have documented the substantial growth in Canada of employment forms that differ from the conventional notion of a full-time, relatively permanent attachment to a single employer. Nonstandard employment now represents about three out of every ten jobs in this country and it has accounted for almost one half of the net job growth over the past decade.

This phenomenon, which has occurred in other developed countries as well, is driven by the reality that nonstandard work forms offer significant advantages to both employers and workers. At the same time, however, it has raised a number of important questions. What are the characteristics of these nonstandard jobs and the workers who occupy them? What factors have been behind the rapid growth? What are the implications of the proliferation of nonstandard jobs for public policy?

We have found that nonstandard employment is generally concentrated most heavily among young people and women. As well, the incidence of these work forms tends to be relatively high in traditional services and small firms. However, an important conclusion of our research is that nonstandard employment has increased over the past 15 years in virtually all segments of the labour market. And while there is a cyclical element to nonstandard employment, particularly part-time work, it has continued to increase regardless of labour market conditions. Our analysis suggests that the growth of these employment forms reflects fundamental changes in the operation of the labour market over this period.

This would not be so important from a public-policy perspective if the quality of nonstandard employment were not an issue; unfortunately, a major feature of these jobs is their generally inferior compensation and security. As our discussion in the final section of this chapter suggests, the policy issues that are raised by the expansion of nonstandard employment are complex. The challenge for policymakers will be to retain the advantages of these work forms while improving the inferior conditions that now characterize them. Otherwise, the continued growth of nonstandard employment will exacerbate the increasing polarization of the labour force.

6 Jobs and Skills in a Service Economy

As we move increasingly towards a high-technology, service-based economy, it is widely agreed that the skill content of jobs is undergoing significant transformation. However, there is less agreement about the nature of these changes. Some observers contend that economic and technological progress inevitably upgrades the nature of work. Others argue that the prevailing trend is towards progressively less-skilled employment structures. The debate has been complicated by the conceptual and methodological problems involved in measuring skill. The methodology traditionally used by economists – essentially proxies of skill based on the wages or the educational attainment of workers – is particularly limited.

We begin with a review of the existing literature. This literature draws heavily from sociological research, which has tended to take a more direct approach to skills analysis by measuring the skill content of occupations or jobs, rather than the characteristics of those occupying them. We then turn to our own analysis of skill trends, which is divided into three parts.

The first part looks at how the occupational structure has changed over time. The dominant trend here has been the growing relative importance of "white-collar," information-based occupations in both the goods and the service sectors. Much of this growth has been in the managerial and administrative, and professional and technical groups which mostly consist of highly skilled occupations.

The second stage of our research considers the skill content of jobs more directly. We base our analysis on "occupational-trait" information which is available from the standard occupational classification system. These data provide details on such elements as the educational and training requirements of occupations and the nature of work. We conclude that overall the skill composition of employment was upgraded between 1971 and 1986.

The third stage of our analysis is based on two surveys where individuals were asked about the nature of their work. While these surveys do not allow us to directly assess trends over time, they do offer a very detailed "snapshot" of job content and an extended view of the skill dimension of employment. Our analysis underlines the heterogeneity of the service sector with respect to job content. A large share of employment in nonmarket and some dynamic services is highly skilled, while lower-skilled jobs are most prevalent in the traditional services. These surveys also indicate that there is a significant concentration of women in low-skilled service employment.

Literature Review

There is no consensus as to how the skill content of jobs is changing. The classic position – what Spenner has called "part of the conventional wisdom of industrialization"[1] – is that skill requirements increase as economies develop. This "postindustrial" view, associated most closely with Daniel Bell,[2] contends that productivity growth, a product mix with higher value-added, and increasingly complex production methods that have evolved with technological change and economic modernization, eliminate menial physical work and place more and more emphasis on high-level technical and professional knowledge. This thesis argues that the "upgrading" of the employment structure is occurring in two ways: first, through progressively higher skill requirements for given occupations, and second, through compositional shifts whereby employment levels decline in low-skilled occupations and increase in high-skilled ones.

In diametrical opposition to this position, the "downgrading" thesis argues that the predominant effect of economic development is to deskill work. This view has received a great deal of attention since the appearance of Harry Braverman's seminal study, *Labor and Monopoly Capital*, in 1974.[3] According to the downgrading argument, technological change and modernization may create a small core of very highly skilled jobs to design and manage the high-technology production systems. However, the remaining jobs in the goods sector will involve routine and systemized tasks requiring very little discretion, and the bulk of employment opportunities will be low-skilled service-sector positions.

Certainly, the absence of consensus over this issue reflects, in no small part, conceptual and methodological problems associated with the measurement of skill levels and their trends over time. In this regard, there is a range of contentious issues including whether skill resides in the worker or the job, what are the appropriate data for observing skill levels, and even what dimensions of skill need to be considered.

Mainstream economists have tended to view "skill" as residing in individuals. An example of this approach is the human capital research of the 1960s and 1970s, represented by the work of Mincer, Becker, Schultz, and others.[4] The primary focus of this literature has been on training and education as an investment with both private and social economic returns. Human capital research has focused virtually exclusively on the supply side of the labour market; it typically has not contemplated the demand side. Accordingly, as countries like Canada have increased their investment in and stock of human capital, analysis in this tradition has supported the thesis that skills are being upgraded.

Researchers outside the mainstream of economics have been more likely to study skill trends based on the attributes of the job structure rather than the labour force – that is, a demand-side orientation. There are a variety of reasons for this. First, technological change and economic development can affect the content of work independent of how it affects the skills that an employee brings to the workplace. Second, the skill requirements of the job may dictate the worker's investment in human capital rather than the reverse.[5] Finally, a supply-side orientation precludes the possibility that workers may be overqualified or underqualified for the job they occupy. There may be compelling reasons, then, for considering both the occupational structure and job content.

Methodological differences and data shortcomings have complicated demand-side analyses of skill trends.[6] Studies of the aggregate composition of the job structure – for example, those using census occupational data over time – have generally found evidence of some upgrading in job skills.[7] On the other hand, case studies focusing on trends in a particular occupation, firm, or industry have often revealed a greater volatility in the skill mix and concluded that skills have been downgraded.[8]

Ultimately, both the statistical and case-study approaches capture only part of the overall story. Trends in skills can be affected by shifts in the occupational composition of employment, and by changes in the actual content of work within occupations. For the most part, aggregate statistical analyses, by tracking the occupational profile over time, permit researchers to consider the first of these – that is, how technological innovation and other changes alter the way the work force is divided into occupations of different skill levels. They generally do not address changing work content, which is really only possible by means of case studies; however, case studies are unable to offer insights into the aggregate compositional picture. Few analyses use both approaches.[9]

Traditional approaches to the study of skill have been limited to studying the objective knowledge and competencies involved in carrying out the job, focusing on the degree of cognitive and physical complexity and the extent of formal expertise required. But more recently, analysts are beginning to adopt a multidimensional, broader approach that incorporates the social context of the job, particularly the degree of autonomy and control it involves. Generally, the narrower approach where the concept of skill is limited to the actual tasks involved has been more likely to conclude that economic development is leading to upgrading of skills, and the approach that focuses on autonomy and control to conclude the opposite.

To complicate things further, our view of the nature of skill is also changing. A number of recent analyses, including a series of case studies conducted by the Economic Council,[10] have documented the growing importance of creativity, adaptability, and communication and interpersonal abilities as employment becomes concentrated in services. Until now, these changes in what constitutes skill have not been adequately incorporated into the literature on trends in skills.

Occupational Shifts and Their Skill Implications

In this section, we examine the changes in the occupational mix over time and across industries by looking at occupational structures to impute shifts in overall skill levels. The drawback of this approach is that it assumes a particular degree of skill for each occupational group. As we will see later in this chapter, there are more sophisticated methodologies to assess intertemporal skill patterns.

Our focus in this chapter is on the impact of the shift to services on jobs and skills. But, as we shall see, the growth of services is not the only cause of the occupational changes that have been occurring in recent years. In fact, it would be more accurate to describe these changes in occupational profiles as a growing resemblance, and perhaps ultimately a convergence, between the goods and service sectors.

The most obvious change in these profiles has been the growth of "white-collar" and the decline of "blue-collar" occupations.[11] Chart 6-1 shows that between 1961 and 1986

Chart 6-1

Distribution of the Labour Force by Blue- and White-Collar Occupations,[1] Canada, Selected Years, 1961-86

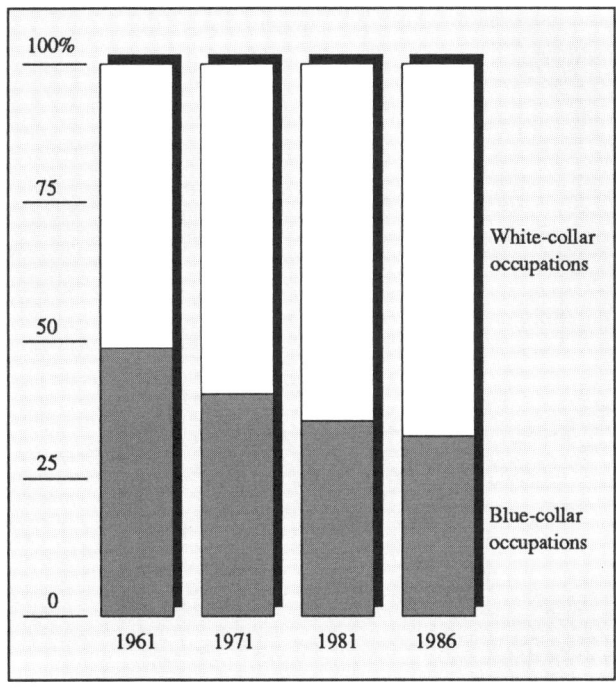

[1] Experienced labour force excluding occcupations not defined or stated.
SOURCE Statistics Canada, Census of Canada.

Table 6-1

Contribution of Occupational Groups to Total Employment Change, Canada, 1971-81 and 1981-86

	Contribution to total employment change	
	1971-81	1981-86
	(Per cent)	
White-collar occupations	78.0	134.5
Managerial, administrative, and related	13.8	34.9
Natural sciences, engineering, and mathematics	5.3	7.2
Social sciences and related	3.1	9.3
Religion	–0.8	–
Teaching and related	4.1	6.6
Medicine and health	5.9	15.6
Artistic, literary, recreational, and related	2.0	5.0
Clerical and related	23.8	6.2
Sales	9.5	18.6
Service	11.2	31.0
Blue-collar occupations	22.1	–34.5
Farming, horticultural, and animal husbandry	–0.7	3.8
Fishing, trapping, and related	0.3	0.1
Forestry and logging	0.1	–0.3
Mining and quarrying (including oil and gas fields)	0.4	–3.0
Processing	3.7	–7.6
Machining and related	1.8	–7.8
Product-fabricating, assembling, and repairing	5.8	–2.2
Construction trades	5.3	–11.5
Transport-equipment operating	3.4	–1.7
Material-handling and related	0.9	–3.6
Other crafts and equipment-operating	0.9	–0.2
	(Thousands)	
Total change[1]	2,985	483

[1] Excludes occupations not classified and not stated.
SOURCE Estimates by the Economic Council of Canada, based on data from Statistics Canada.

there was an increase in the white-collar occupations share of the total labour force of about 16 percentage points from about one half of the work force in 1961 to two thirds by 1986.

When we look at which occupations have contributed most to overall employment growth over the period 1971-86, the white-collar jobs dominate once again (Table 6-1). In 1971-81, total employment increased by nearly 3 million; 80 per cent of this increase was accounted for by white-collar occupations. In particular, managerial and administrative, clerical, sales, and service occupations accounted for almost 60 per cent of the total growth. Most blue-collar occupations contributed very little, if anything, to the overall employment expansion.

This pattern of occupational growth became even more notable during the 1980s. Four white-collar groups – managerial and administrative, medical and health, sales, and service occupations – were responsible for almost all of the net employment creation between 1981 and 1986; managerial and administrative alone accounted for one out of every three new jobs. As Table 6-1 shows, the only deviation from the trend involved clerical occupations whose contribution to employment growth fell from 24 per cent between 1971-81 to 6 per cent over 1981-86. Note that in this latter period, the decline among the blue-collar occupations tended to be even more notable than it had been in the earlier decade.

Occupational Trends by Sector

Traditionally, white-collar occupations have characterized service-industry employment while blue-collar work has been concentrated in the goods sector. Of the workers in the white-collar occupational groups, 86 per cent were employed in service industries in 1986 (Chart 6-2). On the other hand, more than two thirds of blue-collar workers were employed in the goods sector; note, however, that one blue-collar group, transportation equipment operators, was predominantly employed in transportation, a service industry.

While white-collar and blue-collar employment are still strongly associated with particular sectors, there is growing

Chart 6-2

Employment Concentration of Occupations, by Sector, Canada, 1986

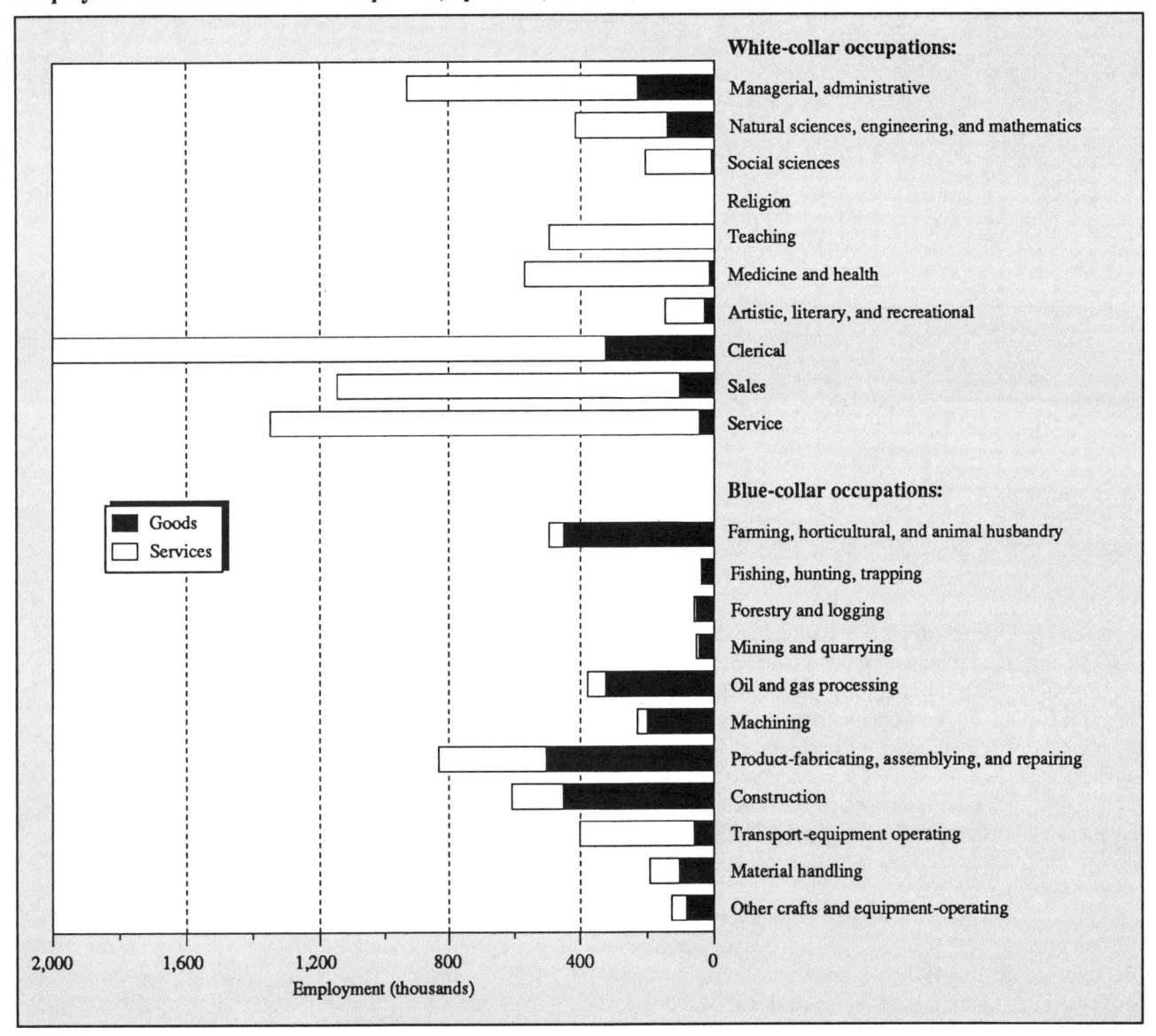

White-collar occupations:
- Managerial, administrative
- Natural sciences, engineering, and mathematics
- Social sciences
- Religion
- Teaching
- Medicine and health
- Artistic, literary, and recreational
- Clerical
- Sales
- Service

Blue-collar occupations:
- Farming, horticultural, and animal husbandry
- Fishing, hunting, trapping
- Forestry and logging
- Mining and quarrying
- Oil and gas processing
- Machining
- Product-fabricating, assemblying, and repairing
- Construction
- Transport-equipment operating
- Material handling
- Other crafts and equipment-operating

Employment (thousands)

Source: Statistics Canada, Census of Canada, unpublished data.

evidence that the occupational profiles of the sectors are becoming more similar, that growth in both goods and services is now concentrated among white-collar occupations. The declining importance of blue-collar employment was evident in both sectors over the period 1971-86, while the occupational profile shifted towards white-collar jobs – specifically in the managerial and administrative, and professional and technical categories – in both goods and services (Table 6-2). Undoubtedly, technological change has been a major factor underlying the increasing concentration of goods-sector growth in white-collar employment and the resulting convergence between the sectors in terms of occupational profiles. As earlier research by the Economic Council has demonstrated, technical innovations are reducing the demand in goods industries for direct production labour and increasing the requirements for a range of professional, technical, and other white-collar workers.[12]

Educational and Skill Implications

What do these changes in the occupational structure tell us about skill trends? In considering this question, we have adopted a classification system sometimes followed by labour market analysts which organizes broad occupational groups into three skill levels.[13] In this categorization, managerial and administrative, and professional and technical occupations are considered "high-skilled"; clerical, sales, and blue-collar occupations are "medium-skilled"; and service occupations are "low-skilled."

In Table 6-3, employment has been broken down into these three categories for the period 1971-86. While the figures in this table can only provide very general insight, they do suggest that shifts in occupational composition have resulted in upgrading of the overall skill profile. Looking at the total economy first, the share of high-skilled occupations in total employment increased nearly 7 percentage points over the 15-year period. The low-skilled group also increased its proportion; however, the gain here was much smaller. Most of the loss was in the medium-skilled group, which experienced a decline in its share of employment of over 7 percentage points.

Table 6-3 indicates that, in both the goods and service sectors, high-skilled occupations experienced significant gains while the low-skilled and, especially, the medium-skilled categories declined. The figures in this table also demonstrate the heterogeneity of the service sector's employment structure. The nonmarket and dynamic services have relatively highly skilled occupational profiles; note that in the nonmarket services, the majority of jobs have been classified as high-skilled, and in the dynamic services virtually all of the employment is either in that or the medium-skilled category. On the other hand, low-skilled employment is by far most heavily concentrated in traditional services with very few jobs classified as high-skilled.

Table 6-2

Change in Occupational Mix, Goods and Service Sectors, Canada, 1971 and 1986

	Goods sector			Service sector		
	1971	1986	Change	1971	1986	Change
	(Per cent)		(Percentage points)	(Per cent)		(Percentage points)
White-collar occupations	23.4	28.0	+4.6	81.6	85.4	+3.8
Managerial and administrative	3.4	7.1	+3.7	5.9	9.5	+3.6
Professional and technical	4.4	6.0	+1.6	20.7	22.1	+1.4
Clerical, sales, and service	15.6	14.9	–0.7	55.0	53.8	–1.2
Blue-collar occupations	76.7	72.1	–4.6	18.5	14.7	–3.8
Total[1]	100.0	100.0	...	100.0	100.0	...

1 Excludes occupations not classified and not stated.
SOURCE Statistics Canada, Census of Canada, unpublished data.

94 Employment in the Service Economy

Table 6-3

Distribution of Employment According to Occupational Skill Level by Sector, Canada, 1971, 1981, and 1986

	High-skilled occupations[1]			Medium-skilled occupations[2]			Low-skilled occupations[3]		
	1971	1981	1986	1971	1981	1986	1971	1981	1986
	(Per cent)								
Goods sector	7.7	11.5	13.1	90.6	87.1	85.6	1.7	1.5	1.4
Service sector	26.2	29.4	31.6	55.6	53.8	51.0	18.2	16.8	17.4
Dynamic services	16.3	22.6	25.5	79.4	73.7	70.5	4.3	3.7	4.0
Traditional services	4.5	6.7	7.5	64.0	61.6	59.1	31.4	31.6	33.4
Nonmarket services	53.4	57.0	60.1	27.0	26.0	23.8	19.7	17.0	16.0
Total	19.2	23.5	26.0	69.0	64.8	61.4	11.9	11.7	12.6

1 Managerial, administrative, professional, and technical occupations.
2 Clerical, sales, and "blue-collar" occupations (the latter include mining, fishing, farming, machining, and construction).
3 Service occupations like food servers, guards, janitors, and clerks.
SOURCE Calculations by the Economic Council of Canada, based on data from Statistics Canada, Census of Canada.

In order to look at future trends, we carried out projections to the year 2000, based on the federal government's Canadian Occupational Projection System (COPS), which are presented in Table 6-4.[14] Under the "fixed coefficient" regime, the occupational make-up of employment in each industry is held constant at its 1986 pattern. In this approach, projected shifts in the overall occupational structure can only reflect changes in the industry distribution of employment. Expected trends in the industry mix (with no intra-industry occupational changes) would result in an occupational structure in the year 2000 that was slightly more oriented towards white-collar jobs than it was in 1986.

The "variable coefficient" projections allow not only for changes in the overall industry employment mix, but also for changes in the occupational mix within industries. The trends in the occupational make-up of each industry between 1981 and 1986 are assumed to continue over the period 1986-2000.[15] Given the patterns of employment growth observed in the 1980s (see Table 6-1), it is not surprising that the projections based on this "variable coefficient" method show an occupational profile in 2000 that is more heavily concentrated in white-collar employment, particularly in managerial and administrative occupations (see Table 6-4). Taken together, these projections suggest that the trends observed over 1971-86 – including the overall occupational upgrading – are likely to continue for the remainder of the century.

Table 6-4

Occupational Employment Structure, Canada, 1986 (Actual) and 2000 (Projected)

		2000	
	1986	Fixed coefficient[1]	Variable coefficient[2]
	(Per cent)		
White-collar occupations	67.8	69.4	71.7
Managerial and administrative	10.2	11.1	14.2
Professional and technical	17.1	17.0	18.2
Clerical, sales, and service	40.6	41.3	39.3
Blue-collar occupations	32.4	30.6	28.3
Total	100.0	100.0	100.0

1 Based on the occupation's share of employment, in each industry in 1986.
2 Based on a methodology which allows the occupational shares of employment in each industry to vary in 1986-2000 as they did in 1981-86.
SOURCE Calculations by the Economic Council of Canada, based on the Canadian Occupational Projection System, and Employment and Immigration Canada, *Success in the Works: A Profile of Canada's Emerging Workforce*, 1989.

Information Content of Jobs

Another dimension of the changing occupational structure is the increasing demand generated by technological change for workers who are specialized in the creation and transmission of information.[16] To assess this trend, we analysed employment using an occupational classification scheme first applied in Canada by Osberg and his colleagues.[17] This classification divides the work force into four occupational groups, two of which are directly involved with information.[18] The first consists of "data" occupations (for example, word processors, clerical workers, salespeople, and bookkeepers) and deals with the production of data, and the second consists of "knowledge" occupations (for example, scientists, engineers, managers, and writers) and is concerned with the development and interpretation of information. In this scheme, knowledge workers tend to be highly skilled information workers while data workers are generally lower-skilled.

In 1971-86, information workers' share of total employment rose from about 45 per cent to over 52 per cent (Table 6-5). Information workers are becoming more important in both sectors: their proportion increased in these years by over 5 percentage points in goods and 4 percentage points in services. Overall the service sector makes considerably greater use of information workers than does the goods sector. But the importance of information employment varies widely among different service industries. At one extreme, personal services have a very low share of information workers, even below those of the goods sector. At the other extreme, the vast majority of employment in financial and business services is accounted for by information occupations.

Table 6-5

Proportion of Information Workers in Each Industry and Ratio of Data- to Knowledge-Workers, Canada, 1971, 1981, and 1986[1]

	Proportion of information workers			Ratio of data- to knowledge-workers		
	1971	1981	1986	1971	1981	1986
	(Per cent)					
Goods sector	22.1	25.8	27.5	2.51	1.51	1.36
Primary industries	9.7	17.9	19.6	0.69	0.70	0.68
Manufacturing	30.0	31.1	33.3	3.23	1.80	1.53
Service sector	59.2	62.8	63.2	6.80	4.62	4.18
Dynamic services	63.8	69.3	70.6	5.81	3.37	3.05
Transportation, communications, and utilities	39.2	43.7	44.4	3.93	2.46	2.23
Wholesale trade	68.9	70.6	72.8	11.26	5.64	4.86
Finance, insurance, and real estate	91.2	93.3	92.9	14.43	5.98	5.25
Business services	86.3	86.2	85.4	2.29	1.74	1.73
Traditional services	50.6	52.7	51.8	24.24	12.18	10.58
Retail trade	73.0	75.9	76.9	38.92	18.60	16.46
Personal services	14.3	17.3	17.8	5.23	3.13	2.91
Nonmarket services	62.3	65.1	66.3	4.84	4.11	3.70
Education, health, and social services	67.9	67.8	68.5	7.25	6.74	5.88
Public administration	52.4	60.0	62.0	2.51	1.97	1.77
All industries	45.1	50.5	52.4	5.35	3.65	3.36

1 Information workers are involved in the creation and transmission of information. They include data workers, who are involved in the production of data (e.g., bookkeepers and word processor operators), and knowledge workers, who are involved in the creation and use of data (e.g., managers and scientists).

SOURCE Estimates by the Economic Council of Canada, based on data from Statistics Canada, Census of Canada.

96   Employment in the Service Economy

The composition of information-based employment in 1971-86 is also shown in Table 6-5. On an economy-wide basis, the ratio of data- to knowledge-workers fell considerably over the period; in fact, in 1986 there were two fewer data workers for every knowledge worker than had been the case in 1971 (3.36 versus 5.35). This implies increasing efficiency in the use of information workers over the period; certainly, the diffusion of computer-based technologies in these years is likely to have been a factor here.

The ratio of data- to knowledge-employment is considerably lower in the goods sector than in the service sector (1.36 versus 4.18 in 1986). Again, a great deal of variation is evident within services. In general, information-based employment is much more highly skilled in dynamic and nonmarket services than it is in traditional services. In particular, business services and public administration have very low data- to knowledge-worker ratios. On the other hand, while retail trade has a high proportion of information workers (77 per cent), the vast majority are lower-skilled data employees, accounting for about 94 per cent of information-based employment.

Occupational-Trait Measures of Skill

In this section, we present the results of a more sophisticated skill-measurement analysis that is based on detailed occupational information incorporated into the Canadian Classification and Dictionary of Occupations (CCDO). With this "occupational-trait" data (sometimes referred to as "worker-trait" data), we can assign dimensions of "skill" and skill levels to each occupation and then use these scores to reconsider the distribution of employment by occupation.[19] This methodology permits a more detailed consideration of skill trends than is possible through a simple tracking of the occupational structure.

However, it should be noted that there are a few concerns about occupational-trait data.[20] First, the CCDO-based factor scores are derived from assessments made in the late 1960s. Consequently, trait analysis of the occupational structure since that time cannot incorporate the impact of recent technological or other developments on the skill content of an occupation. Its usefulness is limited, therefore, to its ability to capture the effects of changes in the occupational distribution of employment. Second, the factor scores are based on occupations rather than jobs. Accordingly, all types of work which fall into a four-digit occupational category are assumed to have the same skill profile when in fact the types of jobs included within any occupational category, while closely related, sometimes differ significantly in terms of their skill requirements.[21] Third, the factor scores reflect the biases of the job raters in an era when work was still oriented towards production industries and male workers. Indeed, an evaluation of the comparable occupational-trait data base in the United States found that reliability fell in the rating of the characteristics of service-type and female-dominated jobs.[22] Finally, the CCDO scores are better suited to assess the objective competency requirements of an occupation (complexity and training requirements) than the amount of autonomy and control involved.

Within these limitations, occupational-trait analysis – based as it is on widely used occupational classification systems that are comprehensive and national in scope, and capable of capturing the multidimensional nature of skills – remains a very useful method of analysing skill trends. The skill measures we used for our analysis are described in the box.

Skill Shifts

Table 6-6, which is based on census data, shows how the skill mix changed between 1971 and 1986 according to these five dimensions. The results for all of the measures suggest that the skills in the work force were upgraded over this period.[23] In specific vocational preparation, for example, in 1986, 25.3 per cent of the employed were in jobs requiring more than two years training, compared to only 20.8 per cent in 1971; at the same time, the proportion in occupations requiring less than one month of training fell 1 percentage point. The same is true of general educational development, where the share of jobs requiring some postsecondary education or the equivalent (levels 5 and 6) grew nearly 3 percentage points between 1971 and 1986, while the proportion requiring less than high school or the equivalent (levels 1 and 2) fell by over 4 percentage points. Overall, Table 6-6 indicates that more and more employment involved higher degrees of cognitive complexity, task diversity, and responsibility.

That skill upgrading took place is also expressed by the indices of net difference which summarize the data in each panel (see Table 6-6). This index measures the probability that a randomly selected individual in 1986 was in a job requiring greater skill than an individual selected in 1971; where the measure is positive, it indicates an upgraded skill structure in 1986 compared to 1971. The specific vocational preparation index, for example, shows that there is a 6 per cent probability that a worker in the later year would be in a job requiring more job-specific training than an individual in the earlier one. In fact, the index of net difference is

> **Skill Measures**
>
> The five skill measures we used are based on occupational-trait data from the Canadian Classification and Dictionary of Occupations (CCDO). In this occupational classification system, associated with every occupational title classification are 52 "traits" that represent the degree of complexity involved, required worker attributes (training and education, and more personal characteristics), and job "environment" conditions.[1]
>
> We used two of these traits, representing the educational and training preparation required for a given occupation – "general educational development" and "specific vocational preparation" – as two of our measures of skill.[2]
>
> *General educational development* (GED) captures the level of reasoning, mathematical, and language development required for satisfactory performance in the corresponding occupation. In the CCDO, GED ranges from 1 (most simple) to 6 (most advanced); the data we used necessitated aggregating levels 5 and 6 in this study.
>
> *Specific vocational preparation* (SVP) measures the amount of job-specific training required to perform the specific occupational task reasonably well. In the CCDO, the SVP ranges from 1 (short demonstration) to 9 (more than 10 years), but in our research results, training categories were aggregated into 3, 4, or 5 groups, depending on the comparison being made in the chart or table.
>
> The other three skill measures we used were selected from eight factor scores that Hunter and Manley computed in order to summarize the original 52 occupational traits.[3] The factor scores we selected were those that related most to skill: "cognitive complexity," "task diversity," and "responsibility." For each factor score, occupations were sorted from low to high, divided into five quintiles, and then assigned a value from 1 (lowest quintile) to 5 (highest quintile).
>
> *Cognitive complexity* (CC) measures the extent to which the occupation involves tasks requiring verbal and quantitative abilities. It is weighted most heavily on the occupational traits of scientific/technical work, numerical and verbal aptitude, educational preparation, and complexity involving people.
>
> *Task diversity* (TD) measures the degree to which the occupation involves a variety of duties or nonroutine activity. It is weighted negatively on the occupational traits of routine work, repetitive operations, working under specific instructions, handling objects, and technical work; and positively on the traits measuring the variety of duties and the extent to which the work involves dealing with people.
>
> *Responsibility* (RESP) measures the degree to which the occupation requires incumbents to supervise, manage, or guide themselves or others. The occupational traits it is weighted on include the variety of duties, directing or controlling ability, interest in work resulting in esteem, working for people's good, and complexity of work involving people.
>
> ---
>
> 1. Canadian occupational-trait data are published for 6,500 (7-digit) occupational titles contained in the Canadian Classification and Dictionary of Occupations, vol. 2, 1971. Since employment by occupation from the census is available only at the 4-digit level (which yields 486 titles), the occupational-trait scores for the 7-digit titles had to be transformed to this more aggregated level. To do this, the "mean" value of each of the job traits was calculated for every 4-digit occupation (based on the simple mean of the scores for the constituent 7-digit occupations).
> 2. Note the basic difference between GED and SVP. The former relates to the amount of general training required, and the latter is concerned with job-specific training. Both SVP and GED can include formal or informal education and training.
> 3. The methodology as applied to Canada is described in full in Alfred A. Hunter and Michael C. Manley, "On the task content of work," *Canadian Review of Sociology and Anthropology* 23, no. 1 (1986).

positive for all five measures, which suggests that skills were upgraded along all the dimensions.

While the results in Table 6-6 do demonstrate an overall trend towards increasing skill requirements, they also show that a large number of workers remain in jobs requiring relatively little skill (for example, the bottom two categories for each measure). Almost one half were still in occupations requiring six months or less of training; close to 30 per cent required only basic reasoning and mathematical and language development; 28 per cent were in jobs demanding few verbal or quantitative skills; nearly 40 per cent were in employment characterized by a repetition of fairly simple tasks; and almost 30 per cent were in jobs where the incumbent was required to give instructions to others in only a limited fashion.

98 Employment in the Service Economy

Table 6-6

Distribution of Employment by Skill Level, and Degree of Skill Transformation, Occupational-Trait Measures, Canada, 1971, 1981, and 1986

	\multicolumn{5}{c}{Skill level from lowest to highest}		Index of net difference,[1]
	1	2	3	4	5	Total	1971-86
	\multicolumn{6}{c}{(Per cent)}	
Specific vocational preparation (SVP)	Up to 30 days	1 to 6 months	6 to 24 months	Over 2 years	...		0.06
1971	16.0	36.0	27.3	20.8	...	100.0	
1981	14.8	35.0	26.7	23.6	...	100.0	
1986	15.0	33.5	26.3	25.3	...	100.0	
General educational development (GED)							0.07
1971	6.4	28.0	36.8	19.1	9.7	100.0	
1981	5.5	25.3	37.4	20.1	11.7	100.0	
1986	5.5	24.4	36.5	21.1	12.5	100.0	
Cognitive complexity (CC)							0.08
1971	19.8	13.2	28.5	20.4	18.1	100.0	
1981	17.1	12.4	29.9	19.2	21.3	100.0	
1986	16.7	11.3	29.8	18.7	23.5	100.0	
Task diversity (TD)							0.05
1971	22.0	20.4	22.3	19.6	15.8	100.0	
1981	20.3	19.1	23.3	19.8	17.5	100.0	
1986	20.0	18.3	23.0	20.3	18.4	100.0	
Responsibility (RESP)							0.06
1971	10.8	23.4	29.6	16.7	19.6	100.0	
1981	10.5	21.7	29.9	17.3	20.7	100.0	
1986	9.6	19.9	30.6	18.2	21.6	100.0	

1 A summary index of skill transformation, measuring the probability a randomly selected individual in 1986 was in a job requiring greater skill than an individual randomly selected in 1971.
SOURCE Calculations by the Economic Council of Canada, based on data from Statistics Canada, Census of Canada.

The occupational-trait data also indicate that women are more likely than men to be in low-skilled jobs and less likely to be in highly skilled ones. Table 6-7 illustrates this for the specific vocational preparation measure, but the findings are applicable on all skill dimensions. In 1986, 17.1 per cent of women compared to only 13.4 per cent of men were in jobs requiring less than one month's training; at the other end, 28.6 per cent of men and only 20.8 per cent of women were in occupations demanding more than two years of training. However, gender-based differences in job skills did diminish between 1971 and 1986.[24]

Relative Skill Levels of Industries

Table 6-8 presents the results of the occupational-trait analysis by industry. Included in the table is the proportion of workers in each industry grouping who are in low-skilled and high-skilled jobs. Here, "low-skilled" jobs are defined as those in the lowest level of each of the five skill measures, while "high-skilled" jobs are those falling into the highest level, except specific vocational preparation, where the proportion shown is for the highest two levels (see Table 6-6). Note that in Table 6-8, dynamic services are disaggregated

Table 6-7

Distribution of Males and Females by Specific Vocational Preparation (SVP) Time Required, Canada, 1971, 1981, and 1986

	Up to 30 days	1 to 6 months	6 to 24 months	Over 2 years	Total
	(Per cent)				
Males					
1971	13.7	34.2	28.3	23.9	100.0
1981	12.5	32.0	28.0	27.5	100.0
1986	13.4	31.2	26.8	28.6	100.0
Females					
1971	20.6	39.8	25.2	14.4	100.0
1981	18.2	39.3	24.8	17.7	100.0
1986	17.1	36.6	25.5	20.8	100.0
Ratio[1]					
1971	1.50			0.60	
1981	1.46			0.64	
1986	1.28			0.73	

1 Proportion of females as a fraction of the proportion of males in lowest- and highest-skilled jobs.
SOURCE Calculations by the Economic Council of Canada, based on data from Statistics Canada, Census of Canada.

into distributive (wholesale trade and transportation, communications and utilities) and information services (finance, insurance, and real estate, and business services). Comparing the goods and service sectors, a higher proportion of service-sector workers are in the high-skill category and, with the exception of specific vocational preparation, a lower proportion are in the low-skill group. Again, however, the service sector's heterogeneity is evident. While traditional services have very large proportions of low-skilled jobs (particularly in terms of specific vocational preparation, cognitive complexity, and task diversity), the other service subsectors are characterized by higher skill profiles. Nonmarket services tend to have the largest share of high-skilled jobs and the smallest share of low-skilled jobs of all the groupings. Information services have a particularly high skill profile.

The skill profiles of the different sectors are also compared in Table 6-9, this time using the index of net difference. Here, each figure shows the probability that an individual in the relevant industry will be in a higher-skilled job than someone randomly selected from the work force at large. The first two rows show positive coefficients on all measures for the service sector and negative ones for the goods sector, which suggests that jobs in the former industries have higher skill requirements than those in the latter. This gap is largest for general educational development, cognitive complexity, and responsibility. The indices also show the variation within services. For all measures but responsibility, traditional services have below-average skill requirements, while information and nonmarket services have high skill profiles.

In Table 6-10, we examine the gender-skills gap in 1986 by industry. The first two lines confirm for both the goods and service sectors what we found earlier for the overall economy: women are overrepresented in low-skilled jobs for most skill measures (ratios are generally above one) and underrepresented in high-skilled ones (ratios are generally below one). One interesting exception is the smaller share of women in jobs with minimal educational requirements. Also notable is the fact that the skills gap between women and men is in some respects less in the service sector than the goods sector. Again, however, the experience varies considerably across the different service subsectors.

Skill Shifts within Industries

In theory, the skill upgrading we have observed over the period of analysis could be the result of changes in the industry mix (i.e., towards higher-skilled industries) or

Table 6-8

Proportion of Workers in Low- and High-Skilled Jobs According to Occupational-Trait Measures, by Industry, Canada, 1986

	\multicolumn{5}{c}{Proportion in lowest level of}	\multicolumn{5}{c}{Proportion in highest level of}
	Specific vocational preparation	General educational development	Cognitive complexity	Task diversity	Responsibility	Specific vocational preparation	General educational development	Cognitive complexity	Task diversity	Responsibility
	\multicolumn{10}{c}{(Per cent)}
Goods sector	13.7	7.9	27.0	21.4	18.8	18.8	7.4	14.0	14.6	14.5
Service sector	15.5	4.4	12.4	19.3	5.7	28.0	14.7	27.5	20.0	24.6
Traditional services	33.8	4.4	23.1	38.2	3.7	18.9	12.2	15.1	14.9	20.0
Distributive services	10.0	3.4	8.2	18.7	14.0	21.8	11.5	18.9	18.6	17.7
Information services	6.9	4.9	6.6	8.8	5.4	32.5	14.9	33.8	21.6	20.2
Nonmarket services	6.0	4.7	7.7	7.8	3.4	37.4	18.5	40.3	24.5	34.9

SOURCE Calculations by the Economic Council of Canada, based on data from Statistics Canada, Census of Canada.

Table 6-9

Relative Skill Levels[1] of Industries According to Occupational-Trait Measures, by Industry, Canada, 1986

	Specific vocational preparation	General educational development	Cognitive complexity	Task diversity	Responsibility
		(Per cent)			
Goods sector	−0.05	−0.16	−0.19	−0.06	−0.24
Service sector	0.02	0.07	0.08	0.03	0.10
Traditional services	−0.24	−0.20	−0.17	−0.21	0.01
Distributive services	−0.05	−0.01	−0.04	−0.06	−0.10
Information services	0.19	0.23	0.27	0.15	0.13
Nonmarket services	0.22	0.27	0.27	0.23	0.28

1 Measured by the index of net difference; each figure represents the probability a worker randomly drawn from an industry will be in a higher- or lower-skilled job (minus sign) than one randomly drawn from the work force at large.
SOURCE Calculations by the Economic Council of Canada, based on data from Statistics Canada, Census of Canada.

changes in the skill mix within industries. In 1988, Myles found that the skill upgrading that took place between 1971 and 1981 was due mainly to the latter factor.[25] Using the same approach as he did, we also concluded that the overall skill upgrading over the period 1981-86 was largely due to skill shifts within industries rather than changes in the industrial composition of employment.[26] Therefore, we used the occupational-trait data to take a closer look at these skill trends within industries.

This analysis is summarized in Table 6-11, which presents the indices of net difference over 1971-81 and 1981-86 for the five skill dimensions, by the major industry groupings. Each figure in the table represents the probability that an individual randomly selected from the relevant industry in the later year (1981 and 1986) would be in a higher-skilled job than one selected in the earlier year (1971 or 1981). The preponderance of positive coefficients indicates upgrading in both 1971-81 and 1981-86 in all of the industry categories. Note that the magnitude of these coefficients tends to be smaller in 1981-86; this may reflect a slowdown in the skill-upgrading trend, or the fact that the length of that period is only one half of the earlier one. Over both periods, skill upgrading was least significant in traditional services; larger increases occurred in distributive, information, and nonmarket services. Particularly in the 1980s, skill upgrading was greatest in communications, finance, insurance, amusement and recreation, health, and public administration.

Skill Measures Based on Reports by Workers

The third stage of our analysis involves worker responses to questions about various aspects of their own jobs. These data provide a perspective on skills that cannot be gained through research based only on occupational-trait data, especially with regard to the shortcomings of the CCDO data (i.e., ratings that are dated, the occupational rather than job base, the potential rater bias, and the limited information on the autonomy-control aspect of skill).

The surveys we used were carried out in the 1980s, thus offering a more recent picture of the nature and content of employment. They also provide information on jobs, rather than occupational groups; there is no limiting assumption, then, that all jobs within an occupation have identical skill profiles. In addition, since the information on job content is based on the assessments of the worker rather than an external assessor, there is no problem of "rater" bias. Finally, the information on job content includes detail on both the objective competency requirements and the autonomy and control aspects.

Certainly, the worker self-report data have their own limitations. First, there is the possibility of respondent bias. Second, they can only provide "snapshots" of the job structure at a particular point in time, and cannot therefore offer direct insight into the question of intertemporal skill

Table 6-10

Ratio of the Proportion of Females to Males in Low- and High-Skilled Jobs According to Occupational-Trait Measures, by Industry, Canada, 1986

	Lowest level of					Highest level of				
	Specific vocational preparation	General educational development	Cognitive complexity	Task diversity	Responsi-bility	Specific vocational preparation	General educational development	Cognitive complexity	Task diversity	Responsi-bility
	(Per cent)									
Goods sector	1.35	0.69	1.51	1.41	1.15	0.55	0.44	0.75	0.52	0.47
Service sector	1.24	0.51	1.04	1.05	0.46	0.68	0.47	0.74	0.48	0.74
Traditional services	1.52	0.39	1.31	1.29	0.38	0.49	0.46	0.52	0.44	0.52
Distributive services	0.65	0.39	0.44	0.95	0.37	0.57	0.44	0.71	0.51	0.60
Information services	0.83	0.72	0.78	0.81	0.89	0.46	0.31	0.46	0.40	0.54
Nonmarket services	0.65	0.47	0.66	0.63	1.18	0.81	0.45	0.84	0.48	0.82

SOURCE Calculations by the Economic Council of Canada, based on data from Statistics Canada, Census of Canada.

Table 6-11

Changes in Skill Levels of Jobs[1] According to Occupational-Trait Measures, by Industry, Canada, 1971-81 and 1981-86

	1971-81					1981-86				
	Specific vocational preparation	General educational development	Cognitive complexity	Task diversity	Responsi-bility	Specific vocational preparation	General educational development	Cognitive complexity	Task diversity	Responsi-bility
	(Per cent)									
Goods sector	0.03	0.04	0.04	0.03	–	0.01	0.01	0.01	0.01	0.02
Service sector	0.03	0.04	0.05	0.03	0.01	0.02	0.02	0.02	0.02	0.02
Traditional services	0.01	0.01	0.02	–	-0.01	0.01	0.01	0.01	0.01	0.01
Distributive services	0.05	0.04	0.05	0.04	0.03	–	–	–	–	0.02
Information services	0.05	0.04	0.05	0.05	0.03	0.03	0.02	0.02	0.03	0.04
Nonmarket services	0.04	0.06	0.06	0.04	0.02	0.03	0.04	0.04	0.03	0.02

1 Measured by the index of net difference; each figure represents the probability a randomly picked person in each industry is in a higher- or lower-skilled job (minus sign) in 1981 or 1986 relative to 1971 or 1981.

SOURCE Calculations by the Economic Council of Canada, based on data from Statistics Canada, Census of Canada.

trends. Also, the samples are not large enough to permit the analysis of very disaggregated subgroups of the labour force.

Nevertheless, they provide a useful tool for looking at the complex question of the skill content of jobs both in themselves and as a complement to the occupational-trait data; we used them particularly to compare the skill structures of the goods and service sectors. Later in this section, we will use the results of our analysis of these data to critically reinterpret the conclusions drawn from the occupational-trait analysis.

Most of the data we used are based on the Canadian Class Structure Survey (CSS), which was carried out in 1982-83, on a household basis.[27] In it, respondents were asked a wide range of questions about the training, complexity, and control aspects of their work, among other things. The sample for the job skills analysis consisted of about 2,000 respondents who were either employed at the time of the survey, or had been in the preceding year, and is broadly representative of the Canadian labour force in 1982 in terms of the age, sex, and industrial and occupational distribution (Table 6-12). A special analysis of the job-content data from the CSS was undertaken by John Myles and Gail Fawcett for the Economic Council of Canada. Our analysis is based on their research.[28]

We also drew from a survey conducted in 1987 which tracked the employment experiences of a sample of about 1,900 high school and university graduates in three Canadian cities two years after their graduation. The particular focus of this survey was on the school-to-work transition. The sample has some biases, specifically: 1) the respondents are young; 2) by definition, they have attained at least a high school diploma; 3) they were situated in urban labour markets; and 4) they were disproportionately employed in the service sector (over 80 per cent). Nevertheless, the survey provides information about the nature of employment in growing service industries, and particularly those that are the major employers of young workers. Our use of these data is based on a study carried out for the Economic Council by Harvey Krahn and Graham Lowe.[29]

Table 6-12

A Comparison of the Canadian Class Structure Survey and the Labour Force Survey: Distribution of the Labour Force, 1982-83, and Employment, 1982, Canada

	Canadian Class Structure Survey (labour force), 1982-83	Labour Force Survey (employment), 1982
	(Per cent)	
Sex		
Males	58.5	58.7
Females	41.5	41.3
Age[1]		
20-24	13.8	15.4
25-34	33.5	30.8
35-44	21.5	23.5
45-54	15.4	17.4
55-64	10.5	11.0
65 and over	1.7	1.9
Industry		
Goods	33.5	30.7
Retail trade	9.3	12.8
Personal services	9.1	11.1
Distributive services	12.4	12.8
Information services	10.3	9.8
Nonmarket services	25.4	22.7
Occupation		
Managerial, administrative, and professional	27.6	24.7
Clerical and sales	25.7	28.3
Service	11.2	13.9
Blue-collar	35.5	33.2
Total	100.0	100.0

1 The Labour Force Survey covers only five-year age groups, and Class Structure Survey data are only available for those 18 years and over; so those under 20 years are excluded here.

SOURCE Estimates by the Economic Council of Canada, based on the Class Structure Survey, and Statistics Canada, the Labour Force Survey.

Job Complexity

Myles and Fawcett developed two measures of job complexity: "thought and attention," which focuses on the degree of difficulty of the problems workers face in their jobs and the degree of experience, knowledge, and analysis that are required to solve them; and "abstract knowledge," which considers the extent to which the job requires an understanding of an underlying body of knowledge and its application to the work. For each measure, respondents were classified as occupying high-, medium-, or low-skilled jobs.

104 Employment in the Service Economy

The skill distributions, by industry group, are shown in Table 6-13. Note that the groupings are slightly different from the classification we have used throughout this report: in all our CSS-based tables, dynamic services are divided into distributive and information services, and traditional services are divided into retail trade and personal services. As Table 6-13 indicates, job complexity varies widely among service sectors. For both the "thought and attention"

Table 6-13

Distribution of the Labour Force According to Two Measures of Job Complexity by Industry, Canada, 1982-83

	\multicolumn{4}{c}{Level of thought and attention}	\multicolumn{4}{c}{Level of abstract knowledge}
	Low	Medium	High	Total	Low	Medium	High	Total
	\multicolumn{8}{c}{(Per cent)}
Nonagricultural goods	28	36	36	100	33	24	43	100
Retail trade	30	41	29	100	34	24	42	100
Personal services	44	30	26	100	49	16	34	100
Distributive services	25	30	45	100	32	20	48	100
Information services	14	32	54	100	18	24	58	100
Nonmarket services	17	26	57	100	17	17	66	100

SOURCE Based on the Class Structure Survey, John Myles and Gail Fawcett, "Job skills and the service economy," Working Paper no. 4, Economic Council of Canada, Ottawa, 1990.

Chart 6-3

Proportion of Males and Females in Jobs Requiring High Levels[1] of Thought and Attention, by Industry, Canada, 1982-83

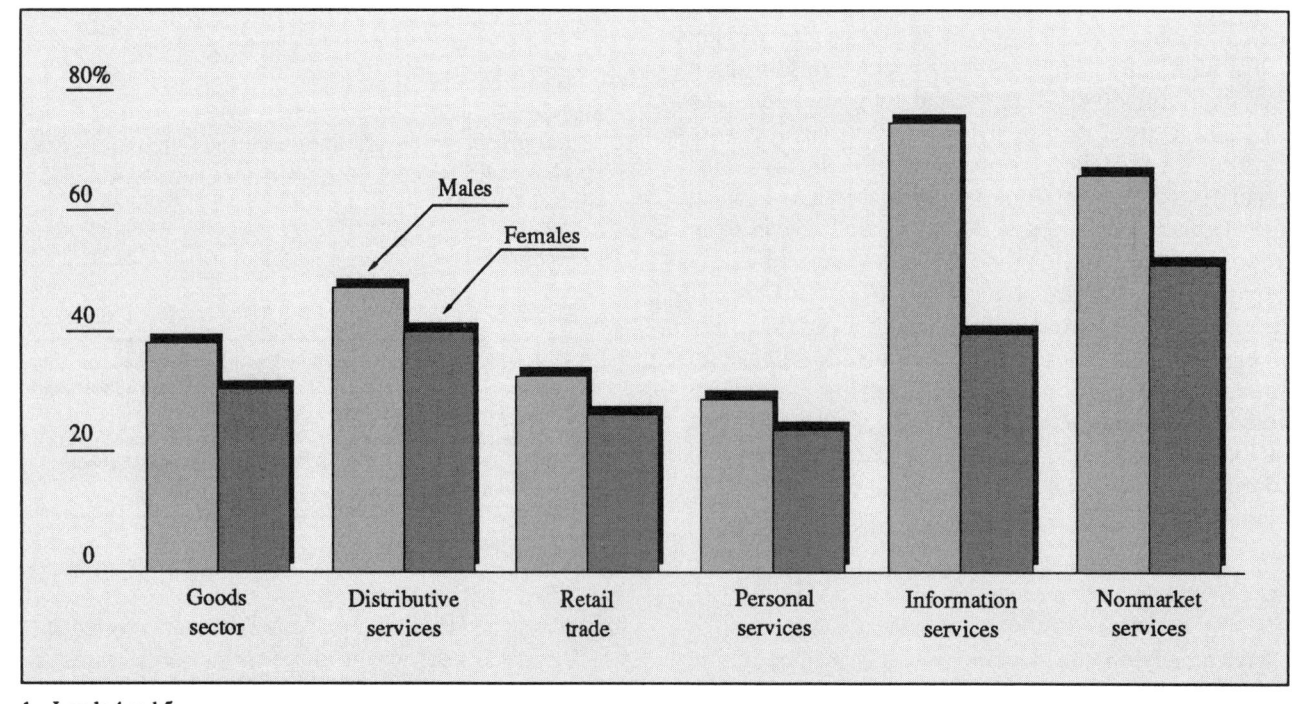

1 Levels 4 and 5.
SOURCE Based on the Class Structure Survey, Myles and Fawcett, "Job skills and the service economy."

and "abstract knowledge" measures, information and nonmarket services have by far the smallest share of low-skilled jobs and the largest share of high-skilled jobs; on the other hand, retail trade and personal services rank below all the others for both indicators. The graduate survey data suggest a similar skill ranking.[30] In general, then, the results of worker self-report data are similar to the sectoral skill profile revealed by the occupational-trait analysis.

The CSS job-complexity measures also offer a tool for comparing the skill content of jobs according to gender. Chart 6-3 focuses on the proportion of workers in jobs requiring high levels of thought and attention by sex and industry. For each industrial grouping, the proportion of males in jobs classified as complex is larger than the proportion of females. Note also that this gender gap is particularly large in information and, to a lesser extent, nonmarket services. While these two subsectors are the most important sources of work involving a high degree of complexity, the CSS data suggest that men are more likely than women to occupy these jobs.[31] These are similar to the conclusions of the occupational-trait analysis – that women are more likely than men to be employed in low-skilled and less likely to be in high-skilled positions.

Training Requirements

Educational and training requirements offer another way of assessing the skill content of work. The CSS asked respondents about the "usual" requirements of their jobs in terms of both general educational development and specific vocational preparation. The results for the first of these measures, the level of education generally needed to do the job, are reported by industry in Table 6-14. They suggest the same industry ranking as in Chart 6-3; that is, information and nonmarket services have the highest educational requirements, retail trade and personal services have the lowest, and distributive services and goods industries are in between. Note the similarity between these results and those indicated by the general educational development factor in Table 6-8.

The CSS also gathered data on training requirements. This measure pertains only to on-the-job training; as such, it is not equivalent to the occupational-trait specific vocational preparation which includes all forms of job-specific training acquired on or off the job. Training requirements by industry group are presented in Table 6-15. The lowest training requirements are in traditional services – retail trade, and particularly personal services, where nearly half of the respondents reported that only a short demonstration was required to learn their job. In contrast to the skill measures shown in Table 6-13, the training-requirement indicator ranks the nonagricultural goods and distributive services at least as high as information and nonmarket services. This result probably reflects the fact that skill-formation traditions vary from industry to industry, with the goods sector and distributive services relying more on industrial training, while information and nonmarket services depend heavily on the educational system.

Chart 6-4 shows job training in the various industries, according to gender. In every industrial group, males were much more likely than females to report that their job had high on-the-job training requirements. While this result is consistent with the gender differences in job complexity reported in Chart 6-3, the gender gap is considerably larger in the case of job-training requirements. This reflects the general unwillingness of employers to invest in the human

Table 6-14

Distribution of the Labour Force According to Educational Requirements by Industry, Canada, 1982-83

	Less than high school diploma	High school diploma	Postsecondary certificate/ diploma	University degree	Total
	(Per cent)				
Nonagricultural goods	48	27	16	9	100
Retail trade	47	35	16	2	100
Personal services	70	17	9	4	100
Distributive services	33	38	20	9	100
Information services	11	38	23	28	100
Nonmarket services	17	18	23	42	100

SOURCE Based on the Class Structure Survey, Myles and Fawcett, "Job skills and the service economy."

Table 6-15

Distribution of the Labour Force According to On-the-Job Training Requirements by Industry, Canada, 1982-83

	Short demonstration	Up to 1 year	Over 1 year	Total
	(Per cent)			
Nonagricultural goods	21	48	31	100
Retail trade	25	54	21	100
Personal services	45	40	15	100
Distributive services	21	48	31	100
Information services	19	55	27	100
Nonmarket services	27	48	25	100

SOURCE Based on the Class Structure Survey, Myles and Fawcett, "Job skills and the service economy."

capital of women; where female employees are in high-skilled jobs, their skill formation tends to have taken place in the educational system.[32] We will take up this question of gender differences in access to employer-based training in the next chapter.

Autonomy and Control

Researchers are increasingly recognizing that in addition to the degree of complexity and objective expertise required, the "skill" level of a job also includes the amount of autonomy and control involved, a more subjective element. The worker self-report data are particularly useful in addressing this issue. In order to assess autonomy and control, Myles and Fawcett developed the "conceptual autonomy" measure. This captures the extent to which the worker is required to originate ideas for and implement

Chart 6-4

Gender Differences in On-the-Job Training Requirements,[1] by Industry, Canada, 1982-83

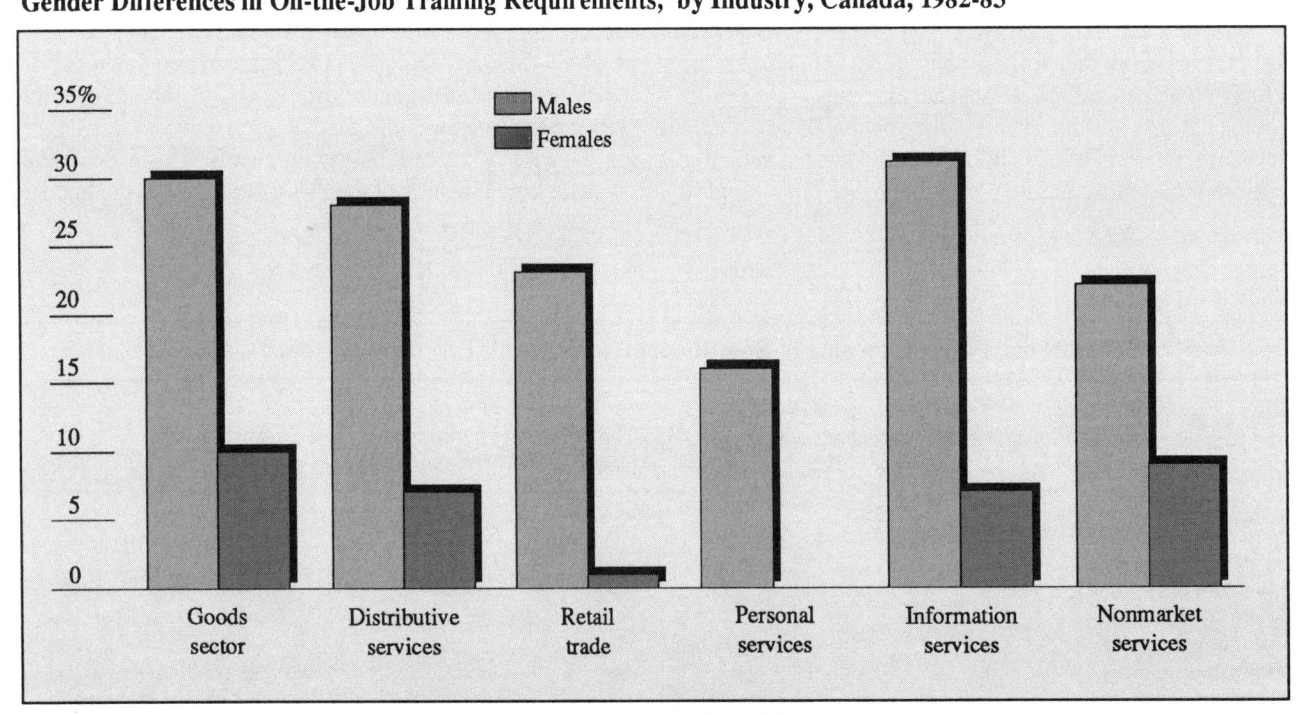

[1] Proportion of males and females in jobs requiring more than two years' on-the-job training.
SOURCE Based on the Class Structure Survey, Myles and Fawcett, "Job skills and the service economy."

important aspects of the job. The results are presented by industry in Table 6-16. The pattern is somewhat similar to that based on job complexity (see Table 6-13). Again, information and nonmarket services rank above the others; note, however, that the differences in conceptual autonomy between the goods industries and distributive services, on the one hand, and retail trade and personal services, on the other, are much less than they were for the job complexity measure. The gender gap for the autonomy-control measure is similar to that for the other skill measures.[33]

The survey of graduates also considered the autonomy-control dimensions of skill. Table 6-17 presents the respondents' assessments of their decision-making autonomy at work. The data from this survey are organized according to different youth labour markets defined jointly by occupation and industry. They indicate that at least among young workers, the amount of autonomy and control are dependent more on occupation than industry; note the higher evaluations for managerial and professional workers than for those in clerical, sales, and service jobs regardless of industry.[34]

Occupational-Trait and Self-Report Skill-Measure Comparisons

Myles and Fawcett also compared the skill content of jobs using evaluations based on the self-report data with those using the occupational-trait scores. This involved comparing one set of jobs (i.e., those reported by CSS respondents) in two ways. To establish the occupational-trait measures, the occupation of each CSS respondent was coded according to the standard classification system and then the trait scores were attributed accordingly. There are two skill areas where comparable measures are available: job complexity and specific vocational requirements.

Do the skill evaluations made by objective raters differ from those made by the job holders?[35] With respect to job complexity, the comparison is based on the occupational-trait factor "cognitive complexity," and the self-report measure "thought and attention." The two skill evaluations are generally similar across industries (Chart 6-5). However, there are some differences; notably, the ranking of goods and retail trade in terms of the proportion of high-skilled jobs depends on which indicator is used. Overall, Chart 6-5 indicates that the occupational-trait evaluators assessed goods-sector and distributive-service work less favourably than job holders do; on the other hand, the reverse is true for much of the service-sector employment.

Table 6-16

Distribution of the Labour Force According to Conceptual Autonomy Required by Industry, Canada, 1982-83

	None or low	Medium	High	Total
	(Per cent)			
Nonagricultural goods	70	18	12	100
Retail trade	69	26	5	100
Personal services	74	19	7	100
Distributive services	68	22	10	100
Information services	49	27	23	100
Nonmarket services	44	13	43	100

SOURCE Based on the Class Structure Survey, Myles and Fawcett, "Job skills and the service economy."

Table 6-17

Decision-Making Autonomy of High School and University Graduates, by Occupational-Industry Groups, Canada, 1985

	Average evaluation score[1]	
	High school graduates	University graduates
Clerical, sales, service occupations		
Personal services	2.87	2.92
Other services	2.75	3.04
Blue-collar	2.76	...
Managerial and professional occupations		
Service sector	3.34	...
Information services	...	3.15
Other services	...	3.42
Goods sector	...	3.70
Teaching	...	3.60

1 Based on respondent evaluations of current job in terms of "freedom to decide what I do in job," (ranging from strongly disagree [1] to strongly agree [5]).
SOURCE Based on the Three-City Graduate Survey, Harvey Krahn and Graham S. Lowe, "Young workers in the service economy," Working Paper no. 14, Economic Council of Canada, Ottawa, 1990.

Chart 6-5

Job Complexity by Industry: A Comparison of Occupational-Trait and Self-Report Measures,[1] Canada, 1982-83

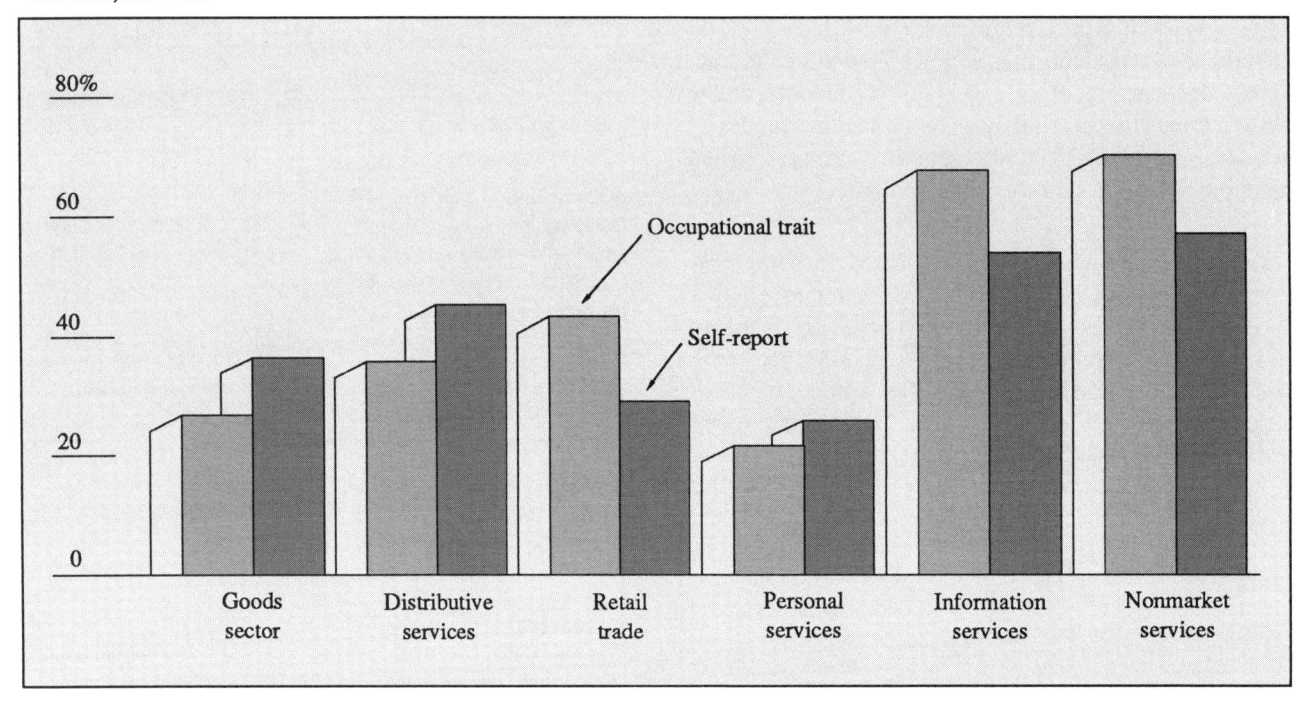

[Bar chart showing Occupational trait and Self-report measures across Goods sector, Distributive services, Retail trade, Personal services, Information services, and Nonmarket services]

1 Proportion of workers in occupations or jobs requiring high levels (4 and 5) of the occupational trait "cognitive complexity" and the self-report measure "thought and attention."
SOURCE Based on the Class Structure Survey, Myles and Fawcett, "Job skills and the service economy."

As this comparison makes clear, the implications of the shift to services for the skill content of employment vary depending on which method is used. In general, the occupational-trait method is more likely to conclude that the shift to services is leading to upgrading of skills than the self-report method. Myles and Fawcett compared trends in job complexity over the period 1951-81 using both indicators. They found that the proportion of higher-skilled employment increased by 7 percentage points with the occupational-trait approach; with the self-report measure, however, the gain was only 2 percentage points.[36]

The two methodologies were also compared in terms of job-specific training using the occupational-trait measure, specific vocational preparation, and a proxy measure (PSVP) based on the worker self-reports (Chart 6-6).[37] The self-report indicator suggests a slightly greater proportion of the work force in high-skilled jobs (with one or more years of preparation) than does the occupational-traits indicator. For jobs requiring less than a year's job preparation, however, there are marked differences between the indicators; specifically, the self-report measure (PSVP) is much more skewed towards less job preparation. Nearly 20 per cent of workers in the self-report survey said that their jobs required only a "short demonstration," while the corresponding figure using the occupational-trait method is only about 1 per cent. Overall, then, the self-report approach produces much more polarized results.

Chart 6-7 presents the proportion of employment in jobs requiring at least one year's preparation using the same indicators (specific vocational preparation and proxy-specific vocational preparation), by industry. In all industries, except agriculture, the share is higher for the self-report measure. Note, though, that the gap is particularly large in the goods sector and distributive services; as was the case with the job-complexity indicator (see Chart 6-5), the occupational-trait ratings estimate skill levels in these two industries to be much lower than do the workers themselves. Here too, then, the implication is that, in considering the transition to a service-dominated economy, the occupational-trait method will be more likely to

Chart 6-6

Job-Specific Training Requirements: A Comparison of Occupational-Trait and Self-Report Measures,[1] Canada, 1982-83

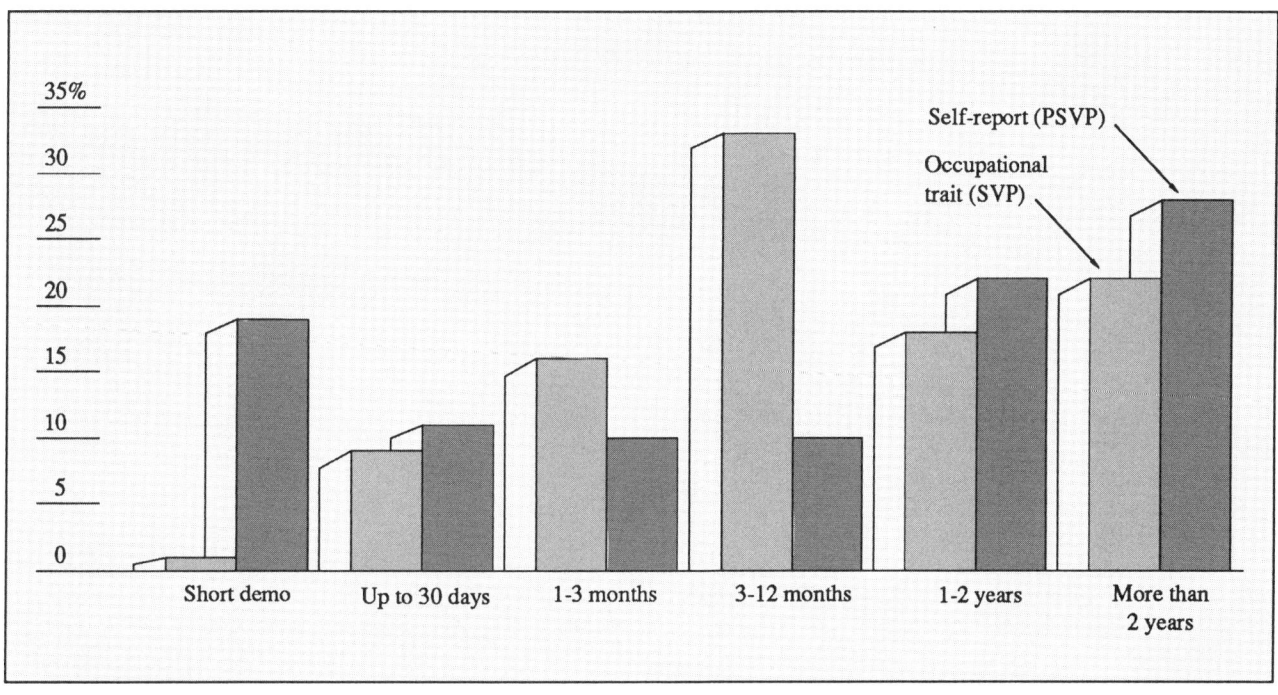

[Bar chart showing percentages by training duration category: Short demo, Up to 30 days, 1-3 months, 3-12 months, 1-2 years, More than 2 years. Two series: Self-report (PSVP) and Occupational trait (SVP).]

1 Proportion of workers in occupations or jobs requiring varying levels of the occupational-trait specific vocational preparation (SVP) and a proxy measure (PSVP) measuring the amount of on-the-job training, with one year added if a postsecondary degree/certificate is required.
SOURCE Based on the Class Structure Survey, Myles and Fawcett, "Job skills and the service economy."

conclude that the result of the shift to services is an upgrading of skills than will the self-report approach.[38]

Conclusion

In this chapter, we have used a variety of analytical approaches to consider trends in the skill content of jobs, in particular, the implications of the ongoing shift towards a service-dominated labour market. There is no consensus in the literature with respect to this issue; indeed, there are various competing hypotheses ranging from the contention that skill requirements are upgraded as we move to an increasingly high-tech service economy, to the opposite argument that this process tends to deskill work.

While the economy continues to generate large numbers of low-skilled jobs, on balance the results of our research support the position that skills are being upgraded. Most obviously, the employment structure continues to shift towards white-collar occupations, with the most rapid growth in relatively highly skilled managerial and professional categories. This development is occurring not only in services, but also in goods industries, suggesting that the occupational make-up of the two sectors will look more and more alike in the future. Our detailed analysis of the changing occupational structure which uses the "occupational traits" of expanding and declining occupations offers further support for the skill-upgrading thesis. We found that over the period 1971-86, employment shifted towards occupations that had relatively complex content and required relatively high levels of educational and training preparation.

What is the role of the shift to services in this process? Our research consistently leads to the conclusion that the changing industrial structure is having a mixed effect on overall skill levels. Some services – notably, the nonmarket and dynamic services – include the most highly skilled jobs in the economy. On the other hand, the skill profile of traditional services is lower than that of any other major industry group. Moreover, the shift to services does not

Chart 6-7

Job-Specific Training Requirements by Industry: A Comparison of Occupational-Trait and Self-Report Measures,[1] Canada, 1982-83

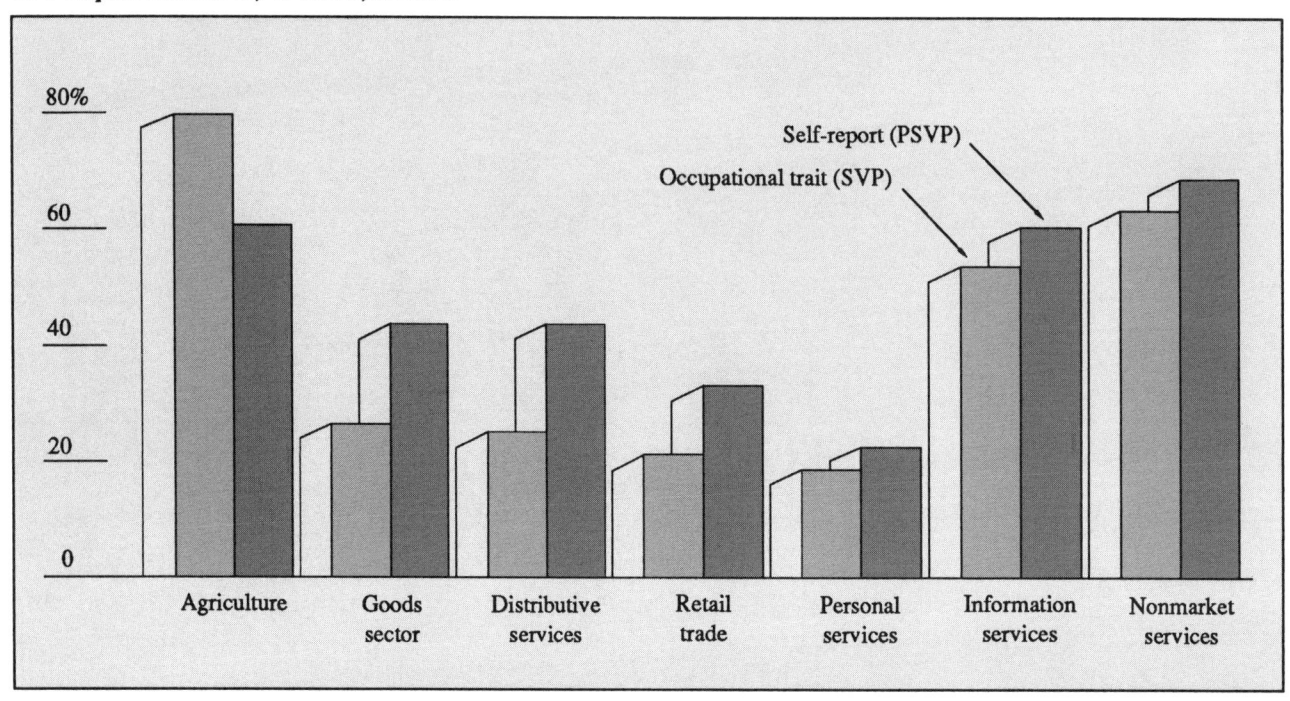

[Bar chart showing percentages for Agriculture, Goods sector, Distributive services, Retail trade, Personal services, Information services, and Nonmarket services, comparing Self-report (PSVP) and Occupational trait (SVP) measures]

[1] Proportion of workers in occupations or jobs requiring over one year of occupational-trait specific vocational preparation (SVP) and a proxy self-report measure (PSVP).
SOURCE Based on the Class Structure Survey, Myles and Fawcett, "Job skills and the service economy."

appear to be reducing the concentration of women in jobs with relatively low-skilled requirements; indeed, the gender gap in skills is particularly large in some of the fastest growing service industries.

In conclusion, our examination of employment in a service economy suggests that the overall upgrading of the employment structure is due less to the shift to services than to a general upgrading of skills in all industries. Overall, a number of factors, most prominently technological change, is leading to a reorganization of production in both goods and services, and employment is increasingly concentrated in more highly skilled jobs. This has obvious implications in terms of training and education. From an aggregate point of view, human capital development will become more and more important as the employment structure is progressively tilted in the direction of work that has higher skill requirements. And from an individual perspective, success in the labour market will increasingly depend on acquiring adequate skills.

7 Issues in Human-Resource Development

Human-resource development is extremely important in a high-technology, service-dominated economy. First, as we have shown in the preceding chapter, work with high skill requirements accounts for an increasing share of overall employment. Accordingly, to meet these demands, the labour force must consist of more and more workers with advanced education and training backgrounds. And, second, as international competition accelerates, high-cost countries such as Canada will be forced to rely on the excellence of their work force to provide a comparative advantage in the global marketplace. While every country must invest in all factors of production including capital and technology, achieving a high return on these investments will require people with the skills and knowledge to exploit their potential; increasingly, the performance of national economies is closely linked to the human factor.

It is not surprising, then, that training and education have been gaining importance within the policy arena in recent years. Currently, there are a number of initiatives in this area in Canada: the Prime Minister's Task Force on Education, the Labour Force Development Strategy, and the related consultation process organized by the Canadian Labour Market and Productivity Centre are particularly prominent examples at the federal level. Human-resource policy reviews also have been initiated in a number of provinces, including the Premier's Council in Ontario and the British Columbia Task Force on Employment and Training. The emphasis being placed on education and training is not unique to this country; indeed, similar exercises are being carried out in most advanced industrial nations and at an international level by organizations such as the OECD.

The research presented in this chapter addresses two sets of issues associated with human-resource development. The first is the relationship between human capital and employment outcomes. We begin here with an analysis of how that relationship has changed. While there has always been a direct link between human capital and success in the labour market, that connection has become stronger over the past 15 years. Specifically, the employment and adjustment problems of individuals with low levels of human capital (as embodied in their educational attainment) appear to have worsened during this period. We then consider two specific aspects of the current relationship between education and the labour market: the transition between school and work, and the ability of workers with different levels of educational attainment to adjust to changes in their employment status.

The message emerging from the first half of this chapter is clear: the poorly educated and unskilled face special difficulties in the emerging labour market. This conclusion has obvious implications for the education system – in particular, the critical imperative of reducing dropout levels. It also brings into focus the importance of skill-formation opportunities outside the formal education sector. This is the issue to which we turn in the second part of the chapter. To begin, we review the evidence on human-resource development within industry. We conclude that industry is not an important source of skill formation for most Canadian workers: many businesses in this country offer no formal training, and where it is provided, it tends to be heavily concentrated among workers who are already well educated and relatively highly skilled.

We then go on to examine recent human-resource development initiatives sponsored by government. The traditional target of public policy has been those in the labour force with no attachment, or only a weak attachment, to a particular employer. At both the federal and provincial levels, there is a growing awareness of the importance of human-resource development and its role in improving the labour market adjustment of these workers; however, on balance, it does not appear that current policies are doing enough to develop skills that would improve their long-term employability.

Education and Employment Outcomes

Over the past three decades, it has been well established that there is an empirical link between human-resource development and economic growth. An important body of evidence has come from "growth accounting" studies which attribute output growth to three sources: increases in labour inputs, increases in capital, and a residual category. Each of these basic sources of growth are then further disaggregated into their various influences: changes in labour inputs, for example, are broken down into changes in educational attainment, the demographic composition of the work force, and average hours worked. Growth-accounting analyses have consistently led to the conclusion that improvements in the educational level of a nation's work force lead to increases in the rate of economic growth.[1]

According to a literature survey carried out by Psacharopoulos, growth-accounting studies estimate that, on average, changes in education have been responsible for roughly 9 per cent of output growth in advanced economies in recent decades.[2] Table 7-1 presents a summary of the conclusions of growth-accounting analyses of the Canadian economy since 1960. These indicate that the increasing educational levels of the Canadian work force have contributed 0.5 to 0.8 percentage points of economic output per year. The contribution of education – both in absolute and relative terms – was highest over the period 1973-81 when the flow of well-educated young people into the labour market was at its peak.

It should be noted that growth accounting has not been without criticism as a methodology for computing the economic returns to education. Some have argued that the technique, in fact, probably underestimates the importance of human capital,[3] because calculations focus only on educational attainment and ignore other (less easily measured) forms of skill development, including training outside the education system. Another concern about growth accounting involves the nature of the conclusions that can be drawn from it. These critics argue that the technique is more suited to identifying the "correlates" than the "causes" of economic growth, and that other types of analyses are necessary for a more precise specification of the link between education and economic growth.

What, then, is the nature of that relationship? Certainly, there are a number of ways in which high levels of educational attainment can contribute to an economy – for example, technological innovation is more rapid in well-educated societies. Our particular interest here is in the economic contribution of education through its role in determining labour quality. In this regard, it is useful to consider the link between education and productive performance at the individual level. The economic literature most relevant to this issue focuses on the positive relationship between educational attainment and wages, which are conventionally viewed as a proxy for productivity and labour quality.[4] While it is well established that highly educated workers tend to be highly paid workers, why this is so remains controversial. Essentially, there are two schools of thought: education as "human capital" and education as a "sorting-and-signalling" device. The former contends that schooling actually creates the skills that directly affect how productive workers are, while the latter argues that the education system simply selects and identifies those who have (or are perceived to have) the potential to be productive.[5]

Testing these hypotheses empirically is complicated by the fact that, in comparing the productive capacities of individuals with varying levels of schooling, it is difficult to separate the effects of education from differences in innate ability. Nevertheless, the soundest estimates of the social and private rates of return to secondary and postsecondary education in advanced countries average between 9 and 12 per cent.[6] Without discounting its "sorting-and-signalling" role, education does seem to play an important part in enhancing worker productivity and quality.

Table 7-1

Growth-Accounting Estimates of the Contributions of Education to Economic Growth, Canada, Selected Years, 1962-88

	Period	Absolute contribution[1]	Relative contribution[2]
		(Per cent)	
Kendrick	1962-73	0.5	8.8
	1973-81	0.6	20.0
Macdonald	1962-73	0.5	8.8
Commission	1973-81	0.8	26.7
CLMPC	1981-88	0.5	16.2

1 Estimate of the number of percentage points added to economic growth per year.
2 Estimate of percentage share of total output growth per year.
SOURCE Canadian Labour Market and Productivity Centre, *Quarterly Labour Market and Productivity Review* (Winter 1989-90).

The Education-Employment Relationship over Time

The fact that there is a relationship between education, work performance, and earnings is borne out by the more favourable employment outcomes of those with high levels of schooling. Traditionally, educational attainment has been associated not only with higher wages, but also with greater labour force participation and lower unemployment rates. In this section, we will examine how these outcomes have changed in the past 15 years, and whether education is becoming a more or less important factor in the labour market.

Although a number of issues undoubtedly come into play here, two – one on the demand side and the other on the supply side – are particularly significant. The first is the changing skill structure. As we saw in the preceding chapter, the overall effect of structural and technological change has been a progressive shift in labour demand towards occupations which have relatively high skill and education requirements.[7] This suggests that the employment situation is likely to become increasingly difficult for the poorly educated.

The second is the changing nature of labour supply, specifically the educational upgrading of the work force.[8] Canadian workers are among the most highly educated in the world; indeed, Canada ranks second only to the United States in terms of the average level of schooling of the labour force.[9] And the educational profile of our working population has improved over the past 15 years (Chart 7-1). While 20 per cent of Canadian workers in 1975 had less than nine years of schooling, this share had dropped to just 9 per cent by 1989. The proportion with at least some postsecondary education increased from 33 to 42 per cent. This rising educational attainment reflects two developments over the period: first, the large (and typically well-educated) baby-boom cohort entering the labour force, and second, increasing enrolment in secondary and postsecondary institutions.[10] The implications of this upgrading for the education-employment relationship are not clear; certainly an important factor here is whether the demand for educated workers has kept up with the supply.

Labour Force Participation

Labour force participation is strongly influenced by the level of schooling. Generally, participation rates rise considerably as educational attainment increases. In 1989, for example, 85 per cent of the adult population (15 years of age or older) with university degrees were in the work force compared to just 37 per cent of those with fewer than nine years of schooling. This relationship between labour force participation and educational attainment is true for all age groups. It also applies to both men and women. Education is a particularly important variable for females; less than one in four women with less than nine years of schooling are in the work force, while the corresponding figure for those with high levels of educational attainment now approaches 80 per cent (Chart 7-2).

The relationship between educational attainment and labour force participation is strengthening for both men and women. Between 1975 and 1989, the aggregate male participation rate dropped slightly from 78.4 to 76.7 per cent, with modest decreases of similar magnitude occurring for most educational-attainment groups (Chart 7-3). Note, however, the substantial decline in the participation of men with less than nine years of schooling: in 1975 the rate was 67.2 per cent, by 1989 it had fallen to 50.8 per cent. Over this period, the absolute gap in the participation rate of these men and those with the highest level of schooling

Chart 7-1

Labour Force by Level of Schooling, Canada, 1975-89

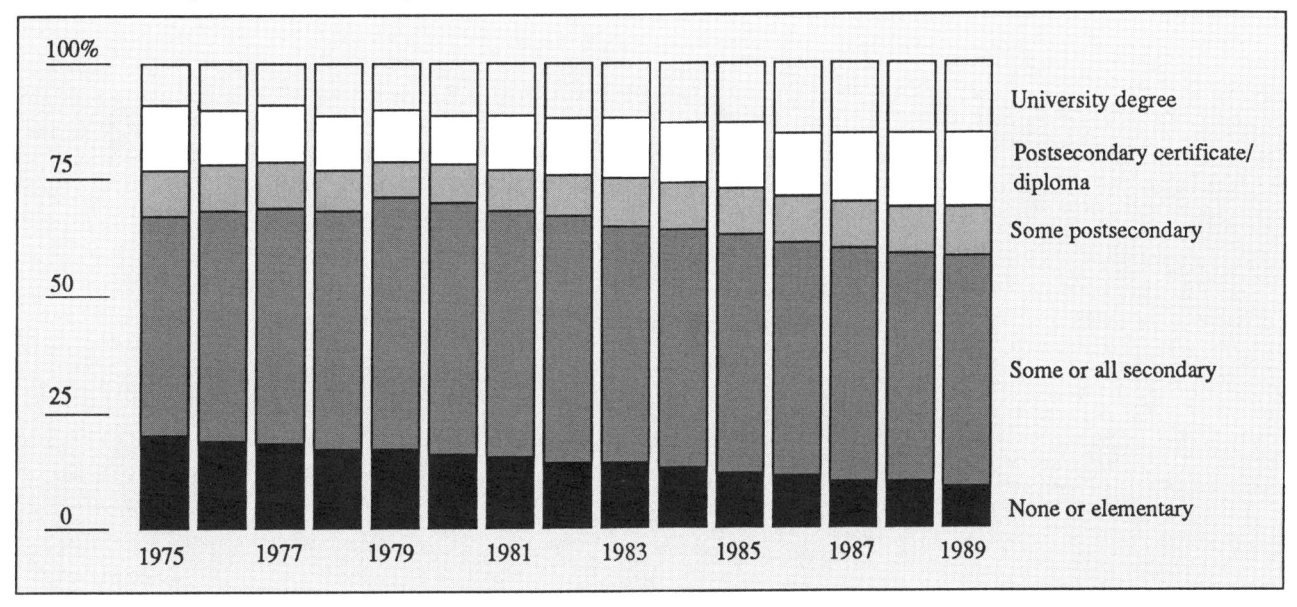

SOURCE Estimates by the Economic Council of Canada, based on data from Statistics Canada.

114 Employment in the Service Economy

Chart 7-2

Labour Force Participation Rates, by Level of Schooling and Sex, Canada, 1989

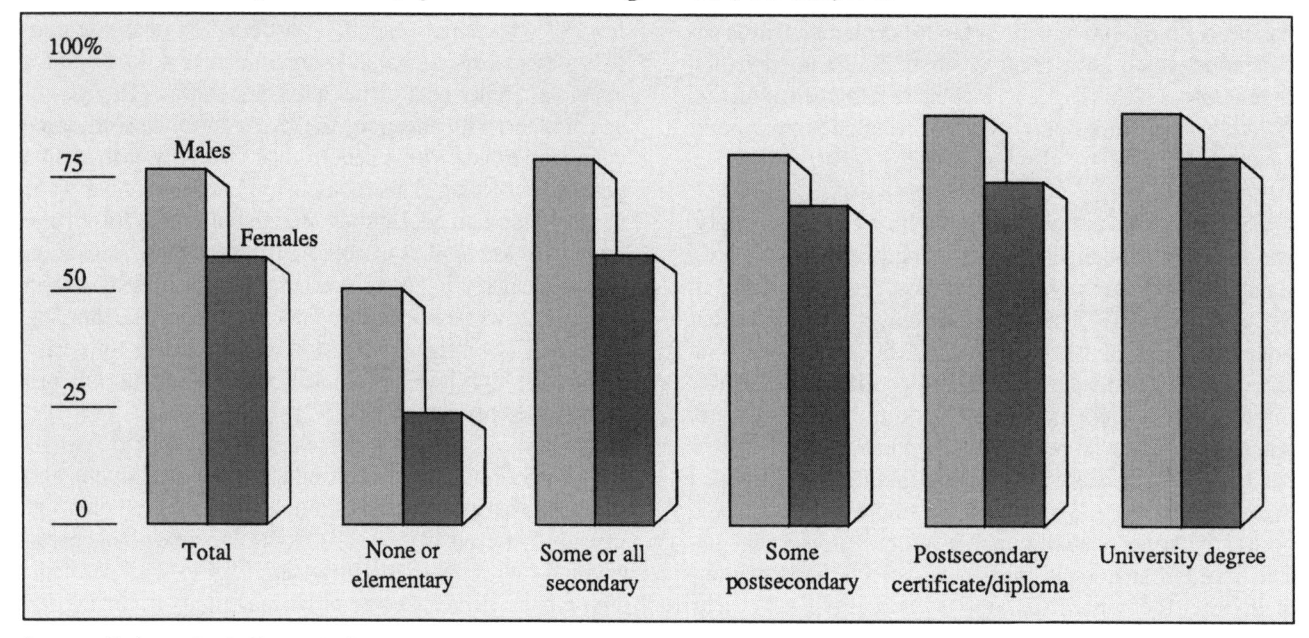

SOURCE Estimates by the Economic Council of Canada, based on data from Statistics Canada.

Chart 7-3

Male Labour Force Participation Rates, by Level of Schooling, Canada, 1975-89

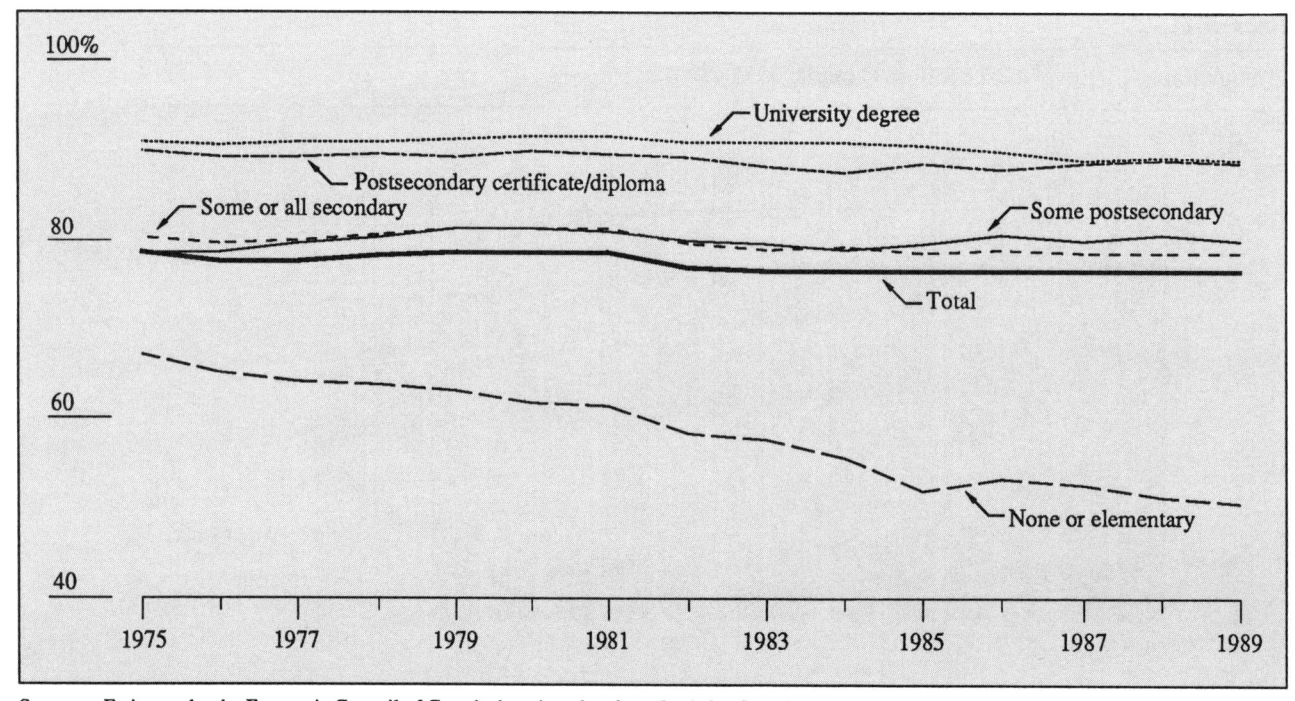

SOURCE Estimates by the Economic Council of Canada, based on data from Statistics Canada.

(postsecondary degree) grew from 24 to 38 percentage points between 1975 and 1989.

During these years, the participation of women in the labour market increased markedly. In 1975, 44.4 per cent of the adult female population were in the work force; by 1989, the proportion had jumped to 57.9 per cent. This trend applied to virtually all educational-attainment groups (Chart 7-4). Poorly educated females, however, are a striking exception. While women with secondary schooling or more entered the labour market in greater and greater numbers, the participation rate for those with fewer than nine years of education actually dropped. As a result, between 1975 and 1989 the absolute difference in participation rates between these women and those with university degrees increased from 41 to 56 percentage points.

Unemployment

Unemployment experiences are also closely linked to educational attainment. In general, the probability of being without a job declines as the level of schooling increases. The unemployment rates in 1989 for labour force groups are organized according to education in Table 7-2. The rate was lowest for those with the most schooling and rose in steps as educational attainment diminished; indeed, the incidence of unemployment for workers with less than nine years of schooling was three times higher than the rate for university graduates.

Table 7-2 also indicates that while this inverse relationship between unemployment and education characterizes all age groups, it is strongest for young workers. This is most evident when we look at the experience of individuals with less than nine years of schooling. As one would expect, these workers had the highest unemployment rates in each of the age groups. Note, however, that the differential between the least educated and the rest of the work force becomes more prominent as age decreases; for the 15-24 age group the unemployment rate in 1989 was 23.2 per cent, over 10 points higher than the rate for those with secondary schooling and more than 17 points above the rate for university graduates! The lack of a good educational foundation, then, is particularly serious for young people entering the labour market.

It appears that the association between educational attainment and unemployment has become stronger over the past 15 years. Chart 7-5 tracks an unemployment "hazard"

Chart 7-4

Female Labour Force Participation Rates, by Level of Schooling, Canada, 1975-89

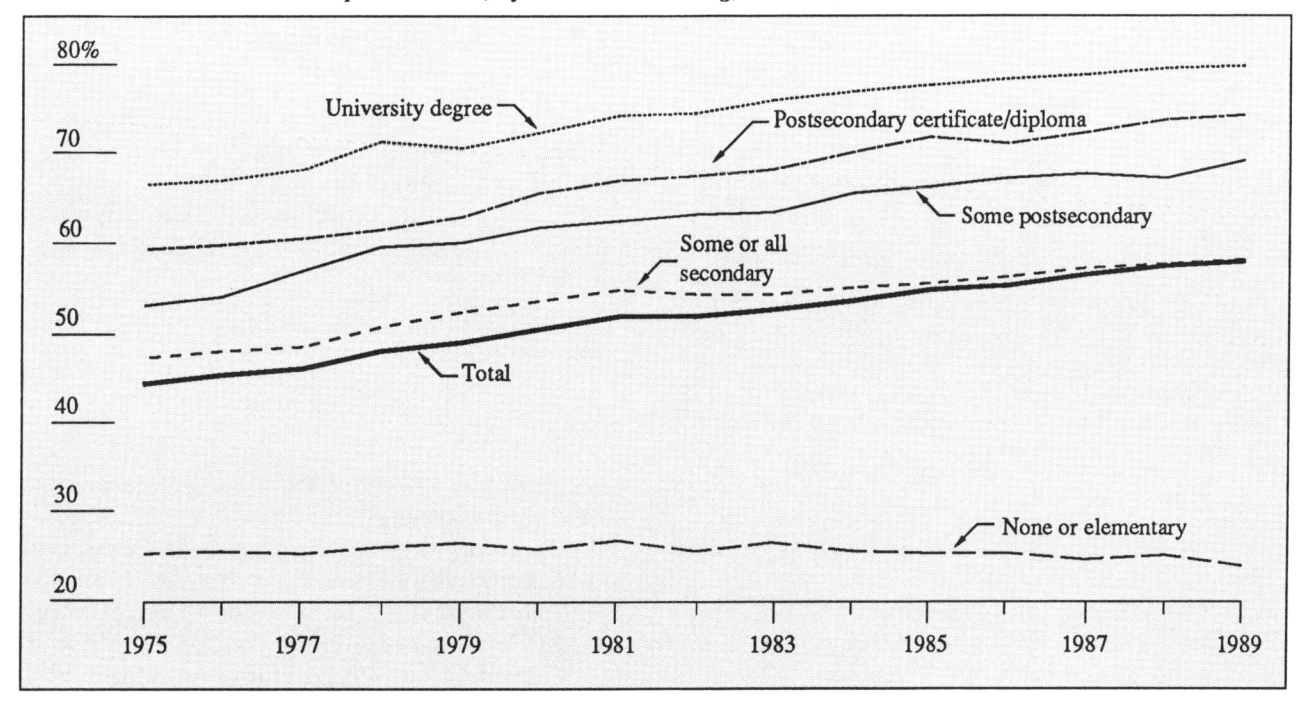

SOURCE   Estimates by the Economic Council of Canada, based on data from Statistics Canada.

116 Employment in the Service Economy

Table 7-2

Unemployment Rates by Level of Educational Attainment, Labour Force Age Groups, Canada, 1989

	Total	15-24	25-44	45 or more
	(Per cent)			
None or elementary	11.1	23.2	13.1	8.2
Some or all secondary	8.9	12.7	8.6	5.3
Some postsecondary	7.3	8.6	7.0	5.3
Postsecondary certificate/diploma	5.2	6.6	5.3	3.9
University degree	3.7	5.9	3.8	2.9
Total	7.5	11.3	7.2	5.4

SOURCE Estimates by the Economic Council of Canada, based on Statistics Canada, the Labour Force Survey.

Chart 7-5

Unemployment "Hazard" Index[1] for Workers with Less than Nine Years' Schooling, Canada, 1975-89

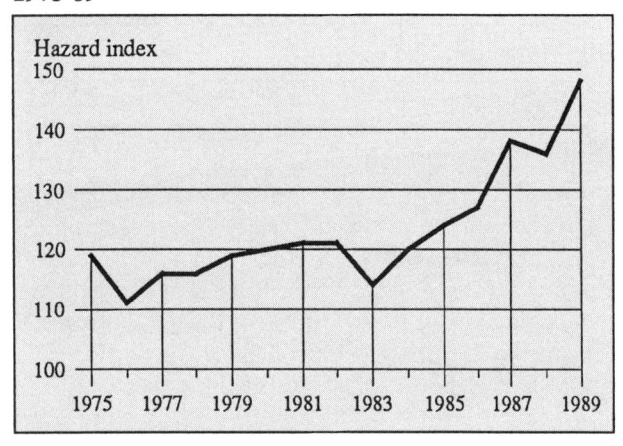

1 Unemployment rate for workers with less than nine years of schooling divided by the aggregate unemployment rate, multiplied by 100.
SOURCE Estimates by the Economic Council of Canada, based on data from Statistics Canada.

index for the poorly educated over the period 1975-89. This measure is calculated as the ratio of the unemployment rate for those with less than nine years of schooling relative to the aggregate unemployment rate. In 1975, the index was 119 which indicates that the unemployment rate for the poorly educated was 19 per cent above the national level in that year. It increased sharply after the 1981-82 recession and in 1989 stood at 148. According to this measure, then, the unemployment hazard specifically associated with having less than nine years of schooling more than doubled over the 15-year period.

Long-term unemployment represents another dimension of the labour market difficulties experienced by the poorly educated. These workers stand a much greater-than-average chance of remaining unemployed for an extended period of time. There was substantial growth between 1976 and 1989 in the overall incidence of long-term joblessness regardless of education level (Chart 7-6). The increase was particularly dramatic, however, for those with less than nine years of schooling. By 1989, about 11 per cent of these workers remained unemployed for at least a year once they were without a job.

Chart 7-6

Long-Term Unemployment, by Educational Attainment Level,[1] Canada, 1976 and 1989

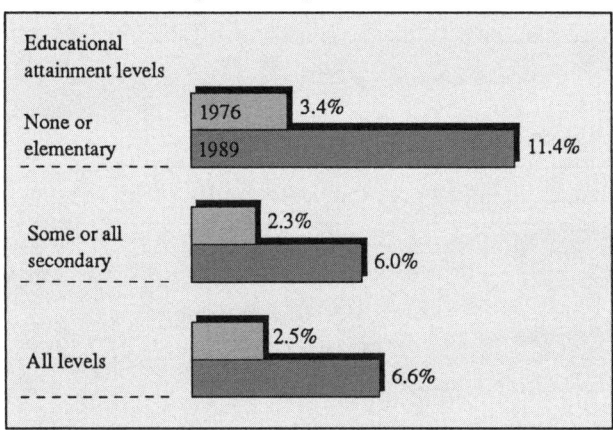

Educational attainment levels	1976	1989
None or elementary	3.4%	11.4%
Some or all secondary	2.3%	6.0%
All levels	2.5%	6.6%

1 Proportion of unemployed at each level who have been unemployed for 53 weeks or more.
SOURCE Estimates by the Economic Council of Canada, based on unpublished data from Statistics Canada.

Earnings

The positive relationship between education and wages has already been noted in this chapter. How have the earnings differentials associated with educational attainment been changing? This question has received more attention in the United States than in Canada. After a period of decline in the late 1960s and early 1970s, the returns to education in the form of higher earnings in the United States have been rising sharply since at least the late 1970s. The reasons for this pattern have generated considerable debate; many observers have argued that labour supply trends associated with the baby-boom cohort have been the determining factor here.[11]

Research on the Canadian situation suggests that, in a very general sense, the trends observed in the United States apply here as well, although to a more moderate extent. Comparing earnings between postsecondary and high school graduates in both countries, Freeman and Needels concluded that the gap for both men and women narrowed in the 1970s but then widened during the 1980s. However, the growth in returns to postsecondary education in Canada in the 1980s has not been as great as that in the United States.[12] Looking at earnings among males employed full time and full year, Dooley found that the education-based differentials were smaller in 1981 than they had been 10 years earlier, with the major compression occurring during the first half of the decade. In a recent update covering the period 1981-87, however, he observed that these differentials, at least between university graduates and those with high school or less, had started to rise again for males under 35.[13]

We looked at earning trends by educational attainment levels for Canadian workers in 1967-86. This analysis is based on data from the Survey of Consumer Finances and includes all Canadians 15 years of age and older who earned at least 5 per cent of the average annual industrial wage in the year under consideration. Tables 7-3 and 7-4 compare the earnings of postsecondary graduates with those having elementary and secondary education. The compensation

Table 7-3

Earnings[1] Ratio of Workers with Postsecondary Degrees Relative to Workers with Up to Eight Years of Schooling, by Age, Canada, Selected Years, 1967-86

	1967	1973	1981	1986
	(Per cent)			
15-24	1.52	1.09	1.34	1.46
25-34	1.87	1.58	1.52	1.67
35-49	2.72	2.37	1.74	1.79
50 or more	3.09	2.53	1.77	1.63
Total	2.39	1.92	1.50	1.50

1 Based on annual earnings of individuals earning at least 5 per cent of the average industrial wage in the year under consideration.
SOURCE Calculations by Statistics Canada and the Economic Council of Canada, based on Statistics Canada, Survey of Consumer Finances, unpublished data.

Table 7-4

Earnings[1] Ratio of Workers with Postsecondary Degrees Relative to Workers with Secondary Education, by Age, Canada, Selected Years, 1967-86

	1967	1973	1981	1986
	(Per cent)			
15-24	1.47	1.20	1.18	1.27
25-34	1.55	1.40	1.26	1.31
35-49	2.14	2.04	1.49	1.52
50 or more	2.31	1.98	1.51	1.45
Total	2.12	1.90	1.48	1.50

1 Based on annual earnings of individuals earning at least 5 per cent of the average industrial wage in the year under consideration.
SOURCE Calculations by Statistics Canada and the Economic Council of Canada, based on Statistics Canada, Survey of Consumer Finances, unpublished data.

premium for the graduates declined significantly from 1967 to 1981; between 1981 and 1986, however, these differentials stabilized.

For a closer understanding of these trends, it is necessary to consider the changing age and educational profile of the Canadian work force over these years. Throughout the 1960s and much of the 1970s, the baby-boom cohort entered the labour market in large numbers. This group was characterized by high levels of educational attainment, and given the cohort's size, the result was a tremendous growth in the supply of workers with advanced schooling. One implication of this development was a narrowing of the premium offered to those with postsecondary education. Between 1967 and 1981, the earnings differential between these workers and those with less than nine years of schooling (Table 7-3) and only secondary schooling (Table 7-4) declined substantially for all age groups.

By the 1980s, however, the bulk of the baby-boom cohort was already in the labour market and had moved into the prime-aged category. While young people, on average, continue to enter the work force with advanced levels of schooling, their smaller numbers have led to slower increases in the supply of well-educated new labour force entrants. (Chart 7-7 shows the relatively stable postsecondary enrolment figures in the 1980s after the tremendous increases of the 1960s and 1970s.) As the growth of well-educated, young labour force entrants has slowed down, the returns to a postsecondary degree have begun to increase again.[14] The mean earnings for these workers compared to those with only elementary schooling grew between 1981 and 1986 from 1.34 to 1.46 per cent in the 15-24 age group, and from 1.52 to 1.67 per cent in the 25-34 group (see Table 7-3); when graduates are compared to workers with secondary education, a similar pattern is observed (see Table 7-4). As the slowdown of young entrants persists through the 1990s, we can expect that the relationship between educational attainment and earnings will continue to strengthen.

Chart 7-7

Full-Time Enrolment in Colleges and Universities, Canada, 1951-90

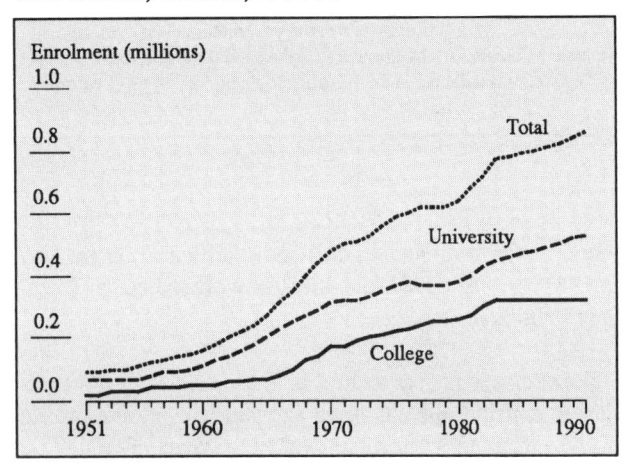

SOURCE Department of the Secretary of State Canada, *Profile of Higher Education in Canada* (Ottawa: Supply and Services Canada, 1990).

The School-to-Work Transition

Another important dimension of the relationship between education and employment involves the school-to-work transition. As would be expected, research has indicated that early labour market experiences are influenced by educational attainment. Surveys of school leavers have highlighted the often unfavourable outcomes for this group, while those studying postsecondary graduates have described more positive transitions.

A recent Ontario government survey documents the transition difficulties for high school "leavers" – that is, individuals who left high school either as dropouts, or as graduates who did not immediately enter a postsecondary institution.[15] Over 40 per cent had been unemployed at some point since their first job. One quarter of the respondents who had experienced some unemployment reported that they had been without work for at least one year since leaving school; those who were in their late twenties had experienced, on average, close to four years of unemployment in total. Employment patterns were particularly unstable for those who had dropped out of high school before graduating. Although respondents did report more work stability with age, a majority of those under 27 expected that their present job would not be permanent. It should be noted that employment outcomes were more favourable for respondents who undertook some form of job-related education or training after leaving school. This was most evident in terms of wages; in fact, the median income for respondents who had pursued some further education or training was 23 per cent above that reported by those who had not.

In contrast to the school leavers, the early labour market experiences of postsecondary graduates tend to be positive. Statistics Canada tracked the school-to-work transitions of 1982 community college and university graduates, in 1984 and 1987.[16] Five years after graduation, the unemployment rate was 3.7 per cent for the university graduates and 5.4 per cent for the college graduates; in comparison, the national rate for their age cohort (25-35 years) was 10.5 per cent. As well, respondents tended to be concentrated in occupations related to their fields of study and the overwhelming majority reported that they were satisfied with their jobs.

In terms of earnings, the graduates also fared well. In 1987, the community-college graduates earned, on average, about $1,000 more than the typical Canadian worker between 25 and 35 years of age. The university graduates reported employment incomes that were about $10,000 above the national average for the age cohort. The survey data, however, did indicate significant differences in the earnings of male and female graduates in 1987. For the university subsample, average earnings for women were 81 per cent of those for men; among college graduates, the corresponding figure was 78 per cent. While individual characteristics, including field of study, can influence incomes, a study of the university group concluded that these factors only accounted for one third of the male-female differential.[17]

In order to get additional insight into the school-to-work transition, we have drawn on the results of the survey of recent high school and university graduates in three Canadian cities, which we introduced in Chapter 6.[18] The respondents completed high school or university in Edmonton, Toronto, and Sudbury in 1985. Follow-up investigations of this sample were carried out 12 and 24 months later. Our analysis is based on the two-year follow-up and includes about 1,900 respondents. The survey included only those with at least a high school diploma, so there is no evidence on the school-to-work transition of dropouts. Nevertheless, the survey offers a longitudinal analysis of the early employment experiences of young people entering a service-dominated labour market. Of particular relevance to this chapter are the results comparing the outcomes experienced by the high school and university graduates.

There are some similarities in the experiences reported by the high school and university subsamples. In both groups, the traditional distinction between student and worker is becoming blurred. On the one hand, a high level of labour force participation is now reported by Canadian students; 68 per cent of the high school sample and 62 per cent of the university sample had held a paying job at some time during the year they graduated. On the other hand, only a minority of the respondents completely terminated their education and entered the labour force upon graduation; even among the university graduates, only about 40 per cent reported that they did not pursue some education in the two years following graduation.

Another similarity between the two subsamples was the concentration of employment in service industries. While approximately 70 per cent of the Canadian labour force is employed in that sector, over 80 per cent of the graduates from both groups who were working two years later had jobs in services (Table 7-5). This dominance was particularly striking among females; over 90 per cent of female high school and university graduates were employed in that sector.

Within services, however, there were important differences between the high school and university graduates. Looking at the less educated group first, about 55 per cent of both the males and females were working in personal services (Table 7-5). These industries are characterized by jobs with relatively low wages, skill content, and stability; indeed, the survey respondents employed in this subsector tended to make observations along these lines about their jobs. On the other hand, while personal services did employ more than a trivial share of the university graduates, they were not nearly as dominant for this group; as Table 7-5 shows, the university subsample was distributed across a wide range of service industries.[19]

There are also differences between the two subsamples when we look at the occupations in which survey respondents were employed in 1987. Table 7-6 shows the concentration of university graduates in managerial and professional positions; in fact, while only 28 per cent of the Canadian labour force was in these occupational groups in 1987, the corresponding figure for university graduates was 74 per cent. Although they were underrepresented in the

Table 7-5

Distribution of Employment by Industry, According to Gender and Educational Level, Canada, 1987

	High school graduates			University graduates		
	Females	Males	Total	Females	Males	Total
	(Per cent)					
Services	93.6	74.7	83.9	90.5	71.5	82.7
Personal services	54.1	55.2	54.7	14.4	13.2	13.9
Distributive services[1]	3.7	5.3	4.5	3.0	7.3	4.7
Information services	15.6	5.0	10.2	15.6	19.2	17.1
Education, health, and social services	11.4	2.5	6.8	46.1	20.2	35.5
Public administration	8.8	6.7	7.7	11.4	11.6	11.5
Goods	6.4	25.3	16.1	9.5	28.5	17.3
Primary industries	2.7	4.0	3.3	2.7	12.3	6.6
Manufacturing	2.1	12.5	7.5	5.9	11.9	8.4
Construction	1.6	8.8	5.3	0.9	4.3	2.3
Total	100.0	100.0	100.0	100.0	100.0	100.0

1 Includes retail trade.
SOURCE The Three-City Graduate Survey, Harvey Krahn and Graham S. Lowe, "Young workers in the service economy," Working Paper no. 14, Economic Council of Canada, Ottawa, 1990.

Table 7-6

Distribution of Employment by Occupation, According to Gender and Educational Level, Canada, 1987

	High school graduates			University graduates		
	Females	Males	Total	Females	Males	Total
	(Per cent)					
Managerial and administrative	0.8	2.0	1.4	13.3	20.5	16.2
Science, engineering, and mathematics	0.5	3.5	2.1	8.7	31.4	18.0
Social sciences	2.9	0.3	1.5	9.8	4.3	7.6
Teaching	1.6	0.3	0.9	35.9	15.8	27.7
Medicine and health	3.7	1.0	2.3	3.7	0.7	2.4
Artistic, literary, and recreational	2.6	2.3	2.4	2.3	2.3	2.3
Clerical	43.9	13.5	28.3	13.5	4.6	9.9
Sales	21.2	15.0	18.0	7.3	9.9	8.4
Service	17.7	24.8	21.4	3.9	5.3	4.5
Primary	2.4	4.3	3.4	0.2	1.0	0.5
Processing and fabricating	1.3	16.5	9.1	0.2	2.0	0.9
Construction	0.3	8.0	4.2	0.2	1.3	0.7
Transportation and communications	1.1	8.5	4.9	0.9	1.0	0.9
Total	100.0	100.0	100.0	100.0	100.0	100.0

SOURCE The Three-City Graduate Survey, Krahn and Lowe, "Young workers in the service economy."

low-wage clerical, sales, and service groups (where 40 per cent of the national work force is employed), note that about 23 per cent did have jobs in these occupations. Among the high school graduates, the clerical, sales, and service occupations dominated, accounting for over two thirds of the group's total employment and for 83 per cent of the jobs held by female high school graduates.

Overall, then, educational attainment seems to have been an important factor in determining where the survey respondents were employed two years after graduation. And, given the concentration of high school graduates in clerical, sales, and service occupations, particularly in traditional services, and the overrepresentation of university graduates in managerial and professional positions, it should not be surprising that the university-educated group reported more favourable work experiences.

Table 7-7 compares the high school and university subsamples in terms of a number of employment outcomes. To begin, the incidence of part-time work was more than twice as frequent among high school graduates than among university graduates. This is primarily because virtually one half of those high school graduates who were in clerical, sales, and service occupations in traditional services were employed on a part-time basis. There are similar differences between the high school and university graduates when we look at involuntary part-time employment.

Respondents with university degrees also earned more on average than those who had only graduated from high school. This was true for both full-time and part-time workers; the gap was particularly large in the case of full-time employment where the mean weekly take-home pay for university graduates was 38 per cent higher than the earnings of high school graduates. As well, on average, the occupational status of jobs held by the university graduates was considerably higher than that of those held by the high school graduates.

Table 7-7 also suggests that respondents in the more educated group experienced more stability in their entry into the labour market. While 44.1 per cent of the employed high school graduates expected to be in their current job for no more than six months, the corresponding figure for the university graduates was far lower, at 28.5 per cent. Moreover, those who had completed only high school reported that they had experienced almost 50 per cent more

Table 7-7

Selected Job Characteristics, by Level of Education, Canada, 1987

	High school graduates	University graduates
	(Per cent)	
Part-time employment share[1]	34.8	15.2
Involuntary part-time share	19.2	9.4
No job permanency[2]	44.1	28.5
	(Dollars)	
Average weekly take-home pay		
Full-time	268.76	374.02
Part-time	121.95	154.78
Average occupational status[3]	34.3	54.8
Average number of months unemployed[4]	2.1	1.5

1 Less than 30 hours per week.
2 Plan to stay in current job for six months or less.
3 Based on the 1987 Blishen Index of socio-economic status, which ranks occupations in ascending order according to earnings and education. See Bernard Blishen et al., "The 1981 socioeconomic index for occupations in Canada," *Canadian Review of Sociology and Anthropology* 24, no. 4 (November 1987).
4 In previous two years.
SOURCE Calculations based on the Three-City Graduate Survey, Krahn and Lowe, "Young workers in the service economy."

unemployment since graduating than those with university degrees (2.2 months versus 1.5 months).

While university graduates did report more favourable school-to-work transitions, the survey results do not suggest that a postsecondary degree will guarantee a "good" job immediately upon graduation. It should be noted, for example, that a sizable minority (9 per cent) of employed university graduates were working in clerical, sales, and service occupations in traditional services. Despite having a university degree and two years of labour market experience, these individuals reported a lot of part-time work, most of it involuntary, and with relatively low wages and occupational status, and the lowest job satisfaction of all 10 job "clusters" analysed by Krahn and Lowe. This underemployment is consistent with results from the Class Structure Survey which indicate a significant degree of overqualification among young workers in traditional services.[20]

In spite of this caveat, however, the findings of this survey of graduates do, on balance, underline the relationship between the level of educational attainment and the ease of transition from school to work. Respondents who had only completed high school clearly had considerably less favourable early labour market experiences compared to the university graduates. In fact, the survey results suggest that without postsecondary education, young workers have a limited range of job opportunities, and that those are predominantly in traditional services.

Education and Labour Market Adjustment

We conclude our analysis of the link between educational attainment and employment by looking at the impact of the level of schooling on labour market adjustment. Is there a relationship between education and job tenure? Do turnover rates differ according to schooling? Are poorly educated workers more likely to lose their jobs? Do they face greater-than-average problems in finding new jobs?

To answer these questions, we analysed labour adjustment using longitudinal data for 1986-87 from the Labour Market Activity Survey (LMAS).[21] Our research is based on the experiences of paid workers who were employed in the first of these two years. We focused particularly on individuals who left their employment (voluntarily or involuntarily) during the 24-month period covered by the survey. This group consists of 3.8 million workers, about 31 per cent of the paid labour force.

The first observation is that the average length of time that individuals had been in their jobs at the time of separation was directly related to their level of education: for example, the mean job duration for those with elementary schooling was just 32 months, compared to 43 months for university degree holders. Consistent with this finding, the likelihood of separating from employment decreased with greater levels of educational attainment. The turnover rate for workers who had completed a postsecondary program was significantly lower than the rate for those who had not; while at least one third of the paid labour force in the latter group separated from their jobs during the survey period, the corresponding figure for workers with a postsecondary certificate or diploma was 26 per cent, and just 20.5 per cent for those with a university degree (Table 7-8).

The reason for separation also differed according to the level of educational attainment. Of the possible reasons – "layoffs" (involuntary loss of a job), "quits" (voluntarily leaving a job), and "other" (for example, retirement, temporary disability, and other personal factors) – layoffs represented a larger share of separations among workers with only elementary education than among any other group. The relative importance of quits, on the other hand, tended to increase with the level of schooling.

Table 7-8

Separation Rates[1] and Distribution by Reason for Separation, According to Educational Attainment Level, Canada, 1986 and 1987

	Separation rate	Distribution of job separators by reason for separation			
		Layoff	Quit	Other	Total
	(Per cent)				
None or elementary	35.9	35.6	26.4	38.0	100.0
Some or all secondary	33.4	29.7	28.3	42.0	100.0
Some postsecondary	36.4	30.4	27.1	42.5	100.0
Postsecondary certificate/diploma	26.0	28.2	30.8	41.0	100.0
University degree	20.5	28.6	33.1	38.3	100.0
Total	31.2	30.2	28.7	41.1	100.0

1 Number of job separators as a percentage of the total number of paid employees in each category.
SOURCE Calculations by the Economic Council of Canada, based on Statistics Canada, the Labour Market Activity Survey.

Of the 3.8 million workers who separated from their jobs, about 2.7 million, or 72 per cent, had found new employment by the end of the period. For those who did find a second job, we investigated the relationship between the duration of joblessness and educational attainment.[22] Our analysis indicates that the period of time without work tended to decrease as educational attainment rose. Workers who had completed a postsecondary program were more likely to be reemployed within four weeks than those who did not have a certificate, diploma, or degree, and the proportion who were jobless at least 27 weeks was significantly higher among the less educated group (Table 7-9). The relationship between joblessness duration and educational attainment was particularly strong where the separation was voluntary: after a quit, the mean joblessness duration for those who had not completed a postsecondary program was 4.1 weeks longer than the duration for those who had.

Does education matter in terms of the wages of workers who change jobs? We considered this question by comparing the hourly wages in the first and second jobs of those workers who did find reemployment, according to their level of schooling. This analysis suggests that there is no clear relationship. Of the job changers, 54 per cent experienced a wage increase while 35 per cent experienced a wage decline; comparing the different educational-attainment groups, those with elementary schooling and those with university degrees – the worst and best educated – were least likely to have a wage gain and most likely to have a wage loss.[23]

Table 7-9

Distribution of Job Separators[1] by Duration of Joblessness, According to Educational Attainment, Canada, 1986 and 1987

	Weeks of joblessness			
	4 or less	5-26	27 or more	Total
	(Per cent)			
None or elementary	23.2	40.7	36.1	100.0
Some or all secondary	25.8	35.4	38.9	100.0
Some postsecondary	25.5	36.8	37.7	100.0
Postsecondary certificate/diploma	32.3	36.7	31.0	100.0
University degree	30.0	40.9	29.2	100.0

1 Based on experience of job separators who found a second job.
SOURCE Calculations by the Economic Council of Canada, based on Statistics Canada, the Labour Market Activity Survey.

Canada's Training Infrastructure

The first half of this chapter has emphasized the importance of human capital, specifically in the form of schooling, in determining employment outcomes. There is a strong relationship between education and success in the labour market, and the evidence we have presented suggests that this link is becoming stronger over time. Certainly, this is partly due to the better-educated work force, which is placing individuals without a lot of schooling in an increasingly disadvantaged position. It also reflects the upgraded skill requirements and the growing role of knowledge in an information-based, high-technology economy.

In light of these facts, the performance of Canada's education systems deserves close attention. In some respects, the evidence suggests that there is a high commitment to education in this country: for example, in terms of relative public expenditures and enrolment rates, Canada places among the world leaders. Some of the education indicators in this country, however, are disturbing: the significant incidence of functional illiteracy, secondary school drop-out rates of around 30 per cent, and mediocre scores at the advanced secondary level in international tests of student achievement in mathematics and science.[24] In looking at the quality of education, it is evident that well-focused research is needed on the performance of Canada's education systems in enhancing the goal of a universally well-educated work force. (The Economic Council has undertaken a study on this subject which is expected to be published in 1992.)

But we must not overlook the importance of skill formation that takes place outside the formal educational system; vocational training activities sponsored by employers and governments are very important sources of human-resource development. For the individual, training can be a means to obtain and upgrade occupational skills, and can ease the process of adjusting to technological and structural change. It can also provide a "second chance" for adults to learn the basic skills that are traditionally acquired through schooling. In general, then, training enhances on-the-job performance and therefore productivity and competitiveness.

In the remainder of this chapter, we will examine various aspects of the training infrastructure in Canada, focusing on the capacity of the training system to provide the skills that enhance individuals' employability and productivity. First, we will review the available evidence on training within Canadian industry. It has often been noted that knowledge in this area has been hampered by a lack of data, and that there have been no definitive assessments of training sponsored by Canadian employers. We have tried to provide a more complete view by assembling the results from those surveys that have been conducted over the past two decades. We will then turn to government-sponsored training activities. Recent trends in federal programs, specifically under the Canadian Jobs Strategy and Unemployment Insurance, will be reviewed. We will also examine developments in selected provincial jurisdictions.[25]

Employer-Sponsored Training

Training in industry is assuming a higher profile on both the corporate and the public-policy agendas. In the debate over this issue, there is consensus regarding the value of employer-sponsored training for workers, organizations, and the economy. To cite one prominent example, the De Grandpré Advisory Council on Adjustment argued that "only private sector training and retraining, on a continuous basis, will allow firms to meet their skill requirements, workers to maximize their abilities, and firms and workers to adjust and win."[26] Similar positions have been articulated by a range of groups including the federal Department of Employment and Immigration, several of the recent task forces coordinated by the Canadian Labour Market and Productivity Centre, the Ontario Premier's Council, and business groups such as the Canadian Manufacturers' Association.[27]

There is empirical evidence on the positive impacts of human-resource development in the workplace. Studies (predominantly in the United States) indicate that employees who receive training have significantly higher wage growth than those who do not.[28] In fact, the rates of return to investments in employer-sponsored training appear to be higher than those for schooling.[29] As well, evidence suggests that employees who receive job training experience lower separation rates and less unemployment than other workers.[30] And there is quantitative support for the contention that human-resource development in the workplace leads to productivity gains for both the individual receiving the training and the employer providing it.[31]

The growing economic importance of workplace training is being increasingly recognized. The American Society for Training and Development concludes that "over the years, the point of learning has moved closer and closer to the point where goods and services are produced."[32] Global competitiveness and technological change are making it more and more difficult for firms to survive and prosper without substantial and ongoing investments in their human resources. As well, as a result of the slowdown in labour force entrants, it seems likely that employers will have little alternative but to rely on retraining existing workers in order to meet new and higher skill requirements.

The question of how to stimulate human-resource development within industry has emerged as an important policy issue in this country. The De Grandpré Advisory Council recommended a mandatory employer tax as an incentive to provide training,[33] and the 1990 Quebec budget included a tax credit for training expenses.[34] The Ontario Premier's Council has also made recommendations to stimulate industry's investment in human-resource development.[35]

Unfortunately, this policy debate is hindered by the fact that we actually know relatively little about industry-sponsored human-resource development. There is no census of training in industry, indeed there is no consensus on what constitutes "training." In this section, we will review existing studies in order to consider the following questions: How much employer-sponsored training takes place in this country? Has this changed over time? What types of employers tend to provide training? What types of employees tend to receive it? How does the Canadian experience compare with that of other countries?

Training Surveys

The following analysis of training in Canadian industry is based on 14 surveys conducted over the past three decades, including the major national surveys undertaken for the most part by federal government agencies.[36] The majority were undertaken in the 1980s; to make some comparisons over time, we also have reviewed some surveys from the 1960s and 1970s. It is important to note that the studies which we have analysed are not strictly comparable. There are important variations among them as to the meaning of "training," and also the population from which the samples were drawn. (For a list of the surveys reviewed and background information, see Figure 7-1.)

In most of the surveys, training is considered in the limited sense of formal activities sponsored by the employer. For example, the Human Resource Training and Development Survey (HRTDS) identifies training as having "an identifiable structured plan and objectives designed to develop a worker's skill and competence."[37] Informal training is not considered; however, it does include all formal programs whether carried out on the job or off-site, during or outside working hours. A few of the surveys do explicitly include informal training, such as the Small Business Panel Survey (SBPS) which considers informal training "acquired by working under normal work or production conditions, either with an experienced worker or under the direction of a supervisor."[38]

The surveys also vary in terms of the nature of their samples. Some are based on responses from workers while, in others, establishments or firms represent the sampling unit. Even within these two broad types, there are differences. For example, among the worker surveys, the Adult Training Survey (ATS) is based on a random sample of labour force participants, while the CLMPC Training Survey includes only full-time employees. Among the establishment surveys, there are some differences in terms of the industries and the size of firms that were covered.

Incidence of Training

According to the most recent comprehensive study, the federal government's Human Resource Training and Development Survey (HRTDS), slightly less than one third (31 per cent) of private-sector firms in Canada supported or directly provided formal training for their employees in 1987.[39] Estimates based on the HRTDS set training expenditures by industry in fiscal year 1986-87 at $1.4 billion.

How does this level of activity compare with earlier estimates? To consider this question, we calculated the training incidence rates from the surveys we have reviewed (Table 7-10). Looking first at those surveys whose scope was limited to formal programs, 25 per cent of Canadian firms provided formal training in 1984-85 according to the Survey of Training in Canadian Industries (STCI); the total training expenditure made by Canadian industry at that time was estimated with STCI data at just over one billion dollars. Studies carried out in the 1960s and 1970s yielded incidence rates from 17 to 27 per cent. A comparison of these figures with the HRTDS suggests that the level of training activity may have been slightly higher in the late 1980s than it was earlier in the decade and in preceding decades. However, while the HRTDS and the STCI and most of the earlier surveys did have broadly comparable methodologies, there were differences, and some caution should be taken in comparing these incidence rates.

When we look at the incidence of training in terms of the percentage of employees receiving formal training, there is no evidence of change over time. Eight surveys in our review published this statistic, and their estimates ranged from 7 per cent in the 1965 Survey of Training in Industry to 19 per cent in the 1963 Survey of Organized Training Programs. All subsequent surveys yielded incidence rates within the bounds established by these early studies.

Using a formal definition, then, most Canadian firms do not provide training, and the vast majority of Canadian workers do not receive any employer-sponsored training. Estimates of human-resource development activity, however, are considerably higher when informal training is recognized. On the basis of this broader definition, 56 per cent of the employees responding to the 1989 Canadian Labour Market and Productivity Centre (CLMPC) Training Survey reported that they had received some training in the previous two years. As well, 68 per cent of the firms

Figure 7-1

Selected Surveys of Employer-Sponsored Training in Canada since 1963

		Sponsor	Sample	Focus
CLMPC High-Tech Survey (CLMPC-HTS)	1989	Canadian Labour Market and Productivity Centre	822 "high-tech" firms	Employer-sponsored formal training
CLMPC Training Survey (CLMPC-TS)	1987-89	Canadian Labour Market and Productivity Centre	960 full-time employees	All training
Small Business Panel Survey (SBPS)	1988	Canadian Federation of Independent Business	1,500 small firms	All employer-sponsored training
Human Resource Training and Development Survey (HRTDS)	1987	Statistics Canada, Employment and Immigration Canada	7,321 firms	Employer-sponsored formal training
Adult Training Survey (ATS)	1984-85	Statistics Canada, Employment and Immigration Canada	93,000 individuals	Formal educational activity for employment-related purposes
Survey of Training in Canadian Industries (STCI)	1984-85	Employment and Immigration Canada	7,652 establishments	Employer-sponsored formal training
Survey of Adult Education (SAE)	1983	Statistics Canada and Secretary of State	92,000 individuals	Employer-sponsored adult education
Survey of Skill Development Leave Programs (SSDLP)	1982	Skill Development Leave Task Force, Employment and Immigration Canada	340 firms	Employer-sponsored leave for skill development
Human Resources Survey (HRS)	1979	Economic Council of Canada	1,354 establishments	All employer-sponsored training
Survey of Educational Leave and Training and Development (SELTD)	1978	Commission of Inquiry on Educational Leave and Productivity, Labour Canada	1,471 establishments	Employer-sponsored formal training
Employer-Sponsored Training Survey (ESTS)	1973	Statistics Canada	30,000 households	Employer-sponsored training
Survey of Training in Industry (STI-2)	1969-70	Statistics Canada, Labour Canada, Economic Council of Canada	41,585 establishments	Employer-sponsored formal training
Survey of Training in Industry (STI-1)	1965	Statistics Canada, Labour Canada, Economic Council of Canada	11,900 establishments	Employer-sponsored formal training
Survey of Organized Training Programs (SOTP)	1963	Statistics Canada, Labour Canada, Economic Council of Canada	11,879 establishments	Employer-sponsored formal training

126 Employment in the Service Economy

Table 7-10

Incidence of Employer-Sponsored Training, Selected Surveys, Canada

	Firms providing training	Employees receiving training
	(Per cent)	
CLMPC High-Tech Survey (1989)	47.0	
CFIB Small Business Panel Survey (1988)[1]	68.3	
CLMPC Training Survey (1987-89)[1,2]		56.0
Human Resource Training and Development Survey (1987)	30.7	
Adult Training Survey (1984-85)[3]		11.3
Survey of Training in Canadian Industries (1984-85)	25.2	11.5
Survey of Adult Education (1983)[4]		6.2
Survey of Skill Development Leave Programs (1982)[5]	52.2	18.1
Human Resources Survey (1979)[1]	61.7	
Survey of Education Leave and Training and Development (1978)	23.0	15.1
Employer-Sponsored Training Survey (1973)[2]		7.9
Survey of Training in Industry (1969-70)	22.9	
Survey of Training in Industry (1965)	26.5	6.9
Survey of Organized Training Programs (1963)	16.8	19.3

1 Formal and informal training.
2 Full-time employees receiving training over a two-year period.
3 Only programs of more than four weeks duration included.
4 Survey of workers taking short-term training.
5 Only firms with at least 100 employees sampled.
SOURCE See Figure 7-1.

participating in the 1988 Small Business Panel Survey (SBPS) provided some form of training.[40] This latter incidence rate is particularly noteworthy given the over-representation of small firms in the SBPS sample. As we will see below, training activity tends to be directly related to establishment size. Over 80 per cent of the SBPS respondents reporting training indicated that they provided on-the-job training, much of it informal, suggesting that the incidence rate yielded by that survey would have been much lower if only formal training had been recognized.

The Training Decision

There are a variety of reasons why employers sponsor training for their workers. Naturally, the standard objective is to improve job performance. Within this overall goal, the reasons vary: a firm may have hired workers, introduced new technology, or simply want to increase productivity or product quality. As well, there are other, quite different reasons for firms to sponsor training, such as to comply with contractual or legislative obligations, and to offer employees an opportunity to develop their personal interests and abilities.

The Human Resource Training and Development Survey asked firms about the objectives of the training they offered. The responses indicate that 58 per cent hoped to improve job performance (Table 7-11). Most of the other significant motivations were also related to job performance in some way or another: at least one quarter of the respondents cited the need to keep employees informed of technical or procedural changes, orientation for new employees, meeting changing skill requirements, and upgrading workers for new positions. Providing an opportunity for employees to develop personal skills and knowledge was identified by 45 per cent of the training respondents. Factors not directly related to job performance – compliance with regulations, affirmative-action goals, and collective agreements, and assisting the relocation of workers to avoid layoffs – were cited relatively infrequently.[41]

From a policy perspective, it is probably of greater interest to understand the reasons why firms do not train.

Table 7-11

Training Objectives Identified by Firms Reporting Formal Training Programs, Canada, 1987

	Proportion of firms citing objective[1]
	(Per cent)
Helping current job performance	57.9
Personal skills and knowledge development	44.7
Keeping employees informed of technical/ procedural changes	31.0
Orientation of new employees	30.9
Meeting changing skill requirements	25.0
Helping employees qualify for future jobs in firm	24.8
Meeting regulatory requirements	14.6
Meeting affirmative-action goals	9.8
Assisting relocation of workers within firm	6.3
Meeting collective-bargaining requirements	2.2

1 Respondents marked all applicable objectives.
SOURCE Statistics Canada, the Human Resource Training and Development Survey, unpublished data.

Unfortunately, most of the available surveys do not provide empirical evidence on this issue. In theory, the classic deterrent to training has been "free-riding," where some firms choose not to invest in training, instead meeting skill requirements by poaching from firms that do. The result is a strong disincentive to train. Concern about this problem and its consequences for overall investment by industry in human-resource development has motivated some policy proposals in recent years; for example, a training tax that would largely eliminate the advantages of free-riding.

How important a deterrent to training is the free-rider problem? The evidence is inconclusive, and it appears that labour market conditions and the type of company are significant factors. In a very tight labour market, free-riding undoubtedly becomes more serious. In a survey conducted by the Ontario Premier's Council in the late 1980s (when unemployment rates were low in Ontario), 41 per cent of the firms reported that poaching was a serious problem; in high growth industries the figure was 58 per cent.[42] However, other surveys conducted when labour market conditions were not so tight present a very different picture. In the 1984-85 Survey of Training in Canadian Industries, only 1 per cent of the nontraining firms identified the risk of losing workers as a reason for not training, but in the 1979 Human Resources Survey, 17 per cent of the non-training establishments said that workers leaving during or after the training period was a deterrent. Obviously, with such a large range of estimates, it is difficult to draw a conclusion about the significance of free-riding.

Certainly, from the surveys that gathered data on deterrents, it is clear that there are other obstacles to providing training. Some firms simply do not have skill requirements that create a need for it; among STCI non-trainers, for example, 16 per cent responded that they did not train because they had few skilled jobs. As well, the surveys have consistently found that a significant number of non-trainers report that the resources required to sponsor formal training (in terms of money, personnel, or space) are a deterrent. According to both the CLMPC High-Tech Survey and the STCI, nearly 30 per cent of the firms who did not provide formal programs said their skill-development needs were better met by informal training.

What Firms Provide Training?

A number of surveys examined the level of training activity by industry and by firm size. There appears to be a relatively consistent ranking by industry; however, the interindustry differences are not particularly large. Firms in manufacturing and in financial and business services typically have the highest incidence rates; among HRTDS respondents, for example, these industries led with 38 per cent and 37 per cent reporting formal training programs, respectively. Construction, and transportation and communications tend to have relatively low proportions of firms sponsoring formal training: the incidence rates among HRTDS respondents in these industries were 23 per cent and 22 per cent, respectively. According to the CLMPC High-Tech Survey, the "high-tech" sector (including various manufacturing and, to a lesser extent, service industries) is comparatively active in terms of training; 47 per cent of the firms reported that they had sponsored formal programs in 1989.

There is strong evidence that human-resource development is most prevalent among large firms. This is true whether formal or informal training is considered. The SBPS, which included both, found that 67 per cent of firms with fewer than 20 employees provided training, while the corresponding figures for those with 20-49 employees and with 50 or more workers were 75 and 84 per cent, respectively. In the CLMPC High-Tech Survey, the formal training incidence rates were 37 per cent for small firms (less than 100 employees), 64 per cent for medium-sized firms (100-999 employees), and 93 per cent for large firms (1,000 or more employees).

The Human Resources Training and Development Survey yields a similar picture. Among respondents with fewer than 10 employees, only slightly more than one quarter reported formal training programs, with the incidence rate increasing for larger firms until it reached 89 per cent for employers with 500 or more workers (Table 7-12). As well, a disproportionate share of the overall training expenditure was made by large firms; while respondents with at least 100 employees represented only 1 per cent of the HRTDS sample, they accounted for 60 per cent of the total money spent. The average expenditure per company was also directly related to firm size.

While these results demonstrate the relationship between firm size and training activity, they do not necessarily indicate that the commitment to human-resource development is greater in large companies. In other words, the higher incidence rates and expenditures may simply reflect differences in the scale of operation. In order to control for firm size, we estimated the training expenditure per employee from the HRTDS data; as Table 7-12 shows, the relationship between size and training activity becomes less clear. In fact, the greatest expenditure per employee was reported by firms in the smallest size-category (less than 10 employees). It is difficult to interpret this result, since it may reflect the fact that small companies cannot benefit from

Table 7-12

Training Activity, by Firm Size, Canada, 1987

	Proportion reporting formal training	Distribution of Employees	Distribution of Training expenditures	Average expenditures Per company	Average expenditures Per worker
	(Per cent)			(Dollars)	
Number of employees					
Less than 10	26.6	82.6	19.6	444	408
10-99	48.3	16.4	19.9	2,270	181
100-499	73.3	0.9	10.0	20,457	147
500 or more	88.8	0.1	50.3	647,848	268
Total	30.7	100.0	100.0	1,872	242

SOURCE Estimates by the Economic Council of Canada, based on Statistics Canada, the Human Resources Training and Development Survey.

---

economies of scale available to larger employers. Relatively high per employee expenditures were also reported by the largest size-category (500 or more workers), and the lowest amounts were reported by firms in the middle range.

Which Employees Receive Training?

Training sponsored by employers tends to be concentrated among certain types of workers – typically those in well-paid and high-skilled jobs who already have relatively high levels of human capital. Undoubtedly, this reflects employers' decisions about where the returns on their training investments would be greatest; however, it also reflects the fact that human-resource development within industry generally has not created training opportunities for the majority of the work force.

This concentration of training is quite evident, for example, from the Adult Training Survey, which provides considerable detail about the characteristics of workers who undertook formal training activities in 1984-85. According to the ATS results, participation rates were higher for men than for women, and for younger than for older employees. The proportion of workers receiving training was greatest among those with postsecondary education and those in professional and technical occupations.[43]

The CLMPC Training Survey gathered data in 1987-89 on who receives employer-sponsored training (Table 7-13). For the most part, it leads to the same conclusions as those that emerge from the ATS. One exception is gender: females were slightly more likely than males to report some training, although the male rate was higher when only longer-term training (20 weeks or more) was considered.[44] Looking at other worker characteristics, the probability of receiving training was greatest for younger workers, full-time employees, those in white-collar occupations, and workers with relatively high household incomes and advanced levels of educational attainment.

International Comparisons

How does Canadian industry's training performance compare with those of other advanced economies? Although it is almost impossible to make absolute comparisons between countries with quite different institutions, we have tried to assemble some comparative measures of training in industry for Canada and a selection of other countries. These indicators, which are summarized in Table 7-14, come from various sources; they are not comprehensive, complete, or perfectly comparable across nations. Nevertheless, they do provide some indication of where to situate Canada's industrial training performance within an international context.

Generally, these figures indicate that Canada's performance does not compare favourably with those of other countries. Looking first at private-sector expenditures on training and education relative to total output, Canada ranks last of the six countries included. According to this measure, U.S. relative expenditures are more than double Canada's, with Japan, Germany, and the United Kingdom standing far above the North American levels. One type of training

Table 7-13

Characteristics of Employees Receiving Job Training, Canada, March 1987 to March 1989

	Proportion reporting	
	Some training	More than 20 days of training
	(Per cent)	
All employees	56	22
Sex		
Males	54	23
Females	57	20
Age		
18-29	65	26
30-44	56	22
45-59	45	15
60 and over	33	16
Employment status		
Full-time	57	23
Part-time	42	4
Occupation		
Professional and administrative	63	26
Technical	55	25
Office, sales, and service	65	23
Skilled and semiskilled	47	19
Unskilled	43	8
Household income in thousands of dollars		
Less than 15	51	17
15-25	51	20
25-35	58	22
35 and more	57	23
Schooling		
0-8 years	34	12
9-13 years	52	21
14 years and over	63	24
University degree	64	20

SOURCE The Canadian Labour Market and Productivity Centre Training Survey, 1989.

for which there are relatively good international statistics is apprenticeship training. That form of training is the strength of the German vocational development system; the number of apprentices there is at least five times that in Canada or in any of the other countries.

A more subjective comparison of the strength of training in industry in various countries was made by the Ontario Premier's Council in its 1988 report, *Competing in the New Global Economy*. Its conclusion was that the training commitment in Canada (along with the United States) was significantly below those of the other countries considered. In terms of the support given by employers to training, both Canada and the United States were rated far below Germany and Japan. While the Canadian (and American) disadvantage relative to Sweden appears to be less, note that government support for training in industry in that country was assessed as "strong" relative to our "weak" evaluation.

Government-Sponsored Training

As the Swedish case demonstrates, governments can also shape a nation's training infrastructure. First, they can support employer-based human-resource development in various ways. Second, and typically the greater policy focus, they are the major player in providing training opportunities for workers who are unemployed, who are at risk of becoming unemployed, or who in some way do not have a strong attachment to a particular employer. In the remainder of this chapter, we will consider the recent activities of Canadian governments – federal and provincial – in providing opportunities for workers to develop employment-related skills.

The Federal Government and Skills Training[45]

Federal government intervention in the labour market includes unemployment insurance, training, job creation, and the national employment agency, as well as special programs targeted to women, young people, older workers, and other groups. Federal financial involvement is substantial; in 1988/89 it represented slightly over 2 per cent of Canada's gross domestic product (Table 7-15). This relative expenditure on labour market programs is slightly below that made by the major countries of western Europe (excluding the United Kingdom),[46] and well above the U.S. and Japanese levels. (While comparable figures are not available for provincial programs, it is likely that, given the decentralized nature of labour market policy in this country, Canada's ranking internationally in terms of public expenditures would be even higher than that indicated in Table 7-15 if all levels of government were included.)

Table 7-15 also presents an international comparison of how labour market expenditures are allocated among income maintenance, training, job creation, and a miscellaneous category which includes special programs for the

Table 7-14

Training Indicators, Selected Countries and Dates, 1982-87

	Private sector expenditures on training and education as a proportion of GDP[1]	Apprentices as a proportion of employment (1987)	Support for training in industry by Employers[2]	Support for training in industry by Government
	(Per cent)			
Canada	0.25	1.1	weak	weak
France	0.48	1.0	..	..
West Germany	1.96	7.1	strong	weak
Japan	1.40	..	strong	weak
Sweden	..	..	modest	strong
United Kingdom	2.17	1.4	..	..
United States	0.66	0.3	weak	weak

1 Data are for 1987 for Canada, the United States, and the United Kingdom; 1985 for France; 1984 for Japan; and 1982 for Germany.
2 Includes apprenticeship training.
SOURCE Based on Wayne Simpson and David Stambrook, "Employer-based training policy in Canada," paper for Employment and Immigration Canada, draft, November 1989; Canadian Labour Market and Productivity Centre, "Apprenticeship," Part 4, Report of the CLMPC Task Forces on the Labour Market Development Strategy, 1990; and Ontario Premier's Council, *Competing in the New Global Economy* (Toronto: Queen's Printer of Ontario, 1988).

Table 7-15

Public Expenditures on Labour Market Programs, Selected Countries and Years, 1988-90

	Year	As a proportion of GDP	Income maintenance[1]	Training[2]	Job creation[3]	Other[4]	Total
			(Per cent)				
Canada	1988/89	2.1	75.6*	12.7	1.8	9.8	100.0
France	1988	2.9	71.8	17.4	4.3	6.1	100.0
West Germany	1989	2.3	57.1	14.8	8.5	19.6	100.0
Japan	1989/90	0.5	66.5	5.3	20.2	6.7	100.0**
Sweden	1989/90	2.4	28.9	21.8	9.6	39.8	100.0
United Kingdom	1989/90	1.7	58.1	29.0	2.6	10.3	100.0
United States	1989/90	0.6	62.1	16.0	6.5	15.4	100.0

*Sickness, maternity, and retirement UI benefits are excluded. Training UI benefits are included under training, and job creation UI benefits are included under job creation.
**Estimate only, therefore figures do not add to 100.
1 Includes payments for early retirement except in Canada, Japan, and the United Kingdom. These are generally fairly small except for France where they constitute 28 per cent of total labour market expenditures.
2 Includes training programs aimed at youth in France, West Germany, the United Kingdom, and the United States.
3 Includes job creation programs aimed specifically at youth, except Germany and Japan.
4 Mainly administration costs and costs of programs for the disabled, except in Canada where there is no program specifically aimed at the disabled. In Sweden, programs for the disabled constitute 30 per cent of total labour market expenditures.
SOURCE Estimates by the Economic Council of Canada, based on Organisation for Economic Co-operation and Development, *Labour Market Policies for the 1990s*, Paris, OECD, 1990.

disabled as well as administrative costs. Canada's labour market policies have emphasized income maintenance, mostly through the Unemployment Insurance (UI) system. In 1988/89, this category accounted for three quarters of the expenditures at the federal level. While income maintenance is also the most important cost component for the other countries (with the exception of Sweden), none is as high proportionally as Canada's.

Canada places less emphasis on "active" strategies, notably training and job creation, than do the other countries, particularly Sweden and Germany. Focusing specifically on training, these expenditures represented slightly less than 13 per cent of all federal spending on labour market programs in 1988/89. This percentage is significantly above the figure for Japan and below all other shares. Note that in Japan the base (in terms of relative public labour market expenditures) is much lower, indicating a further diminished government role in skill development in that country; however, as we have seen, Japanese industry plays a substantially greater role in training than does Canada's industry.

The strong orientation of federal labour market policy towards income maintenance has been the subject of considerable discussion in recent years. While major differences of opinion exist with respect to the role of unemployment insurance, there does appear to be a fair degree of consensus that public policy must become more "active" in the sense of supporting workers in becoming employable in the long term, particularly through training.[47] Certainly this is the position expressed by the federal government in its April 1989 policy paper, *Success in the Works*.[48] Nevertheless, the share of federal labour market spending allocated to training actually decreased slightly in the last half of the 1980s (despite declines in unemployment rates that reduced the demand for income-maintenance funding) from 13.4 per cent in 1985/86 to 12.7 per cent in 1988/89. For all of the other countries, the relative share accounted for by training increased in these years.[49]

Overall federal expenditures on training were slightly more than $1.7 billion in 1989/90. This money is essentially spent through two programs: the Canadian Jobs Strategy (CJS) and Unemployment Insurance, with the former accounting for over 85 per cent of the total. The CJS was introduced in 1985 as the umbrella structure for federal government labour market initiatives. The stated intention of the strategy was to provide programs that were flexible and responsive to market needs. It was meant to encourage competition among suppliers of training (in contrast to the previous situation where federal training dollars were predominantly directed towards provincial community colleges). The other important feature of the CJS was its focus on those most in need.

The Canadian Jobs Strategy is organized into six programs:

1 Job Development focuses on the needs of the long-term unemployed;

2 Job Entry is targeted at the entry of young people and the reentry of women into the work force;

3 Skill Shortages assists employers facing occupational skill shortages;

4 Skill Investment is addressed to workers threatened by technological or market changes;

5 Community Futures supports a range of development activities in economically depressed communities; and

6 Innovations supports pilot and demonstration projects designed to develop employment.

How have these programs contributed to the skill development of the Canadian work force? Unfortunately, the CJS data are organized on the basis of the six constituent programs rather than the activity undertaken, and while training is an important aspect of each of the programs, and the most important aspect of many, none is exclusively concerned with training. In our analysis of the CJS, we make the assumption that all of the expenditures are on training, with the exception of the Challenge option of Job Entry which clearly emphasizes employment creation.[50] Given that job creation, as well as counselling, adjustment assistance, and a range of other activities take place under the CJS umbrella, this assumption will lead to some overstatement of the strategy's actual contribution to skill development.[51]

Table 7-16 shows the annual level of CJS expenditures (in 1989 dollars) in 1986/87, the first complete fiscal year for the strategy, and 1989/90, the most recent year for which data are available. The first point to note is that total expenditures in real terms declined over this period; funding for the programs was more than $150 million lower in 1989/90 than it was in 1986/87. A major reason for this decrease was the substantial decline in expenditures on Job Development (targeted at the long-term unemployed); indeed, real annual expenditures for this program were more than twice as great in 1986/87 than in 1989/90. While funding for the other components did increase in real terms, the magnitude of these gains did not compare to the decrease for job development. Particularly notable is the very modest increase for skill shortages, a program which would be especially useful as labour markets tighten; while expenditures on this program did increase by 23 per cent in 1986/87 and 1987/88, they have only risen slightly since then.

Evaluations undertaken for the federal government offer mixed reviews of the effects of participation in the two largest CJS components on the subsequent employability and earnings of participants. An assessment of Job Development found clear improvements in employability and real wage gains in just one of three program options studied.[52] The evaluation of Job Entry was somewhat more favourable; positive impacts were identified for two of the three program options analysed.[53] However, even when sophisticated program evaluations are carried out, caution must be exercised in interpreting the results. What appear to be effects of training may, in fact, be the result of "unobservable" factors for which it is impossible to control. As well, evaluations such as those carried out for the federal government are based on relatively short-term follow-ups and cannot offer information on long-term effects.

Putting aside questions of evaluation, the major limitation of the CJS as an instrument for human-resource development is its selective targeting. As we have noted, the strategy is explicitly targeted at those most in need; about two thirds of the approximately 300,000 people participating in CJS programs in 1988/89 – excluding Challenge – had experienced long-term unemployment or problems entering the labour market, or were threatened by technological or market changes. Targeting available funds at these groups may well be the most appropriate way to allocate CJS resources; however, the CJS cannot be considered a human-resource development option for most Canadian workers.

The other major avenue for federal involvement in training is the UI system. Typically, UI claimants must be available for work and, as such, cannot normally undertake training on any significant basis. Section 26 of the Unemployment Insurance Act, however, does provide for claimants to obtain training in certain circumstances. In these situations, unemployed workers continue to receive their benefits and may also have their training costs paid for. One objective of the recent reforms to the Unemployment Insurance Act is to make training a more important option for claimants. To this end, the proportion of the UI fund allocated for training and other "developmental" purposes (job creation and work sharing) will be raised significantly.[54]

Until now, Section 26 activity has represented a minor aspect of the UI system. In 1989/90, about 85,000 UI beneficiaries received training under Section 26, with total expenditures amounting to slightly less than $300 million. In terms of both participants and costs, this represented about 2.5 per cent of the overall program. Moreover, the relative importance of training within the UI system did not increase during the 1980s; real expenditures remained between $220 million and $300 million throughout the decade. In fact, Section 26 activity accounted for a slightly higher proportion of beneficiaries and benefits just prior to the 1981-82 recession than it does now; during the recession, the shares of both dropped by about 1 percentage point and they have remained at that lower level since then (Chart 7-8).

The minor role played by training within the UI system is the result of a number of factors. We have already mentioned the budget ceiling for developmental uses of the UI fund. In addition, there have been restrictions regarding access to training for claimants and the choice of courses available. In fact, apprentices collecting UI benefits while on block release make up a large part of the Section 26 clientele, accounting for 49 per cent of the individuals receiving training benefits who started their claim period in 1989. It is not surprising, then, that the demographic profile of apprentices – essentially young men – dominates the demographic profile of claimants who receive benefits under Section 26. About 64 per cent of UI training beneficiaries in 1989/90 were male, compared to only 53 per cent

Table 7-16

Canadian Jobs Strategy Annual Expenditures, by Program, 1986/87 – 1989/90[1]

	1986/87	1987/88	1988/89	1989/90*
(Millions of 1989 dollars)				
Job Development	937	647	504	462
Job Entry	256	401	388	394
Skill Shortages	208	255	258	267
Skill Investment	55	71	85	96
Community Futures	72	78	123	140
Innovations	17	39	40	32
Subtotal	1,545	1,485	1,399	1,391
Challenge (Job Entry)	132	133	134	128
Total CJS	1,677	1,618	1,533	1,519

*Estimated.
1 Fiscal years, beginning April 1.
SOURCE Estimates by the Economic Council of Canada, based on Employment and Immigration Canada, Annual Reports, and unpublished figures.

Chart 7-8

Training Component of Unemployment Insurance Benefits and Beneficiaries,[1] Canada, 1978-89

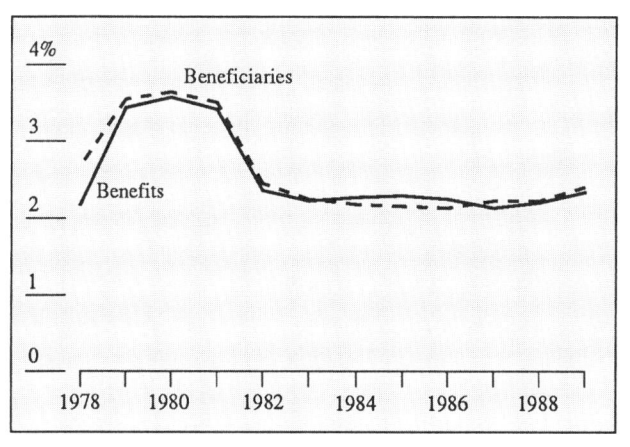

1 Based on annual monthly average.
SOURCE Estimates by the Economic Council of Canada, based on Statistics Canada, Cat. 73-202S.

of all beneficiaries, and those under 35 years of age were over-represented (Chart 7-9). As a result of the restrictions in its application, then, the training option within UI has tended to serve a very limited group of Canadian workers.

Chart 7-9

Distribution of Unemployment Insurance Training Beneficiaries[1] and Total Beneficiaries by Age, Canada, 1989/90

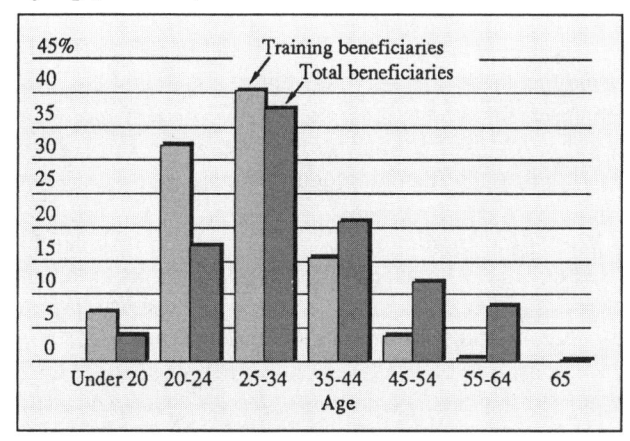

1 Based on annual monthly average.
SOURCE Estimates by the Economic Council of Canada, based on Statistics Canada, Cat. 73-001.

Provincial Governments and Skills Training

The provinces, with constitutional jurisdiction over all levels of education, play a critical role in human-resource development. Most obviously, their primary, secondary, and postsecondary school systems shape Canada's future work force. Also, their own labour market programs include training and adult education initiatives. The activities sponsored by each province vary considerably, making it impossible to reduce the provincial experience to a singular description. While we have not conducted a comprehensive analysis of all provincially sponsored training efforts, we have researched developments in a selection of provinces. We found that the awareness of the economic importance of skill formation was enhanced in all jurisdictions in the 1980s; however, differences in provincial economies, including differences in available resources, have led to significant variations in how much the provinces have done in this area.

An Economic Council review of labour market policies in Newfoundland and New Brunswick reveals that the constraints faced by small provinces in developing a training strategy are considerable.[55] It should be noted that there are some important differences between these two provinces, especially the focus in Newfoundland in recent years on preparing for the labour demands of the Hibernia project. Prior to the 1980s, human-resource development represented a very minor policy area in Newfoundland and New Brunswick; in both jurisdictions it was essentially limited to a small postsecondary education system and apprenticeship training. Certainly, during the past decade, the emphasis on training and adult education in Newfoundland and New Brunswick has increased and policies have been reorganized to reflect changes in industrial structure and the composition of the labour force. Both provinces have gone through major policy reviews, established strategic planning functions, and expanded and diversified their postsecondary and vocational training systems.

However, the scarcity of resources in government and industry severely limit the ability of the Newfoundland and New Brunswick governments to develop and implement provincial policies. Consequently, they must rely heavily on federal funding to directly and indirectly support their training infrastructures. While the general response to the Canadian Jobs Strategy, and especially the flexibility it offers, has been positive in Newfoundland and New Brunswick, it has created some difficulties. For example, the relatively short-term orientation of the CJS training programs often does not deal with the long-term structural problems that exist in these provinces.[56] But the most serious problems associated with the federal strategy for policymakers in Newfoundland and New Brunswick have involved funding.

Prior to the introduction of the CJS in 1985, federal training support to the provinces was overwhelmingly concentrated in the "direct" purchase of seats in community colleges. An explicit objective of the new strategy has been to designate more of these funds to "third parties" – employers, and industry and community associations – and less to the colleges directly. Direct federal expenditures dropped from nearly $19 million in 1984/85 in each province to $10.4 million in New Brunswick and $12.4 million in Newfoundland in 1988/89 (Table 7-17). While third-party sponsors may themselves buy training at the colleges, these "indirect" purchases have not made up for the decline in direct purchases in these provinces. In New Brunswick, for example, indirect training purchases in public institutions amounted to $4.4 million in 1988/89; when this figure is added to the $10.4 million in direct purchases, the total amount of federal funds received by the colleges was still well below pre-CJS levels.

A major problem is the fact that these provincial economies are dominated by small employers in seasonal industries that are less likely to invest in human-resource development, and therefore do not generate much demand for third-party funding from the federal government.[57] In the absence of this impetus, federal training funds have dropped significantly in both provinces, despite increased awareness of the economic importance of a skilled work force.[58]

Table 7-17

Direct Federal Government Training Expenditures[1] **in New Brunswick and Newfoundland, 1982/83 – 1988/89**

	New Brunswick	Newfoundland
	(Millions of dollars)	
1982/83	16.2	18.7
1983/84	17.0	18.9
1984/85	18.6	18.4
1985/86	17.6	17.8
1986/87	15.8	16.0
1987/88	13.4	13.9
1988/89	10.4	12.4

1 Purchase of seats in provincial colleges and training institutions.
SOURCE Elizabeth Beale, "Labour market policies in two eastern provinces: Newfoundland and Labrador, and New Brunswick," a paper prepared for the Economic Council of Canada, Ottawa, 1990.

The Council also commissioned a review of labour market policy in three western provinces: Manitoba, Alberta, and British Columbia.[59] These provinces also raised the priority of human-resource development and reevaluated their approaches in this area in the 1980s. However, the experiences in these provinces differ from those of the Atlantic provinces in some important respects, including in terms of the general economic and labour market environment and the resource capacity to develop a training infrastructure.

All three western provinces have now established a range of human-resource development initiatives. Increasingly, their philosophical approach is that training must be a shared responsibility among business, labour, government, individuals, and the educational institutions, and market responsiveness has therefore become a higher priority.

Traditionally, institutional training has been the cornerstone of these provinces' skill-development policies. During the 1980s, however, the colleges and training institutions changed in many respects. While training in the trades, especially for construction and the resource industries, continues to be important, course offerings have shifted somewhat to reflect the growth of services. The institutions have also tried to become more responsive in terms of delivering training to smaller and more remote communities; for example, British Columbia has instituted a remote-learning agency, Winnipeg's community college has established satellites in smaller communities, and Alberta's colleges have become involved in meeting the needs of major resource projects.

To some extent, these changes have been driven by the Canadian Jobs Strategy, just as they have been in Newfoundland and New Brunswick. Direct federal purchases from the colleges and training institutions declined by 39 per cent in Manitoba, Alberta, and British Columbia in the first three years after the implementation of the CJS. However, the western economy is able to generate more demand for institutional programs through third-party training than the Atlantic economy does.

Workplace training initiatives are most developed in Alberta, largely because the apprenticeship system in that province is among the most active in the country. While the three provinces have participated in human-resource development within industry in various ways other than apprenticeship training, the overall level of involvement has been somewhat limited. For most of the 1980s, the major policy instrument here was the use of wage-subsidy incentives for employers. Increasingly, however, British Columbia and Alberta have seen this approach as supporting only short-term, firm-specific skills development, and are moving towards a system of funding actual training costs.

With economies that are more subject to external competitive pressure and with greater resources, Manitoba, Alberta, and British Columbia have established a more developed and autonomous training infrastructure than New Brunswick and Newfoundland. In particular, the training institutions in the western jurisdictions have been better placed to respond to and benefit from the federal policy changes associated with the introduction of the Canadian Jobs Strategy. Nevertheless, according to our review, some skill-related issues are still not addressed very effectively in the western provinces; for example, employer-based initiatives tend to be limited, there are basic literacy needs, and training for disadvantaged groups remains a concern. However, in the current economic environment, with the decline in federal funding and the competitive economic pressures within the region, it is difficult for these provinces to make further headway in developing their human resources.

Not surprisingly, Quebec and Ontario have the most comprehensive training programs of all of the provinces. Certainly, even in these large jurisdictions, Ottawa's dollars are an important source of funding. As well, provincial initiatives in Quebec and Ontario tend to be developed as complements to the federal government's programs. Increasingly, however, these two provinces appear to be interested in establishing their own approaches to skills development and labour market policy. For example, the Quebec government introduced a training tax credit in the 1990 budget, which is a marked departure from prevailing federal policy. Under this new arrangement, Quebec employers will be eligible to receive a refundable tax credit on costs associated with establishing a human-resource development plan.

To get a sense of the breadth of the training initiatives in a large province, we have reviewed the current situation in Ontario. The human-resource development infrastructure in Ontario was built around a very extensive community college system. In recent years, the province has also developed a more eclectic training approach. The 1989/90 expenditures on training programs by the Ministry of Skills Development are set out in Table 7-18. Overall, the ministry spent about $270 million on a wide range of programs.

The initiatives identified in Table 7-18 reflect the dual focus of Ontario's training effort: skills development in the workplace and training for youth. The major skills-development programs, introduced as part of the Ontario Training Strategy in 1986, are the Training Consulting

Table 7-18

Ontario Training Expenditures,[1] by Program, Canada, 1989/90

	Expenditures
	(Millions of dollars)
Industrial training[2]	
Training consulting service	17.9
Ontario skills	33.7
Trades updating	4.0
Basic skills	25.6
Ontario Training Corporation	6.8
Technician/technologists skills updating	3.6
Transitions	4.0
Apprenticeship (administration and seat purchases)	23.7
Apprentice Tool Fund	4.4
Special support allowances	2.3
Special Projects Fund	1.3
Community industrial training committees	2.3
Ontario training trust funds	2.0
International marketing interns	2.0
Youth/community training	
Futures	90.3
Summer employment	5.4
Summer experience	10.5
Youth employment counselling centres	6.5
Environmental youth corps	11.0
Youth venture capital	2.3
Student venture capital	0.9
Community literacy	6.0
Community Action Fund	–
Ontario Help Centres	1.5
Total	268.0

1 As funded by the Ministry of Skills Development. Training undertaken in other ministries (for example training for the disabled in the Ministry of Community and Social Services) is excluded.
2 A certain amount of industrial training is done under youth training programs. Including such training, industrial training represents over one half of the ministry's total budget.
SOURCE Estimates by the Economic Council of Canada, based on Ontario Premier's Council, *People and Skills in the New Global Economy* (Toronto: Queen's Printer of Ontario, 1990), and information from the Ontario Ministry of Skills Development.

Service, which assists small and medium-sized businesses to establish human-resource development plans; Ontario Skills, which supports training in these firms; and Basic Skills, which concentrates on literacy and numeracy.[60] These complement the longstanding apprenticeship system. Since then, a number of smaller workplace training initiatives have also been introduced in Ontario, including Transitions, which supports the re-employment of older workers, and the Technicians and Technologists Skills Updating program. Youth training is dominated by Futures, which is directed towards preparing disadvantaged young people for employment. With expenditures of $90 million in 1989/90, Futures is the largest single program in Ontario and comparable in size to some of the CJS programs.

The Ontario government has recently been engaged in a comprehensive review of provincial human-resource policy through the Premier's Council, and Vision 2000, which focused on the future of the community college system.[61] Their recommendations call for major changes in the province's skills-development infrastructure. The net result of these proposals, if they are implemented, would be a more comprehensive "made-in-Ontario" approach to training which enlarges the province's sponsorship of human-resource development.

Conclusion

In this chapter, we have seen that human capital matters a great deal and that its importance is increasing. As Canada moves into an information-based, service economy, both individual outcomes in the labour market and the national economic performance will be significantly influenced by the skills that we possess.

The infrastructure for developing human resources, then, is a critical dimension of a nation's economic profile. That infrastructure includes both education systems – from the primary to the postsecondary levels – and training systems sponsored by industry and governments, which are often closely linked to the education sector. In this chapter, we have focused on the training component and considered the activities of Canadian employers and governments in the area of human-resource development.

Some parts of the work force appear to be fairly well served now. For example, highly educated, young, male professionals employed by large firms obtain a disproportionate amount of employer-based training. Similarly, the groups targeted by the Canadian Jobs Strategy as facing severe employment difficulties receive a large percentage of the federal government training funds. As well, the biggest provinces are able to use their resources to sponsor additional training within their jurisdictions. However, for the majority of the work force there is little, if any, possibility for skills development. In the final analysis, our review suggests that Canada's training infrastructure compares unfavourably to those of many other nations, where there is greater access to skill formation either through employer- or state-sponsored programs. This does not augur well for those individuals who do not have access to training opportunities, or for the long-run competitive position of the Canadian economy.

8 The Distribution of Earnings

Important changes have taken place in the distribution of earnings in Canada over the past two decades. In particular, in a study with Statistics Canada, we found that earnings inequality and polarization increased between 1967 and 1986. Our analysis reveals that these trends cannot be attributed to any significant degree to the shift to a service-based economy. We do conclude that changes in labour force composition – particularly the entry of the baby-boom generation and the increasing participation of women – partially explain the distributional changes. But in the final analysis we are unable to completely account for the increase in earnings disparities.

To set the stage for our examination of distributional trends, we begin with a brief look at trends in compensation levels. In real terms, overall labour income has stagnated in this country. Hourly wages and salaries – by far the major component of total labour compensation – peaked in Canada in 1976. Our analysis indicates that there have been some gains in supplementary labour income (compensation other than wages and salaries). However, the growth in this area has not been significant enough to offset the declines in real wages.

Trends in Compensation Levels

Labour compensation is made up of wages and salaries, and supplementary labour income (non-wage benefits). Traditionally, wages and salaries have been the dominant component, accounting for well over 90 per cent of total labour income. In the past two decades, however, supplementary labour income has become more important.

Wages and Salaries

Throughout the late 1960s and first half of the 1970s, Canadian workers enjoyed real gains in hourly wages and salaries of over 4 per cent per year (Chart 8-1).[1] However, after peaking in 1976, this wage trend levelled off; in fact, from 1976 to 1989, real wages actually declined by an annual average of 0.3 per cent.

What was the reason for this stagnation? Wage and salary trends can be explained in terms of two interrelated

Chart 8-1

Hourly Wages and Salaries, Canada, 1967-89

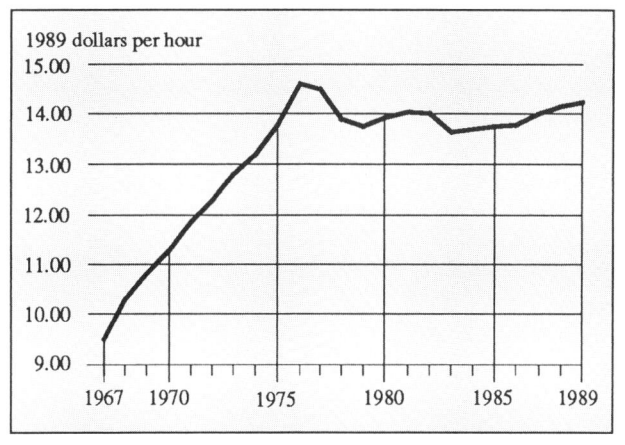

SOURCE   Calculations by the Economic Council of Canada, based on data from Statistics Canada, the Labour Force Survey, and data from the Labour Division.

factors: first, the growth in labour productivity, and second, labour's bargaining power and the resulting distribution of the income among the various contributors to the production process. Labour income was negatively affected by both of these factors during the past decade.

In theory, compensation levels are determined by the value of the output produced. Over the long run, therefore, one would expect wages and salaries and labour productivity to grow at about the same rate. Between 1967 and 1976, labour productivity grew at an annual rate of about 3 per cent per year (Chart 8-2),[2] which allowed for rapid wage growth during that period. However, since 1976, productivity growth has slowed appreciably, with annual increases averaging 1 per cent for the period to 1989. Inevitably, this has had a depressing impact on wage and salary growth.

The productivity slowdown, though, does not by itself explain the wage losses. During 1967-76, labour received wage increases that were greater than the significant productivity growth rates. In fact, wages and salaries grew at an average annual rate that was about one third higher than the gains in labour productivity. During the period 1976-89

Chart 8-2

Average Annual Growth Rates of Hourly Wages and Salaries, and Labour Productivity[1] (1989 dollars), Canada, 1967-76 and 1976-89

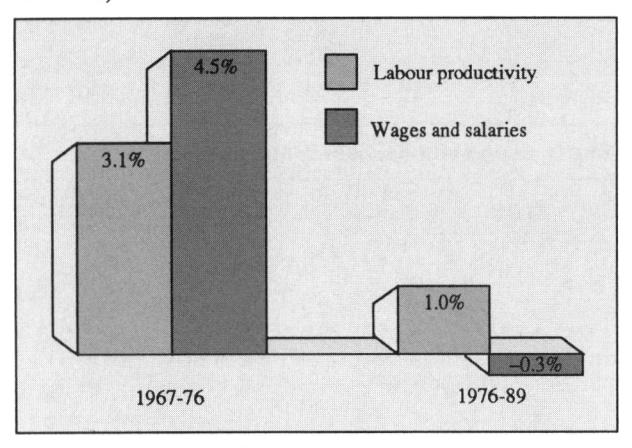

1967-76: Labour productivity 3.1%, Wages and salaries 4.5%
1976-89: Labour productivity 1.0%, Wages and salaries -0.3%

1 Total ouput per actual hour worked.
SOURCE Calculations by the Economic Council of Canada, based on data from Statistics Canada.

the relationship between wage and productivity trends reversed, with wages falling behind productivity.[3] An explanation for stagnant wage and salary growth, then, must also consider the apparent reduction in the ability of workers to capitalize fully on those productivity gains that have occurred since the mid-1970s. Indeed, evidence of the decline in labour's bargaining power is available from National Income and Expenditure Accounts data on the distribution of total domestic income. Between 1965 and the early 1970s, labour's share increased by about 2 percentage points; since 1975, however, it has declined by 5 percentage points.

Certainly, the rise in unemployment rates constitutes an important element of the explanation for the erosion in labour bargaining power. Before 1976, the aggregate unemployment rate in Canada had never been above 7 per cent (at least in the postwar period); since 1976, it has never been below it. When unemployment rates are high, workers are unlikely to make high wage demands, and when they do, employers generally have the capacity to resist them.

Chart 8-3

Employment Growth and Unionization Rates,[1] by Industry, Canada, 1981-89

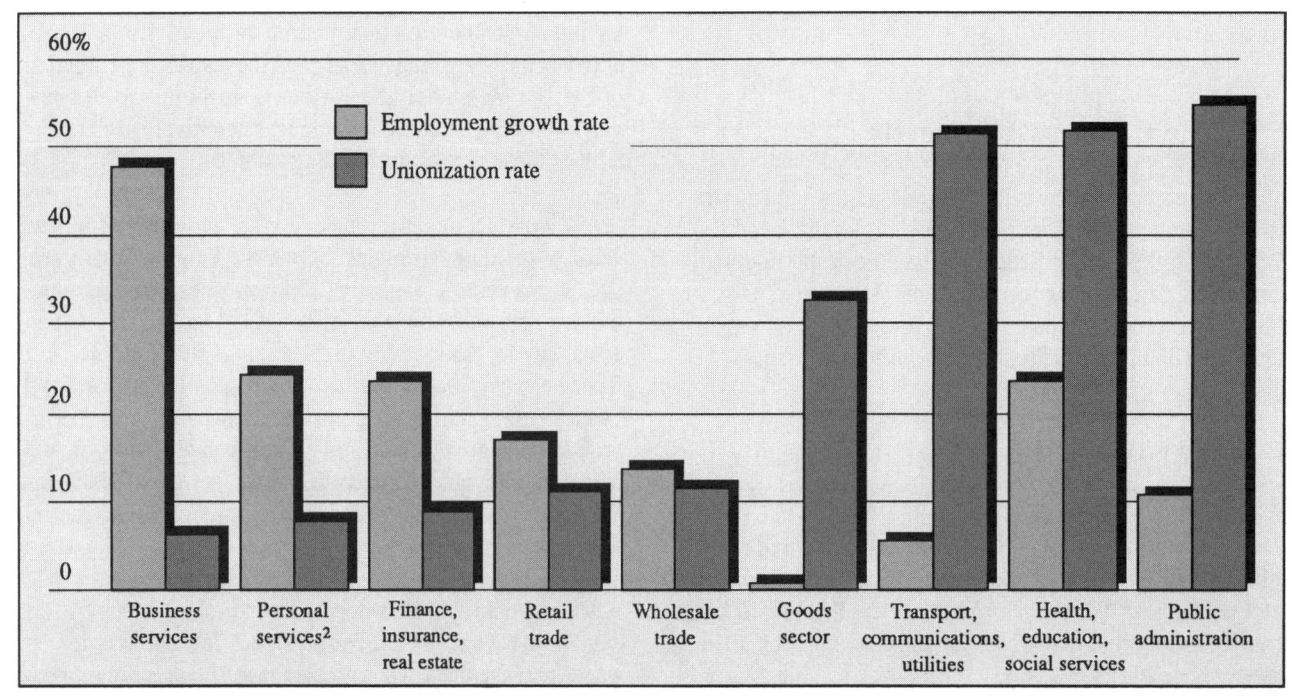

1 Unionization rates are for 1986.
2 Includes all traditional services except retail trade.
SOURCE Estimates by the Economic Council of Canada, based on data from Statistics Canada.

The coverage and bargaining power of unions also exert an effect on the ability of labour to capture real wage gains. Unions influence the wages of not only their members, but also of nonunionized workers indirectly through spill-over effects. Unionization levels in Canada have been stagnant and have even declined somewhat in recent years. One reason for this has been the concentration of employment growth in sectors with traditionally low rates of unionization. Of the six industry divisions that experienced significant employment gains in the 1980s, only one – health, education, and social services – has a high union density; the other five have unionization rates far below the national average (Chart 8-3). There is also evidence that since the recession of the early 1980s, union priorities have shifted and labour has increasingly used its bargaining "chips" to negotiate issues such as job security, rather than compensation.[4]

Finally, employment growth has generally been most rapid in the 1980s among groups of workers who are not well positioned to obtain wage increases. As we saw in Chapter 5, a large proportion of new jobs have been created in nonstandard work forms such as temporary, part-time, and contract work, in which hourly earnings (and fringe benefits) have always been relatively low. As well, and related to this, much of the job growth has taken place in small businesses (see Chapter 2), which typically offer lower levels of compensation than larger firms; in 1986, for example, the average hourly wage in firms with less than 20 employees was two thirds of the average wage in firms with more than 500 workers.[5] And employment expansion has also been rapid in such low-wage service industries as retail trade and personal services, an issue we will discuss later in this chapter.

Supplementary Labour Income

The other major aspect of labour compensation is the nonwage portion – supplementary labour income (SLI), or fringe benefits. Technically, "supplementary labour income" measures the value of the employer's contributions to various employee benefit plans – both private (for example, employer-sponsored pension and insurance plans) and public (Unemployment Insurance, Workers' Compensation, and the Canada/Quebec Pension Plans).[6]

There is a strong correlation between supplementary labour income and wage and salary income. This is evident from Table 8-1, which presents data on employer-provided benefits by industry (public benefits are not included here because they do not vary greatly by industry). While there are some exceptions, those industries with the highest hourly

Table 8-1

Hourly Wages and Salaries, and Supplementary Labour Income, by Industry, Canada, 1989

	Supplementary labour income	Wages and salaries
	(Dollars)	
Public administration	2.37	16.18
Nonagricultural primary industries	2.27	18.13
Transportation, communications, and utilities	2.13	16.56
Manufacturing	2.01	15.16
Health, education, and social services	1.77	15.01
Wholesale trade	1.42	16.69
Finance, insurance, and real estate	1.41	20.14
Construction	1.38	14.73
Business and personal services	0.85	12.47
Retail trade	0.79	9.23
Agriculture	0.10	6.44
All industries	1.49	14.22

SOURCE   Calculations by the Economic Council of Canada, based on data from Statistics Canada, the Labour Force Survey, and data from the Labour Division.

wages and salaries also tend to have the highest levels of employer-provided benefits. Benefit levels are greatest in public administration, followed by nonagricultural primary industries; transportation, communication and utilities; manufacturing; and health, education, and social services; these industries also have above-average wages.

Overall, supplementary labour income has become an increasingly important part of total labour compensation, nearly doubling its share between 1967 and 1989 from 5.6 to 9.5 per cent (Chart 8-4). Indeed, during the first half of that period (1967-77), it grew by 122 per cent, well over twice as much as did wage and salaries (Table 8-2). In the period 1977-89, when real wages and salaries declined by 2 per cent, supplementary labour income continued to grow, although only by 15.5 per cent. However, it represents a small part of total labour income and its growth over the past decade could not compensate for the fall in wages and salaries, so total income fell by 0.5 per cent over these years.[7]

Chart 8-4

Supplementary Labour Income as a Proportion of Total Labour Income, Canada, 1967-89

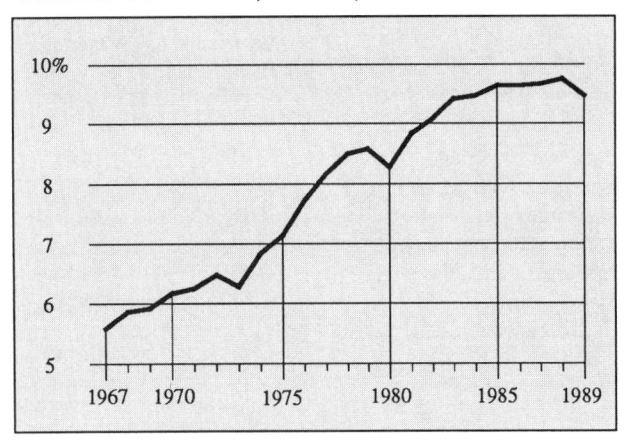

SOURCE Calculations by the Economic Council of Canada, based on data from Statistics Canada, the Labour Division.

Table 8-2

Growth in Hourly Labour Income,[1] by Source of Income, Canada, 1967-77 and 1977-89

	1967-77	1977-89
	(Per cent)	
Wages and salaries	47.8	–2.0
Supplementary labour income	122.4	15.5
Total labour income	51.9	–0.5

1 In 1989 dollars.
SOURCE Calculations by the Economic Council of Canada, based on data from Statistics Canada, the Labour Force Survey, and data from the Labour Division.

Trends in the Distribution of Earnings

The recent literature on trends in earnings distributions has been rather controversial. The debate during the 1980s was initially popularized by Robert Kuttner's article, "The declining middle," which appeared in 1983.[8] Kuttner argued that the shape of income distribution was being redrawn as a result of labour market polarization. Where previously the bulk of employment had been in middle-income jobs, it was increasingly being clustered at the upper and lower extremes. According to Kuttner, this was driven by a number of forces, including deindustrialization, globalization, and technological change, which were contributing to the demise of middle-earnings jobs in manufacturing, and the creation of high- and low-wage service-sector jobs.

Following the appearance of Kuttner's article, there was a substantial number of empirical tests of the "declining middle" thesis – particularly in the United States – which generated considerable disagreement.[9] A number of methodological issues, some of which we will touch upon later, muddied the waters further. The results of the more recent work have, for the most part, supported and in some cases even extended Kuttner's argument as it applies to the American experience.[10] It is now generally accepted that the share of total employment in jobs with mid-level earnings in the United States has decreased since the mid-1970s, and the share in jobs with low-level and high-level earnings has increased. Some analysts have found that, along with the polarization, there has been growing earnings inequality.[11] As well, certain studies have extended these distributional trends from individual earnings to the earnings of families and total family income.[12]

In Canada less attention has been paid to the issue. Early analyses were inconclusive, generally conceding a modest tendency towards increased earnings inequality and polarization,[13] or finding overall stability in family income inequality.[14] More recent work in Canada, however, has been more supportive of the declining middle/polarization thesis, particularly for individual earnings, but also to a lesser extent for total family income.[15] The degree of inequality of family income, however, appears to have remained relatively stable.[16]

While most researchers now agree that there has been some earnings polarization over the past two decades, there is no consensus regarding its causes. American studies, for example, can be organized into three groups: demand-side, supply-side, and cyclical. The initial emphasis, including Kuttner's, was on demand-side explanations – for example, the effect of technological innovation and changing global economic patterns in the shift in employment from medium-wage manufacturing jobs to low- and high-wage jobs in services. Empirical studies have offered relatively little support to the shift-to-services explanation, often finding, in fact, that the distributional changes were taking place in all industry groups.[17]

A more recent demand-side explanation sees changes in the way work is being organized as a cause of the declining middle.[18] This hypothesis is driven by the observation that, within most goods and service industries, employers are relying increasingly on nonstandard workers (see Chapter 5) and two-tier wage systems to reduce labour costs. Little empirical work has been undertaken to test this hypothesis.

Supply-side hypotheses focus on changes in the composition of the labour force rather than changes in the characteristics of jobs. In this view, the growing labour market participation of women, who traditionally have lower average wages and more polarized distributions than prime-aged males, is set out as a factor in the growing disparity in earnings. The research here has generally concluded that gender shifts can only partially account for the increased earnings disparity, which, in fact, has risen faster among men than women.[19] Another supply-side explanation is the theory of the maturation of the postwar baby-boom generation. According to this hypothesis, as the large numbers of baby boomers move into prime-age categories, competition for middle-level (and middle-earnings) positions increases, which depresses the wages these jobs offer. Though some researchers have found empirical support for this explanation,[20] most analysts see growing polarization and inequality of both earnings and total income in all age brackets.[21]

Explanations that focus on the distributional impacts of the business cycle see the declining middle, in effect, as a temporary, rather than a secular, phenomenon.[22] Recessions generally have a depressing effect on earnings, owing to layoffs and downward wage pressure; however, high earners with a lot of human capital and/or seniority are best able to protect themselves. Indeed, short-term analyses of the 1980s risk capturing fundamentally cyclical trends; that is, the distributional impacts of a recession/recovery phase. However, while earnings distributions clearly are affected by business conditions, research that uses long-term data and controls for cyclical effects has tended to find a secular decline in the middle-earnings group.[23]

To this point, the literature we have reviewed on growing earnings disparities has been restricted to Canada and the United States. Does the same trend characterize the Japanese and European economies? Comparable cross-national data sets are difficult to assemble and the problems increase when these databases extend to observations over a period of time. Indeed, most analyses compare distributions in various countries in a single year.[24] This cross-sectional evidence suggests the following ranking of countries, based on various inequality measures and income shares in various income strata: the United States, and perhaps Japan with the most unequal income distributions; Canada, the United Kingdom, Australia, and possibly Switzerland occupying a second stratum; West Germany and the Netherlands in a third; with the most equal distributions in Norway and Sweden.

In addition to Canada and the United States, we have only been able to satisfactorily document distributional trends over time for the United Kingdom.[25] The experience in that country is one of increased income inequality up to the early 1970s, a slight decline for both income and earnings disparities through most of the rest of that decade, and a significant increase during the 1980s. While the American experience follows this broad pattern, the reversal of the equalizing trend in that country occurred in the mid-1970s, rather than later in the decade.

Of this literature review three aspects are particularly relevant to this study. First, a consensus seems to be emerging that over the last two decades there has been increased earnings disparity and polarization in Canada, the United States, and also the United Kingdom. Second, there is a lack of agreement on the causes of the distributional trends, which has led to some controversy over whether the declining middle is a short-term or a more durable phenomenon. Demand-side explanations focusing on global economic patterns, technological change, the growth of services, and changes in work organization are more likely to see the changes as structural and relatively permanent in nature. On the other hand, supply-side hypotheses based on

---

Methodology of Income Distribution Analysis[1]

Type of income	• Earnings from employment plus self-employment • Total (money) income
Accounting period	• Annual • Hourly
Population	• ELFPs[2] • ELFP census families • All census families
Time period	• 1967, 1973, 1981, 1986 • 1951-67 and 1981-88
Measures	• Polarization: population share of earnings groups defined by distance from median • Inequality: Gini coefficient • Income shares of quintiles • Income cutoff of lowest and highest quintiles
Analytical techniques	• Descriptive • Standardization

1 See Appendix B for details.
2 Effective labour force participants – individuals earning at least 5 per cent of the average industrial wage.

demographic shifts lead to the view that the changes are to some extent temporary and self-correcting. As well, there are supporters of the view that cyclical factors, specifically the severe recession of the early 1980s, have been the major cause of the observed declining middle. Third, methodological issues are at the root of many of the disagreements surrounding the declining middle. Researchers have used a variety of data sources and types of measurements, all of which affect the analytical results. The methodology used by the Economic Council and Statistics Canada is summarized in the box on p. 141 (for more details, see Appendix B).

Results

The Economic Council-Statistics Canada study of income distribution upon which the present report is based draws primarily on data from Statistics Canada's Survey of Consumer Finances (SCF). For our purposes, this is a comprehensive database: the SCF offers information on annual income (and its component parts, including earnings) for individuals and for families; it also provides data on individual and family characteristics that are relevant for the study of income distribution trends. Our analysis used SCF data for 1967, 1973, 1981, and 1986.

Individual Earnings

We begin with descriptive evidence of trends in the earnings distribution of individuals in these years. As Table 8-3 shows, between 1967 and 1986, polarization increased among "effective labour force participants" (ELFPs), which includes all individuals with earnings of at least 5 per cent of average industrial earnings. The share of the work force in the middle stratum (those within 25 per cent of median earnings on either side) declined by 5.3 percentage points, and the shares of the lower and upper earnings strata increased by 3.0 and 2.2 percentage points, respectively.[26] Thus, of the "declining middle," nearly three fifths was redistributed into the lower group, and the remainder into the upper group. At the same time, the share of earnings held by those in the middle declined by 5.4 percentage points, a loss that was absorbed almost entirely by the upper earners.

The mean earnings of the lower stratum (relative to the population average) fell over the sample period by slightly over 2 percentage points, while those of the upper group rose nearly 4 percentage points (Table 8-4). In 1986, then, there was a larger upper group with higher average earnings than in 1967, and a larger lower group with smaller average earnings.

Reporting distributional trends for three strata has the virtue of descriptive simplicity; however, it does not offer much detail about where along the distribution the changes took place. The shifts in work force share are organized into more finely defined earnings levels in Chart 8-5. Here, earnings levels 1 and 2 make up the lower earnings group of Table 8-3; levels 3, 4, and 5 comprise the middle stratum,

Table 8-3

Earnings Distribution of ELFPs,[1] Canada, Selected Years, 1967-86

		Distribution by earnings stratum[2]								
		Work force				Earnings				Gini coefficient[3]
	Median	Lower	Middle	Upper	Total	Lower	Middle	Upper	Total	
	(1986 $)				(Per cent)					
1967	15,088	36.4	26.8	36.9	100.0	12.4	23.7	63.8	100.0	0.389
1973	17,285	37.2	23.7	39.1	100.0	12.0	20.1	67.9	100.0	0.407
1981	18,046	38.2	23.4	38.3	100.0	12.5	20.4	67.0	100.0	0.402
1986	17,395	39.4	21.5	39.1	100.0	12.5	18.3	69.2	100.0	0.418
					(Percentage points)					
Change		+3.0	−5.3	+2.2	...	+0.1	−5.4	+5.4	...	+0.029

1 Effective labour force participants – individuals earning at least 5 per cent of the average industrial wage.
2 Lower, middle, and upper strata consist of ELFPs earning 0-75, 75-125, and more than 125 per cent of the median, respectively.
3 The traditional measure of inequality which rises with the degree of inequality.
SOURCE Calculations by Statistics Canada and the Economic Council of Canada, based on Statistics Canada, Survey of Consumer Finances, unpublished data.

The Distribution of Earnings 143

Table 8-4

Relative Mean ELFP[1] Earnings,[2] by Earnings Stratum, Canada, Selected Years, 1967-86

	Earnings stratum[3]		
	Lower	Middle	Upper
	(Per cent)		
1967	34.1	88.4	172.9
1973	32.3	84.8	173.7
1981	32.7	87.2	175.1
1986	31.7	85.1	176.5

1 Effective labour force participants – individuals earning at least 5 per cent of the average industrial wage.
2 Mean earnings of each stratum as a proportion of the overall mean.
3 Lower, middle, and upper strata consist of ELFPs earning 0-75, 75-125, and more than 125 per cent of the median, respectively.
SOURCE Calculations by Statistics Canada and the Economic Council of Canada, based on Statistics Canada, Survey of Consumer Finances, unpublished data.

and 6 and 7 the upper level. All the work force share gains between 1967 and 1986 took place at the very extremes of the distribution; i.e., among individuals earning either less than 50 per cent or more than 150 per cent of the median. All of the losses were experienced by those earning within 50 per cent of the median on either side, with the losses rising with earnings level.[27]

Turning now to earnings inequality, from 1967 to 1986 the Gini coefficient rose by about 30 "basis" points (from 0.389 to 0.418), an amount which can be considered statistically significant. (For a description of the Gini coefficient, see Appendix B.)[28] The growing earnings inequality is graphically depicted in Chart 8-6, which portrays the 1967 and 1986 (cumulative) earnings distributions in the form of Lorenz curves. The diagonal straight line going from the lower left corner to the upper right corner describes a hypothetical situation of perfect income equality. In any given year, the actual distribution, as shown by the Lorenz curve, is more unequal the farther it is from the diagonal. The curve in 1986 indicates more inequality throughout the distribution than the 1967 curve.

Further insights into the distribution trends can be found in the analysis of population quintiles; this method arrays the work force into five equal groups according to earnings. The gap between the earnings of the lower and upper quintiles grew over the period under analysis (Table 8-5). Between 1967 and 1986, the upper earnings cutoff of the lowest quintile (or lowest fifth of the work force) fell from 37 to 30 per cent of the median; during the same years, the lower cutoff of the highest rose from 144 to 155 per cent of the median. Thus the gap between the highest and lowest fifths of the work force expanded by 18 points. In terms of earnings shares of the quintiles, everyone of the bottom three groups lost ground while both of the upper two gained. The result was a 3-percentage-point shift of the total

Chart 8-5

Change in Work Force Share by Detailed Earnings Level,[1] Canada, 1967-86

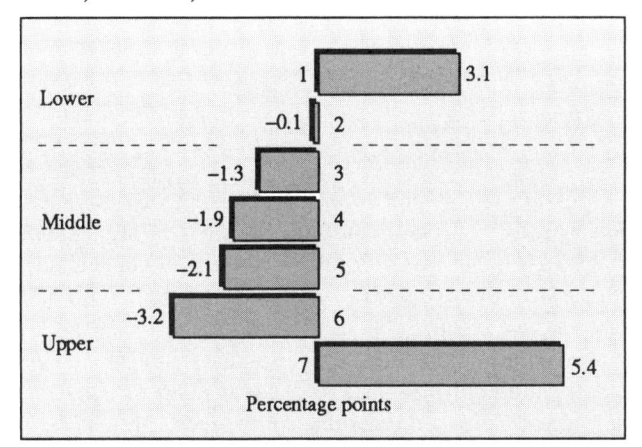

Level		Percentage points
Lower	1	3.1
	2	-0.1
	3	-1.3
Middle	4	-1.9
	5	-2.1
	6	-3.2
Upper	7	5.4

1 Levels 1-7 are less than 50 per cent, 50 per cent, 75-85 per cent, 85-115 per cent, 115-125 per cent, 125-150 per cent, and 150 per cent or more of the median, respectively.
SOURCE Calculations by Statistics Canada and the Economic Council of Canada, based on data from Statistics Canada.

Chart 8-6

Earnings Distribution – Lorenz Curves, Canada, 1967 and 1986

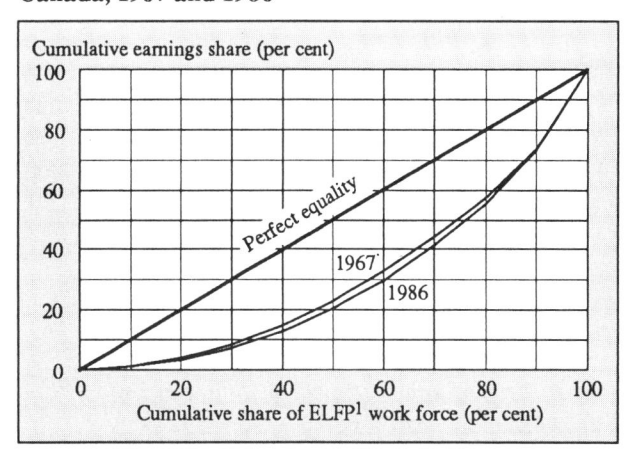

1 Effective labour force participants – individuals earning at least 5 per cent of the average industrial wage.
SOURCE Calculations by Statistics Canada and the Economic Council of Canada, based on Statistics Canada, Survey of Consumer Finances, unpublished data.

Table 8-5

Quintile[1] Measures of Changes in the Earnings Distribution of ELFPs,[2] Canada, Selected Years, 1967-86

	Earnings cutoffs as a proportion of median		Earnings share of	
	Ceiling of quintile 1	Floor of quintile 5	Bottom 3 quintiles	Top 2 quintiles
	(Per cent)			
1967	37	144	32.8	67.1
1973	33	150	31.0	69.0
1981	33	154	31.2	68.8
1986	30	155	29.9	70.1
	(Percentage points)			
Change	–7	+11	–2.9	+3.0

1 Quintiles are five equal groups of ELFP individuals, sorted according to earnings.
2 Effective labour force participants – individuals earning at least 5 per cent of the average industrial wage.
SOURCE Calculations by Statistics Canada and the Economic Council of Canada, based on Statistics Canada, Survey of Consumer Finances, unpublished data.

earnings share from the lowest three fifths of the ELFP work force to the upper two fifths.

To this point we have considered only the endpoints of 1967-86 without examining trends throughout the period. In fact, all or most of the observed increases in both polarization and inequality took place in 1967-73 and 1981-86; during the middle years between 1973 and 1981 the earnings distribution was relatively stable. For example, the proportion of the work force in the middle stratum decreased by almost 3 percentage points during the early period, declined only marginally (0.3 points) in the middle period, and then decreased significantly again (by almost 2 points) during the last period (recall Table 8-3). The Gini coefficient increased (signifying growing inequality) between 1967 and 1973 and again between 1981 and 1986; during the middle period, on the other hand, earnings inequality abated. The quintile results also indicate that the distributional shifts were concentrated in the first and third periods (see Table 8-5).

An important question concerns the sensitivity of our results to the criteria used to determine a) who is an "effective labour force participant" and b) how we define the various earnings strata. Regarding a), in order to capture those with more than a trivial attachment to the labour market, recall that our analysis included only those who earned at least 5 per cent of the average industrial wage. What would happen if this arbitrary threshold of 5 per cent were adjusted up or down? In Table 8-6 the threshold is adjusted down to 2.5 per cent and up to 10 per cent, and the observed declining middle and increasing inequality remain when the ELFP boundary is changed in either direction.

Regarding the earnings strata thresholds, our results were based on a definition of the middle stratum that includes those workers earning within 25 per cent of the current year median on either side (between $13,050 and $21,744 in 1986). Would the distribution trends change with a different definition? Table 8-7 indicates that earnings polarization occurred over 1967-86 whether we widen the middle-group boundaries (from 75 per cent to 150 per cent of the median), or narrow them (85 per cent to 125 per cent).

Distributions over the Longer Term

Our analysis uses the unpublished Survey of Consumer Finances (SCF) database for 1967-86, the longest possible series for which satisfactory data (in terms of content and sample size) were available. This raises the question of what the trends were before 1967 and what they have been since 1986. To consider the latter, we examined published SCF data on the employment income of earners. Since these data have already grouped individuals into broad earnings categories, they do not offer the same analytical flexibility as the unpublished file. Therefore, we have only been able to roughly reproduce the approach described above of organizing effective labour force participants into three earnings categories according to their distance from the median.

Table 8-6

Sensitivity Analysis of the ELFP[1] Criterion, Earnings Distribution Trends, Canada, Selected Years, 1967-86

	Work force share of middle earnings stratum[2]				Gini coefficient[3]			
	1967	1973	1981	1986	1967	1973	1981	1986
	(Per cent)							
Proportion of average industrial wage								
5 per cent	26.8	23.7	23.4	21.5	0.389	0.407	0.402	0.418
2.5 per cent	25.4	22.5	22.4	20.3	0.403	0.421	0.418	0.434
10 per cent	29.6	26.2	25.9	24.1	0.363	0.380	0.374	0.391

1 Effective labour force participants – individuals earning at least 5 per cent of the average industrial wage.
2 Lower, middle, and upper strata consist of ELFPs earning 0-75, 75-125, and more than 125 per cent of the median, respectively.
3 The traditional measure of inequality which rises with the degree of inequality.
SOURCE Calculations by Statistics Canada and the Economic Council of Canada, based on Statistics Canada, Survey of Consumer Finances, unpublished data.

Table 8-7

Sensitivity Analysis of Middle Earnings Cutoffs, Trends in the ELFP[1] Work Force Share of the Middle Stratum, Canada, Selected Years, 1967-86

	Work force share of middle earnings stratum			
	1967	1973	1981	1986
	(Per cent)			
Proportion of median				
75-125 per cent	26.8	23.7	23.4	21.5
75-150 per cent	39.3	34.3	33.6	30.8
85-125 per cent	21.6	18.2	19.1	17.6

1 Effective labour force participants – individuals earning at least 5 per cent of the average industrial wage.
SOURCE Calculations by Statistics Canada and the Economic Council of Canada, based on Statistics Canada, Survey of Consumer Finances, unpublished data.

The published SCF data over 1967-86 (column A, Table 8-8) do match quite closely the results reported in Table 8-3 based on the unpublished SCF data. Significant polarization took place between 1981 and 1984 (column B); indeed, this is what we would expect during and immediately following a severe recession. Since then, the middle group has expanded somewhat (column C); however, by 1988, it had not regained its prerecession work force share (column D), despite a prolonged period of sustained economic growth.

The published SCF data also allow us to make some observations about the period prior to 1967. Information on earnings alone, however, was not available before 1967, so we used data on the total income of those individuals whose major source of income was wages and salaries (which only roughly approximates the employment income of earners). For this exercise, income-share quintile data were organized into three groups: the lowest, the middle three, and the highest quintiles. With the analytical limitations of the data, it is difficult to draw any conclusions regarding trends in earnings distributions between 1951 (the earliest year of published SCF data) and 1967, other than relative stability with a modest decline in the share of total income going to the lowest quintile (Table 8-9).

Regional Trends

Table 8-10 describes the trends in the earnings distributions for the five major regions of the country. The general patterns of earnings polarization and growing inequality observed for Canada as a whole did occur in all regions; in each case, the proportion of the work force in the middle group was significantly smaller in 1986 than it had been in 1967, and the Gini coefficient rose as well. As was the case nationally, the regional polarization and inequality trends tended to be most characteristic of 1967-73 and 1981-86.

Although on one level the experience is similar across the country, there is also some evidence of considerable regional differences. First, the level of polarization and inequality throughout the sample period was greatest in the

Table 8-8

Earnings Distribution of ELFPs,[1] Published Grouped Data,[2] Canada, Selected Years, 1967-88

	1967	1981	1984	1986	1988	Change 1967-86 (A)	Change 1981-84 (B)	Change 1984-88 (C)	Change 1981-88 (D)
	(Per cent)					(Percentage points)			
Stratum[3]									
Lower	34.6	36.1	36.8	36.5	36.7	+1.9	+0.7	−0.1	+0.6
Middle	27.3	22.0	19.0	19.7	20.8	−7.6	−3.0	+1.8	−1.2
Upper	38.1	41.9	44.2	43.8	42.5	+5.7	+2.3	−1.7	+0.6
Total	100.0	100.0	100.0	100.0	100.0	...	...	...	...

1 Effective labour force participants – individuals earning at least 5 per cent of the average industrial wage.
2 Based on published data already grouped into income categories which do not correspond with the categories used in the rest of the chapter.
3 Lower, middle, and upper strata consist of ELFPs earning 0-75, 75-125, and more than 125 per cent of the median, respectively.
SOURCE Calculations by the Economic Council of Canada, based on Statistics Canada, Survey of Consumer Finances, unpublished data.

Table 8-9

Distribution of Total Income of Those Whose Major Source of Income Are Wages and Salaries, by Income Quintiles,[1] Canada, Selected Years, 1951-67

	Quintile income shares			
	Lowest	Middle three	Highest	Total
	(Per cent)			
1951	4.2	55.6	40.3	100.0
1957	4.5	56.1	39.4	100.0
1961	3.7	56.0	40.3	100.0
1967*	2.8	54.7	42.5	100.0

*Includes farmers (they were excluded in earlier years).
1 Quintiles are five equal groups of ELFPs, sorted according to income.
SOURCE Estimates by the Economic Council of Canada, based on Statistics Canada, Survey of Consumer Finances.

Atlantic provinces and lowest in Ontario and Quebec. The latter two provinces, though, suffered the biggest absolute decreases in the middle (8.2 and 6.6 percentage points, respectively) and the largest gains at the low end (3.6 and 4.9 percentage points). But the greatest increase in inequality was experienced by the Atlantic provinces. In this region, which had the most unequally distributed earnings in 1967, the Gini coefficient had grown by 50 basis points by 1986. The Prairie provinces had the smallest shrinking middle (3.9 percentage points) and the least increase in inequality (22 basis points).

Families

Although the major focus of our analysis of distributional trends is on the earnings of individuals, we also considered the distribution of family earnings and the total incomes of families. In Table 8-11, family distribution trends over 1967-86 are presented along with the earnings distributions of individuals. The second line consists of census (nuclear) families which include at least one ELFP individual whose total earnings represent at least 50 per cent of their total income. In 1986 earnings were less polarized and more equally distributed among this sample of ELFP families (29.6 per cent in the middle and a Gini of 0.347) than among ELFP individuals (21.5 per cent and 0.418). This indicates that additional workers in a family expand the middle stratum and decrease the inequality of employment income. The second point is that the difference in size between the middle stratum of families and individuals has not changed over the years, implying that earnings polarization has increased in much the same way for families as for individuals. The same may be said about changes in earnings inequality; the rise in the Gini coefficient for family earnings from 0.329 to 0.347 was only slightly less than the corresponding increase for individuals.

The story changes, however, when we examine the distribution of total family income. Over our sample period the composition of total family income (employment,

Table 8-10

Earnings Distribution Trends, by Region, Canada, Selected Years, 1967-86

	Distribution of ELFP[1] work force by earnings stratum[2]				Gini coefficient[3]
	Lower	Middle	Upper	Total	
	(Per cent)				
Atlantic provinces					
1967	37.6	23.4	39.1	100.0	0.399
1973	38.6	23.6	37.9	100.0	0.414
1981	39.7	20.3	40.1	100.0	0.424
1986	40.6	18.5	40.9	100.0	0.449
Quebec					
1967	33.9	29.7	36.4	100.0	0.374
1973	35.7	26.6	37.7	100.0	0.391
1981	36.8	25.4	37.8	100.0	0.389
1986	38.8	23.1	38.1	100.0	0.404
Ontario					
1967	35.2	30.6	34.1	100.0	0.380
1973	37.7	24.5	37.8	100.0	0.399
1981	38.5	23.1	38.4	100.0	0.402
1986	38.8	22.4	38.8	100.0	0.413
Prairie provinces					
1967	37.5	24.8	37.7	100.0	0.403
1973	36.8	23.7	39.4	100.0	0.422
1981	37.7	24.0	38.4	100.0	0.407
1986	39.7	20.9	39.4	100.0	0.425
British Columbia					
1967	37.9	24.9	37.3	100.0	0.383
1973	39.2	22.5	38.4	100.0	0.403
1981	37.6	23.2	39.2	100.0	0.391
1986	39.9	19.4	40.7	100.0	0.414

1 Effective labour force participants – individuals earning at least 5 per cent of the average industrial wage.
2 Lower, middle, and upper strata consist of ELFPs earning 0-75, 75-125, and more than 125 per cent of the median for each region, respectively.
3 The traditional measure of inequality which rises with the degree of inequality.
SOURCE Calculations by Statistics Canada and the Economic Council of Canada, based on Statistics Canada, Survey of Consumer Finances, unpublished data.

investment, transfers, and other income) has changed, with the relative share of earnings declining and the share of the other components, particularly transfers, increasing (Chart 8-7). Also note from Table 8-12 that between 1973 and 1988 this partial replacement of employment income by transfer and investment income was evident at all income levels except the lowest, where the share of investment income fell.[29] As would be expected, the lowest quintile depends upon the transfer system for the bulk of its income; the reliance on the labour market as an income source rises with the income level. Returning to Table 8-11, the distribution of total income for all census family units was more polarized in 1986 than employment income. However, the increase in polarization of total income and employment income has been, in relative terms, about the same; in terms of total income, the decline in the population share of 3.8 points in the middle stratum from 1967 to 1986 was only slightly less than it was in terms of employment income (4.8 points). Turning to income inequality of families, note that the Gini coefficient did increase when only earnings are considered; when total family income is considered, however, the rise in inequality was insignificant.

Table 8-11

Income Distribution Trends, ELFPs[1] and Census Family Units,[2] Canada, Selected Years, 1967-86

	Population share of middle stratum				Gini coefficient[3]			
	1967	1973	1981	1986	1967	1973	1981	1986
	(Per cent)							
Earnings, ELFPs	26.8	23.7	23.4	21.5	0.389	0.407	0.402	0.418
Earnings, ELFP families[4]	34.4	31.9	31.8	29.6	0.329	0.335	0.330	0.347
Total income, all families	26.1	22.5	23.1	22.3	0.398	0.413	0.395	0.404
After-tax income, all families	--	25.1	25.8	25.1	--	0.385	0.368	0.373
Total income, all families, EAU[5]	28.0	27.0	28.0	27.0	0.360	0.360	0.380	0.380

1 Effective labour force participants – individuals earning at least 5 per cent of the average industrial wage.
2 A husband and wife with or without never married children living at home, or a lone parent with one or more never married children, or unattached individual(s).
3 The traditional measure of inequality which rises with the degree of inequality.
4 Census families with at least one ELFP, whose earnings are at least 50 per cent of total family income.
5 Effective adult unit: standardizing by family size and earning ability of family members.
SOURCE Calculations by Statistics Canada and the Economic Council of Canada, based on Statistics Canada, Survey of Consumer Finances.

Chart 8-7

Income Composition of Census Family Units,[1] Canada, 1965-88

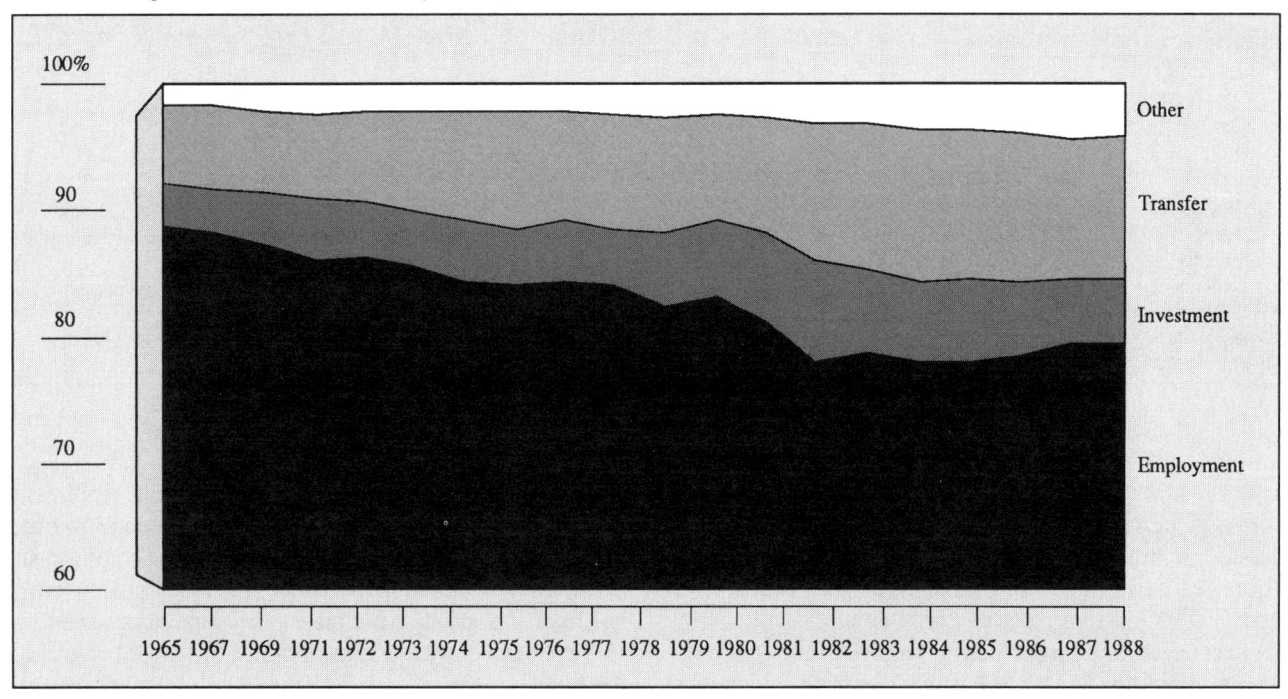

1 Census family unit – a husband and wife with or without never married children living at home, or a lone parent with one or more children, or unattached individual(s). Data for 1965 and 1967 are for economic family units, that is, unattached individuals, or groups of individuals having a common dwelling unit and related by blood, marriage, or adoption.
SOURCE Estimates by the Economic Council of Canada, based on Statistics Canada, Survey of Consumer Finances.

Table 8-12

Distribution of Total Income in Each Quintile by Income Source, Economic Family Units,[1] Canada, 1973 and 1988

	Quintile									
	Lowest		Second		Middle		Fourth		Highest	
	1973	1988	1973	1988	1973	1988	1973	1988	1973	1988
	(Per cent)									
Employment	31.7	28.3	69.4	53.9	86.3	76.0	91.1	85.9	91.1	88.9
Transfer income	55.6	61.8	19.8	31.2	7.3	13.1	4.4	6.3	2.6	3.1
Investment income	7.0	4.9	5.4	6.6	3.7	4.9	3.0	4.1	5.1	5.5
Other	5.6	5.0	5.3	8.3	2.6	6.0	1.5	3.7	1.3	2.5
Total	100.0	100.0	100.0	100.0	100.0	100.0	100.0	100.0	100.0	100.0

1 Unattached individuals or groups of individuals having a common dwelling unit and related by blood, marriage, or adoption. Income composition by quintile was not available by census family units, the unit of family analyses used elsewhere in this chapter.

SOURCE Estimates by the Economic Council of Canada, based on Statistics Canada, Survey of Consumer Finances.

This assessment of family income trends suggests increasing polarization and inequality of earnings, and polarization but not growing inequality of total income. A closer look at Table 8-11, however, indicates considerable stability in the distribution of total family income. First, since 1973 the population share of the middle-income group has remained constant, both in terms of pre-tax income and after-tax income. Moreover, the Gini coefficient actually declined in both cases between 1973 and 1986, implying growing equality. Second, when we control for changes in family size (the last line of Table 8-11), the distribution of total family income has remained essentially unchanged since 1967, both in terms of polarization and inequality.

Explanations of Increased Earnings Disparity

Supply-Side Explanations: A Changing Labour Force

Supply-side factors focus on the shifting composition and earnings of the work force and their distributional impacts. We considered three trends that significantly altered the labour force over the sample period: the increased participation of women in the labour force; the changing age structure driven by the labour force entry and maturation of the "baby boom" generation; and the growth in nonstandard employment.[30] What part did these developments play in the observed polarization and growing inequality? We will address this question first by looking at earnings trends by sex, age, and employment status, and then by using standardization techniques to isolate the impact of these factors.

It is well known that on average women have earned less than men; however, the gap did narrow between 1967 and 1986 (Table 8-13). Female earnings are also more polarized and more inequitably distributed than male earnings. The increasing female share of the work force would thus be expected not only to increase the number of individuals in low-wage jobs, but also to increase overall earnings inequality and polarization. While polarization within the female sample remains higher than that among males, the middle declined much more rapidly for men between 1967 and 1986 (11.1 percentage points) than it did for women (2.4 percentage points). In terms of inequality, the Gini coefficient increased by roughly similar magnitudes for both sexes.[31]

The entry of the large cohort of postwar baby boomers has altered the age composition of the work force. During the 1960s and 1970s, this generation inflated the numbers in the under-25 age group; in the 1980s, the baby-boom cohort has become part of the 25-34 and, more recently, the 35-49 groups. Within this period, then, it is not surprising that the relative earnings of the two younger categories (less than 35 years) have fallen, while those of the two older groups (greater than 35 years) have increased (Table 8-14). While this offers evidence that a large cohort depresses the relative wages of its members, note that in terms of polarization and inequality, all age groups have

Table 8-13

Earnings Distribution Trends by Gender, Canada, Selected Years, 1967-86

	Work force share	Relative mean[2]	Distribution of work force by earnings stratum[1]				Gini coefficient[3]
			Lower	Middle	Upper	Total	
	(Per cent)		(Per cent)				
Males							
1967	69.4	1.18	32.4	35.9	31.6	100.0	0.350
1973	65.5	1.21	35.0	31.1	33.8	100.0	0.364
1981	59.0	1.22	35.9	29.8	34.1	100.0	0.363
1986	57.0	1.21	37.9	24.8	37.2	100.0	0.390
Females							
1967	30.3	0.59	38.2	23.7	38.1	100.0	0.375
1973	34.1	0.60	38.8	22.9	38.3	100.0	0.390
1981	40.6	0.69	38.7	22.2	39.1	100.0	0.393
1986	43.0	0.72	38.5	21.3	40.3	100.0	0.405

1 Lower, middle, and upper strata consist of ELFPs earning 0-75, 75-125, and more than 125 per cent of the median, respectively.
2 Relative to the overall mean.
3 The traditional measure of inequality which rises with the degree of inequality.
SOURCE Calculations by Statistics Canada and the Economic Council of Canada, based on Statistics Canada, Survey of Consumer Finances.

experienced increases. This suggests that pervasive factors affecting the entire population, and not any particular age group, have been acting to increase earnings disparities.

Table 8-15 presents data on trends in earnings levels and distributions on the basis of employment status: for full-time, full-year workers, on the one hand, and for those without full-time, full-year employment, on the other. As we can see, the work force share of the latter group (which approximates nonstandard workers) increased significantly over the sample period. As expected, the annual earnings of nonstandard workers are significantly lower than those of full-time, full-year employees (0.49 vs. 1.31 of the overall mean in 1986), which reflects the former group's fewer hours worked and typically lower wages. As well, the earnings of nonstandard workers are also more polarized and unequally distributed than those of full-time, full-year employees (in 1986, 19 per cent vs. 34 per cent in the middle group and Gini coefficient of 0.460 vs. 0.316, respectively). This suggests that the trend towards nonstandard employment may be contributing to the rise in inequality and polarization. On the other hand, the observed polarization trend was stronger over the period 1967-86 for full-time, full-year workers; that group experienced a decline in the middle group of 4.4 percentage points, while there was little change within the nonstandard sample. For the full-time, full-year population, however, all of the movement away from the middle was towards the upper stratum.

The Gini coefficient remained relatively stable for both groups.

Standardizing by Labour Force Changes

What does this descriptive analysis of earnings trends for the various age, sex, and employment status groups tell us about the role of supply-side factors in explaining the overall polarization and growing inequality of earnings over the period 1967-86? On the one hand, polarization and inequality have increased in varying degrees for virtually all segments of the labour force groups that we have examined; on its own, this suggests that the overall trends in the earnings distribution have been driven by factors beyond shifts in the make-up of the labour force. On the other hand, however, the compositional changes have tended to be in the direction of labour force groups which have high levels of earnings disparities – females and nonstandard workers are the most striking examples.

To more systematically analyse the impact of supply-side changes on the observed distributional trends, we have conducted a series of "standardization" exercises. This standardization technique (described in Appendix B) is designed to measure how much of the change in the income distribution over a given period of time is due to the changing make-up of the population (the "composition"

Table 8-14

Earnings Distribution Trends by Age Group, Canada, Selected Years, 1967-86

	Work force share	Relative mean[2]	Distribution of work force by earnings stratum[1]				Gini coefficient[3]
			Lower	Middle	Upper	Total	
	(Per cent)		(Per cent)				
Less than 25 years							
1967	23.3	0.56	41.2	18.1	40.7	100.0	0.393
1973	25.4	0.52	41.2	17.2	41.6	100.0	0.407
1981	24.1	0.56	41.4	16.5	42.1	100.0	0.430
1986	20.7	0.49	41.2	15.9	43.0	100.0	0.452
25-34 years							
1967	21.6	1.09	32.0	38.1	29.9	100.0	0.310
1973	24.4	1.09	33.5	32.8	33.7	100.0	0.329
1981	28.0	1.05	34.6	29.6	35.7	100.0	0.340
1986	29.1	1.01	36.2	27.6	36.1	100.0	0.357
35-49 years							
1967	29.9	1.21	33.4	33.9	32.7	100.0	0.352
1973	26.8	1.28	35.2	30.1	34.7	100.0	0.364
1981	26.5	1.24	36.0	28.2	35.6	100.0	0.360
1986	30.6	1.24	36.6	25.6	37.8	100.0	0.373
More than 50 years							
1967	24.9	1.08	35.6	28.6	35.9	100.0	0.398
1973	23.2	1.10	36.5	26.4	37.2	100.0	0.394
1981	21.2	1.13	36.3	26.5	37.2	100.0	0.391
1986	19.6	1.16	37.8	23.5	38.7	100.0	0.403

1 Lower, middle, and upper strata consist of ELFPs earning 0-75, 75-125, and more than 125 per cent of the median, respectively.
2 Relative to the overall mean.
3 The traditional measure of inequality which rises with the degree of inequality.
SOURCE Calculations by Statistics Canada and the Economic Council of Canada, based on Statistics Canada, Survey of Consumer Finances.

factor) and how much is due to changes in earnings – both level and distribution – within groups (the "income" factor).

Table 8-16 presents the impact on polarization and inequality of standardizing for labour force changes with respect to age, sex, and employment status over the period 1967-86. The first two lines describe the actual earnings distribution in 1967 and 1986 (from Table 8-3). The next three lines report the standardization results. These demonstrate what the 1986 middle-group size and Gini coefficient would have been had there been no change in the work force composition, the relative mean earnings of the various population subgroups, and the shapes of the earnings distributions of the various groups.

In line *a* of Table 8-16, the first figure indicates the hypothetical size of the middle stratum in 1986, freezing the age, sex, and employment status make-up of the work force at its 1967 composition (but still allowing for actual changes in the relative mean and earnings distributions of the groups). According to this standardization, had the labour force composition remained constant, earnings polarization would have occurred but not by as much as it actually did. In other words, if between 1967 and 1986 female work force participation, the age structure of the labour force, and the standard/nonstandard employment status mix had not changed, the middle-earnings group in 1986 would have represented a larger share of the population (23.3 per cent) than was actually the case (21.5 per cent). These results indicate that changes in the make-up of the work force have contributed to greater polarization; of the 5.3 percentage-point decline in the middle, 1.8 points (roughly one third) can be attributed to the composition factor. With respect to inequality, compositional changes do not appear to have

152 Employment in the Service Economy

Table 8-15

Earnings Distribution Trends by Employment Status, Canada, Selected Years, 1967-86

	Work force share	Relative mean[2]	\multicolumn{4}{c	}{Distribution of work force by earnings stratum[1]}	Gini coefficient[3]
			Lower	Middle	Upper	Total	
	(Per cent)		\multicolumn{4}{c	}{(Per cent)}	
Full-time, full-year employees[4]							
1967	75.2	1.19	30.8	38.4	30.9	100.0	0.318
1973	63.7	1.29	30.7	37.5	31.8	100.0	0.302
1981	61.7	1.30	30.0	37.5	32.5	100.0	0.298
1986	62.4	1.31	30.9	34.0	35.1	100.0	0.316
All other employees							
1967	24.8	0.44	39.0	20.4	40.5	100.0	0.468
1973	36.3	0.49	38.4	20.9	40.7	100.0	0.466
1981	38.3	0.51	38.9	19.9	41.2	100.0	0.455
1986	37.6	0.49	39.7	19.2	41.2	100.0	0.460

1 Lower, middle, and upper strata consist of ELFPs earning 0-75, 75-125, and more than 125 per cent of the median, respectively.
2 Relative to the overall mean.
3 The traditional measure of inequality which rises with the degree of inequality.
4 Defined as those who worked 50 weeks or more on a full-time basis.
SOURCE Calculations by Statistics Canada and the Economic Council of Canada, based on Statistics Canada, Survey of Consumer Finances.

Table 8-16

Work Force Share of the Middle Earnings Stratum, and Gini Coefficient, Standardized for Demographic Shifts, Canada, 1967 and 1986 (Actual), and 1986 (Hypothetical)

	Work force share of middle stratum	Gini coefficient
	(Per cent)	
Actual 1967	26.8	0.389
Actual 1986	21.5	0.418
Hypothetical 1986, standardized for		
a Composition (work force shares)	23.3	0.414
b Relative mean incomes	20.3	0.391
c Earnings distributions	23.7	0.415

SOURCE Calculations by Statistics Canada and the Economic Council of Canada, based on Statistics Canada, Survey of Consumer Finances, unpublished data.

played a significant role; the hypothetical 1986 Gini coefficient (based on the 1967 labour force composition) was very similar to the actual coefficient (0.414 vs. 0.418).

Line *b* of Table 8-16 presents the results of standardizing for changes in the relative mean earnings of the different labour force groups (while allowing for the actual shifts in composition and within-group distributions). The marked increase in relative earnings for women, older workers, and full-time, full-year employees, and the decline in those of younger workers in 1967-86 that we observed earlier, were not behind the growing polarization. After standardizing for shifts in relative earnings, the size of this hypothetical middle stratum in 1986 is in fact even smaller than it really was.

However, trends in relative earnings do appear to have been an important factor behind the growing inequality of earnings. As we can see from line *b* of Table 8-16, freezing the relative mean earnings of the different labour force segments at their 1967 levels eliminates virtually all of the observed increase in the Gini coefficient between 1967 and 1986. Further univariate standardizations suggest that changes in the relative mean earnings along all three dimensions considered here – age, sex, and employment status – played a part in the growing inequality over the sample period.

Line *c* of Table 8-16 presents the results of standardizing for changes in the earnings distributions of the population groups. Recall that for most of the work force groups, polarization and growing inequality were observed to some extent. Once we hold the distributions within these groups constant at their 1967 shapes, we find that the 1986 middle-earner category becomes larger (by 2.2 percentage points) than it actually was in that year. This indicates the importance of within-group polarization in driving the overall declining middle. However, changes in the distribution within the labour force groups did not play a part in the increasing Gini coefficient.

To summarize from our supply-side standardizations: first, the observed increase in earnings inequality over the period 1967-86 appears to have been the product of changes in the relative earnings of the various work force groups; and second, two labour force developments contributed to the polarization between 1967 and 1986 – the changing age, sex, and employment status composition of the work force, and the growing polarization within the various labour force groups. When each of these developments is controlled for (lines *a* and *c* of Table 8-16), between 33 and 42 per cent of the polarization observed during the sample period is eliminated. (Unfortunately, the standardization technique is limited in that it is not additive – that is, the impact of each of the standardizations cannot be summed to a total effect of supply-side factors.) Our results do suggest, therefore, that part of the declining middle can be accounted for by changes in the composition of the labour force. However, the changes do not explain the majority of the polarization, nor do they explain why earnings distributions *within* work force groups became more polarized between 1967 and 1986.

Demand-Side Explanations:
The Shift to Services

Demand-side factors are concerned with the distributional impacts of changes in the structure of employment, most notably shifts in its industrial and occupational make-up. These shifts reflect developments such as technological change and changing international economic patterns. Here, we will focus on how the shifting industrial structure – specifically the growth of services – has affected earnings distributions.

As is the case with supply-side hypotheses, these shifts can have implications for distributions either through a composition effect or an income effect. The former changes the make-up of employment by industry (i.e., the shift from goods to services); the latter has two dimensions – first, changes in interindustry wage levels, and second, changes in the wage distribution within industries. We will examine the evidence on the compositional and income factors as they apply to the industrial structure. Since the SCF database does not provide accurate coding of employment by industry for 1967, our analysis is limited to the period 1973-86. During this truncated period, the middle-earnings segment of the labour force declined only 2.2 percentage points and the Gini coefficient increased by only 11 basis points. Because of these relatively small changes, we have not been able to incorporate the standardization technique into the analysis, and our consideration of the distributional implications of the shift to services has been limited to descriptive analysis.

The Changing Industrial
Composition of Employment

How important has the growth of services been in altering earnings distributions? Recall that the "deindustrialization" hypothesis argues that the shift from middle-wage goods employment to high- and low-wage services has been behind the observed polarization and growing inequality in earnings. To examine this hypothesis, we looked at the trends regarding employment growth and hourly earnings by sector and industry. In Table 8-17, the first two columns tell the familiar story of the rapid growth of employment in services and the major contribution of that sector to overall growth during the past 15 years. In terms of hourly earnings, jobs in the goods industries paid, on average, $12.55 in 1987, compared to $11.90 for those in the service industries.[32] However, because the wage structure in the service sector is very heterogeneous, the average wage rate for that sector as a whole does not accurately represent the rates of its constituent industries.

This is evident when we look at the individual service industries where employment gains were most concentrated. Seven of these were particularly significant sources of employment growth between 1974 and 1989, contributing at least 5 per cent to overall employment expansion: finance, insurance, and real estate; business services; retail trade; accommodation, food, and beverages; education; health and social services; and public administration (see Table 8-17). An examination of average earnings in these high-growth services underlines that sector's wage heterogeneity. The two traditional services, retail trade and accommodation, food, and beverages had hourly wages in 1987 that were roughly 74 per cent and 55 per cent of the all-industry

Table 8-17

Employment Growth, 1974-89, and Average Hourly Earnings, by Industry, Canada, 1987

	Employment, 1974-89		Average hourly earnings,[1] 1987	
	Average annual growth	Contribution to growth	Level	Proportion of total
	(Per cent)		(Dollars per hour)	(Per cent)
All industries	2.1	100.0	12.09	100.0
Goods sector	0.7	10.7	12.55	103.8
Agriculture	–0.7	–1.5	7.28	60.2
Other primary	1.7	1.9	15.00	124.1
Manufacturing	0.6	5.3	12.63	104.5
Construction	1.7	5.0	12.76	105.5
Service sector	2.8	89.3	11.90	98.4
Dynamic services	2.9	30.0	13.01	107.6
Transportation, communications, and utilities	1.3	4.8	14.28	118.1
Wholesale trade	2.1	4.6	11.75	97.2
Finance, insurance, and real estate	3.1	8.1	12.53	103.6
Business services	7.0	12.5	12.57	104.0
Traditional services	3.1	34.1	8.29	68.6
Retail trade	2.2	13.4	8.94	73.9
Accommodation, food, and beverages	4.6	10.9	6.63	54.8
Amusement and recreation	4.4	2.1	9.32	77.1
Personal services	3.2	3.5	6.61	54.7
Other traditional services[2]	4.3	4.2	9.60	79.4
Nonmarket services	2.4	25.1	13.74	113.6
Education	1.7	5.5	15.30	126.6
Health and social services	3.2	13.4	11.88	98.3
Public administration	1.9	6.3	14.47	119.7

1 Total wages and salaries divided by the total hours worked in paid jobs in each industry.
2 Includes photographic, car rental, and janitorial services.
SOURCE Calculations by the Economic Council of Canada, based on Statistics Canada, the Labour Force Survey, unpublished data, and Cat. 71-529, and data from the Labour Market Activity Survey.

average, respectively. At the other end of the spectrum, education and public administration had average hourly wages that exceeded the national average by about 27 per cent and 20 per cent, respectively. The wages of the three remaining high-growth services – financial services, business services, and health and social services – were close to the all-industry average.

Certainly, the employment growth nodes in the service sector include industries with widely varying average wages. While some of these can be characterized as high-paying and others as low-paying, it must be noted that a significant proportion of the shift to services involved industries with hourly wage levels that are close to the all-economy mean and within the range of average wages describing the goods industries.

Changes in Interindustry Wage Levels

Changes in interindustry wage levels can also affect the overall earnings distribution. Even in the absence of compositional changes, polarization can occur where the gap between high-wage and low-wage industries grows over time. American studies suggest that wage gaps between industries have been widening throughout much of the postwar period in that country.[33] The Canadian evidence is less conclusive. One problem in this country has been the

Table 8-18

Earnings[1] Dispersion among Industries, Canada, 1973, 1981, and 1986

	Standard deviation	Coefficient of variation[2]
1973	0.287	3.22
1981	0.317	3.32
1986	0.330	3.36

1 Based on the natural log of the annual earnings of 15 industries.
2 Standard deviation divided by (log) industry mean.
SOURCE Calculations by the Economic Council of Canada, based on Statistics Canada, Survey of Consumer Finances, unpublished data.

lack of time-series data at a level of industry disaggregation that is detailed enough to compute meaningful measures of dispersion.[34]

Table 8-18 presents our estimates of earnings dispersion across 15 industries in 1973, 1981, and 1986. Using the natural log of average annual earnings for these industries, both the standard deviation and the coefficient of variation (the standard deviation scaled by average earnings) increased slightly between 1973 and 1986. While indicating growing earnings dispersions across industries during this period, the trend in Canada is much smaller than comparable American estimates. As well, our small sample size calls for caution in interpretation.

Changes in Earnings Distributions within Industries

The other factor associated with the industry effect involves changes in the earnings distributions within industries. Table 8-19 presents distributional trends for the four major industrial sectors: goods, traditional services, dynamic services, and nonmarket services. With 23 per cent of its work force in the middle group in 1986, the goods sector

Table 8-19

Earnings Distribution Trends by Industry, Canada, 1973, 1981, and 1986

	Work force share	Distribution of work force by earnings stratum[1]				Gini coefficient[2]
		Lower	Middle	Upper	Total	
	(Per cent)	(Per cent)				
Goods sector						
1973	33.3	35.2	29.6	35.2	100.0	0.350
1981	32.2	37.0	25.8	37.1	100.0	0.374
1986	29.7	38.5	22.7	38.7	100.0	0.392
Traditional services						
1973	16.8	38.1	22.1	39.8	100.0	0.425
1981	23.1	40.1	18.3	41.6	100.0	0.447
1986	24.9	40.8	18.7	40.6	100.0	0.470
Dynamic services						
1973	19.1	34.2	30.4	35.4	100.0	0.364
1981	22.6	33.6	29.3	37.1	100.0	0.364
1986	22.5	35.1	27.5	37.4	100.0	0.380
Nonmarket services						
1973	19.7	33.5	32.4	34.2	100.0	0.356
1981	21.3	34.9	27.5	37.6	100.0	0.379
1986	22.4	35.4	27.7	36.8	100.0	0.378

1 Lower, middle, and upper strata consist of ELFPs earning 0-75, 75-125, and more than 125 per cent of the median, respectively.
2 The traditional measure of inequality which rises with the degree of inequality.
SOURCE Calculations by Statistics Canada and the Economic Council of Canada, based on Statistics Canada, Survey of Consumer Finances, unpublished data.

distribution lies within the extremes describing the service subsectors. Polarization was greatest in traditional services, where the middle group accounted for about 19 per cent of that subsector's labour force. On the other hand, corresponding shares for nonmarket and dynamic services were very high, at nearly 28 per cent. The distributional impact of the employment shift from goods to services, then, is indeterminate: movements to traditional services have had a polarizing effect, while shifts to both dynamic and nonmarket services have had the opposite effect.

Note also that all four industrial groupings experienced polarization over the sample period (Table 8-19). In fact, this was most marked in goods, where the middle group shrank by 6.9 points. The decline was 3.4, 2.9, and 4.7 points in traditional, dynamic, and nonmarket services respectively. While the standardization technique would have permitted us to draw a more conclusive picture, these descriptive results suggest that rising earnings disparities are more accurately described as the product of distributional changes within industries than the shift to the service sector.

The apparent pervasiveness of the polarization implies that it may be caused by something more fundamental, more systemic within industries, which is affecting the overall distribution of earnings. Certainly, the supply-side changes documented earlier represent an important factor, but as we have discussed, they are only part of the explanation. A complete explanation for the observed earnings polarization continues to elude us.

The Durability of the Declining Middle

Is the declining middle that we have observed between 1967 and 1986 a relatively permanent trend or is it merely a transitory phenomenon of the period we have studied? Our research has shown that distributional trends are not static over time. Just as the period 1967-86 was one of growing earnings disparities, earlier or later periods may not have been. Indeed, to the extent that we have been able to consider trends outside our sample years – for example, 1951-67 – we have seen evidence of earnings stability rather than polarization. Moreover, even within the two decades encompassed by our analysis, the distributional trend has not been simply one of progressive polarization. While the middle did decline in 1967-73 and 1981-86, the earnings distribution was relatively stable in the intervening period between 1973 and 1981.

Changing Labour Force Demographics

An important point to consider in terms of the durability of the declining middle is the future demographic composition of the labour force and its effect on distributional patterns. One demographic feature of the changes in work force composition that partially explains the earnings polarization is the major inflows of women and young people into the labour market during the sample period. This influx of workers whose income distributions were more polarized and unequal than the work force as a whole heightened overall disparities.

To some extent these compositional changes were specific to the period under analysis. It is certainly clear, for example, that large numbers of young workers entering the labour force will not be part of the picture in the immediate future. We carried out some projections to estimate some of the future implications of the changing demographics. Our analysis of traditional services is especially illustrative because young people are most heavily concentrated in these industries, so it is here that the aging work force is likely to have its greatest impact.

On the basis of these projections, we estimate that the youth share of total traditional-service employment will decline over the next decade.[35] Since strong growth in traditional services is anticipated, employers will increasingly have to look to other sources of labour supply. But to attract such workers they will probably have to offer higher compensation. As fewer young people become available, and as the composition of employment in traditional services changes, the wage patterns within this and other sectors that have relied on young workers can be expected to change as well.

While the aging work force will likely act as a moderating influence, it cannot be expected to reverse the polarization trend, since there are other factors at play. Picot et al., using the micro SCF database for the same years (1967-86) as we did, took a close look at the impact of demographic variables for the different subperiods.[36] Their analysis clearly shows that the growing female and youth share of the labour force did explain much of the polarization observed between 1967 and 1981. However, these factors did not play a role in 1981-86, essentially because the trends underlying them had changed considerably. While the female participation rate increased by 40 per cent in the 1970s, the increase was only 15 per cent between 1980 and 1989. And the increase in the youth share of the total labour force peaked in 1974 and has declined ever since (Chart 8-8).

Chart 8-8

Youth Labour Force[1] as a Share of Total Labour Force, Canada, 1966-89

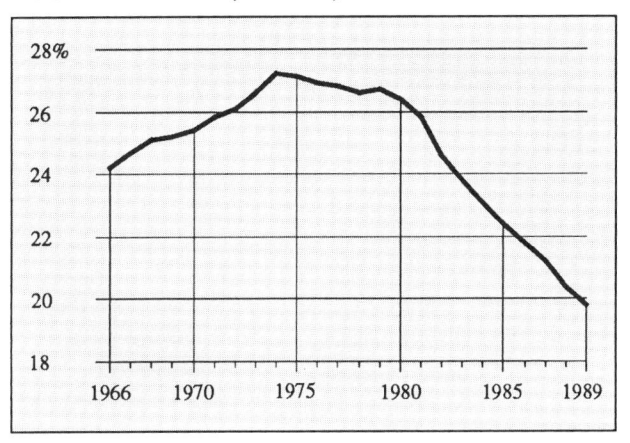

[Line chart showing youth labour force share rising from about 24% in 1966 to a peak of about 27% around 1975, then declining to about 20% by 1989.]

1 Those aged 15-24.
SOURCE Estimates by the Economic Council of Canada, based on data from Statistics Canada, the Labour Force Survey.

Conclusion

In this chapter we have highlighted two trends that have characterized earnings in Canada in recent years – stagnant real compensation levels, and growing disparities in employment income. With respect to the former, average real wages had not recovered by the end of the 1980s to the peak level of 1976. While supplementary (non-wage) labour income has increased since then, this has not offset the decline in wages. The result is that there were no gains in total labour compensation during the 1980s.

The trend that we have focused on is the increase in polarization and inequality in the employment income of Canadian workers between 1967 and 1986. More specifically, disparities increased in 1967-73 and 1981-86. For Canadian families, the distribution was relatively stable once all income sources and changes in the composition of families were taken into account. These results suggest that nonemployment income in the form of transfers is largely offsetting the increasing polarization and inequality emanating from the labour market. In the present context of large budgetary deficits and mounting public debt, the transfer system could be stretched even further as it faces an added redistributive challenge because of growing disparities in incomes from work.

How serious the polarization and growing inequality of earnings between 1967 and 1986 is depends on whether this is part of a longer term trend. The fact that we do not have the appropriate data, and that there is so far no complete explanation for these observations, makes it difficult to assess this issue. It is clear that the make-up of the labour force will not contribute to earnings disparities in the future as it did in the 1960s and 1970s. In particular, the relative decline in the supply of young workers is likely to change the composition of the work force and its wage distribution. However, the earnings disparities observed during the 1980s appear not to have been driven by demographic factors. The evidence that there are disparities within all industrial groupings suggests that fundamental changes are taking place within Canadian workplaces. More research is necessary to enable us to have a better understanding of what these factors are, and to assess whether the polarization is likely to continue in the future.

Part C: Conclusions

9 Conclusions and Policy Implications[1]

Our analysis suggests that the Canadian labour market in the 1990s will be defined by the following features:

– slow growth of the work force, with an older age profile;

– increasing employment in service activities;

– more work with high knowledge content;

– concentration of "good" jobs in large cities;

– growth of nonstandard employment forms; and, possibly,

– widening disparities in the quality of jobs and in the degree of economic security they provide for workers.

These changes are likely to have far-reaching consequences for all Canadians. They will shape the education and training decisions of young people and the career patterns of the adult work force. They will influence the roles and concerns of Canada's social institutions, from families to unions. And they will undoubtedly affect the approaches of industry to the management of human resources.

Our portrait of the emerging labour market also has important consequences for a wide range of public policies. The growth of services, along with the information explosion and the internationalization of business activity, is fuelling the demand for an increasingly well-educated and skilled work force. Canada's future economic welfare will be dictated in no small measure by its capacity to develop human resources. The "education-and-training" imperative will also be compelling for individuals, since employment experiences will be less and less favourable for those who have skill deficiencies. In fact, our analysis suggests that the segmentation of the labour market into "good job" and "bad job" sectors is likely to raise considerable challenges for policymakers concerned with the economic security of Canadians. Certainly, the presence of competitive industries is essential for a robust labour market that can provide that security. We have found that the quality and efficiency of service deliverers and their integration with goods producers is increasingly critical to this competitiveness; accordingly, economic development policies must recognize and support the role of services.

Labour market policies will have to adapt to these transformations; indeed, our research suggests that some institutions no longer "fit" the needs of Canadian workers and employers. In the pages that follow, we look at how policies might be reshaped to support job creation and to maximize the contribution of Canada's human resources in the changing environment. We reiterate here the three interrelated principles that should, in our view, underlie a strategy that recognizes the new dynamics of the labour market:

1 strengthen the commitment to the development of human resources;

2 promote economic security for workers; and

3 recognize the role of services in economic growth.

In making our recommendations, we are aware that actions taken today have implications for future generations. Indeed, that was the theme of the Council's Annual Review for 1989, entitled *Legacies*, which highlighted two elements – the capacity to develop Canada's human resources and the public debt – that have a direct bearing on the policy discussion that follows.

We believe that human-resource development is an investment in the future. Canada's success in the emerging information-based service economy will depend heavily on its capacity to develop a first-rate work force; and that capacity must be put in place now. In emphasizing the role of education and training, we note that a macroeconomic context that supports high rates of employment growth is an important condition for realizing that goal.

To some extent, however, Canada's human-resource objectives lie in direct conflict with the legacy of the public debt. Canada cannot achieve its labour force goals simply by digging deeper into the public purse. Accordingly, we have not made any recommendations that would increase government spending over the next several years. Rather, our suggestions are intended, in large part, to shift policy emphasis in order to better reflect the changing environment. Some of our proposals would, however, require new spending by the private sector, because there are areas where current efforts are inadequate.

In recent years, the Economic Council has drawn attention to the rapid changes in the economic environment and to their implications for Canadians. Generally, we have advocated adaptation to market forces as the best approach to meet the challenges of an increasingly competitive global economy; this has been our perspective in supporting trade liberalization, more rapid adoption of new technologies, and less regulation in product markets. In advocating that approach, we recognize the growing pressure on the labour market, both to generate the skills that are so critical to competitiveness and to provide mechanisms for individuals to adjust to the accelerating changes they face. This perception has been reinforced by the research that we have undertaken for this research report.

The Council believes that, as much as possible, the goals of human-resource development and labour adjustment should be achieved through the actions of employers, unions, and individual workers, responding to market forces. At the same time, however, there is an important role for governments in the functioning of labour markets and in cushioning the hardships inflicted on individuals. Public policies must work with market forces to strengthen the commitment to human resources and to promote the economic security of workers, thereby maximizing the contributions of all Canadians.

Strengthen the Commitment to the Development of Human Resources

The development of human resources contributes to competitiveness and employment growth, and it plays a significant part, as well, in achieving distributional objectives. While this has always been the case, a number of trends – including technological change, the information revolution, and intensifying global competition – are combining to make human-resource development more critical than ever before.

Our research indicates that work with high skill and educational requirements represents a growing share of overall employment. Many high-skilled jobs in both the goods-producing industries and services are trade-sensitive, if not directly dependent on trade; as global competition accelerates, high-cost countries such as Canada will be forced to rely increasingly on the excellence of their work force to provide a comparative advantage in the global marketplace.

A growing number of jobs are information-based; even those which do not have a high skill content demand basic literacy and numeracy. To gain employment – particularly, stable, well-compensated employment – people now need an adequate educational base. The unskilled and poorly educated are experiencing greater disadvantage in the labour market and, in particular, are facing special problems in adjusting to the changing employment structure.

While every country must invest in all factors of production – including capital and technology – the achievement of a high return on these investments will require people with the skills and knowledge to exploit their potential. Increasingly, then, the performance of national economies is closely linked to the human factor. To put it simply, Canadians should not expect to improve – or even maintain – their standard of living unless, as a nation, they attach a high priority to the quality of the work force. Thus effective education and training policies will be absolutely fundamental to Canada in the coming decades.

Human-resource development must be a major priority for policymakers. Accordingly, industry, labour, educators, and governments must aggressively pursue a human-resource strategy that will emphasize, on the one hand, a broadly based education system and, on the other, an active, industry-based training system, with the primary focus to be on the development of specific vocational skills.

Education

In terms of labour force preparation, Canada's education systems must meet two imperatives. The first is to ensure that basic levels of competency are universally held: all Canadians must have literacy and numeracy skills and, more generally, the analytical tools to "navigate" in an information-based society. The second imperative is to pursue a standard of excellence through the development of highly educated individuals. These two objectives involve all education levels, from primary to postsecondary.

The Economic Council is concerned about the performance of the Canadian education systems, when measured against such criteria. While recognizing that there have been some positive developments, we have noted, in Chapter 7, a number of disturbing indicators that raise serious questions about the quality of education in this country. At first glance, these concerns do not seem to be the result of inadequate "inputs." Although real expenditure per student at the postsecondary level has declined over the past decade, spending on primary and secondary students has been rising steadily. Overall, Canada's public expenditures on education, as a percentage of gross domestic product, are among the highest of the developed countries; indeed, this country's financial commitment to education rivals that of any other nation.

Our review of education performance has led us, then, to ask why Canada, as a nation, does not appear to be getting a greater economic return on its substantial investments in this area. Indeed, the growing public debate on education and the increased calls for some action suggest that this concern is becoming more widespread. The usefulness of any policy dialogue on education and the future quality of Canada's workers will depend, however, on the availability of better empirical analysis. Hard and well-focused research is badly needed on how Canada's education systems can prepare a high-quality, competitive work force, capable of adapting to a rapidly changing knowledge-based economy.

Accordingly, we believe that a major empirical study into the state of education in Canada must be undertaken, with a view to evaluating concerns about the quality of education in this country. The focus of the study should be the link between education and economic goals – specifically the future competitiveness of Canada's work force in a knowledge-based economy. This is largely uncharted territory, raising formidable questions about concepts and measurements. It also brings to the fore sensitivities among educators, industry, and governments. Nonetheless, a stronger body of empirical research is bound to enhance the reform process within the various education systems across the country.

Training and Labour Adjustment

While high-quality education represents the essential precondition for a first-class work force, the development of vocational skills must be based in the training system. Training is essential for enhancing on-the-job performance and thus industrial competitiveness. It is also critical for facilitating labour adjustment. As changes in consumer demand and production methods accelerate, and as comparative advantages shift, the need for "retooling" is intensifying. The challenge for Canada's training system is to provide individuals with the ongoing opportunity to acquire productive skills that are needed in the marketplace.

In our view, the current training effort in this country is not satisfactory. It is beset by two major problems. First, the investment by Canadian industry in the development of human resources is insufficient; that situation is very unfortunate, especially in view of the substantial body of evidence showing that training is most effective when it is employment-based. Second, public policy continues to have a "damage-control" orientation, emphasizing income maintenance and short-term training for the long-term unemployed. Current programs do not offer adequate opportunities for developing skills that would improve real long-term employability.

Governments must play a dual role in this area if Canada is to develop the capacity for skill formation that we believe will be necessary in the future. First, they must provide training and adjustment opportunities for workers who are jobless, who face the prospect of unemployment, or who do not have a strong "attachment" to a particular employer. Second, governments must consider ways of stimulating the development of human resources within industry.

Policies Aimed at "Unattached" Workers

The conventional view of the labour market has been that individuals would work for the same employer for extended periods of time and that breaks in that relationship would be infrequent and would typically be associated with "cyclical" unemployment resulting from business downturns. That image of the labour market has been transformed, however, partly because of persistently high unemployment rates, partly because of the accelerating pace of economic change, and partly because of the proliferation of nonstandard employment forms. A growing proportion of the labour force has no attachment, or only a weak attachment, to a particular employer. Thus it will become more important in the 1990s for public policy to deal directly with those "unattached" workers, many of whom experience substantial economic insecurity. As well, the slowdown in the growth of the labour force will heighten the need to ensure that all Canadian workers can participate productively in the labour market.

In Chapter 7, we saw that Canada's level of public expenditure on labour market programs is comparable to that of the major countries of Western Europe and well above the U.S. and Japanese levels. More than most, however, Canadian public policy has emphasized short-term income maintenance and not "active" strategies aimed at supporting workers in the acquisition of long-term employability; about 75 per cent of federal spending on labour market programs is allocated to income maintenance, mostly under the Unemployment Insurance Act.

Income maintenance through a traditional unemployment insurance (UI) system has an important adjustment role in providing earnings replacement in cases where unemployment is cyclical or seasonal or where some time is needed to locate a job opening. As this Council emphasized in its Annual Review for 1988, however, in the present context of rapid industrial and technological change, skill obsolescence, and growing regional imbalances, a large – and growing – proportion of unemployment is "structural" in nature. As a consequence, training, mobility, and counselling services need to play a much larger role. The Council believes that public policy in this country must reflect the emerging labour market by more appropriately addressing the changing nature of labour adjustment; this does not necessarily require additional funding but rather a shift in emphasis towards a more active orientation. As a consequence,

1 **We recommend that reform of the federal government's labour market strategy move in the direction of supporting skill development and employability as the primary objective. As a long-run goal, we endorse a transition from the existing unemployment insurance fund to an "employment insurance" fund.**

The intention of this recommendation is to set out a broadly defined policy target. As we envisage it, the "employment insurance" (EI) fund would not be added to the UI fund but, rather, would be the end-product of a gradual transformation of the existing scheme into one that can more appropriately address the adjustment needs of Canadians. Unemployed workers could draw on the EI plan for income support in the event of unemployment (as is generally the case now); in addition, these workers would be able to use the fund for such purposes as skill development, mobility, and counselling. The actual form of the benefit would be determined by the insured worker, in consultation with Employment Centre counsellors, and it would depend on the individual's situation and on labour market conditions. If, for example, an unemployed worker had employable skills and if the period of joblessness were clearly temporary, income maintenance would be the appropriate approach; however, where immediate employment prospects were poor, benefits could be used for training or one of the other "active" measures.

The nature of the Canadian labour market now demands an adjustment strategy that will offer a range of options to unemployed workers – to receive straight income support, to improve employability, or to pursue some combination of the two. This imperative underlies our proposal for an EI fund.

Without dealing here with all of the specific design issues, many of the basic administrative principles of the existing UI system do seem to suit the needs of the new adjustment instrument we are calling for – e.g., benefit eligibility and benefit levels tied to the length of employment, as well as joint employee/employer contributions. These features could be preserved in the proposed EI scheme.

While we do not intend to set out the detailed fiscal arrangements that the proposed EI fund should entail, we would like to briefly discuss two financing aspects: first, the responsibilities of workers, employers, and government; and second, the overall funding levels that would be required. Regarding the former, the fund would involve both employee/employer contributions and public financing. While the financing responsibilities would have to be negotiated, in principle, government contributions should cover initiatives under the EI fund that are perceived to have "social" benefits for all Canadians; these would involve the "active" options of the fund and would include, for example, the direct costs of training and counselling expenses. On the other hand, employee/employer contributions should be applied principally towards the income-maintenance component of the fund. Undoubtedly, some expenses would fall into a "gray" area, and their financing would require both study and negotiation.

What would be the overall cost implications of the EI proposal? To the extent that the "active" options were pursued, the transition to the EI fund would likely imply higher costs, at least in the short run, than in a system where benefits are predominantly taken in the form of straight income maintenance, as is the case under the current UI system. Clearly, some of the incremental costs could be met through transfers of appropriate parts of the budget for the Canadian Jobs Strategy. If, however, the take-up rates for the active options were very high, thereby creating cost pressures on the fund, and if the current fiscal restrictions on the federal government remained, it might be necessary to limit the amount of financial support available under the active options.

Ultimately, we believe that by more effectively addressing labour adjustment through the principle of promoting employability, an EI fund would result in net savings through lower adjustment costs and a more productive work force.

As well, it is important to recognize that we are proposing that a labour market policy built on this sort of approach be implemented gradually. In that regard, an important transition step would be to increase the scope for the unemployed to acquire training while collecting UI benefits. Although Section 26 of the Unemployment Insurance Act does allow for retraining in some circumstances, training activity represents a minor part of the overall UI system, primarily because the share of UI funds allocated to Section 26 remains relatively small and because there have been substantial restrictions regarding eligibility and the choice of courses.

2 **We strongly support the principle of greater accessibility of training for the recipients of unemployment insurance benefits. Accordingly, we recommend that the federal government increase the UI funds available for retraining and relax the eligibility restrictions for training under the UI program.**

In making this recommendation, we support the proposal, made by the federal government in its April 1989 discussion paper on employment policy (entitled *Success in the Works*), to increase substantially the UI-fund allocations to training UI recipients under Section 26. We believe that the structure of the UI program – namely, the individual accounts and the contributory nature – is an appropriate one for supporting skill development. Indeed, this lies behind our vision of an EI fund. However, we do have reservations about another proposal in that document, aimed at reallocating additional UI funds, built up through universal employer/employee contributions, to programs outside the UI system that are not universally available. While we believe that UI claimants should have far greater access to training, their contributions should not be financing the expansion of federal labour market programs that are not necessarily targeted to the adjustment of unemployed workers.

We turn now to more selective policies for those categories of workers experiencing special problems in adapting to the changing employment structure. Two groups that are of particular concern are older workers and workers who have been laid off. Reintegrating those individuals into productive employment should be an important policy objective, particularly as Canada moves into an era of slow work force growth, where changing patterns of employment cannot be met by relying on new entrants.

In this country, the conventional public-policy approach regarding older workers has been to compensate them for loss of employment. This philosophy underlies the Program for Older Worker Adjustment (POWA) – currently the major initiative in this area – which provides for compensation for permanently laid-off older workers. In a 1987 report, *Managing Adjustment*, which was released shortly after POWA had been announced, the Economic Council supported the notion of a program specifically concerned with the adjustment difficulties of older workers. Since then, we have undertaken more research on older-worker adjustment and POWA. Our findings have raised concerns about certain features of POWA, including its limited and somewhat subjective eligibility conditions.

A more fundamental concern, however, stems from our belief that the approach to older-worker adjustment should be centred on a positive reintegration strategy that emphasizes retraining and job-search counselling. Compensation programs like POWA are expensive and, by necessity, have very restricted coverage. Moreover, they do not adequately recognize the principle that productive employment is a key to full participation in our society. As Canada's work force continues to grow more slowly, the contribution of older workers to the economy will become more critical. Canada simply must learn to use its older workers effectively.

Certainly, the adjustment difficulties faced by these workers should not be minimized. Some are understandably reluctant to change jobs or careers, both for personal reasons and because the benefits they have built up may be jeopardized; with respect to the latter consideration, enhancing the portability of benefit plans is clearly an important objective. There is also a general reluctance, on the part of employers, to hire older people; this attitude is bound to change in the future, however, as employers will increasingly come to realize that older workers must be the solution for the labour shortages that they will face.

On balance, the Council finds that there are strong arguments supporting a policy strategy primarily aimed at reintegration rather than compensation. As well, some experiments with a focus on assisting older workers to acquire new employment skills suggest that reintegration is a viable approach to adjustment. We note, for example, the demand for the Transitions program in Ontario, which provides vouchers to institutions or employers offering training to individuals aged 45 years or more.

3 **We strongly endorse the principle of reintegration as the cornerstone of adjustment policy for older Canadians. In this regard, we recommend that publicly funded programs for these workers emphasize retraining and employment counselling.**

The reintegration principle is also important in the case of laid-off workers. We have noted the adjustment difficulties of these workers with respect to the length of time needed to find another job and to the frequency with which they experience wage cuts. Research indicates that reemployment outcomes are much more favourable when workers are informed in advance that they will be laid off. Adjustment is also assisted when labour and management work together to develop redeployment solutions for the employees affected.

Canadian jurisdictions currently have some minimum standards for providing advance notice to laid-off workers. While notice-period requirements vary considerably, in general they depend on either the employee's length of service or the number of workers who are being laid off. In the event of group layoffs, some jurisdictions also include positive redeployment measures, such as the advance provision of the profile of laid-off employees to the government or the creation of a firm-level adjustment committee.

The report of the federal government's Advisory Council on Adjustment – the De Grandpré Council – which was published in 1989, recommended minimum national standards regarding the advance notice of layoffs. The length of notice provided by the employer would depend on the number of workers involved in the layoff: two weeks would be required when fewer than five employees were to be laid off, with the notice period increasing in stages – up to 16 weeks when the layoff included 50 or more. Advance notice would be given to full-time and "regular" part-time workers; in the case of group layoffs, the employer would be required to provide the appropriate government with a profile of the affected employees and with a proposed compensation and redeployment package.

4 **We recommend that the federal, provincial, and territorial governments implement the national minimum advance-notice standards suggested by the De Grandpré report. The minimum notice period should be two weeks in the case of layoffs involving between one and four persons, four weeks where between five and nine persons are to be laid off, eight weeks where 10 to 49 persons are to be laid off, and 16 weeks in the case of layoffs of 50 people or more.**

The principle of this recommendation – that advance-notice requirements should depend on the magnitude of the layoff – reflects the fact that the adjustment problem tends to increase with the number of workers involved. In the event of a major layoff, large numbers of workers with similar skills and experience must search for new jobs at one point in time, frequently in industries and localities where job opportunities are relatively scarce. As a consequence, the challenges of a major layoff often can require more than advance notice.

In these situations, the re-employment possibilities of those who have lost their jobs may benefit significantly from adjustment plans developed at the firm level. These plans, typically developed by representatives of management and labour, address issues such as the skill profile of the laid-off workers, likely re-employment prospects, and appropriate counselling, mobility, and retraining options. While the government involved acts as a facilitator, provides information on labour market conditions and programs, and covers the administrative costs of the committee, it is the parties themselves that must work out a solution. As this Council has noted before, labour/management adjustment committees coordinated by the federal Industrial Adjustment Service (IAS) have a very positive and cost-effective record in layoff situations with respect to the re-employment of laid-off workers and the post-layoff climate within the firm itself; indeed, in two recent Statements, *Making Technology Work* and *Managing Adjustment*, we have expressed our strong support for the IAS committees.

Currently, industrial adjustment committees are required in the federal jurisdiction in the case of major layoffs (involving 50 or more workers); Quebec, Ontario, and Manitoba provide for the establishment of such committees at the request of the Minister of Labour. In practice, a high degree of flexibility exists in the application of this employment standard. In the federal jurisdiction, for example, the requirement for a committee is waived where the parties have established their own adjustment arrangement or where it would be a real burden, such as in a bankruptcy situation.

5 **We recommend that all jurisdictions establish a labour standard providing for the creation of a committee that will include management and labour representatives, to develop and implement a re-employment package for laid-off workers involved in a major layoff.**

Without identifying a precise definition of what constitutes a "major" layoff, we note that the most prevalent standard in Canadian jurisdictions is a loss of jobs for 50 workers or more.

The requirements set out in the two preceding recommendations are intended for situations where workers must seek new employment opportunities; they would not apply in cases where layoffs are seasonal or short-term in nature. In light of accelerating economic change, the re-employment problems faced by laid-off workers, and the observed benefits of advance-notice and adjustment committees, we believe that these proposals, which would clearly strengthen existing standards in most jurisdictions, would contribute to smoother adjustment in the Canadian labour market without imposing undue demands on employers.

Employer-Based Human-Resource Development

It is the Council's position that the overwhelming responsibility for job-related skill formation rests with business and labour. Indeed, the role of the private sector in human-resource development is crucial. We have already emphasized that employer-based training is the most effective approach for developing vocational skills and that, increasingly, human-resource development within industry is essential to Canada's competitiveness.

Ideally, a strong "training culture" should be created by forces operating at the firm level – by employers viewing skill formation as an essential element of human-resource management, by unions making training a priority, and by employees taking initiative to update existing skills and to acquire new ones. Certainly, there are examples of Canadian firms where this commitment to training by all parties exists. However, our review in Chapter 7 of the available information suggests that the extent of private-sector training in this country is inadequate.

Overall, Canadian employers and employees need to make a much stronger commitment to training. This raises the question of what kinds of instruments might be effectively used to stimulate human-resource development at the level of the firm. There are a variety of "training triggers" that could be considered, including earned time off for training, employer-sponsored educational leave, and firm-level training trust funds. The most frequently discussed triggers are the grant-and-levy scheme and other tax-based arrangements. While there are a number of possible designs, a "training tax" would involve the imposition of an earmarked corporate tax that is refunded to firms up to the full amount, depending on the extent of training provided. This would create a financial incentive for firms to provide training and at the same time generate a pool of funds to finance training to fill gaps in the employer-sponsored effort.

Indeed, Canada's apparent "training gap" and a growing awareness of the harm that it can potentially inflict on this country in a globally competitive, information-based economy have led to increased calls for some kind of universally applied policy intervention to stimulate skill formation throughout the private sector. The credibility of this position as a serious option was established by a recommendation of the De Grandpré report for a training levy.

After reviewing training taxes and other types of triggers, however, we would not recommend the institution of a universally applied standard at this time. Any across-the-board intervention would need to be based on a number of principles: a simple administrative format; no new spending by governments; recognition of differences in training incentives for firms of different sizes and in different industries; access to training for all employees; a flexible definition of "training" that would extend beyond the traditional notion of formal courses; and no additional costs for firms already meeting the agreed-upon standards. Clearly, these requirements pose substantial design problems that could not be solved easily.

While ruling out the use of a universal instrument to stimulate training, we believe that a commitment to training could, in some industries where business and labour recognize that more skills formation is needed, be effectively created by planning at the sector level. We have noted some recent initiatives where employers and workers, together, identify skill needs in their industry and develop and implement an appropriate training plan. Sectoral initiatives can take on a variety of forms, depending on the nature of the industry, its organization, and its key human-resource issues. These approaches are not meant to replace but, rather, to encourage firm-level training plans.

Where there is no existing tradition of human-resource development, the Council sees considerable potential in sectoral approaches; while our remarks here focus on sector-based plans, we also note the effectiveness of some initiatives operating at the regional or local level.

The electrical-product and automotive-repair sectors are examples of industries that have created committees, involving both labour and management, that are charged with identifying and addressing sectoral human-resource issues. In some respects, the example of the automotive-repair scheme is of particular interest. That industry, like many of the growing service industries, is dominated by small firms and does not have well-established formal organizations on either the employer or the labour side. While at first glance these characteristics would not seem to be amenable to a sectorwide initiative, the automotive-repair experience demonstrates that a fragmented industry can be coordinated. Indeed, there may be a particular need for sector-based plans in industries of this type, which typically do not have a strong training record at the firm-level.

While a sector-based human-resource approach may not be suitable for all industries – and indeed may be redundant in industries with an established training record – we believe that these initiatives have a number of attributes that could make them interesting for sectors that do not have a strong tradition in this area. First and foremost, they can promote the private-sector responsibility that we see as being so critical. As well, there are advantages associated with being close to the scene, in terms of diagnosing the real problems and identifying tailor-made responses. Furthermore, these approaches offer a forum for labour and management to work together – and that, in itself, is a virtue.

Ultimately, business and labour in any industry must determine whether a sectoral training plan is appropriate; where it is, the initiative must come from the industry itself, with respect to both the commitment and the resources. Government can make a significant contribution simply by facilitating the creation of the industry committee and the development of its priorities. The Industrial Adjustment Service, for example, played a key role in the start-up of the electrical-product and automotive-repair initiatives. However, the ability of the IAS to support the creation of other industry-level plans is restricted by the relatively limited funds available for this purpose ($1 million in 1988-89).

6 **We encourage the provincial and federal governments to facilitate the emerging trend towards sector-based human-resource development initiatives. To this end, we recommend that the federal government allocate increased funds to the Industrial Adjustment Service to be used as "seed money" for the development of sector-specific human-resource plans in industries that have chosen to initiate such plans.**

168 Employment in the Service Economy

The Council believes that the level of skills development in Canadian industry is an issue of national concern. In our view, more active employer-based training represents a major challenge. The necessary investment in human resources should be generated by employers responding more realistically to the needs of the marketplace, by unions more frequently placing training issues on the bargaining table, and in some instances by industry-based human-resource committees implementing training plans more aggressively. One way or the other, training must become a fundamental activity for Canadian employers and a fundamental right for Canadian workers. Tomorrow's economy will require nothing less.

Promote Economic Security for Workers

The research undertaken for this report suggests that employment is becoming increasingly polarized into two categories – good jobs and bad jobs. This is most apparent when we look at trends in the distribution of employment income: over the past two decades there has been a notable decline in the share of the work force with middle-level earnings. At the same time, the growth in nonstandard employment forms is leading to the emergence of a related dichotomy within the labour force: workers with well-paid, relatively stable jobs and with extensive legal protections; and workers in employment forms that are often more tenuous, usually less well compensated, and nearly always less protected.

This polarization raises policy dilemmas in the prevailing context of restraint, since it appears to have increased the redistributive task facing the transfer system. It is difficult to determine an appropriate response to the evidence on income distribution, as it is not yet fully clear what factors underlie the observed polarization and whether it is a transitory or permanent phenomenon. We do believe, however, that employment must be the fundamental source of economic security in Canada; the capacity of the labour market to meet the economic security needs of workers should therefore be strengthened.

The suggestions that we have made with respect to training should contribute to the economic security of workers. While training is not a panacea, many individuals experiencing difficulties in the labour market are severely constrained by a lack of education or by limited access to training. Improvements in those areas can substantially raise their prospects for upward mobility.

We believe, also, that stronger policies to protect nonstandard workers represent an important means of addressing some of the causes of the growing earnings inequality, since many low-income workers occupy those kinds of jobs. In coming to this conclusion, we have been struck by the complex nature of nonstandard employment and by the tensions involved in applying labour policies to those work forms.

Traditionally, employment standards and benefit programs were designed to fit stereotyped images of an average worker – typically a male employed full time in the goods sector. While there has been progress, some regulations and benefits still afford a lesser degree of protection or coverage to certain groups of nonstandard workers.

Should employment standards and benefits be further extended to offer wider coverage to workers in nonstandard jobs? We are aware that there are strong arguments in opposition to this course of action. Some nonstandard workers are most concerned with their immediate cash flow – e.g., those with income problems and those who have only a casual attachment to the labour force. To the extent that improved security and benefits will result in less take-home pay, the short-run interests of these individuals will not be served by stronger policies in support of nonstandard employees. Another effect might well be to create disincentives to hire workers in nonstandard job forms, thereby reducing employment options for many workers and diminishing the operational flexibility of employers.

Although these arguments are valid, the Council ultimately supports the principle that nonstandard workers with an ongoing attachment to the labour force should not be excluded from the protections and benefits offered to those in full-time, more permanent jobs. The notion of labour force attachment has changed, and policies to support the working population must keep pace. Moreover, many workers are involuntarily in nonstandard jobs and would prefer full-time, full-year positions if they could find them. Our concern here is heightened by the fact that the incomes, benefits, and job security of workers in nonstandard jobs are generally lower than for people doing similar types of work in more conventional employment forms.

Our analysis does lead us to the conclusion that the recent growth of nonstandard employment is part of a long-term trend. If that is indeed the case, steps must be taken to ensure that nonstandard work will offer more benefits and greater protection. This may well have social consequences too; indeed, we have noted the growing frequency of labour disputes where the central issue for labour is security.

Policymakers must bear in mind the new employment diversity and explicitly address the situation of workers in the new employment forms. In doing so, they face the dilemma of providing the intended support to nonstandard employees without undermining the flexibility needs of these workers or of employers.

Employment Standards

Some of the current employment standards should be extended to certain nonstandard employment forms. The case is perhaps most compelling with respect to part-time workers, specifically those who develop a continuous and regular relationship with an employer. Indeed, part-time employees often have an attachment to their employer and to the labour market that is comparable to that of full-time employees. For example, some individuals (often those with household responsibilities) enter into an explicit arrangement with an employer to work part-time on a continuing basis; for other part-time workers, an ongoing relationship with a particular employer develops over time. We believe, partly on grounds of equity, that part-time employees who develop such ongoing relationships with employers should be entitled to receive the same benefits, prorated, as full-time workers. And beyond considerations of fairness, access to employee benefits is an important step in improving the prospects of many workers, very frequently women, for achieving economic security through employment. Many of those benefits, from pensions to various types of insurance, have the effect of reducing the number of people who need the safety nets provided by public benefit programs. Accordingly,

7 **We support the adoption of legislation in all jurisdictions that will provide for the inclusion of part-time employees with an ongoing employer attachment, on a prorated basis, in all employee-benefit programs normally available to full-time employees.**

Although we have provided above a couple of general examples of what we mean by an "ongoing employer attachment," we recognize that they constitute less than a complete definition. Developing such a definition is an appropriate subject for consultation among the groups affected.

Public Benefit Programs

The economic security of nonstandard workers would also be favourably affected by ensuring that they are not unreasonably excluded from public benefit programs. Here, too, policymakers must recognize that the nature of labour force attachment – the "litmus test" for coverage – is changing.

8 **As a general principle, we urge that awareness of the new employment diversity be incorporated into the design of public benefit programs, with a view to ensuring that workers in nonstandard employment forms are not excluded from these benefits.**

To offer one example, the unemployment insurance system has traditionally determined eligibility for benefits, in part, on the basis of labour force attachment; in some ways, however, the criteria used to establish the degree of attachment have not kept pace with changing labour market realities. At present, in order to qualify for benefits, employees must earn at least 20 per cent of the UI earnings ceiling or work 15 or more hours per week, for a specified number of weeks depending on their geographical location. As a result, a part-time employee may be ineligible even though he/she may have accumulated more hours of employment than, for instance, a full-time employee with the minimum number of weeks of employment.

Pensions

Relative to the working-age population, the economic status of Canadians aged 65 and over has improved substantially over the past two decades. And undoubtedly, they will benefit in the future as a result of improvements during the 1980s in pension-standards legislation in jurisdictions that cover 80 per cent of the Canadian labour force. Benefits, protection, and portability will continue to be enhanced for those who are members of pension plans. As well, a larger proportion of the labour force has purchased registered retirement savings plans (RRSPs).

Pension reform has not helped those who are not covered by a work-related plan, however. And it is important to note that the proportion of the work force taking part in employer pension plans has been declining – from 40 to 37 per cent between 1980 and 1986. The locus of employment growth in the 1980s – largely in nonstandard employment forms and in small firms – is very likely to have contributed to this decrease. We know, for example, that pension coverage is only about 15 per cent both among part-time workers and among workers employed in firms with fewer than 20 employees.

This recent decline in work-related pension coverage gives cause for concern. The design of Canada's public pension system (which includes Old Age Security, the Guaranteed Income Supplement, and the Canada and Quebec Pension Plans) is effectively predicated on the premise that Canadians will acquire private pension entitlements throughout their working lives. If the trends observed during the 1980s persist, however, they may call into question the validity of that assumption. In light of these considerations,

9   We urge governments to evaluate on an ongoing basis the adequacy of Canada's combined private and public pension systems. Governments should be alert to the possibility that labour market trends may necessitate further rethinking of the overall approach to retirement income security in the 1990s.

Recognize the Role of Services in Economic Growth

While the main focus of our research has been on labour market policy, our study has led us to recognize that the shift to services also has profound implications for economic development. Although specific recommendations in that area are beyond the scope of this report, we suggest general directions for economic development policies, in light of the changing contribution of services to economic growth.

A strong conclusion of our examination of the growth of the service economy is that a successful economic strategy must not only reinforce the importance of both resources and manufacturing industries, but must also recognize the contribution of services to overall economic growth. Service industries are important sources of employment and output. Competitiveness and productivity growth are keys to an economy in which more and more people are working in services, especially since services are becoming increasingly internationalized.

The efficiency and the quality of the service industries themselves must become a key focus of economic development policy. Policies that identify and foster linkages between goods and service producers, and that improve the quality and effectiveness of those linkages, should be encouraged.

Industrial Policy

Historically, Canadian industrial policy has focused on the resource and manufacturing sectors. Eligibility requirements for access to government grant, subsidy, and tax-relief programs have tended to apply to capital investments in plant and equipment for the production of goods. As the efficiency and quality of the service sector become increasingly important to overall living standards, however, those biases must be eliminated. Governments must become explicitly aware of the unintended "steering effects" built into policies and programs that were designed for a goods-based economy. Public policy that focuses on general economic development should, in fact, be neutral in its treatment of goods and services.

One important example of the bias towards goods producers involves technology policy. Innovation and technological change are fundamental to productivity growth and competitiveness in both goods and service industries. Canadian policy in this area, however, focuses on the development of new technologies by the goods industries. Little research has been done on how the processes of innovation and diffusion take place in the service sector, although some pioneering work suggests that service-sector innovation patterns may be quite different from those in the goods sector. Innovation in the service sector does not come from scientists working in laboratories, for example, but rather involves new ways of organizing and delivering services. Accordingly,

10 We urge governments to review their overall policy stance towards innovation and the service sector. They should discuss these issues with the appropriate industry associations and with experts in the field, for the purpose of developing an innovation policy that would reflect the contribution of R&D and technological change to economic growth in services.

Some key questions need to be answered: How does the pace of innovation among Canadian service producers compare with that of their counterparts elsewhere? Are there identifiable problems in the process of innovation diffusion? If so, what actions could be taken by industry and governments? Are some service producers more in need than others of policy support to improve their innovation performance?

Innovation represents just one example of non-neutrality in industrial policy. Industry, Science and Technology Canada (ISTC) is now undertaking a series of consultations with other federal departments to determine the degree to which anti-service-sector biases are built into a range of policies and programs. This effort is essential, in our view, and we urge all departments to regard this review as being of the utmost importance.

Linking Goods and Services

An important emphasis of industrial policy should be on facilitating linkages between goods and service industries. Some programs recently initiated by ISTC incorporate that emphasis. A good example of this type of approach is a program developed by the Canadian Textiles Institute, the Canadian Apparel Manufacturers Institute, and the Retail Council of Canada in cooperation with ISTC. The Canadian

Manufacturers and Retailers Council (CANMARC) provides a centralized source of specialized information to assist manufacturers and retailers in the coordinated use of technologies such as bar-coding and electronic data interchange.

CANMARC has only recently been established, and it remains to be seen whether its efforts will be successful. In our view, however, it has many attractive features: its purpose is to facilitate industry linkages; its development heavily involved the private sector; and the industries that joined together have traditionally lagged in the introduction of new technologies.

Other industries could benefit from similar types of arrangements; indeed, interest has been expressed by some of them. CANMARC-type programs could be especially useful in regions with a resource-based economy; those regions which are based on agriculture or fishing, in particular, face difficult problems in fostering linkages between sectors, since awareness and use of both the services themselves and of the technologies so important for linkages are relatively low in those industries.

11 We urge industry associations and governments to work together to develop programs that contain "linkage" features, such as those of CANMARC, for other groups of industries that are connected through customer/supplier relationships. Furthermore, we recommend that an early emphasis be placed upon involving resource producers.

Government's role in the development of such programs should be to act as facilitator, bringing complementary industries together to develop cooperative arrangements. No new public spending commitments are implied.

Service Infrastructure

Given the largely intangible nature of service outputs, the key elements of that sector's infrastructure are telecommunications and computer technology: these are the "highways" that "transport" those "products" nationally and internationally. A nation or region that lacks an up-to-date infrastructure will lag behind others in attracting and developing dynamic services; not only will job opportunities in services suffer, but – given the synergies – the goods sector will be adversely affected as well. Traditional services (notably, retail trade) are also critical components in an interdependent economy, since they represent the final contact between the commercial marketplace and the producers of consumer products. Consequently, the infrastructure linking producers and consumers through retailers must also be a priority.

Canada's telecommunications system is among the most technologically sophisticated in the world. It has the potential to provide Canadian industry with a comparative advantage in the current shift to information-intensive activities. That potential can only be fully realized, however, if a conscious effort is made to shape the telecommunications infrastructure so that it will help to foster the establishment and growth of a vibrant service sector in Canada. In addition, given the growing importance of human-resource development, combined telecommunications and computer technologies can increasingly play a strategic role in education and training.

The August 1989 ruling of the Supreme Court of Canada – stating that the federal government has sole constitutional jurisdiction over all of the major telephone companies in Canada (including those previously held to be under provincial jurisdiction) – provides the opportunity for the development of an appropriate set of rules for telecommunications across the country. With the removal of Crown immunity for some companies that were previously regulated at the provincial level, there is scope for designing a single set of rules for telecommunications across the country, eliminating the inefficiencies and inequalities associated with a jurisdictionally fractured system.

A detailed prescription for a Canadian telecommunications and computer policy that would promote the development of a diversified, efficient, and high-quality service sector and of effective linkages between goods and services is far beyond the scope of this research report. However, there is no question that Canadian telecommunications policy must evolve as the structure of the global economy changes and as new technologies appear. That evolution will necessarily involve a large number of regulatory issues and key decisions regarding standards for the content and format of the information to be exchanged. An important issue will be the extent to which competition is used to achieve the desired results.

It is also likely that regional issues will play a growing role in decision making in this area. Natural market forces will almost certainly create the strongest pressures for the introduction of new telecommunications capabilities in the highly developed parts of the country. Those areas which are lagging in terms of the range of telecommunications services offered will find it increasingly difficult to compete with the more advanced regions. Policy must therefore ensure that all regions in Canada are given equal opportunity to develop information-based industries by having the necessary telecommunications capabilities in place.

12 We therefore urge the federal and provincial governments to view the Canadian telecommunications and computer infrastructure "proactively" as a vital component of an internationally competitive, diversified, information-based economy. At least four dimensions must be considered in shaping such an infrastructure: the technological capabilities of the system; the availability of enhanced services; the cost structure; and the adoption of international standards.

Regional Development

The labour market trends evoked in the present research report cannot help but make the job of reducing regional disparities more difficult. Since a detailed analysis of the implications of the growth of services for regional policy was not an explicit element of our research, we offer only general observations here.

How can lagging regions improve their performance? Unfortunately, given the new economic realities, the fundamental challenge is to prevent further widening of the existing gaps – between urban and rural areas in general, and between smaller urban areas and major metropolitan centres, most of which are located in the already highly developed regions, in particular.

The development of dynamic services in the less-developed regions is constrained by the frequent lack of integration of branch plants with local service producers and by the fact that the head offices of multi-branch firms tend to be located in the highly developed regions. The possibilities for a decentralized development of dynamic services therefore appear to be limited to services that respond to the needs of locally controlled businesses, to services that have been decentralized to less costly locations by multi-branch firms, to tradable specialized services that have developed on the basis of expertise related to the local industrial base, and to services that respond to public-sector demand through procurement. With respect to the last of these, the federal Department of Supply and Services has recently initiated changes in procurement policy that appear to be based on a recognition of the role that this instrument can play in regional development. While competitive pricing should unquestionably remain as the basis for awarding contracts, efforts must be made to ensure that goods and service producers have equal opportunity to bid on government contracts, regardless of location.

Regional development efforts should build upon the complementarities that exist between services and the regional industrial base. In this country, that base is often resource-oriented; given the particularly strong stimulative effect (suggested by our analysis) of several resource activities on the demand for services, this traditional strength of the Canadian economy may be well-suited to generating growth in dynamic services. To make this happen, firms in the resource sector – and indeed in other sectors of the regional economy – must have computer-based technologies in place. Regional lags in the diffusion of these technologies will handicap the entire regional economy because of the linkages between industries. Those concerned with regional development must, therefore, view the spread of technological change as an essential part of building the infrastructure of the 1990s and beyond.

In other cases, services based on specialized local expertise often develop in association with universities, local research centres, or other specialized facilities. Here, too, the key is to capitalize on local skills, opening the door perhaps to other markets in Canada and abroad.

It is not inconceivable that, at some point in the 21st century, new technologies – and, perhaps equally important, social innovations – will lead to more dispersed patterns of economic activity. For now, however, dynamic services remain an overwhelmingly urban phenomenon; and while subregional centres based on special skills may develop, extensive decentralization is not likely over the medium term. Therefore, regional planners must pay special attention to the health of their largest urban areas as a means of ensuring that disparities across regions do not widen. And by promoting competitiveness, especially in those services which are linked to local resource and manufacturing firms, those local firms will themselves benefit from higher-quality inputs. In that way, growth can spread throughout regions as well.

Finally, a necessary condition for regional growth will be the development of a well-educated and skilled work force. Increasingly, cities that are able to offer specialized pools of skills will attract new business activities in unique niches. Those concerned with regional development, therefore, will have to be concerned with the issues related to training and education discussed in this research report.

Measuring the Service Economy

Economic policy would benefit from better data on service activity. Major problems have been consistently identified in the measurement of service output, productivity growth, and trade. In undertaking our research on services, we identified a number of other data problems. For example, the instruments for tracking the business cycle – such as new and unfilled orders, productive capacity, and inventories – must be reshaped to reflect more accurately an economy in which the service sector has become so important. Also, data are needed on the in-house service activities of goods-producing firms; such information would provide insights into an important component of real service employment and would make possible a better assessment of the magnitude of the contracting-out of services by goods-producing firms. To offer another example, methods of estimating productivity growth rates by sector need to be improved; estimates appear to be biased in such a way that the share of economy-wide productivity gains allocated to the goods sector is inflated, while the service sector's share is biased downward. As well, some of the key components of an information-based economy have yet to be defined and measured successfully; for example, there are simply no objective yardsticks for the concepts of "skill" and "knowledge."

What is required is an extension and rethinking of the measures that economists have traditionally used. We strongly support the request, made by Statistics Canada, for resources to review the national statistical base in order to improve its capacity to measure service activity. Better information on services, by improving the basis for decision-making, would, in the final analysis, benefit all Canadians.

* * * * *

The Canadian economy, along with the economies of other highly developed countries, is undergoing tremendous change. The remarkable growth of the service sector is, at the same time, both a cause and a manifestation of that change. In this research report we have stressed the contribution that services now make to competitiveness and overall performance – both in their own right and through their role in the production of goods. In the new interdependent economy, the distinctions between goods and services are becoming blurred, and the success of one depends on the efficiency and growth of the other.

Many Canadians still think of the service economy as "second rank" – as a source of weak productivity and bad jobs. That perception is true, but it is only half of the story. The service sector is also a source of good jobs and high productivity, providing new avenues for wealth creation and new scope for building stronger, more competitive industries.

The trends that we have described raise major challenges for both workers and employers, on the one hand, and for governments, on the other. In the face of the polarization of the labour market and of the acceleration in economic restructuring, Canadian workers must commit themselves to a life-long personal strategy of skill formation and adjustment to change. In our view, Canadian employers will play a particularly critical role in the process of adaptation to the "double-edged" labour market. They must adopt a much stronger focus on human resources by investing more in people and, where possible, by transforming bad jobs with low pay, benefits, and stability into better jobs that provide greater economic security. The slowdown in the growth of the labour force and anticipated shortages of skilled workers will create some pressure to move in that direction. The degree of change required, however, will not occur unless more employers become highly committed to the development of human resources.

While emphasizing the importance of the actions of employers and workers, the Council believes there is also an essential role for public policy in the emerging labour market. The bad-jobs side of the story is heightening the stakes for effective training and labour-adjustment programs and for other programs that influence the economic security of workers. The good-jobs side is placing new demands on Canada's education and training systems, and on industrial policies.

Ultimately, many of Canada's traditional institutions and patterns of behaviour must be reshaped by governments and market forces acting in concert to build competitive industries and to enhance the security of Canadian workers.

Appendices

A The Calculation of Stimulative Power by Industry

In an economic system, industry (gross) output minus intermediate input is by definition equal to final demand, which includes consumption, investment, inventories, exports, imports, and gross current government expenditures on goods and services. The well-known Leontief input-output system derives from this accounting identity and by simple matrix operation:

$$g = (I - A)^{-1} * f$$

| output by industry | intermediate input requirement by industry | final demand by industry |

I is an identity matrix and all other symbols are either matrices or vectors, whose definitions are noted above. The model states that output by industry is equal to the product of the total multiplier matrix (also known as the Leontief inverse) and final demand. After the system completes all transactions required for one production pass, the ultimate industry output of the economy can be calculated from the right of the equation for any given final demand. These are the cornerstones of input-output analysis. However, because this approach focuses on the impacts of final demand on industry outputs, information on the nature of the underlying industry transactions is not provided explicitly and little attention has been paid in the literature to the details of interindustry input-output relationships, with the exception of Miyazawa.[1]

Miyazawa first partitions the total economy into individual sectors and then applies the input-output technique to them individually. By setting up each sector as an economy in its own right, while keeping all other parts of the economy unchanged, the importance of the interactions of the industries in the sector with the rest of the economy can be calculated. This is, of course, a partial equilibrium analysis. The merit of this technique is that it unambiguously captures the effect of each set of sectoral activities on the rest of the system. For example, it enables the calculation of the demand of the goods industries for the outputs of individual service industries, based entirely on activity within the goods sector alone. The most fundamental difference between Leontief's and Miyazawa's approaches is that Leontief's approach calculates the effect of the interactions of the total economic system, thus showing the ultimate effect of any change on the economy. Unlike Miyazawa's approach, however, it does not quantify the "pure" effect of one sector's activities on the other.[2]

We adapted Miyazawa's methodology for the Canadian input-output data in the following way. First, the input matrix of the input-output table – that is, the matrix which shows the goods and services needed to produce one unit of output in each of the industries in the system – is partitioned into submatrices reflecting the goods and service inputs for goods production and the goods and service inputs for service production:

$$\text{Input matrix} = \begin{bmatrix} P & P_1 \\ S_1 & S \end{bmatrix} \begin{matrix} \text{goods} \\ \text{services} \end{matrix}$$

P shows the goods needed to produce one unit of output in each of the goods industries; P_1 shows the goods required to produce one unit of output in each of the service industries; S_1 shows the services required to produce one unit of output in each of the goods industries; and S shows the services required to produce one unit of output in each of the service industries.

The goods sector is treated separately from the service sector, and following the same procedure used for input-output analysis of the total economy, the internal multiplier matrix is derived for each of the two sectors. For the goods sector, then:

$$B = (I - P)^{-1}$$

This means that because each goods industry requires other goods as inputs to the production process, one unit of output in each goods industries leads to the production of additional outputs in the industries supplying those goods. The B matrix therefore provides information on the total units of goods to be produced by each goods industry.

When the S_1 and the B matrices are multiplied, the product is an estimate of the stimulative power of the goods industries on services, that is, the units of services required to satisfy the demand of goods production. Similarly, the stimulative power of services on goods also can be calculated.

The end result is a matrix showing the stimulative power of the industries in each sector on each of the industries in the other sector (see Tables A-1 and A-2). To find the stimulative power of each industry in one sector on the whole of the other sector, the columns are simply totalled (see Charts 3-4 and 3-5).

Table A-1

The Stimulative Power of Each Goods Industry[1] on Each Service Industry, 1985

	Goods industry[2]								
	1. AG	2. FIS	3. FOR	4. MIN	5. PET	6. QUAR	7. FOOD	8. BEV	9. TO
	(1981 dollars)								
Service industry[3]									
1. TRAN	0.0045	0.0098	0.1144	0.0131	0.0023	0.0587	0.0096	0.0031	0.0040
2. PIPE	0.0023	0.0027	0.0008	0.0028	0.0005	0.0018	0.0025	0.0030	0.0012
3. STOR	0.0001	0.0002	0.0034	0.0004	0.0001	0.0018	0.0003	0.0001	0.0001
4. COMM	0.0054	0.0022	0.0023	0.0027	0.0014	0.0046	0.0067	0.0069	0.0056
5. UTIL	0.0158	0.0034	0.0024	0.0278	0.0122	0.0225	0.0147	0.0143	0.0109
6. WTR	0.0355	0.0239	0.0136	0.0244	0.0074	0.0413	0.0436	0.0216	0.0219
7. RTR	0.0064	0.0079	0.0120	0.0038	0.0043	0.0161	0.0078	0.0048	0.0041
8. FIN	0.0357	0.0216	0.0539	0.0424	0.1971	0.0301	0.0238	0.0215	0.0219
9. INSU	0.0058	0.0034	0.0084	0.0069	0.0331	0.0041	0.0038	0.0033	0.0034
10. ROY	0.0065	0.0038	0.0093	0.0077	0.0370	0.0046	0.0042	0.0037	0.0039
11. DWE	0.0000	0.0000	0.0000	0.0000	0.0000	0.0000	0.0000	0.0000	0.0000
12. BSER	0.0049	0.0046	0.0050	0.0172	0.0212	0.0063	0.0078	0.0137	0.0116
13. ED	0.0000	0.0000	0.0000	0.0000	0.0000	0.0000	0.0000	0.0000	0.0000
14. HEAL	0.0000	0.0000	0.0002	0.0000	0.0001	0.0001	0.0000	0.0000	0.0000
15. ACC	0.0002	0.0003	0.0005	0.0002	0.0007	0.0005	0.0001	0.0001	0.0001
16. AMUS	0.0000	0.0000	0.0000	0.0000	0.0001	0.0000	0.0000	0.0000	0.0000
17. PSER	0.0023	0.0029	0.0101	0.0028	0.0029	0.0130	0.0031	0.0033	0.0028
18. OSER	0.0032	0.0040	0.0129	0.0043	0.0046	0.0166	0.0043	0.0047	0.0040
Total services	0.1293	0.0914	0.2501	0.1573	0.3258	0.2228	0.1329	0.1049	0.0962

	Goods industry[2]									
	10. RU	11. PL	12. LE	13. TX	14. CL	15. WD	16. FU	17. PA	18. PR	19. PME
	(1981 dollars)									
Service industry[3]										
1. TRAN	0.0018	0.0019	0.0021	0.0017	0.0017	0.0366	0.0045	0.0159	0.0041	0.0042
2. PIPE	0.0032	0.0038	0.0017	0.0035	0.0010	0.0018	0.0020	0.0048	0.0015	0.0050
3. STOR	0.0000	0.0000	0.0001	0.0000	0.0000	0.0011	0.0001	0.0005	0.0001	0.0001
4. COMM	0.0079	0.0098	0.0082	0.0079	0.0083	0.0047	0.0080	0.0051	0.0225	0.0037
5. UTIL	0.0168	0.0224	0.0099	0.0177	0.0083	0.0173	0.0121	0.0547	0.0158	0.0289
6. WTR	0.0229	0.0297	0.0423	0.0335	0.0397	0.0362	0.0611	0.0281	0.0302	0.0349
7. RTR	0.0029	0.0044	0.0061	0.0034	0.0020	0.0097	0.0040	0.0079	0.0037	0.0034
8. FIN	0.0334	0.0211	0.0252	0.0195	0.0220	0.0317	0.0227	0.0221	0.0243	0.0163
9. INSU	0.0054	0.0033	0.0040	0.0031	0.0036	0.0048	0.0036	0.0033	0.0039	0.0025
10. ROY	0.0061	0.0037	0.0044	0.0034	0.0040	0.0053	0.0040	0.0037	0.0043	0.0028
11. DWE	0.0000	0.0000	0.0000	0.0000	0.0000	0.0000	0.0000	0.0000	0.0000	0.0000
12. BSER	0.0152	0.0119	0.0096	0.0091	0.0122	0.0077	0.0144	0.0087	0.0152	0.0088
13. ED	0.0000	0.0000	0.0000	0.0000	0.0000	0.0000	0.0000	0.0000	0.0000	0.0000
14. HEAL	0.0000	0.0000	0.0000	0.0000	0.0000	0.0000	0.0000	0.0000	0.0000	0.0000
15. ACC	0.0001	0.0001	0.0002	0.0001	0.0001	0.0003	0.0001	0.0002	0.0001	0.0001
16. AMUS	0.0000	0.0000	0.0000	0.0000	0.0000	0.0000	0.0000	0.0000	0.0000	0.0000
17. PSER	0.0023	0.0035	0.0037	0.0028	0.0015	0.0076	0.0025	0.0049	0.0026	0.0028
18. OSER	0.0036	0.0050	0.0052	0.0040	0.0025	0.0099	0.0039	0.0065	0.0040	0.0040
Total services	0.1225	0.1214	0.1233	0.1103	0.1075	0.1755	0.1438	0.1671	0.1331	0.1180

Table A-1 (concl'd.)

	Goods industry[2]								
	20. FME	21. MACH	22. TEQ	23. ELEC	24. NME	25. RPE	26. CH	27. OMA	28. CON
	(1981 dollars)								
Service industry[3]									
1. TRAN	0.0028	0.0017	0.0053	0.0029	0.0034	0.0021	0.0031	0.0021	0.0094
2. PIPE	0.0024	0.0015	0.0011	0.0012	0.0083	0.0191	0.0121	0.0016	0.0014
3. STOR	0.0001	0.0000	0.0001	0.0001	0.0001	0.0001	0.0001	0.0000	0.0003
4. COMM	0.0069	0.0092	0.0045	0.0139	0.0064	0.0026	0.0110	0.0117	0.0043
5. UTIL	0.0130	0.0096	0.0069	0.0086	0.0308	0.0124	0.0294	0.0094	0.0065
6. WTR	0.0326	0.0353	0.0175	0.0259	0.0239	0.0085	0.0277	0.0346	0.0498
7. RTR	0.0038	0.0026	0.0034	0.0024	0.0089	0.0040	0.0055	0.0027	0.0120
8. FIN	0.0180	0.0153	0.0091	0.0164	0.0255	0.1079	0.0366	0.0289	0.0184
9. INSU	0.0028	0.0024	0.0013	0.0026	0.0037	0.0180	0.0058	0.0047	0.0026
10. ROY	0.0031	0.0027	0.0014	0.0029	0.0042	0.0201	0.0065	0.0052	0.0029
11. DWE	0.0000	0.0000	0.0000	0.0000	0.0000	0.0000	0.0000	0.0000	0.0000
12. BSER	0.0108	0.0119	0.0312	0.0115	0.0108	0.0164	0.0152	0.0156	0.0352
13. ED	0.0000	0.0000	0.0000	0.0000	0.0000	0.0000	0.0000	0.0000	0.0000
14. HEAL	0.0000	0.0000	0.0000	0.0000	0.0000	0.0000	0.0000	0.0000	0.0000
15. ACC	0.0001	0.0001	0.0001	0.0001	0.0003	0.0004	0.0002	0.0001	0.0002
16. AMUS	0.0000	0.0000	0.0000	0.0000	0.0000	0.0000	0.0000	0.0000	0.0000
17. PSER	0.0031	0.0020	0.0029	0.0019	0.0076	0.0030	0.0043	0.0020	0.0057
18. OSER	0.0044	0.0031	0.0050	0.0030	0.0100	0.0045	0.0061	0.0033	0.0087
Total services	0.1045	0.0981	0.0904	0.0939	0.1444	0.2197	0.1644	0.1227	0.1581

1 The increase in the output of each service industry that results from a one-dollar increase in the output of each goods industry.

2 Goods industries: 1. AG – agriculture; 2. FIS – fishing and trapping; 3. FOR – logging and forestry; 4. MIN – mining; 5. PET – crude petroleum and gas; 6. QUAR – quarries and sand pits; 7. FOOD – food; 8. BEV – beverages; 9. TO – tobacco; 10. RU – rubber; 11. PL – plastics; 12. LE – leather; 13. TX – textiles; 14. CL – clothing; 15. WD – wood; 16. FU – furniture and fixtures; 17. PA – paper and allied industries; 18. PR – printing and publishing; 19. PME – primary metals; 20. FME – fabricated metals; 21. MACH – machinery; 22. TEQ – transportation equipment; 23. ELEC – electrical goods; 24. NME – nonmetalic minerals; 25. RPE – refined petroleum and coal; 26. CH – chemicals; 27. OMA – other manufacturing; 28. CON – construction.

3 Service industries: 1. TRAN – transportation; 2. PIPE – pipeline transportation; 3. STOR – storage; 4. COMM – communications; 5. UTIL – utilities; 6. WTR – wholesale trade; 7. RTR – retail trade; 8. FIN – finance and real estate; 9. INSU – insurance; 10. ROY – government royalties on natural resources; 11. DWE – owner-occupied dwellings; 12. BSER – business services; 13. ED – educational services; 14. HEAL – health services; 15. ACC – accommodation, food, and beverages; 16. AMUS – amusement and recreation; 17. PSER – personal services; 18. OSER – other services.

SOURCE Estimates by the Economic Council of Canada, based on input-output data from Statistics Canada.

Table A-2

The Stimulative Power of Each Service Industry[1] on Each Goods Industry, 1985

	Service industry[2]								
	1. TRAN	2. PIPE	3. STOR	4. COMM	5. UTIL	6. WTR	7. RTR	8. FIN	9. INSU
	(1981 dollars)								
Goods industry[3]									
1. AG	0.0007	0.0001	0.0005	0.0003	0.0001	0.0014	0.0080	0.0004	0.0007
2. FIS	0.0000	0.0000	0.0000	0.0000	0.0000	0.0000	0.0000	0.0000	0.0000
3. FOR	0.0001	0.0000	0.0000	0.0000	0.0000	0.0007	0.0000	0.0000	0.0000
4. MIN	0.0004	0.0007	0.0006	0.0002	0.0260	0.0003	0.0006	0.0008	0.0005
5. PET	0.0034	0.0698	0.0037	0.0010	0.0033	0.0018	0.0031	0.0043	0.0044
6. QUAR	0.0001	0.0000	0.0000	0.0000	0.0000	0.0000	0.0000	0.0000	0.0000
7. FOOD	0.0051	0.0011	0.0036	0.0025	0.0008	0.0054	0.0054	0.0035	0.0033
8. BEV	0.0004	0.0001	0.0003	0.0002	0.0000	0.0005	0.0003	0.0004	0.0004
9. TO	0.0000	0.0000	0.0000	0.0000	0.0000	0.0000	0.0000	0.0000	0.0000
10. RU	0.0052	0.0002	0.0013	0.0006	0.0002	0.0008	0.0014	0.0007	0.0006
11. PL	0.0010	0.0002	0.0057	0.0006	0.0002	0.0032	0.0028	0.0007	0.0006
12. LE	0.0004	0.0000	0.0001	0.0001	0.0000	0.0001	0.0001	0.0001	0.0001
13. TX	0.0011	0.0001	0.0027	0.0004	0.0001	0.0008	0.0011	0.0003	0.0003
14. CL	0.0003	0.0001	0.0003	0.0002	0.0000	0.0002	0.0008	0.0002	0.0002
15. WD	0.0002	0.0000	0.0002	0.0001	0.0000	0.0020	0.0004	0.0001	0.0002
16. FU	0.0000	0.0000	0.0000	0.0001	0.0000	0.0000	0.0000	0.0001	0.0000
17. PA	0.0015	0.0004	0.0155	0.0010	0.0003	0.0070	0.0103	0.0013	0.0013
18. PR	0.0085	0.0033	0.0088	0.0103	0.0025	0.0147	0.0129	0.0151	0.0133
19. PME	0.0015	0.0001	0.0004	0.0002	0.0000	0.0017	0.0003	0.0002	0.0003
20. FME	0.0029	0.0005	0.0023	0.0015	0.0004	0.0038	0.0029	0.0017	0.0016
21. MACH	0.0011	0.0002	0.0010	0.0012	0.0002	0.0008	0.0005	0.0008	0.0007
22. TEQ	0.0137	0.0003	0.0022	0.0012	0.0003	0.0014	0.0009	0.0010	0.0010
23. ELEC	0.0039	0.0008	0.0026	0.0155	0.0006	0.0028	0.0017	0.0029	0.0031
24. NME	0.0007	0.0000	0.0003	0.0002	0.0000	0.0004	0.0002	0.0002	0.0002
25. RPE	0.0895	0.0048	0.0340	0.0095	0.0202	0.0248	0.0164	0.0128	0.0084
26. CH	0.0042	0.0007	0.0031	0.0019	0.0006	0.0036	0.0019	0.0020	0.0018
27. OMA	0.0013	0.0002	0.0017	0.0014	0.0006	0.0013	0.0013	0.0009	0.0009
28. CON	0.0409	0.0202	0.0334	0.0235	0.0284	0.0063	0.0097	0.0458	0.0178
Total goods	0.1896	0.1050	0.1256	0.0751	0.0859	0.0871	0.0843	0.0975	0.0631

182 Employment in the Service Economy

Table A-2 (concl'd.)

	Service industry[2]

	10. ROY	11. DWE	12. BSER	13. ED	14. HEAL	15. ACC	16. AMUS	17. PSER	18. OSER
	(1981 dollars)
Goods industry[3]
1. AG	0.0000	0.0000	0.0004	0.0006	0.0005	0.0158	0.0017	0.0007	0.0007
2. FIS	0.0000	0.0000	0.0000	0.0000	0.0000	0.0007	0.0000	0.0000	0.0000
3. FOR	0.0000	0.0000	0.0000	0.0000	0.0000	0.0001	0.0000	0.0001	0.0000
4. MIN	0.0000	0.0000	0.0002	0.0009	0.0008	0.0006	0.0007	0.0004	0.0003
5. PET	0.0000	0.0001	0.0012	0.0046	0.0013	0.0035	0.0019	0.0021	0.0018
6. QUAR	0.0000	0.0000	0.0000	0.0000	0.0000	0.0000	0.0000	0.0000	0.0000
7. FOOD	0.0000	0.0001	0.0034	0.0050	0.0038	0.1622	0.0071	0.0033	0.0054
8. BEV	0.0000	0.0000	0.0003	0.0004	0.0003	0.0062	0.0007	0.0002	0.0004
9. TO	0.0000	0.0000	0.0000	0.0000	0.0000	0.0000	0.0000	0.0000	0.0000
10. RU	0.0000	0.0000	0.0007	0.0013	0.0010	0.0004	0.0014	0.0017	0.0013
11. PL	0.0000	0.0000	0.0007	0.0012	0.0010	0.0026	0.0016	0.0007	0.0014
12. LE	0.0000	0.0000	0.0001	0.0002	0.0001	0.0000	0.0006	0.0008	0.0002
13. TX	0.0000	0.0000	0.0004	0.0005	0.0037	0.0044	0.0008	0.0071	0.0006
14. CL	0.0000	0.0000	0.0002	0.0004	0.0004	0.0007	0.0005	0.0001	0.0005
15. WD	0.0000	0.0000	0.0002	0.0002	0.0001	0.0001	0.0002	0.0092	0.0003
16. FU	0.0000	0.0000	0.0000	0.0000	0.0000	0.0002	0.0000	0.0000	0.0000
17. PA	0.0000	0.0000	0.0018	0.0021	0.0015	0.0071	0.0029	0.0025	0.0033
18. PR	0.0000	0.0002	0.0124	0.0205	0.0088	0.0059	0.0320	0.0048	0.0142
19. PME	0.0000	0.0000	0.0002	0.0004	0.0003	0.0001	0.0006	0.0003	0.0014
20. FME	0.0000	0.0000	0.0017	0.0027	0.0021	0.0011	0.0057	0.0017	0.0041
21. MACH	0.0000	0.0000	0.0007	0.0011	0.0009	0.0004	0.0013	0.0003	0.0013
22. TEQ	0.0000	0.0000	0.0010	0.0017	0.0011	0.0009	0.0018	0.0010	0.0016
23. ELEC	0.0000	0.0001	0.0026	0.0031	0.0029	0.0014	0.0037	0.0011	0.0034
24. NME	0.0000	0.0000	0.0002	0.0003	0.0004	0.0012	0.0004	9.0002	0.0004
25. RPE	0.0000	0.0002	0.0091	0.0123	0.0124	0.0137	0.0131	0.0203	0.0232
26. CH	0.0000	0.0000	0.0021	0.0032	0.0060	0.0016	0.0038	0.0255	0.0039
27. OMA	0.0000	0.0000	0.0010	0.0012	0.0054	0.0011	0.0055	0.0010	0.0026
28. CON	0.0000	0.0559	0.0042	0.0246	0.0043	0.0092	0.0108	0.0037	0.0034
Total goods	0.0000	0.0567	0.0462	0.0900	0.0602	0.2426	0.1004	0.0902	0.0769

1 The increase in the output of each goods industry that results from a one-dollar increase in the output of each service industry.
2 Service industries: 1. TRAN – transportation; 2. PIPE – pipeline transportation; 3. STOR – storage; 4. COMM – communications; 5. UTIL – utilities; 6. WTR – wholesale trade; 7. RTR – retail trade; 8. FIN – finance and real estate; 9. INSU – insurance; 10. ROY – government royalties on natural resources; 11. DWE – owner-occupied dwellings; 12. BSER – business services; 13. ED – educational services; 14. HEAL – health services; 15. ACC – accommodation, food, and beverages; 16. AMUS – amusement and recreation; 17. PSER – personal services; 18. OSER – other services.
3 Goods industries: 1. AG – agriculture; 2. FIS – fishing and trapping; 3. FOR – logging and forestry; 4. MIN – mining; 5. PET – crude petroleum and gas; 6. QUAR – quarries and sand pits; 7. FOOD – food; 8. BEV – beverages; 9. TO – tobacco; 10. RU – rubber; 11. PL – plastics; 12. LE – leather; 13. TX – textiles; 14. CL – clothing; 15. WD – wood; 16. FU – furniture and fixtures; 17. PA – paper and allied industries; 18. PR – printing and publishing; 19. PME – primary metals; 20. FME – fabricated metals; 21. MACH – machinery; 22. TEQ – transportation equipment; 23. ELEC – electrical goods; 24. NME – nonmetalic minerals; 25. RPE – refined petroleum and coal; 26. CH – chemicals; 27. OMA – other manufacturing; 28. CON – construction.
SOURCE Estimates by the Economic Council of Canada, based on input-output data from Statistics Canada.

B Income Distribution Analysis: Methodology

Type of Income

Data on incomes can take the form of "total (money) income" or its constituent parts: employment earnings, income from investments, and income from government transfers. Naturally, distributional trends vary according to the type of income under consideration. Given the labour market perspective of this study, the analysis in Chapter 8 concentrates on employment earnings (which is the largest of the three income components). Earnings from both employment (wages and salaries) and self-employment are included in our definition of employment income.

Accounting Period

The accounting period refers to the period covered by each data observation. This could be hourly, daily, weekly, monthly, yearly, or even longer. Research on trends in earnings typically use hourly or annual employment income. Analysis based on an annual accounting period reflects the impacts of changes in both hours worked and the wage rate per hour; the hourly accounting period only includes the latter. Trends in hours worked are going in the opposite direction from wage rate trends, and studies based on annual earnings can yield outcomes that are different again from those based on hourly earnings. In fact, analyses based on both accounting periods have found evidence of increasing inequality and polarization.[1] For this reason, and also because the variation in hours available to job holders is an important aspect of the distribution question, we report results using annual earnings in Chapter 8.

Population

Some researchers are interested in the distribution of individual income, while others focus on family incomes. The trends for these two populations can be quite different. For instance, changing family composition (more single parents, fewer children) and the increase in two-earner families are factors that do not necessarily affect individual earnings significantly but which obviously have direct implications for the income of families. We recognize the importance of family incomes and some of our results for this population are reported in Chapter 8. However, given our primary interest in the labour market (which most directly affects incomes at the individual rather than the family level), we focus on individual earnings distributions. The analysis is restricted to workers with some degree of attachment to the labour market. Here, we use the concept of "effective labour force participant" (ELFP), which we generally define as those who earned at least 5 per cent of the average industrial wage (roughly equivalent to two and one-half weeks for someone with average earnings). We also report results using other ELFP selection criteria.

Time Period

Ideally, the analysis of distribution trends should cover a long time period so that secular (and not just cyclical) trends can be observed. But often research is hampered by lack of appropriate data. The formal analysis of our study is based on data from 1967 to 1986, and we also make some observations on both earlier and more recent developments. With respect to cyclical factors, comparisons between years at different points in the business cycle would confound the results. Accordingly, our analysis is based on four observation points – 1967, 1973, 1981, and 1986 – which were roughly at the mid-point of each economic cycle.[2]

Measures

Research on income distribution trends has tended to focus on two phenomena: inequality and polarization. While these concepts have much in common, they are not identical. "Inequality" relates to differences in the proportion of income held by individuals or families in the entire population; "polarization" reflects the extent to which the population tends to cluster at the two extremes of the income distribution.[3] While inequality and polarization are often observed together, it is possible to observe different trends for the two within a given income distribution. In the Economic Council of Canada-Statistics Canada study, both types of distributional concepts were included.

To measure income inequality, we use the Gini coefficient which is the traditional indicator of inequality. In essence, the Gini measures the "distance" that the observed income distribution is from the state of perfect equality – that is, where any given percentage of the population receives the identical percentage of the population's income. The Gini rises with the degree of inequality, ranging from 0 (perfect equality) to 1 (complete inequality).[4]

The principal index we use to gauge polarization involves calculating the proportion of the population falling into particular strata of the income (earnings) distribution. The most common type of polarization measure, and the one used in this study, defines three income groups (low, medium, and high) by those individuals (or families) whose income is within particular percentages of the current year median: for example, we included in the lower stratum those individuals who earn up to 75 per cent of the median; in the middle stratum those earning between 75 and 125 per cent; and in the upper stratum those over 125 per cent. Since the selection of the thresholds used to determine the income strata is arbitrary, we also report some results from sensitivity analyses in which we have changed the boundaries of these strata.

Standardization

It is important to identify the factors underlying any observed changes in the income distribution over time. Many analyses simply compare inequality and polarization trends across various population subgroups to suggest reasons for distributional shifts. While such an approach – for example, comparing the pattern of income polarization in different industry groups – can be a useful descriptive mechanism, it cannot empirically establish the contribution of different factors to the overall picture. We therefore report our results using more sophisticated "standardization" techniques.[5] The standardization method is based on the premise that shifts in the distribution of income can result from changes in the composition of the population, and/or changes in the income of the members of that population. We label the first the "composition" factor, and the second the "income" factor.

To offer a stylized example, assume that there is only one characteristic – say, education – that affects an individual's income. Now, suppose that during a 20-year period the income distribution is observed to have become more unequal. This could be completely due to the "composition" factor (i.e., education became more unequally distributed, but the returns to different levels of education remained unchanged); to the "income" factor (i.e., the returns to different levels of education became more unequal, however the distribution of the education characteristics of the population stayed constant); or to some combination of both factors.

The essential idea of our standardization technique is to measure how much of the change in the income distribution can be explained by each of these factors. It does this by "freezing" one of the factors (e.g., the education characteristics of the population) for the entire time period at its state in the first year of the period. We can then observe how the hypothetical (standardized) income distribution trends differ from the actual (observed) trends. If there is no difference, the "standardized" factor (here, educational composition) has not been an important one; if the difference is large, the factor is obviously a significant determinant. The standardizations reported in Chapter 8 address the "compositional" factor (i.e., changing population shares of different population subgroups) and the "income" factor. With respect to the latter, we used two types of standardization: one to control for changes in the shape of the income distribution of population subgroups, and the other to control for changes in the mean earning levels of these subgroups.

Notes

Chapter 1

1. In 1986, Industry, Science and Technology Canada (then known as the Department of Regional Industrial Expansion) sponsored the Service Industries Study Program (SISP). Two of the major participants in the research were the Fraser Institute and the Institute for Research on Public Policy. Over the two years of the program, over 80 studies addressing a range of issues relating to the service sector, including trade, were carried out. For a summary, see Industry, Science and Technology Canada, *The Service Sector in the Canadian Economy*, Interdepartmental Discussion Paper, July 1989. Details on the analysis have been published by the organizations that conducted the research. For overviews of the economics studies, see Herbert G. Grubel and Michael A. Walker, *Service Industry Growth: Causes and Effects* (Vancouver: The Fraser Institute, 1988); and A. R. Dobell and H. E. English, "Canada's trade in services: An overview," Working Paper, Institute for Research on Public Policy, Halifax, 1988. The major provincially sponsored study was carried out in Ontario; see George Radwanski, *Ontario Study of the Service Sector* (Toronto: Ministry of Treasury and Economics, 1986).

2. Economic Council of Canada, *Good Jobs, Bad Jobs: Employment in the Service Economy* (Ottawa: Supply and Services Canada, 1990).

Chapter 2

1. This section is based on H. H. Postner, "The goods/services convergence hypothesis: An analysis," a paper prepared for the Economic Council of Canada, Ottawa, 1990.

2. A.G.B. Fisher, "Production: Primary, secondary, and tertiary," *Economic Record* 15 (June 1939):24-38.

3. For the conventional view, see T. P. Hill, "On goods and services," *Review of Income and Wealth* 23, no. 4 (December 1977):315-38; and "The economic significance of the distinction between goods and services," a paper presented at the Conference of the International Association for Research in Income and Wealth, August 1987.

4. For the implications of this for the economic analysis of service activity, see T. P. Hill, "The economic significance of the distinction between goods and services"; and P. Petit, "Services," *Palgrave Dictionary of Economics* (New York: Stockton Press, 1987).

5. A less conventional view of services identifies their storability as embodied in the skills of people.

6. Some of these issues have been discussed with reference to the current revision of the United Nations System of National Accounts. See C. Carson, "Revision of the United Nations System of National Accounts: A revision for the 21st century," a paper presented at the American Economic Association Meetings, December 1989.

7. Also included in the traditional services subsector is that part of the education and health industries that operates in the business sector of the Canadian economy (as opposed to the bulk of those industries that is found in the nonmarket sector).

8. Gordon Betcherman and Kathryn McMullen, *Working with Technology: A Survey of Automation in Canada*, Economic Council of Canada (Ottawa: Supply and Services Canada, 1986); Economic Council of Canada, *Innovation and Jobs in Canada* (Ottawa: Supply and Services Canada, 1987); Communications Canada/Industry, Science and Technology Canada, *Technologies in Services* (Ottawa: Supply and Services Canada, 1990); and Communications Canada, Industry, Science and Technology Canada, Employment and Immigration Canada, and Statistics Canada, "Diffusion of technology survey in the service industries," September 1989.

9. Communications Canada/Industry, Science and Technology Canada, *Technologies in Services*.

10. Communications Canada et al., "Diffusion of technology survey in the service industries."

11. W. J. Coffey and M. Polèse, "Service activities and regional development: A policy-oriented perspective," a paper prepared for the 35th North American Meetings of the Regional Science Association, Toronto, 11-13 November 1988.

12. For a discussion of private and social rates of return to R&D spending, see Economic Council of Canada, *The Bottom Line: Technology, Trade, and Income Growth* (Ottawa: Supply and Services Canada, 1983).

13. R. Barras, "Towards a theory of innovation in services," *Research Policy* 15, no. 4 (1986):161-73; and "Information technology and the service revolution," *Policy Studies* 5, no. 4 (1985):14-24.

14. James Brian Quinn, "Technology in services: Past myths and future challenges," in *Technology in Services: Policies for Growth, Trade, and Employment*, eds. Bruce R. Guile and James Brian Quinn (Washington, D.C.: National Academy Press, 1988), pp. 16-46.

15 W. J. Perry, "Cultivating technological innovation," in *The Positive Sum Strategy: Harnessing Technology for Economic Growth*, eds. R. Landau and N. Rosenberg (Washington, D.C.: National Academy Press, 1986), pp. 443-51; and R. N. Foster, *Innovation: The Attacker's Advantage* (New York: Summit Books, 1986).

16 R. Barras, "Interactive innovation in financial and business services: The vanguard of the service revolution," *Research Policy* 19, no. 3 (June 1990):215-37.

17 The same conclusion is reached in A. R. Dobell and H. E. English, "Canada's trade in services: An overview," Working Paper, Institute for Research on Public Policy, Halifax, 1988. This study was part of the federally sponsored Service Industries Study Program.

18 The Council has recently examined the Canadian financial system in the context of the internationalization of financial markets. See Economic Council of Canada, *A New Frontier: Globalization and Canada's Financial Markets*, and *Globalization and Canada's Financial Markets* (Ottawa: Supply and Services Canada, 1989 and 1990).

19 The above analysis of service trade in 1986 is based on J. J. McRae, "An exploratory analysis of Canada's international transactions in service commodities," a paper prepared for the Economic Council of Canada, November 1989.

20 R. G. Harris and D. Cox, "The service sector and trade in the Canadian economy: An input-output analysis," Discussion Paper, The Fraser Institute, Vancouver, 1988.

21 Harris and Cox, "The service sector and trade in the Canadian economy."

22 Coffey and Polèse, "Service activities and regional development."

23 W. J. Coffey et al., *Service Industries in Regional Development* (Halifax: Institute for Research on Public Policy, 1989).

24 Coffey et al., *Service Industries in Regional Development*.

25 W. J. Coffey and M. Polèse, "Trade and location of producer services: A Canadian perspective," *Environment and Planning* 19 (1987):597-611; and "Intrafirm trade in business services: Implications for the location of office-based activities," *Papers of the Regional Science Association* 62 (1987):71-80.

26 Coffey et al., *Service Industries in Regional Development*.

27 A. Gillespie et al., "Information and communications technology and regional development: An information economy perspective," *STI Review*, no. 5 (April 1989):86-111.

28 Coffey and Polèse, "Intrafirm trade in business services."

29 Coffey et al., *Service Industries in Regional Development*.

30 A. Gunter Pauli, *Services: The Engine of the European Economy*, ESIF 1 (Aylesbury, Buckinghamshire: Hazell Watson and Viney Limited, 1987).

31 See, for example, Gillespie et al., "Information and communications technology and regional development"; Barry Lesser, "A chance for the disadvantaged," *Policy Options* 7, no. 10 (December 1986):32-33; Maurice Estabrooks and Rodolphe Lamarche, eds., *Telecommunications: A Strategic Perspective on Regional, Economic and Business Development* (Moncton: The Canadian Institute for Research and Regional Development, 1987); Rodolphe Lamarche, "High technology, telecommunications and regional development: A survey of the literature," *Canadian Journal of Regional Science* 9, no. 3 (Autumn 1986):341-51; and Science Council of Canada and the Canadian Advanced Technology Association, *Firing Up the Technology Engine: Strategies for Community Economic Development* (Ottawa: The Council, 1990).

32 For a detailed discussion of the definition and calculation of the "average labour unit" (ALU), see Statistics Canada, *Developing a Longitudinal Database on Businesses in the Canadian Economy: An Approach to the Study of Employment*, Cat. 18-501 (Ottawa: Supply and Services Canada, 1988).

33 David L. Birch, *Job Creation in America: How Our Smallest Companies Put the Most People to Work* (New York: The Free Press, 1987).

Chapter 3

1 Colin Clark, *The Conditions of Economic Progress* (London: Macmillan, 1st ed. 1940, 3rd ed. 1957).

2 W. Baumol, "Macroeconomics of unbalanced growth: The anatomy of urban crisis," *American Economic Review* 57, no. 3 (1967):415-26; Victor R. Fuchs, *The Service Economy* (New York: National Bureau of Economic Research, 1968).

3 Rudiger Dornbusch et al., *The Case for Manufacturing in America's Future* (Rochester: Eastman Kodak Company, 1988); and Gregory Schmid, "Manufacturing: The key to future jobs," *Challenge* (November-December 1988):54-56.

4 Different sample periods, functional forms, and specifications may affect the estimate of marginal propensity to consume. We experimented with a number of functional forms. Although the estimates are inevitably different, depending on the specifications and the different ways in measuring income, the marginal propensity to consume goods was consistently higher than for service consumption. Space limitations would not allow us to include all of the estimated equations here.

5 See, for example, Fuchs, *The Service Economy*; and Sunder Magun, "The rise of service employment in the Canadian economy," *Relations Industrielles* 37, no. 3 (1982):528-56.

6 H. G. Grubel and M. A. Walker, *Service Industry Growth: Causes and Effects* (Vancouver: The Fraser Institute, 1988).

7 Fuchs, *The Service Economy*; and Magun, "The rise of service employment."

8 R. Wisner and M. Bédard, "The measurement of productivity by sector: A brief survey," a paper prepared for the Economic Council of Canada, Ottawa, July 1988, for an alternative analysis of the productivity performance of the goods and service sectors based on estimates of total factor productivity (TFP). Wisner and Bédard also review the quality of the data that measures gross domestic product. Because it was not possible to group the TFP results to conform to the typology of the service sector used in this report, and because our primary interest in this report is to explain employment growth, the discussion in the text focuses on measures of labour productivity.

9 Andrew Sharpe, "The measurement of constant dollar gross domestic product – How good are the data?," Canadian Labour Market and Productivity Centre, mimeo., Ottawa, 1986.

10 Sharpe, "The measurement of constant dollar gross domestic product," p. 2.

11 Statistics Canada, "Sources and methods for service industries in the Canadian input-output tables," vol. 2, mimeo., Ottawa, 1988.

12 Researchers in the United States have used stock-market returns as a proxy for measuring productivity growth in services, thereby avoiding the problem altogether. See, for example, G. R. Faulhaber, "Sectoral productivity measurement and capital markets," in *The Service Economy*, Coalition of Service Industries, vol. 3, no. 3 (July 1989). While there is no Canadian evidence on the extent of the bias, Postner and Wesa have developed a methodology to bypass the problem of the misallocation of service-sector productivity. It focuses on productivity growth by end-product; for example, the production of food, clothing, leisure, and personal services, rather than on productivity by industry. See H. H. Postner and L. M. Wesa, *Canadian Productivity Growth: An Alternative (Input-Output) Analysis*, Economic Council of Canada (Ottawa: Supply and Services Canada, 1983); and in the United States, see E. F. Denison, *Estimates of Productivity Change by Industry: An Evaluation and Alternative* (Washington, D.C.: The Brookings Institution, 1989).

13 H. H. Postner, "The contracting-out problem in service sector analysis: Choice of statistical unit," *The Review of Income and Wealth* 36, no. 2 (June 1990):177-86.

14 Grubel and Walker, *Service Industry Growth*.

15 D. B. McFetridge and D. A. Smith, *The Economics of Vertical Disintegration* (Vancouver: The Fraser Institute, 1989).

16 H. H. Postner and L. M. Wesa, "Sources of Canadian employment change: A decomposition analysis," Discussion Paper no. 339, Economic Council of Canada, Ottawa, October 1987.

17 W. F. Empey, "Contracting-out of services by manufacturing industries," Institute for Research on Public Policy, Victoria, B.C., 1988; and McFetridge and Smith, *The Economics of Vertical Disintegration*.

18 J. Niosi, "The rise of the conglomerate economy," a report to the Social and Economic Studies Division, mimeo., Statistics Canada, Ottawa, 1987.

19 For a more detailed discussion, see Postner, "The contracting-out problem."

20 H. H. Postner, "Problems of identifying and measuring intermediate (producer) services in the compilation and use of input-output tables," *The Review of Income and Wealth* 28, no. 2 (June 1982).

21 Statistics Canada, "Report on a survey of the use and sources of business services," a paper prepared by the Services Division, Ottawa, September 1989.

22 That the utilities industry sold so little of its services to consumers can be explained by the fact that a large part of that industry's output went to a final demand component called "personal expenditures on electricity, gas and other fuels." The question is whether one labels electricity, gas and other fuels as goods or services. If they are counted as services, the figure would have to be much higher.

23 The fact that 5.5 per cent of retail trade's output went to consumer services may also appear low. This is a result of the treatment of retail trade statistics in the input-output system and the difference between the retail trade margins on goods and on services. In the input-output accounting framework, the retail trade stores are shown as producers of retail margins, defined as sales of goods and services less the cost of goods and services purchased for resale. Thus, when a consumer makes a purchase, he/she buys the retail margin directly from the retailer and simultaneously pays the retailer for the cost of the product. In everyday life, the person pays a sum for the transaction, but the input-output system treats the transaction as if the person pays for two separate items. In Canada, retail margins on services are normally lower than those on goods. Explaining the low figure for consumer expenditure on personal services is more complicated. In 1985, other than selling a large amount of services to other industries, the industry sold $433.3 million (constant 1981 dollars) worth of output to the final demand component called "personal expenditure on motor vehicle parts and repairs," and $443.7 million (constant 1981 dollars) to "government current expenditure on goods and services." These two components accounted for 22.6 per cent of the total output of the personal services in 1985. Since government could not be counted as the general public, the $443.7 million presented no accounting problem. However, since a fraction of the $433.3 million was for consumer's spending on auto repairs, it should really be included as consumer expenditure on services. Unfortunately, this unscrambling job is not possible with this data. Therefore, the figure is an underestimate of the real consumer spending on personal services.

188 Employment in the Service Economy

24 See, for example, D. Bell, *The Coming of Post-Industrial Society* (New York: Basic Books, 1973); and R. K. Shelp, *Beyond Industrialization: Ascendency of the Global Service Economy* (New York: Praeger, 1981).

25 Dornbusch et al., *The Case for Manufacturing in America's Future.*

26 S. Cohen and J. Zysman, *Manufacturing Matters: The Myth of the Post-Industrial Economy* (New York: Basic Books, 1987).

27 D.C.A. Curtis and K.S.R. Murthy, "Goods sector-service sector structural change and Canadian economic growth: A dynamic multisectoral modelling analysis," a paper prepared for the Economic Council of Canada, Ottawa, 1989.

28 In the real world, policymakers would have to face many more political and economic constraints than the ones considered in the model simulations.

29 Wassily W. Leontief, *Input-Output Economics* (New York: Oxford University Press, 1966).

30 For more detail on the applications of the input-output model, see Statistics Canada, *The Input-Output Structure of the Canadian Economy, 1961*, vols. 1 and 2, Cat. 15-501 and 15-502 (Ottawa: Supply and Services Canada, 1969).

31 K. Miyazawa, *Input-Output Analysis and the Structure of Income Distribution* (Heidelberg: Springer-Verlag-Berlin, 1976).

32 For a more detailed discussion of the methodology and results of the input-output analysis, see Tom Siedule, "The interdependence of industrial activities," a paper prepared for the Economic Council of Canada, Ottawa, 1990.

33 The information given in Tables A-1 and A-2 is summarized in Charts 3-4 to 3-7 in the text. Chart 3-4 corresponds to the column totals of Table A-1; Chart 3-5 corresponds to the column totals of Table A-2; Chart 3-6 corresponds to the row totals of Table A-1; and Chart 3-7 corresponds to the row totals of Table A-2.

34 One could argue that, since the input-output data are disaggregated into more goods than service industries, the size of the stimulation to services given by a one-dollar increase in output in each goods industry would be larger than the amount of stimulation given to goods by a one-dollar increase in output in each service industry. However, when the size of the stimulation given by the two sectors is converted to a common base, the relative impacts on each industry in the "receiving" sector remain essentially unchanged.

35 The results for 1982-85 are not shown because they are not directly comparable to those for the earlier period. The data for 1982-85 are in constant 1981 dollars, while those for 1971-81 are in constant 1971 dollars.

36 See Economic Council of Canada, *Legacies,* 26th Annual Review (Ottawa: Supply and Services Canada, 1989). This was the most recent base case at the time our analysis was undertaken.

Chapter 4

1 For more detailed analyses of the composition of service-sector growth through time for a number of OECD countries (excluding Canada), see Tom Elfring, *Service Sector Employment in Advanced Economies: A Comparative Analysis of its Implications for Economic Growth* (Aldershot: Avebury, 1988); and "New evidence on the expansion of service employment in advanced economies," *Review of Income and Wealth* 35, no. 4 (December 1989):409-40; and Robert Bednarzik, "Employment profile of the service sector in selected OECD countries," Project on Technological Change and Human Resource Development in the Service Sector, OECD, Centre for Educational Research and Innovation, draft, Paris, 31 May 1989.

2 Economic Council of Canada, *Back to Basics*, 25th Annual Review (Ottawa: Supply and Services Canada, 1988).

3 For a detailed discussion on the sectoral shifts hypothesis, see D. M. Lilien, "Sectoral shifts and cyclical unemployment," *Journal of Political Economy* 90, no. 4 (1982):777-93. For empirical Canadian evidence, see Lucie Samson, "A study of the impact of the sectoral shifts on aggregate unemployment in Canada," *Canadian Journal of Economics* 18, no. 3 (1985):518-30.

4 This interindustry employment dispersion measure is defined as the standard deviation of the employment growth rates of the individual industries from the average employment growth (in all industries) weighted by the share of each industry in total employment.

5 See Surendra Gera and Syed Sajjadur Rahman, "Sectoral labour mobility and Canadian unemployment: Evidence from the 1980s," a paper prepared for the Economic Council of Canada, Ottawa, 1990; Janet Neelin, "Sectoral shifts and Canadian unemployment," *Review of Economics and Statistics* 69, no. 4 (1987):718-23; and Andrew Burns, "Unemployment in Canada: Frictional, structural, and cyclical aspects," Working Paper no. 1, Economic Council of Canada, Ottawa, 1990. For a critical discussion of the American results, see K. G. Abraham and L. Katz, "Cyclical unemployment: Sectoral shifts or aggregate disturbances," *Journal of Political Economy* 94, no. 3, Part 1 (1986):507-22.

6 This section is based on Syed Sajjadur Rahman, "Has the rise of the service sector moderated cyclical fluctuations in employment?," a paper prepared for the Economic Council of Canada, Ottawa, 1990.

7 See G. H. Moore, "The service industries and the business cycle," *Business Economics* 23, no. 2 (April 1987); and J. B. Quinn et. al., "Technology in services," *Scientific American* 257, no. 6 (December 1987).

8   Recessionary periods are characterized by an absolute decrease in the level of real gross national product. For more details on the recent Canadian experience, see Ranga Chand, "Employment during recessions: The boost from services," *Canadian Business Review* (Summer 1986):37-40. For an extensive discussion on the dating of the Canadian business cycles, see Philip Cross, "Special study: The business cycle in Canada, 1950-1981," *Current Economic Analysis*, Statistics Canada (Ottawa: Supply and Services Canada, March 1982), pp. xxii-xxxi.

9   Garnett Picot and John Baldwin, "Patterns of quits and layoffs in the Canadian economy," *Canadian Economic Observer*, Statistics Canada (October 1990).

10 The separation count is based on the number of ROE forms issued by employers, while the "person-job" count is based on the number of T4 income tax forms issued by employers. Note that the administrative file is potentially subject to some biases, due for the most part to a failure on the part of the employer to submit either an ROE or a T4 form. In order to evaluate the validity of the estimates based on these data, a comparison for 1986 was made with separation rates calculated from the Labour Market Activity Survey, a household survey which gathered information from workers on their labour-market experiences over the preceding year. While there were some differences, the volume of separations and the reasons for separation were very similar between the two sources. For additional information, see Marcel Bédard, "A comparison of separations from the ROE and LMAS files," a paper prepared for the Economic Council of Canada, 1990; and Picot and Baldwin, "Patterns of quits and layoffs."

11 Although the LMAS gathered information on up to five jobs from respondents, we have restricted our analysis to the period encompassing the first two jobs only. This was because the number of observations involving a third, fourth, or fifth job was too low for meaningful statistical analysis.

12 For a discussion of separation patterns over the business cycle, see Picot and Baldwin, "Patterns of quits and layoffs."

13 These statistics are based on the sample of LMAS respondents who reported they had separated from the first job they had held in 1986. The 78.6 per cent who indicated that they had obtained another job before the end of 1987 were not necessarily still in it at the end of 1987; some were no longer employed while others had gone on to yet another job.

14 The distinction among respondents who had not found another job between those who wanted another job and those who did not is based on their responses at the end of the survey period (the last week of 1987). Naturally, these responses need not reflect the preferences of the job separators throughout their period of joblessness; for example, some respondents who reported that they did not want to find another job were undoubtedly discouraged workers who had searched unsuccessfully for reemployment.

15 See, for example, Garnett Picot and Ted Wannell, "Job loss and labour market adjustment in the Canadian economy," *The Labour Force*, Statistics Canada, Cat. 71-001 (Ottawa: Supply and Services Canada, March 1987); and Diane E. Herz, "Worker displacement in a period of rapid job expansion, 1983-87," *Monthly Labour Review* 113, no. 5 (May 1990): 21-33.

Chapter 5

1   See Organisation for Economic Co-operation and Development, *Flexibility in the Labour Market: The Current Debate* (Paris: OECD, 1986).

2   See Bennet Harrison and Barry Bluestone, "The dark side of labour market 'flexibility': Falling wages and growing income inequality in America," Labour Market Analysis and Employment Planning, Working Paper no. 17, International Labour Organization, Geneva, 1987; and Guy Standing, "European unemployment, insecurity and flexibility: A social dividend solution," Labour Market Analysis and Employment Planning, Working Paper no. 23, International Labour Organization, Geneva, 1989.

3   See Eileen Appelbaum, "Restructuring work: Temporary, part-time and at-home employment," in *Computer Chips and Paper Clips: Technology and Women's Employment*, ed. Heidi Hartmann (Washington, D.C.: National Academy Press, 1987).

4   There have been a number of studies of some of its components, particularly part-time work. For example, see Labour Canada, *Part-Time Work in Canada: Report of the Commission of Inquiry into Part-Time Work* (Ottawa: Supply and Services Canada, 1983).

5   See A. E. Polivka and T. Nardone, "On the definition of 'contingent work'," *Monthly Labor Review* 112, no. 12 (December 1989):9-16; and Richard S. Belous, *The Contingent Economy: The Growth of the Temporary, Part-Time, and Sub-Contracted Workforce* (Washington, D.C.: National Planning Association, 1989).

6   Polivka and Nardone, "On the definition of 'contingent work'."

7   Catherine Hakim, "Trends in the flexible workforce," *Employment Gazette* (November 1987):549-60.

8   Belous, *The Contingent Economy*.

9   Note that this operational definition of "contingency" departs from the notion of a long-term attachment with an employer. A significant number of part-time workers, for instance, do have such an attachment and are, by any standard, part of their employer's "regular" labour force. Likewise, many workers in the business service industry, which Belous includes because it is the "primary provider of subcontracted human resource services to employers," have an ongoing attachment to their own employers, albeit not to those businesses to which services are provided. For more details, see Belous, *The Contingent Economy*.

10 Hakim, "Trends in the flexible workforce."

11 C. Büchtemann and S. Quack, "'Bridges' or 'traps'? Non-standard forms of employment in the Federal Republic of Germany," in *Precarious Jobs in Labour Market Regulation: The Growth of Atypical Employment in Western Europe*, eds. Gerry and Janine Rodgers (Geneva: International Labour Organization, 1989).

12 Note that a series break occurred in the data in 1975. Before that, Statistics Canada defined part-time as less than 35 hours work per week, while since 1975, it has been defined as less than 30 hours per week.

13 Statistics Canada, *Family Expenditures in Canada, 1986* (Ottawa: Supply and Services Canada, March 1989), pp. 130 and 131.

14 Based on calculations from the Labour Market Activity Survey, 1986.

15 According to data on the incidence of promotions, part-time employees are also relatively poorly situated for future compensation gains. In the federally regulated sector, information collected to meet the requirements of the Employment Equity Act shows that full-time workers were twice as likely to be promoted as part-time workers: in 1988, 12.2 per cent of all full-time workers were promoted, compared with only 5.7 per cent of part-time workers. The disparity is evident even when comparing employees in the same occupational category: among clerical workers (who account for 73 per cent of all part-time workers in this sector and are the single largest occupational group of full-time workers), 14 per cent of full-time employees received promotions in 1988 but only 6.7 per cent of part-timers. See Employment and Immigration Canada, *Employment Equity Act Annual Report, 1989* (Hull: EIC, 1989).

16 These figures come from the Labour Market Activity Survey. The situation is similar for other fringe benefits. For instance, a survey by Hewitt Associates indicates that the following benefits are available to over 90 per cent of full-time employees of larger firms, but to less than one quarter of employees who work fewer than 20 hours per week: life insurance, pension plans, long-term disability insurance, supplemental medical insurance, dental benefits, and payment of provincial Medicare premiums where applicable. See Hewitt Associates, *Benefits for Canadian Part-Time Employees*, a report for Labour Canada (Toronto: Hewitt Associates, 1985).

17 Gordon Betcherman, "Union membership in a service economy," in *Industrial Relations Issues for the 1990s*, ed. Michel Grant, Proceedings of the 26th Conference of the Canadian Industrial Relations Association, 1989.

18 This temporary-employment share excludes jobs that were identified as seasonal in nature. An additional 8.7 per cent of the completed jobs in 1987 were seasonal; therefore, if both seasonal and nonseasonal work were considered, the temporary-employment share would rise to 20 per cent. It should be noted that temporary jobs (both seasonal and nonseasonal) identified in the Labour Market Activity Survey did not have any duration criterion.

19 The LMAS data cover work experiences through the 1987 calendar year. By using this selection criterion, then, we were able to have at least six months of information (weeks 27 to 52) for every job reported in the first half of 1987. Data on this length of time enabled us to identify which jobs from the first six months lasted 26 weeks or more and which did not.

20 The major assumption is one of a "steady-state" world where eventual job duration is not related to the specific (calendar) time when the ongoing job tenure is observed. In such a state, there is an equal probablility that a spell in progress observed by the Labour Force Survey has been captured at any point along the eventual spell-length. Thus the point of capture by the LFS is, on average, halfway through the completed spell. In other words, the estimated mean job duration is two times the observed mean tenure. For more details regarding this estimation procedure, see Stephen A. Salant, "Search theory and duration data: A theory of sorts," *Quarterly Journal of Economics* 91, no. 1 (February 1977):39-57; and the Organisation for Economic Co-operation and Development, *Employment Outlook 1984* (Paris: OECD, 1984), pp. 55 and 56.

21 The Labour Market Activity Survey has two subfiles; in one, the unit of analysis is the worker, while in the other, it is the job. In the discussion that follows, the unit of analysis is the job.

22 We also examined the relationship between firm size and the incidence of temporary employment. There was very little association between these variables as temporary employment accounted for 11.4 per cent, 9.1 per cent, 11 per cent, and 11.9 per cent of job terminations in firms with less than 20, 20-99, 100-499, and 500 employees or more, respectively.

23 Statistics Canada, *Employment, Earnings and Hours*, Cat. 72-002 (Ottawa: Supply and Services Canada, March, June, September, and December 1989).

24 Dennis Maki, *The Market for Employment, Personnel and Security: A Service Sector Analysis* (Vancouver: Fraser Institute, 1988); The DPA Group Inc., "The role and operation of private sector employment agencies and temporary help service firms in Canada," prepared for the Program Evaluation Branch, Employment and Immigration Canada (Vancouver: The DPA Group, 1988); and Ernest Akyeampong, "The changing face of temporary help," *Perspectives on Labour and Income* (Summer 1989):43-49.

25 The DPA Group Inc., "The role and operation."

26 Margaret White and Marcy Cohen, "The impact of computerization on temporary office workers: Some empirical evidence," Women's Skill Development Society, mimeo., Vancouver, September 1988, pp. 12 and 13.

27 These statistics come from Akyeampong, "The changing face of temporary help."

28 Lawrence Fric, "A study of the temporary help labour market: Differences from part-time – characteristics – fringe benefits," Federation of Temporary Help Services, mimeo., Toronto, 1985; and Marcy Cohen and Margaret White, "The impact of computerization and economic restructuring on women's employment opportunities: A research and policy analysis," a paper prepared for Labour Canada, Technology Impact Program, Vancouver, 1987.

29 Cohen and White, "The impact of computerization and economic restructuring."

30 As well, fringe benefits for temporary-help workers are generally minimal. See Fric, "A study of the temporary help labour market."

31 Akyeampong, "The changing face of temporary help."

32 The DPA Group Inc., "The role and operation."

33 In assessing the earnings of temporary-help workers on an annual basis, it is important to note that three quarters of temporary-help workers are employed only on a part-year basis: the average for this group is just 13 weeks. See Akyeampong, "The changing face of temporary help."

34 While many analyses of nonstandard employment incorporate all of the self-employed within their frame of reference, we have excluded here those self-employed persons who have employees. These individuals are employers and they tend to have quite different economic experiences (which are less "contingent") than the own-account group. For purposes of comparison with other studies, we do provide some sample calculations based on total self-employment.

35 Gary Cohen, *Enterprising Canadians: The Self-Employed in Canada*, Statistics Canada, Cat. 71-536 (Ottawa: Supply and Services Canada, 1988).

36 Over the same period, growth in total self-employment accounted for 21 per cent of all new jobs and the overall work force share of the self-employed rose from 10.8 per cent to 13.4 per cent.

37 At a finer level of disaggregation than is shown in the table, high OASE incidence rates were registered in personal services (where it represented 43 per cent of total employment in 1989), fishing and trapping (40 per cent in 1986), amusement and recreation (16 per cent in 1989), insurance and real estate (11 per cent in 1986), and services to business management (12 per cent in 1989).

38 Cohen, *Enterprising Canadians*.

39 These data on hours worked, as well as the figures on OASE job-tenure and earnings come from Cohen, *Enterprising Canadians*. The hours and tenure data apply to 1986 while the earnings statistics are for 1985.

40 The calculations on aggregate nonstandard employment are based on estimates that have taken into account the overlap existing between the various forms.

41 Many of the foreign studies include all forms of self-employment. When this is done for Canada, the share of nonstandard employment was slightly more than 35 per cent in 1985, which would have placed Canada in the middle, for example, of the dominant range estimated by Hakim for the European Economic Community in that year. See Hakim, "Trends in the flexible workforce."

42 Our analysis is based on employment in the first six months in order to be able to identify short-term jobs (26 weeks or less). Note that the LMAS estimate is higher than the nonstandard incidence rate derived from the LFS. This may be explained by the different methodologies, particularly associated with removing the overlap between nonstandard employment forms. With the LMAS, out of the jobs in existence in the first half of 1987, we first identified all short-term jobs, that is, those ending in six months or less. Of the remaining (long-term) paid jobs, we identified those which were part-time and then out of the remaining (full-time) jobs we selected the temporary ones (i.e., those ending because they were temporary nonseasonal). Then, among the remaining (long-term) unpaid jobs, we added all the own-account self-employed and the part-time employers. As part-time/full-time information was not available for unpaid jobs, the part-time proportion of employers was assumed from the LFS (about 5 per cent). With the LFS, we began by identifying all part-time workers (i.e., the monthly average of those captured by the survey). Of the remaining (full-time) workers, we identified those employed in short-term positions (i.e., ongoing tenure of less than three months). Finally, among the (full-time, long-term) workers that remained, we identified the own-account self-employed (the part-time and short-term OASE would have already been captured in the first two steps). Because it was impossible to identify full-time, long-term OASE in the LFS data we had at our disposal, we used a long-term proportion of 90 per cent taken from Cohen, *Enterprising Canadians*. One source of difference between the LFS and LMAS estimates of total nonstandard employment is that the former, in capturing workers at a single point in time in each month, would likely miss a number of short-term jobs that workers had left, or were about to enter, at other points in time during the months. The LMAS, on the other hand, provides an accurate estimate of all jobs throughout the first half of the year. Another reason for the differences between the LMAS and LFS is that only in the latter were we able to identify temporary jobs. Finally, in each file, estimates necessitated assumptions which were not identical.

43 In our analysis the factors that affect the overall nonstandard employment incidence rate are changes in the demographic (age, sex) and industrial structure of employment and changes in the incidence rates of the various sex, age, and industry groups. In applying shift-share analysis, we applied 1975 age, sex, and industry employment proportions to the 1988 individual incidence rates, thus isolating the impact of the changing work force composition on the overall incidence rate. It should be pointed out, however, that in this procedure we are not considering the effect on the overall incidence rate of the changing incidence rates of individual groups or of the interaction between changing composition and incidence.

44 The most notable initiative was the Wallace Commission on Part-Time Work, which conducted a comprehensive review of many of these questions in the early 1980s. See Labour Canada, *Part-Time Work in Canada* (Ottawa: Supply and Services Canada, 1983). Since that time, the predominance of women in the part-time labour force has caused a number of women's organizations to press actively to keep issues related to part-time work on the public agenda.

45 Own-account self-employment raises somewhat different policy issues. On the one hand, it is a form of employment that yields inferior and unstable incomes for the majority, with corresponding low levels of benefit coverage. On the other hand, market forces, including the element of risk, are inherent to entrepreneurship and its proliferation: only those who are most successful at finding and exploiting a market niche thrive and grow, while the others gain far less and may eventually go out of business. If there is a role for policy intervention in this area of the labour market, it presumably lies in the direction of helping to enhance the longer-term economic security of the OASE individuals without interfering, in the short term, with appropriate market signals.

46 For estimates of the additional costs to employers of prorating benefits to part-time employees, see Frank Reid and Gerald S. Swartz, "Prorating of fringe benefits for part-time workers," Centre for Industrial Relations, Toronto, 1982.

Chapter 6

1 Kenneth I. Spenner, "Deciphering Prometheus: Temporal change in the skill level of work," *American Sociological Review* 48 (December 1983):824-37.

2 Daniel Bell, *The Coming of Post-Industrial Society* (New York: Basic Books, 1973).

3 Harry Braverman, *Labor and Monopoly Capital: The Degradation of Work in the Twentieth Century* (New York: Monthly Review Press, 1974).

4 See, for example, Gary S. Becker, *Human Capital* (New York: National Bureau of Economic Research, 1964, 2nd ed. 1975); Jacob Mincer, *Schooling Experience and Earnings* (New York: National Bureau of Economic Research, 1974); and Theodore W. Schultz, *Investment in Human Capital: The Role of Education and of Research* (New York: The Free Press, Collier MacMillan, 1971).

5 See, in particular, Melvin L. Kohn and Carmi Schooler, "Job conditions and personality: A longitudinal assessment of their reciprocal effects," *American Journal of Sociology* 87, no. 2 (May 1982):1257-86.

6 See Spenner, "Deciphering Prometheus"; and Gordon Betcherman, "Computer technology, work and society," *Canadian Journal of Sociology* 15, no. 2 (Spring 1990): 195-201.

7 John Myles, "The expanding middle: Some Canadian evidence in the deskilling debate," *Canadian Review of Sociology and Anthropology* 25, no. 3 (August 1988):335-64.

8 For U.S. research on skill downgrading, see Michael Wallace and Arne L. Kalleberg, "Industrial transformation and the decline of craft: The decomposition of skill in the printing industry, 1931-1978," *American Sociological Review* 47 (1982):307-24; and for research on skill downgrading, upgrading, and polarization, see M. R. Kelley, "Programmable automation and the skill question: A reinterpretation of cross-national evidence," *Human Systems Management* 6 (1986):223-41; and Harley Shaiken, *Work Transformed: Automation and Labor in the Computer Age* (New York: Holt, Rhinehart, Winston, 1984). For an interesting perspective on this, see Thomas A. Diprete, "The upgrading and downgrading of occupations: Status redefinition vs deskilling as alternative theories of change," *Social Forces* 66, no. 3 (March 1988):725-46. He argues that case-study findings of deskilling within particular occupations should be considered in the wider context of functional hierarchies where occupational boundaries get redefined and positions get "professionalized." For example, while technology has undoubtedly downgraded (simplified) the work content of U.S. public service clerical workers, it has also transformed and extended what a clerk is capable of doing, enabling individual clerks to do the work of managers and technical officers.

9 Examples of those that do use both methods are Ivar Berg, *Education and Jobs: The Great Training Robbery* (New York: Praeger, 1970); Russell W. Rumberger, *Overeducation in the U.S. Labor Market* (New York: Praeger, 1981); and Paul Osterman, "The impacts of computers on the employment clerks and managers," *Industrial and Labor Relations Review* 39, no. 2 (1986):175-86.

10 Gordon Betcherman et al., eds., *Two Steps Forward: Human Resource Management in a High-Tech World*, Economic Council of Canada (Ottawa: Supply and Services Canada, 1990). We have also conducted a set of less formal studies of human-resource planning in selected service-sector firms which underlie the comments here.

11 The term "white collar" refers to those occupations in which the worker deals mainly with persons or information. This group includes managerial, administrative, professional (doctors, scientists, economists, etc.), technical (technologists, etc.), clerical, and sales and service workers. "Blue collar" refers to those occupations where manual labour constitutes an important part of the job. They include miners, loggers, processors, and mechanics, to offer a few examples.

12 Economic Council of Canada, *Innovation and Jobs in Canada* (Ottawa: Supply and Services Canada, 1987).

13 For example, this classification system is used in Sara Natelson Krulwich, "Job projections evaluated by education or training requirements," *Looking Ahead*, National Planning Association, vol. 3, no. 2 (February 1985):8-10. It is based on educational requirements for the broad occupational categories.

14 The occupational composition of employment by industry is based on this projection system while the projection of total employment comes from the fall 1988 solution of the Conference Board forecasting model (adapted by the Council). Because there was little detail on industries in the latter model, the projected employment was broken down into its constituent industries using the projected industry employment shares of the Canadian Occupational Projection System (COPS). The resulting figures were then entered into the COPS model to come up with occupational employment projections.

15 While the "variable coefficient" projections do have the virtue of predicting shifts in the occupational mix of any industry, the changes in the occupational pattern which are incorporated into projections are driven by the specific period in which employment composition trends are observed. In our projections, we used 1981 and 1986 as the years of observation; it should be noted that these years mark out a period when Canada experienced a severe recession, in response to which there was major rationalization within industry. Both occurrences undoubtedly influenced the pattern of employment by occupation.

16 Economic Council of Canada, *Innovation and Jobs*; F. Machlup, *Knowledge and Knowledge Production* (New Jersey: Princeton University Press, 1980); and Marc Porat, "The information economy: Definition and measurement," Special Publication 77-12(1), Office of Telecommunications, U.S. Department of Commerce, Washington, D.C., 1977.

17 Lars Osberg et al., *The Information Economy: The Implications of Unbalanced Growth* (Halifax: Institute for Research on Public Policy, 1989).

18 While it could be argued that all workers create, interpret, and transmit information, this typology attempts to isolate those occupations where these functions are central to the work.

19 In Canada, the data come from Manpower and Immigration Canada, *Canadian Classification and Dictionary of Occupations, 1971* (Ottawa: Supply and Services Canada, 1971) and in the United States, from the U.S. Department of Labor, *Dictionary of Occupational Titles*, 4th ed. (Washington, D.C.: U.S. Government Printing Office, 1977). Although "worker traits" are in fact the accepted term for these, we use the term "occupational traits" because such information describes the occupation or the job, not necessarily the worker. Occupational-trait-based skill analyses in Canada include Alfred A. Hunter, "Formal education and initial employment: Unravelling the relationship between schooling and skills over time," *American Sociological Review* 53 (October 1988):753-65; and Myles, "The expanding middle"; in the United States, see Berg, *Education and Jobs*; and Rumberger, *Overeducation in the U.S. Labor Market*.

20 The CCDO occupational-trait data were not developed for the purposes of analysing skill trends, but were intended primarily for use in job counselling.

21 See Employment and Immigration Canada, "Background to the NOC development" and "Principles/objectives of the NOC," unpublished mimeos., Ottawa, 1989. In 1984, Employment and Immigration Canada initiated work on a new occupational classification system, the National Occupational Classification (NOC) system, based primarily on the unifying principle of skill level as indicated by the training requirements, complexity and responsibility of the occupation. It is expected to be in place for the 1991 census.

22 Pamela S. Cain and Donald J. Treiman, "The dictionary of occupational titles as a source of occupational data," *American Sociological Review* 46, no. 3 (June 1981):253-78.

23 This result is consistent with previous studies (predominantly in the United States) based on "occupational-trait" data which generally have supported the skill-upgrading thesis. Examples include Berg, *Education and Jobs*; Rumberger, *Overeducation in the U.S. Labor Market*; Myles, "The expanding middle"; and Hunter, "Formal education and initial employment."

24 This is corroborated by Monica Boyd, "Sex differences in occupational skill: Canada, 1961-1986," *Canadian Review of Sociology and Anthropology* 27, no. 3 (August 1990): 285-315; and "Employment and skill: Men and women in Canada's service economy, 1971-1986," a paper presented at the 1990 annual meeting of the Canadian Sociological and Anthropological Association, Victoria, B.C., June 1990. Using the same data, she found that the gender gap has closed somewhat from the perspectives of both occupations and industry.

25 Myles, "The expanding middle."

26 Based on unpublished data provided by John Myles.

27 The CSS was part of an international project called the International Class Structure Project. See Erik Olin Wright and Bill Martin, "The transformation of the American class structure, 1960-1980," *American Journal of Sociology* 93, no. 1 (July 1987).

28 See John Myles and Gail Fawcett, "Job skills and the service economy," Working Paper no. 4, Economic Council of Canada, Ottawa, 1990.

29 See Harvey Krahn and Graham S. Lowe, "Young workers in the service economy," Working Paper no. 14, Economic Council of Canada, Ottawa, 1990.

30 Respondents were asked two questions that are generally relevant for assessing job complexity: the degree to which their job was interesting and the extent to which their work drew on their skills and abilities. The lowest average scores for both were found in those employed in clerical, sales, and service occupations in consumer services (which roughly approximate our "traditional" subsector).

31 Myles and Fawcett, "Job skills and the service economy," Table C-1. This conclusion is supported by the occupational-trait data in the case of information services but not for nonmarket services (recall Table 6-10).

32 Myles and Fawcett, "Job skills and the service economy," p. 22.

33 Myles and Fawcett, "Job skills and the service economy," p. 27.

34 Myles and Fawcett also draw this conclusion, at least in terms of what they call "task autonomy," which appears to be similar to the type of autonomy considered by Krahn and Lowe.

35 While this is the central question here, it should be noted that any differences could be the result of changes in job content between the late 1960s, when the occupational-trait scores were established, and the 1980s, when the CSS self-reports were conducted.

36 Myles and Fawcett, "Job skills and the service economy," p. 35.

37 The latter was calculated by adding 12 months to the on-the-job training time for jobs requiring a postsecondary education.

38 More detailed calculations by Myles and Fawcett confirmed this. They calculated that over the period 1951-81, the growth in the proportion of jobs requiring at least one year of specific vocational preparation was 5 percentage points using specific vocational preparation and 3 points using proxy-specific vocational preparation. See Myles and Fawcett, "Job skills and the service economy," p. 36.

CHAPTER 7

1 The origin of growth-accounting analysis is associated with Edward Denison, *Accounting for U.S. Economic Growth, 1929-1969* (Washington, D.C.: The Brookings Institution, 1974).

2 George Psacharopoulos, "Future trends and issues in education," in *Perspective 2000*, eds. K. Newton et al., Proceedings of a conference sponsored by the Economic Council of Canada, December 1988 (Ottawa: Supply and Services Canada, 1990).

3 See George Psacharopoulos, "The contribution of education to economic growth," in *International Comparisons of Productivity and Causes of the Slowdown*, ed. J. W. Kendrick (Cambridge: Ballinger Publishing Co., 1984). Ultimately, much of the criticism is due to the assumptions underlying the growth-accounting methodology. These are addressed in "Review of education and training in Canada," and "The linkages between education and training and Canada's economic performance," *Quarterly Labour Market and Productivity Review* (Spring 1989; and Winter 1989/90).

4 While wages are only a proxy measure of quality, more direct measures of physical output, for example, also support the positive influence of education. See, for example, Organisation for Economic Co-operation and Development, "Educational attainment of the labour force," Chapter 2 of *Employment Outlook, 1989* (Paris: OECD, 1989).

5 There are variants and extensions of these two positions. For a more complete discussion, see OECD, "Educational attainment of the labour force."

6 George Psacharopoulos, "Returns to education: A further international update and implications," *Journal of Human Resources* 20, no. 4 (1985):583-604. While these estimates are undoubtedly biased upwards because of unobserved individual abilities, there appears to be a consensus that this accounts for only a relatively small part of the calculated rates of return. See Sherwin Rosen, "Human capital: A survey of empirical research," in *Research in Labour Economics*, ed. R. C. Ehrenberg (Greenwich, Conn.: JAI Press, 1977).

7 Additional support is offered in Ann P. Bartel and Frank R. Lichtenberg, "The comparative advantage of educated workers in implementing new technology," *Review of Economics and Statistics* 69, no. 1 (February 1987):1-11. They found that sectors characterized by high rates of innovation create a relatively high demand for the well-educated.

8 In using the conventional approach of equating years of schooling with educational attainment, a caveat should be made about possible changes in the quality of education and, hence, the quantity of education that is "consumed." We do not have sufficient information to definitely establish that the quality of education in Canada has changed and, therefore, that the number of years of schooling do not mean the same

thing over time. In the United States, however, research indicates that this is the case. See Congressional Budget Office, *Trends in Educational Achievement*; and *Educational Achievement: Explanations and Implications of Recent Trends* (Washington: U.S. Congress, April 1986 and August 1987).

9   OECD, "Educational attainment of the labour force," Table 2-1.

10 Among those aged 15-19 years, the proportion of full-time students increased from 52 per cent in 1980 to 62 per cent in 1989. Full-time enrolment for the 20-24 age group also increased in the 1980s, from 10 per cent in 1980 to 16 per cent in 1989.

11 For some examples of recent U.S. research, see McKinley L. Blackburn et al., "The declining economic position of less-skilled American males," in *A Future of Lousy Jobs?*, ed. Gary Burtless (Washington, D.C.: The Brookings Institution, 1990); Barry Bluestone, "The impact of schooling and industrial restructuring on recent trends in wage equality in the United States"; and Marvin H. Kosters, "Schooling, work experience, and wage trends," both in the American Economics Association Annual Meeting Papers and Proceedings, *American Economic Review* 80, no. 2 (1990):303-12.

12 Richard Freeman and Karen Needels, "Educational attainment and returns in the U.S. and Canada," a paper presented to the 24th Annual Meeting of the Canadian Economics Association, Victoria, British Columbia, June 1990.

13 For the original analysis, see Martin Dooley, "The overeducated Canadian: Changes in the relationships among earnings, education and age for Canadian men: 1971-81," *Canadian Journal of Economics* 19, no. 1 (1986):142-59; and, for the update, see Martin Dooley, unpublished comments on the session "Inequality in North America – A comparative perspective," at the Annual Meeting of the Canadian Economics Association, Victoria, British Columbia, June 1990.

14 A comparison of the bottom rows of Tables 7-3 and 7-4 indicates that, in the aggregate, there is virtually no return for a secondary education (relative to a primary education). The age-composition factor also accounts for this result. When we compare these two tables, it becomes clear that, once age is held constant, workers with secondary schooling do receive a wage premium relative to those with only primary schooling.

15 In Ontario, approximately two thirds of those entering high school fall into this category. The survey results are described in Ontario Ministry of Skills Development, *Pathways, A Study of Labour Market Experiences and Transition Patterns of High School Leavers* (Toronto: OMSD, May 1989).

16 For a summary of the findings, see Ernest B. Akyeampong, "The graduates of '82: Where are they?," *Perspectives on Labour and Income* (Spring 1990).

17 Ted Wannell, "Male-female earnings gap among recent university graduates," *Perspectives on Labour and Income* (Summer 1990).

18 Harvey Krahn and Graham S. Lowe, "Young workers in the service economy," Working Paper no. 14, Economic Council of Canada, Ottawa, 1991.

19 The importance of education, health, and social services as an employer partially reflects the character of the original university subsample which had significant representation from education faculties. Even if these graduates are excluded, however, almost 20 per cent of the remaining university respondents were employed in that subsector.

20 Myles and Fawcett, "Job skills and the service economy."

21 The material reported in this section is part of a larger labour adjustment analysis using Labour Market Activity Survey data. Other aspects of that research were reported in Chapter 4. There are some differences in the sample used in that chapter and the one we employ here. In Chapter 4, we focused only on those workers who separated from a job in 1986, and individuals between 65 and 69 years of age were excluded, as were those who held two jobs simultaneously for four weeks or more. In Chapter 7, the base sample includes all individuals who reported paid employment in 1986.

22 An analytical problem with the Labour Market Activity Survey involves distinguishing workers who moved from one job to another from individuals who held two positions simultaneously. We are interested in the former group here. In our analysis of job changers, we only look at workers who had at least one week of joblessness before finding a second position. This reduced our sample to 1.8 million individuals.

23 These findings are confirmed by analyses of displaced workers surveys, in Canada, Garnett Picot and Ted Wannell, "Job loss and labour market adjustment in the Canadian economy," Statistics Canada, *The Labour Force*, Cat. 71-001 (March 1987); and in the United States, Paul Swaim and Michael Podgursky, "Do more educated workers fare better following job loss?," *Monthly Labor Review* 112, no. 8 (August 1989).

24 For detailed discussions of these international comparisons of student achievement, see David F. Robitaille, "Canadian participation in the Second International Mathematics Study"; and Robert K. Crocker, "Science achievement in Canadian schools: National and international comparisons," Working Paper nos. 6 and 7, Economic Council of Canada, Ottawa, 1990.

25 Too often, analysts do not recognize that both levels of government must be considered in an examination of public training policy in this country. Indeed, in the largest urban areas, municipal programs should also be considered. For the programs offered by all three levels of government in Metropolitan Toronto, for example, see Armine Yalnizyan and David A. Wolfe, *Target on Training: Meeting Workers' Needs in a Changing Economy* (Toronto: Social Planning Council of Metropolitan Toronto, 1989).

26 Report of the Advisory Council on Adjustment, *Adjusting to Win*, A. Jean de Grandpré, Chairman (Ottawa: Supply and Services Canada, March 1989).

27 Employment and Immigration Canada, *Success in the Works, A Policy Paper: A Labour Force Development Strategy*, Public Affairs and Strategic Policy and Planning (Hull: CEIC, April 1989); Canadian Labour Market and Productivity Centre, *Report of the CLMPC Task Forces on the Labour Force Development Strategy* (Ottawa: CLMPC, 1990); Ontario Premier's Council, *People and Skills in the New Global Economy* (Toronto: Queen's Printer of Ontario, 1990); and Canadian Manufacturers' Association, *The Aggressive Economy: Daring to Compete* (Toronto: CMA, 1989).

28 See, for example, Harvey S. Rosen, "Taxation and on-the-job training decisions," *Review of Economics and Statistics* 64 (1982):442-49; G. Lillard and H. Tan, "Private sector training: Who gets it and what are its effects," Rand Corporation Monograph no. R-3331-DOL/RC, Santa Monica, Calif., 1986; Jacob Mincer, "Job training, wage growth and labor turnover," and Harry J. Holzer, "The determinants of employee productivity and earnings: Some new evidence," Working Paper nos. 2680 and 2782, National Bureau of Economic Research, Cambridge, Mass., 1988; and James N. Brown, "Why do wages increase with tenure? On-the-job training and life cycle wage growth observed within firms," *American Economic Review* 79, no. 5 (December 1989): 971-91.

29 Jacob Mincer, "Job training: Costs, returns, and wage profiles," Working Paper no. 3208, National Bureau of Economic Research, Cambridge, Mass., 1989.

30 Mincer, "Job training."

31 Ann P. Bartel, "Formal employee training programs and their impact on labor productivity: Evidence from the Human Resource Survey," Working Paper no. 3026, National Bureau of Economic Research, Cambridge, Mass., 1989. Bartel observes, however, that "the increase in productivity attributable to training is largely due to the fact that businesses that train rely heavily on screening of job applicants which significantly enhances labor productivity" (p. 27).

32 American Society for Training and Development, *Training America: Learning to Work for the 21st Century* (Alexandria, Virginia: ASTD, 1989), p. 2.

33 Advisory Council on Adjustment, *Adjusting to Win*.

34 Quebec Department of Finance, *Budget, 1990-1991*, Budget Speech and Supplementary Information, Quebec, April 1990.

35 Ontario Premier's Council, *People and Skills*.

36 There have been some comprehensive provincial surveys, most notably in Ontario. See the Ontario Manpower Commission, *Training in Industry: A Survey of Employer-Sponsored Programs in Ontario* (Toronto: OMC, 1986); and Ontario Ministry of Skills Development, *The Training Decision: Training in the Private Sector* (Toronto: OMSD, 1989).

37 Statistics Canada, "Human resource training and development survey," Distribution Report, Education, Culture and Tourism Division, Ottawa, 1990.

38 Canadian Federation of Independent Business, "Skills for the future: Small business and training in Canada," Toronto, 1989.

39 The HRTDS covered a 12-month period ending in November 1987.

40 Both formal and informal training were included in the Human Resource Survey. Over 60 per cent of the respondents reported some training activity. See Gordon Betcherman, *Meeting Skill Requirements: Report of the Human Resources Survey*, Economic Council of Canada (Ottawa: Supply and Services Canada, 1982).

41 The HRTDS list of objectives is identical to the list used by the Ontario Ministry of Skills Development in a 1987 employer survey. See Ontario Ministry of Skills Development, *The Training Decision*.

42 Ontario Premier's Council, *People and Skills*.

43 This finding regarding occupational concentration is consistent with the results of most surveys. An interesting exception was the SBPS, where professional and managerial employees had relatively low participation rates in training programs. According to the SBPS report, respondents (mostly small businesses) tended to rely on recruiting individuals in these categories who were already qualified. See Canadian Federation of Independent Business, "Skills for the future," p. 20.

44 This is consistent with analyses based on Statistics Canada's Survey of Adult Education and the Annual Work Patterns Surveys of 1982 and 1983, which found that, while female participation in short-term and part-time training was comparable to male rates, females had lower incidences of full-time training. See Garnett Picot, "The participation in training by women, the unemployed, and the disadvantaged," Research Paper no. 24, Social and Economics Studies Division, Statistics Canada, Ottawa, May 1986.

45 Note that this was written at a time of serious debate about the directions for labour market policy in this country. As issues surrounding the federal government's Labour Force Development Strategy and the related consultation process are resolved, and as policy reform in a number of provinces is completed, the emphasis and contribution of governments to the human-resource development of Canadian workers may change significantly.

46 Labour market expenditures as a proportion of GDP recently dropped significantly in the United Kingdom in the late 1980s. Indeed, in 1988 the ratio was higher in that country than in Canada.

47 For example, the Advisory Council on Adjustment, *Adjusting to Win*, used the metaphor of a "trampoline" rather than a "safety net" as the preferred orientation of public policy.

48 Employment and Immigration Canada, *Success in the Works*.

49 Organisation for Economic Co-operation and Development, *Labour Market Policies for the 1990s* (Paris: OECD, 1990).

50 This option is directed towards summer employment for students. In making this assumption, we are following the OECD's organization of the CJS. See OECD, *Labour Market Policies for the 1990s*.

51 A number of observers contend that very little of what is funded through CJS actually is concerned with real skill development that will aid long-run employability. A House of Commons Committee review of the strategy, for example, heard the criticism that much of the training under CJS was really just wage subsidization. See House of Commons, *A Review of the Canadian Jobs Strategy*, Second Report of the Standing Committee on Labour, Employment and Immigration, Claude Lanthier, Chairman, Issue no. 55, Ottawa, 12 April 1988.

52 Employment and Immigration Canada, *Evaluation of the Job Development Program, Final Report*, prepared for the Program Evaluation Branch, Strategic Policy and Planning, Hull (Quebec), August 1989.

53 Employment and Immigration Canada, *Evaluation of the Job Entry Program, Final Report*, prepared for the Program Evaluation Branch, Strategic Policy and Planning, Hull (Quebec), July 1989.

54 In 1990 the proportion allocated to developmental programming was about 4 per cent. Under the new act, the statutory ceiling will be 15 per cent as of 1 January 1992. Note, however, that the real incremental budget for developmental activity will be somewhat less than this reform suggests because of changes in the way training expenses under Section 26 are accounted for.

55 This discussion of Newfoundland and New Brunswick is based on Elizabeth Beale, "Labour market policies in two eastern provinces: Newfoundland and Labrador, and New Brunswick," a paper prepared for the Economic Council of Canada, Ottawa, 1990.

56 This is evident from evaluations of CJS programs where the assessments for Atlantic Canada are less favourable than those elsewhere in the country. See Beale, "Labour market policies in two eastern provinces," pp. 55 and 56.

57 One strategy has been to encourage industry and community associations to organize training initiatives (for example, in the hospitality industry). See Beale, "Labour market policies in two eastern provinces," pp. 44-47.

58 As well, it should be noted that postsecondary institutions have been receiving less money under the Established Program Financing arrangement, which has further reduced the overall resources available.

59 This discussion of Manitoba, Alberta, and British Columbia is based on Elisabeth Wagner, "The changing labour market – Some provincial policy responses," a paper prepared for the Economic Council of Canada, Ottawa, 1989.

60 Ontario Ministry for Skills Development, *Breaking New Ground: Ontario's Training Strategy* (Toronto: OMSD, 1988).

61 See Ontario Premier's Council, *People and Skills*; and Ontario Ministry of Colleges and Universities, *Vision 2000: Quality and Opportunity, A Review of the Mandate of Ontario's Colleges* (Toronto: OMCU, 1990).

CHAPTER 8

1 Wages and salaries refer to remuneration paid to workers for their services, including directors' fees, bonuses, commissions, gratuities, income in kind, and net farm income, but excluding military pay. Wages and salaries are taken from Statistics Canada, *Estimates of Labour Income*, Cat. 72-005. Analysis in this chapter comparing hourly wages and salaries across industries and examining various supplementary labour components makes use of unpublished data from the Labour Division, the unit responsible for Cat. 72-005. Net farm income is a National Income and Expenditure Accounts entry. To calculate average hourly rates, annual wages and salaries were divided by annual "actual hours." Hours figures are from Statistics Canada, *The Labour Force*, Cat. 71-001, and *Labour Force Annual Averages*, Cat. 71-529. Industry comparisons of hours of work are based on published and unpublished data obtained from the Labour Force Survey. To calculate real wage rates, the annual hourly compensation figures were deflated by the current year Consumer Price Index (CPI). The hours figures include the hours of the self-employed while the compensation figures from Labour Division exclude the earnings of the self-employed apart from net farm income. In their hourly compensation figures, the Input-Output Division of Statistics Canada do include imputations of self-employed earnings. However, their compensation figures are only available by industry for the business sector and are not sufficiently detailed for our purposes. Moreover, the data do not permit separate analysis of supplementary income. Comparisons between our hourly income series and the input-output hourly compensation figures yield similar trends overall. For more details, see Norm Leckie, "An alternative measure of hourly labour compensation: A note," a paper prepared for the Economic Council of Canada, Ottawa, November 1989.

2 Labour productivity here is measured as gross domestic product divided by total actual hours worked (from the Labour Force Survey). Traditionally, labour productivity has been calculated on the basis of person-hours worked generated by National Accounts, but we used this hours series to be consistent with our hourly compensation computations, as outlined in note 1. The relative performance of productivity and wages is not affected by the choice of the hours divisor, however.

3 Over the entire period 1967-89, the average annual rate of increase for wages and salaries was 1.6 per cent and for labour productivity it was 1.8 per cent.

4 Richard B. Freeman and Morris M. Kleiner, "The impact of new unionization on wages and working conditions," *Journal of Labour Economics* 8, no. 1, part 2 (1990):S8-S25.

5 Calculated on the basis of the Labour Market Activity Survey (1986), the average hourly wages were $8.72 and $13.26 for firms employing fewer than and more than 500 employees, respectively.

6 Strictly speaking, supplementary labour income, as a measure of employer contributions, is neither a true benefit nor true income in the sense of money actually received by workers. Treated in this way, SLI can be viewed as deferred income – contributions made by employers for the future benefit of workers.

7 For additional details on supplementary labour income in Canada, see Christina Caron and Norm Leckie, "Recent trends in supplementary labour income," a paper prepared for the Economic Council of Canada, Ottawa, 1990.

8 Robert Kuttner, "The declining middle," *The Atlantic Monthly* (July 1983):60-72. Kuttner in fact popularized a debate originally fuelled by Barry Bluestone and Bennett Harrison in *The Deindustrialization of America* (New York: Basic Books, 1982).

9 For an analytical example counter to the declining-middle thesis, see Marvin H. Kosters and Murray N. Ross, "A shrinking middle class?," *The Public Interest* 90 (Winter 1988):3-25.

10 See, in particular, Barry Bluestone and Bennett Harrison, "Increasing inequality and the proliferation of low-wage employment: A review of the debate and some new evidence," draft mimeo, February 1989. In this work, they attempt to answer some of the methodological criticisms levelled at their earlier analyses, such as "The great American job machine: The proliferation of low-wage employment in the U.S. economy," a study prepared for the U.S. Joint Economic Committee, Washington, D.C., 1986.

11 For example, see Bennett Harrison et al., "Wage inequality takes a great U-turn," *Challenge* 29, no. 1 (March/April 1986):26-32; and Norton W. Grubb and Robert H. Wilson, "Sources of increasing inequality in wages and salaries, 1960-80," *Monthly Labor Review* 112, no. 4 (April 1989): 3-13.

12 For example, Katherine L. Bradbury, "The shrinking middle class," *New England Economic Review* (September/October 1986):45-55; and McKinley L. Blackburn and David E. Bloom, "What is happening to the middle class?," *American Demographics* 7, no. 1 (1985):18-25.

13 See Chapter 5 of Economic Council of Canada, *Innovation and Jobs in Canada* (Ottawa: Supply and Services Canada, 1987). For more details on this research, see Norm Leckie, "The declining middle and technological change: Trends in the distribution of employment income in Canada, 1971-84," Discussion Paper no. 342, Economic Council of Canada, Ottawa, 1988.

14 Michael C. Wolfson, "Stasis amid change: Income inequality in Canada, 1965-1983," *Review of Income and Wealth* 32, no. 4 (December 1986):337-70.

15 Garnett Picot et al., "Good jobs/bad jobs and the declining middle, 1967-1986," Research Paper series no. 28, Statistics Canada, Ottawa, 1990; Michael C. Wolfson, "Inequality and polarization: Is there a disappearing middle class in Canada?," a paper presented to the Statistics Canada Symposium on Analysis of Data in Time, Ottawa, October 1989; and Catherine J. McWatters and Charles M. Beach, "Factors behind the changes in the family income distribution and the share of the middle class," *Relations Industrielles* 45, no. 1 (1990):118-33.

16 Wolfson, "Inequality and polarization."

17 For example, in the United States, Grubb and Wilson, "Sources of increasing inequality"; and in Canada, Picot et al., "Good jobs/bad jobs and the declining middle."

18 Patrick J. McMahon and John H. Tschetter, "The declining middle class: A further analysis," *Monthly Labor Review* 109, no. 9 (September 1986):22-27; Grubb and Wilson, "Sources of increasing inequality"; Bluestone and Harrison, "Increasing inequality"; and Robert B. Reich, "As the world turns," *The New Republic* (1 May 1989).

19 For example, Robert Z. Lawrence, "Sectoral shifts and the size of the middle class," *Brookings Review*, no. 3 (Fall 1984):3-11; Leckie, "The declining middle and technological change." However, Lester C. Thurow claims in "A surge in inequality," *Scientific American* 256, no. 5 (1987), that rising female participation in the labour force has increased inequality.

20 Lawrence, "Sectoral shifts"; Dan A. Black et al., "Demographic change and inequality in the size distributions of labor and non-labor income," *Review of Income and Wealth* 35, no. 3 (September 1989):283-96.

21 For example, Bradbury, "The shrinking middle class"; Bennett Harrison and Barry Bluestone, "The dark side of labour market 'flexibility': Falling wages and growing income inequality in America," Labour Market Analysis and Employment Planning, Working Paper no. 17, International Labour Organization, Geneva, October 1987; and Leckie, "The declining middle and technological change."

22. Janet L. Norwood, "The job machine has not broken down," *The New York Times* (22 February 1987).

23. Gary Burtless, "Earnings inequality over the business and demographic cycles," in *A Future of Lousy Jobs?: The Changing Structure of U.S. Wages*, ed. Gary Burtless (Washington D.C.: The Brookings Institution, 1990).

24. John Coder et al., "Inequality among children and elderly in ten modern nations: The United States in an international context," Papers and Proceedings of the 101st Annual Meeting of the American Economics Association, New York, December 1988, in *American Economic Review* 79, no. 2 (1989); Timothy M. Smeeding, "Poverty, affluence and the income costs of children: Cross-national evidence from the Luxembourg Income Study (LIS)," *Journal of Post Keynesian Economics* 11, no. 2 (1988-89):222-40; Michael O'Higgins et al., "Income distribution and redistribution: A microdata analysis for seven countries," *Review of Income and Wealth* 35 no. 2 (June 1989):107-31; Pan A. Yotopoulos, "Distributions of real income: Within countries and by world income classes," *Review of Income and Wealth* 35, no. 4 (December 1989):357-76; Daniel B. Radner, "Family income, age, and size of unit: Selected international comparisons," *Review of Income and Wealth* 31, no. 2 (June 1985):103-26; and Gary Burtless, "Inequality in America: Where do we stand?," *The Brookings Review* 5, no. 3 (1987):9-16.

25. Mark Adams, "The distribution of earnings, 1973 to 1986," Employment Market Research Unit, Research Paper no. 64, United Kingdom Department of Employment, 1988; Mark Adams et al., "Trends in the distribution of earnings, 1973 to 1986," *Employment Gazette* (United Kingdom, February 1988); Brian Nolan, "Macroeconomic conditions and the size distribution of income: Evidence from the United Kingdom," *Journal of Post Keynesian Economics* 11, no. 2 (1988-89): 196-221; and Dilip Mookherjee and Anthony Shorrocks, "A decomposition analysis of the trend in U.K. income inequality," *Economic Journal*, no. 92 (December 1982): 886-902.

26. It should be made clear that these data are not longitudinal, that is, they do not follow the same group of individuals throughout the time period under consideration. We are merely observing, in each of the four years, a snapshot of the earnings distribution of a group of individuals that is different from year to year. The cross-sectional/time-series analysis we employ here cannot capture the actual number of individuals falling out of, or into, the various earnings groups, but rather gives us a *net* picture of the changes in the distribution.

27. John Myles et al., provide a more detailed picture of this polarization in the 1980s. They examine the changes in the hourly wage distribution in 1981-86 among 10 wage classes, and find that the largest shift was from the lower-middle into the bottom of the wage distribution, with smaller shifts out of the middle wage levels and into top wage levels. John Myles et al., "Wages and jobs in the 1990s: Changing youth wages and the declining middle," Social and Economic Studies no. 17, Statistics Canada, Ottawa, 1988.

28. According to Wolfson, "Inequality and polarization," a change in the Gini of more than 16 basis points is statistically significant.

29. The similarity in relative importance of investment income across quintile groups according to the Survey of Consumer Finances is unexpected but may be accounted for by the way investment income is handled in the survey. Accrued interest income, rental income, and indirectly received investment income from holding companies is not reported. Thus it is likely that investment income is underestimated, particularly for higher income groups who are more apt to rely on such income sources than lower income groups.

30. Note that we are treating the growth in nonstandard employment as a supply-side phenomenon even though it is also a function of demand-side factors as discussed in Chapter 5.

31. Note that in comparing the distributional trends of males and females we are calculating Ginis and earnings groups based on the parameters of each population subgroup. Thus, for example, we computed the work force share of the middle earnings stratum of females on the basis of the female median earnings, not the overall median. Similarly, we calculate the distributional parameters for all the population subgroups defined by each of the other factors considered in this analysis: age, employment "status," and industry.

32. Our interest here is in wage rates rather than annual earnings, so we have used Labour Market Activity Survey data as opposed to Survey of Consumer Finances data. The former data base allows for earnings to be adjusted for the number of hours worked. Note that the unit of analysis is the "job" rather than the "worker."

33. See, for example, Organisation for Economic Co-operation and Development, "Relative wages, industrial structure and employment performance," Chapter 5 of *Employment Outlook, 1985* (Paris: OECD, 1985); and Linda A. Bell and Richard B. Freeman, "The facts about rising industrial wage dispersion in the U.S.," in *Proceedings of the Thirty-Ninth Annual Meeting of the Industrial Relations Research Association*, ed. Barbara D. Dennis, 28-30 December 1986, New Orleans (Madison, WI: Industrial Relations Research Association, 1987).

34. While input-output data does provide total compensation over the period 1961-88 for 21 manufacturing industries, this level of disaggregation is not available for the service sector. The Survey of Employment, Payrolls, and Earnings (SEPH) database reports earnings at a detailed industry level; however, comparisons between periods before and after 1983 are difficult since the survey was significantly altered in that year.

35. For details on the methodology and results, see Marcel Bédard, "Low-wage services, demographic trends and employment needs," a paper prepared for the Economic Council of Canada, 1990.

36 Picot et al., "Good jobs/bad jobs."

CHAPTER 9

1 This chapter is essentially reproduced from the final section of the Economic Council of Canada, *Goods Jobs, Bad Jobs: Employment in the Service Economy* (Ottawa: Supply and Services Canada, 1990).

APPENDIX A

1 K. Miyazawa, *Input-Output Analysis and the Structure of Income Distribution.*

2 A detailed discussion of Miyazawa's methodology and a comparison of Miyazawa's and Leontief's approaches can be found in Tom Siedule, "The interdependence of industrial activities," a paper prepared for the Economic Council of Canada, Ottawa, 1990.

APPENDIX B

1 For example, in Canada, Myles et al., "Wages and jobs"; Picot et al., "Good jobs/bad jobs"; and in the United States, Bluestone and Harrison, "The great American job machine" and "Increasing inequality."

2 Specifically, economic growth and unemployment were not at extreme levels in those years. In 1967, 1973, 1981, and 1986, the rate of economic growth (real increase in the gross domestic product) was 2.9, 7.7, 3.7, and 3.1 per cent, respectively, and the rate of unemployment was 3.8, 5.5, 7.5, and 9.5 per cent, respectively; within the context of each business cycle, these figures were in the middle range.

3 For a discussion of the difference between inequality and polarization, see Wolfson, "Inequality and polarization."

4 Other measures of inequality are available and have been used, but they generally yielded results similar to those using the Gini coefficient, although each has its weakness. For example, McWatters and Beach, "Factors behind the changes," have used quantile (quintile) income shares, but these have been found not to reflect changes within quantiles and whether the entire income pie is shrinking. Grubb and Wilson, "Sources of increasing inequality," used the Theil measure which, along with variance-log measures, has been found to be sensitive to changes in lower income ranges. Kosters and Ross, "A shrinking middle class?," have used the coefficient of variation, said to be sensitive to the upper ranges of the distribution. Even the Gini coefficient is sensitive to changes in the middle, and like all measures but the quantile indicator, cannot pinpoint the location of inequality changes. Nevertheless, because the Gini enjoys wide acceptance, we use it here, along with quintile income shares for comparative purposes. For a detailed empirical discussion of all of the above measures, see Roger Love and Michael C. Wolfson, *Income Inequality: Statistical Methodology and Canadian Illustrations,* Statistics Canada, Cat. 13-559, March 1976.

5 Others have used the standardization methodology including Wolfson, "Stasis amid change"; Bradbury, "The shrinking middle class?"; and Myles et al., "Wages and jobs."

List of Tables, Charts, and Figures

Tables

2-1	Average Annual Growth in Machinery and Equipment Capital Stock, 1966-88, and Share of Total Machinery and Equipment Capital Stock, Seclected Years, 1961-88, by Industry, Canada	11
2-2	Machinery and Equipment Investment as a Share of Total Investment, by Industry, Canada, 1960s, 1970s, and 1980s; and 1988	11
2-3	Expenditure on Machinery and Equipment per Employee, 1966 and 1988, and Average Annual Growth Rate, 1966-88, by Industry, Canada	12
2-4	Adoption of Computer-Based Technology, by Service Industry, Canada, 1980-85	13
2-5	Current Intramural R&D Expenditures as a Proportion of Performing Company Sales (Revenues), by Industry, Canada, 1979, 1983, and 1987	13
2-6	Service Exports and Imports as a Proportion of Total and Non-Auto-Pact Exports and Imports, Canada, Selected Years, 1961-88	16
2-7	Service Exports and Imports of Major OECD Countries, 1984	16
2-8	Distribution of Service Exports and Imports by Service-Trade Category, Canada, Selected Years, 1961-89	17
2-9	Exports and Imports of Selected Business Services, by Type of Service, Canada, 1969 and 1988	18
2-10	Exports as a Proportion of Output and Export-Dependent Employment in the Service Sector, Canada, 1988	19
2-11	Index of Employment Concentration, Dynamic Services, Selected Cities and Towns, Canada, 1986	22
2-12	Index of Employment Concentration, by Occupation, Selected Cities and Towns, Canada, 1986	24
2-13	Distribution of Employment Growth in the Goods and Service Sectors by Firm Size, Canada, 1978-86	28
2-14	Distribution of Employment in the Goods and Service Sectors by Firm Size, Canada, 1978, 1984, and 1986	28
2-15	Distribution of Employment by Firm Size, Canada, First Half of 1989	29
3-1	Distribution of Total Final Expenditures on Goods and Services, Canada, 1971, 1981, and 1988	32
3-2	Average Annual Rate of Growth in Output per Employee, Canada, 1967-89	33
3-3	Distribution of Service Industry Output According to Intermediate and Final Demand, Canada, 1985	36
3-4	Sectoral Interdependency: Selected Indicators of the Impacts of Three Sets of Policy Simulations on Goods- and Service-Sector Growth, Canada, Selected Years, 1971-86	42
3-5	Output per Employee, by Sector, Canada, 1966, 1981, and 1989	51
3-6	Growth in Gross Domestic Product and Employment, by Sector, Canada, 1972-88 and Projected 1989-93	52
4-1	Output Growth, 1967-89, and Output Share, 1967 and 1989, by Industry, Canada	58

4-2	Employment Growth, 1967-89, and Employment Share, 1967 and 1989, by Industry, Canada	58
4-3	Distribution of Employment by Sector, Selected OECD Countries, Early 1960s, 1973, 1982, and 1984; and Canada, 1984	60
4-4	Changes in Employment between Business Cycle Peaks and Troughs, by Industry, Canada, 1970s and 1980s	62
4-5	Changes in Real GDP during Recessions, by Industry, Canada, 1970s and 1980s	63
4-6	Changes in Real Consumer and Government Expenditures during Recessions, Canada, 1970s and 1980s	63
4-7	Job Separation Rates, by Industry Group, Canada, 1986	64
4-8	Profile of Job Finders: Distribution by Sectoral Movement, Canada, 1986-87	65
4-9	Profile of Job Separators: Distribution by Postseparation Status, Canada, 1986-87	66
4-10	Profile of Job Finders: Distribution by Duration of Joblessness, Canada, 1986-87	67
4-11	Profile of Job Finders: Distribution by Wage Outcome, Canada, 1986-87	68
5-1	Net Employment Growth, by Employment Status, Canada, 1980-89	73
5-2	Distribution and Incidence of Part-Time Employment by Industry Group, Canada, 1989	73
5-3	Distribution of Part-Time and Full-Time Paid Jobs by Firm Size, Canada, 1987	74
5-4	Part-Time Paid Jobs: Average Hourly Earnings and Earnings Relative to Full-Time Earnings, by Industry Group, Canada, 1987	76
5-5	Incidence and Distribution of Short-Term Paid Jobs by Industry Group, Canada, 1987	78
5-6	Own-Account Self-Employment as a Share of Total Employment, by Industry, Canada, 1975 and 1989	80
5-7	Distribution of Paid Employees and Own-Account Self-Employed by Sex and Age, Canada, 1989	80
5-8	Distribution and Incidence of All Nonstandard Jobs by Industry, Canada, 1987	82
5-9	Distribution and Incidence of All Nonstandard Jobs by Sex and Age, Canada, 1987	82
5-10	Shift-Share Analysis of Nonstandard Employment Trends, Canada, 1975 and 1988 (Actual) and 1988 (Hypothetical)	84
6-1	Contribution of Occupational Groups to Total Employment Change, Canada, 1971-81 and 1981-86	91
6-2	Change in Occupational Mix, Goods and Service Sectors, Canada, 1971 and 1986	93
6-3	Distribution of Employment According to Occupational Skill Level by Sector, Canada, 1971, 1981, and 1986	94
6-4	Occupational Employment Structure, Canada, 1986 (Actual) and 2000 (Projected)	94
6-5	Proportion of Information Workers in Each Industry and Ratio of Data- to Knowledge-Workers, Canada, 1971, 1981, and 1986	95
6-6	Distribution of Employment by Skill Level, and Degree of Skill Transformation, Occupation-Trait Measures, 1971, 1981, and 1986	98
6-7	Distribution of Males and Females by Specific Vocational Preparation (SVP) Time Required, Canada, 1971, 1981, and 1986	99
6-8	Proportion of Workers in Low- and High-Skilled Jobs According to Occupational-Trait Measures, by Industry, Canada, 1986	100

6-9	Relative Skill Levels of Industries According to Occupational-Trait Measures, by Industry, Canada, 1986	101
6-10	Ratio of the Proportion of Females to Males in Low- and High-Skilled Jobs According to Occupational-Trait Measures, by Industry, Canada, 1986	102
6-11	Changes in Skill Levels of Jobs According to Occupational-Trait Measures, by Industry, Canada, 1971-81 and 1981-86	102
6-12	A Comparison of the Canadian Class Structure Survey and the Labour Force Survey: Distribution of the Labour Force, 1982-83, and Employment, 1982, Canada	103
6-13	Distribution of the Labour Force According to Two Measures of Job Complexity by Industry, Canada, 1982-83	104
6-14	Distribution of the Labour Force According to Educational Requirements by Industry, Canada, 1982-83	105
6-15	Distribution of the Labour Force According to On-the-Job Training Requirements by Industry, Canada, 1982-83	106
6-16	Distribution of the Labour Force According to Conceptual Autonomy Required by Industry, Canada, 1982-83	107
6-17	Decision-Making Autonomy of High School and University Graduates, by Occupational-Industry Groups, Canada, 1985	107
7-1	Growth-Accounting Estimates of the Contributions of Education to Economic Growth, Canada, Selected Years, 1962-88	112
7-2	Unemployment Rates by Level of Educational Attainment, Labour Force Age Groups, Canada, 1989	116
7-3	Earnings Ratio of Workers with Postsecondary Degrees Relative to Workers with Up to Eight Years of Schooling, by Age, Canada, Selected Years, 1967-86	117
7-4	Earnings Ratio of Workers with Postsecondary Degrees Relative to Workers with Secondary Education, by Age, Canada, Selected Years, 1967-86	117
7-5	Distribution of Employment by Industry, According to Gender and Educational Level, Canada, 1987	119
7-6	Distribution of Employment by Occupation, According to Gender and Educational Level, Canada, 1987	120
7-7	Selected Job Characteristics, by Level of Education, Canada, 1987	121
7-8	Separation Rates and Distribution by Reason for Separation, According to Educational Attainment Level, Canada, 1986 and 1987	122
7-9	Distribution of Job Separators by Duration of Joblessness, According to Educational Attainment, Canada, 1986 and 1987	122
7-10	Incidence of Employer-Sponsored Training, Selected Surveys, Canada	126
7-11	Training Objectives Identified by Firms Reporting Formal Training Programs, Canada, 1987	126
7-12	Training Activity, by Firm Size, Canada, 1987	128
7-13	Characteristics of Employees Receiving Job Training, Canada, March 1987 to March 1989	129
7-14	Training Indicators, Selected Countries and Dates, 1982-87	130
7-15	Public Expenditures on Labour Market Programs, Selected Countries and Years, 1988-90	130
7-16	Canadian Jobs Strategy Annual Expenditures, by Program, 1986/87 – 1989/90	132
7-17	Direct Federal Government Training Expenditures in New Brunswick and Newfoundland, 1982/83 – 1988/89	134

7-18	Ontario Training Expenditures, by Program, Canada, 1989/90	135
8-1	Hourly Wages and Salaries, and Supplementary Labour Income, by Industry, Canada, 1989	139
8-2	Growth in Hourly Labour Income, by Source of Income, Canada, 1967-77 and 1977-89	140
8-3	Earnings Distribution of ELFPs, Canada, Selected Years, 1967-86	142
8-4	Relative Mean ELFP Earnings, by Earnings Stratum, Canada, Selected Years, 1967-86	143
8-5	Quintile Measures of Changes in the Earnings Distribution of ELFPs, Canada, Selected Years, 1967-86	144
8-6	Sensitivity Analysis of the ELFP Criterion, Earnings Distribution Trends, Canada, Selected Years, 1967-86	145
8-7	Sensitivity Analysis of Middle Earnings Cutoffs, Trends in the ELFP Work Force Share of the Middle Stratum, Canada, Selected Years, 1967-86	145
8-8	Earnings Distribution of ELFPs, Published Grouped Data, Canada, Selected Years, 1967-88	146
8-9	Distribution of Total Income of Those Whose Major Source of Income Are Wages and Salaries, by Income Quintiles, Canada, Selected Years, 1951-67	146
8-10	Earnings Distribution Trends, by Region, Canada, Selected Years, 1967-86	147
8-11	Income Distribution Trends, ELFPs and Census Family Units, Canada, Selected Years, 1967-86	148
8-12	Distribution of Total Income in Each Quintile by Income Source, Economic Family Units, Canada, 1973 and 1988	149
8-13	Earnings Distribution Trends by Gender, Canada, Selected Years, 1967-86	150
8-14	Earnings Distribution Trends by Age Group, Canada, Selected Years, 1967-86	151
8-15	Earnings Distribution Trends by Employment Status, Canada, Selected Years, 1967-86	152
8-16	Work Force Share of the Middle Earnings Stratum, and Gini Coefficient, Standardized for Demographic Shifts, Canada, 1967 and 1986 (Actual) and 1986 (Hypothetical)	152
8-17	Employment Growth, 1974-89, and Average Hourly Earnings, by Industry, Canada, 1987	154
8-18	Earnings Dispersion among Industries, Canada, 1973, 1981, and 1986	155
8-19	Earnings Distribution Trends by Industry, Canada, 1973, 1981, and 1986	155
A-1	The Stimulative Power of Each Goods Industry on Each Service Industry, 1985	179
A-2	The Stimulative Power of Each Service Industry on Each Goods Industry, 1985	181

Charts

1-1	Employment Share of the Goods and Service Sectors, Canada, Selected Years, 1946-89	1
3-1	Total Service Input as a Proportion of Total Intermediate Input, by Goods Industry, Canada, 1971, 1981, and 1985	37
3-2	Total Service Input as a Proportion of Gross Output, by Goods Industry, Canada, 1971, 1981, and 1985	37

3-3	Total Service Input as a Proportion of Gross Output, by Service Industry, Canada, 1971, 1981, and 1985	38
3-4	Stimulative Power of Goods Industries on Service-Sector Output, Canada, 1985	46
3-5	Stimulative Power of Service Industries on Goods-Sector Output, Canada, 1985	47
3-6	Sensitivity of Service Industries to Goods-Sector Output, Canada, 1985	47
3-7	Sensitivity of Goods Industries to Service-Sector Output, Canada, 1985	48
3-8	Stimulative Power of Each Goods Industry on All Other Goods Industries, Canada, 1985	48
3-9	Stimulative Power of Each Service Industry on All Other Service Industries, Canada, 1985	49
3-10	Stimulative Power of Goods Industries on Service-Sector Output, Canada, 1971 and 1981	50
3-11	Sensitivity of Service Industries to Goods-Sector Output, Canada, 1971 and 1981	51
4-1	Goods and Service Sectors' Share of Total Employment, Selected OECD Countries, Early 1960s, 1973, and 1984	59
5-1	Part-Time Employment as a Proportion of Total Employment, Canada, 1953-89	73
5-2	Part-Time Employment as a Proportion of Total Employment, by Age Group, Canada, 1979 and 1989	74
5-3	Involuntary Part-Time Employment as a Proportion of Total Part-Time Employment, and Unemployment Rate, Canada, 1975-89	75
5-4	Hourly Earnings of Part-Time Paid Jobs Relative to Full-Time Paid Jobs, by Firm Size, Canada, 1987	76
5-5	Short-Term Paid Jobs, as a Proportion of All Paid Jobs, by Age, Canada, 1987	78
5-6	Nonstandard Employment as a Proportion of Total Employment, Canada, 1975-89	81
5-7	Incidence of Nonstandard Employment Forms and Unemployment Rate, Canada, 1975-89	85
6-1	Distribution of the Labour Force by Blue- and White-Collar Occupations, Canada, Selected Years, 1961-86	91
6-2	Employment Concentration of Occupations, by Sector, Canada, 1986	92
6-3	Proportion of Males and Females in Jobs Requiring High Levels of Thought and Attention, by Industry, Canada, 1982-83	104
6-4	Gender Differences in On-the-Job Training Requirements, by Industry, Canada, 1982-83	106
6-5	Job Complexity by Industry: A Comparison of Occupational-Trait and Self-Report Measures, Canada, 1982-83	108
6-6	Job-Specific Training Requirements: A Comparison of Occupational-Trait and Self-Report Measures, Canada, 1982-83	109
6-7	Job-Specific Training Requirements by Industry: A Comparison of Occupational-Trait and Self-Report Measures, Canada, 1982-83	110
7-1	Labour Force by Level of Schooling, Canada, 1975-89	113
7-2	Labour Force Participation Rates, by Level of Schooling and Sex, Canada, 1989	114
7-3	Male Labour Force Participation Rates, by Level of Schooling, Canada, 1975-89	115
7-4	Female Labour Force Participation Rates, by Level of Schooling, Canada, 1975-89	115

7-5	Unemployment "Hazard" Index for Workers with Less than Nine Years' Schooling, Canada, 1975-89	116
7-6	Long-Term Unemployment, by Educational Attainment Level, Canada, 1976 and 1989	116
7-7	Full-Time Enrolment in Colleges and Universities, Canada, 1951-90	118
7-8	Training Component of Unemployment Insurance Benefits and Beneficiaries, Canada, 1978-89	133
7-9	Distribution of Unemployment Insurance Training Beneficiaries and Total Beneficiaries by Age, Canada, 1989/90	133
8-1	Hourly Wages and Salaries, Canada, 1967-89	137
8-2	Average Annual Growth Rates of Hourly Wages and Salaries, and Labour Productivity (1989 dollars), Canada, 1967-76 and 1976-89	138
8-3	Employment Growth and Unionization Rates, by Industry, Canada, 1981-89	138
8-4	Supplementary Labour Income as a Proportion of Total Labour Income, Canada, 1967-89	139
8-5	Change in Work Force Share by Detailed Earnings Level, Canada, 1967-86	143
8-6	Earnings Distribution – Lorenz Curves, Canada, 1967 and 1986	143
8-7	Income Composition of Census Family Units, Canada, 1965-88	148
8-8	Youth Labour Force as a Share of Total Labour Force, Canada, 1966-89	157

Figures

3-1	Partial Illustration of the Types of Intermediate Transactions Involved in Production, Food-Processing Industry, Canada, 1985	45
3-2	Links between Goods and Services	49
7-1	Selected Surveys of Employer-Sponsored Training in Canada since 1963	125

Project Contributors

The authors of Economic Council research reports are the staff economists and, in some cases, outside researchers working under contract for the Council. *Employment in the Service Economy* is the product of the following contributions:

Chapter	Principal author	Additional contributions
1	Gordon Betcherman	
2	Kathryn McMullen	Norm Leckie Harry Postner
3	Tom Siedule	Kathryn McMullen Harry Postner Marcel Bédard
4	Gordon Betcherman	Surendra Gera Sajjad Rahman Marcel Bédard Tom Siedule Kathryn McMullen
5	Christina Caron	Gordon Betcherman Norm Leckie Marcel Bédard
6	Norm Leckie	Gordon Betcherman
7	Gordon Betcherman	Norm Leckie Marcel Bédard
8	Norm Leckie	Marcel Bédard Christina Caron Gordon Betcherman
9	Economic Council*	

*Chapter 9 is reproduced from the Economic Council Statement, *Good Jobs, Bad Jobs*.

Consultants

Elizabeth Beale
"Labour market policies in two eastern provinces: Newfoundland and Labrador, and New Brunswick," mimeo (March 1990).

Laurence Kelly, IR Research Services
"Decentralization of labour market policy," mimeo (June 1989).

Harvey Krahn and Graham Lowe, University of Alberta
"Young workers in the service economy," Working Paper No. 14, Ottawa, 1991.

James J. McRae, University of Victoria
"An exploratory analysis of Canada's international transactions in service commodities," mimeo (November 1989).

D.C.A. Curtis and K.S.R. Murthy, Trent University
"Goods sector-service sector structural change and Canadian economic growth: A dynamic multisectoral modelling analysis," mimeo (September 1989).

John Myles and Gail Fawcett, Carleton University
"Job skills and the service economy," Working Paper No. 4, Ottawa, 1990.

Elisabeth Wagner
"The changing labour market – Some provincial policy responses," mimeo (May 1989).

Klaus Weiermair, York University
"Service sector development, restructuring and public policy response in West Germany, Japan and Sweden," mimeo (June 1989).

Special thanks are due to the Informatics Division, the Publications Division, and the Registry Service, for their contribution to this Report.